Architecture and Authority in Japan

Architecture is one of the most inspired manifestations of Japanese civilization, a pillar of both traditional society and the modern state. The rugged walls of Himeji Castle, the pristine perfection of the Ise Shrine, and the soaring sky-scrapers of modern Tokyo are all examples of consummate artistic inspiration harnessed to building technology in the service of religion or the state. These buildings offer a unique opportunity to identify the ideas and institutions of authority, both religious and secular, embodied in built form.

William Coaldrake argues that there is a symbiotic relationship between architecture and authority throughout Japanese history. Examination of Nara and Heian palaces, Kamakura temples and Momoyama castles reveals the changing countenance of aristocratic and warrior power. The study also shows how some buildings helped to mould power relations by creating a physical presence to intimidate and subordinate those under imperial and shogunal rule, such as the Palace of Nijō Castle. More recently, Western architectural styles have been used to restructure the way Japan presents itself to the outside world.

Relating buildings to the political ambitions and religious beliefs of the age, this book makes a significant contribution to Japanese studies. By examining architecture as an expression of authority, William Coaldrake highlights many defining moments in Japanese history, opening up new avenues for study on both traditional and contemporary Japan.

William H. Coaldrake is Foundation Professor of Japanese at the University of Melbourne, Australia.

The Nissan Institute/Routledge Japanese Studies Series

Architecture and Authority in Japan

William H. Coaldrake

London and New York

First published 1996
by Routledge
11 New Fetter Lane, London EC4P 4EE

Simultaneously published in the USA and Canada
by Routledge
29 West 35th Street, New York, NY 10001

Routledge is an International Thomson Publishing company

THIS PUBLICATION WAS MADE POSSIBLE BY A
GENEROUS GRANT FROM TOSHIBA INTERNATIONAL
FOUNDATION.

A Foreign Publication Assistance Grant was also awarded by
the Suntory Foundation.

Typeset in Galliard by Florencetype Limited, Stoodleigh, Devon
Printed and bound in Great Britain by Redwood Books,
Trowbridge, Wiltshire

British Library Cataloguing in Publication Data
A catalogue record for this book is available from the
British Library

Library of Congress Cataloguing in Publication Data
A catalogue record for this book has been requested

ISBN 0–415–05754–X (hbk)
ISBN 0–415–10601–X (pbk)

To M.S.C.

Contents

Series Editor's Preface

> . . . we are a people whose glorious history will bear to be held up to the gaze
> of Western nations. We have learned a great many things from the West, but
> there are some instances of our having outstripped our tutors.

So wrote Count Okuma in *Fifty Years of New Japan*, published in 1910, some
five years after Japan had emerged victorious in the Russo-Japanese war. Over
the 86 years that have elapsed since those words were written, the history of
Japan's relations with the rest of the world has passed through phases more turbu-
lent than Okuma could have imagined. The tragic and terrible history of the
1930s and 1940s gave way, however, to decades in which the Japanese forged an
amazing (and mostly deserved) reputation for economic development and effi-
ciency. The idea of the Japanese outstripping their tutors is no longer as exotic
as it must have sounded to an English-speaking readership in 1910, but its content
has been radically changed with the passage of time. At the same time, as current
controversies testify, Japan is far from escaping from the dilemma that aspirations
to forge a distinctively Japanese identity and practice in many areas of human
endeavour come up against forceful pressures to conform to the norms of a world
which is globalising along lines over which Japan has only a limited degree of
control. How the Japanese seek to resolve that dilemma is fascinating to watch.

The Nissan Institute/Routledge Japanese Studies Series seeks to foster an
informed and balanced, but not uncritical, understanding of Japan. One aim of
the series is to show the depth and variety of Japanese institutions, practices and
ideas. Another is, by using comparison, to see what lessons, positive and negative,
can be drawn for other countries. The tendency in commentary on Japan to resort
to outdated, ill-informed or sensational stereotypes still remains, and needs to be
combated.

In this splendid book William Coaldrake shows how closely architecture and
authority have been linked together throughout Japanese history. Japanese architects have been resourceful and innovative creators of architectural forms, but far
from working in a political or religious vacuum, they have often catered to the
power-projection needs of those employing them. In the process, over the centuries
they have created many wonderful buildings, which can be enjoyed by the spec-
tator long after their religious or political significance has ceased to be relevant.
On one level this book informs the reader and assists with the appreciation of
many architectural gems. On another level it relates architecture to history and
helps the reader to understand the forces which drove that history. It is a book
to be read at home, and to be carried on trips around Japan.

J.A.A. Stockwin

Figures

Acknowledgements

I am indebted first and foremost to John M. Rosenfield, Professor Emeritus of Harvard University, who supervised my doctoral research from 1976 to 1983 and provided me with the opportunity to participate in lecturing at Harvard, from my initial year of graduate study and later as a member of the Fine Arts faculty. Many of the ideas in this book grew out of that decade of creative collaboration. In addition I shall always be in the debt of Wilma and John Fairbank for their freely offered encouragement and intellectual stimulus. It is not only the China field which owes them so much.

I must express my gratitude to friends and colleagues at the University of Oxford for their sustained interest and stimulation, and to the undergraduates whose questions cast new light on the buildings we studied together. In particular I should like to thank Arthur Stockwin, Brian Powell and I. James McMullen for the opportunity to present these lectures to their undergraduates. Oxford itself drew my attention once again to the rich artistic and intellectual legacy of John Ruskin (1819–1900), Slade Professor of Fine Art in the University of Oxford, whose extraordinary drawings and watercolours of Venetian Gothic I had first encountered at an exhibition in the Fogg Art Museum, Harvard, in 1977.

I am most grateful to Henry D. Smith II of Columbia University for reading and making suggestions on the first draft of the manuscript, and to James L. McClain of Brown University for extensive and valuable comments on the final draft manuscript. I am also indebted to Maurice Bairy, S.J., of Sophia University, Tokyo, Martin Collcutt of Princeton University and Joy Hendry of Oxford Brookes University for reading and commenting on the manuscript at various stages.

The Kenzō butsuka of Bunka-chō, Tōgū-shoku of Kunai-chō and Ise Jingū provided invaluable assistance with photographic materials and publishing permissions.

I also acknowledge with gratitude the assistance of James Ackerman, Beatrice Bodart-Bailey, Michael Cooper, S.J., Kim Dovey, Mark Elvin, Andrew Fraser, the late John Freeman, Mark Hudson, Eizō Inagaki, Nobuo Itō, Sanae Konno, Fumihiko Maki, Jeffrey Mass, Kate Wildman Nakai and Masao Takemura. Margaret Thiery helped me transcribe lecture notes into a first draft and Susan Tyler was indefatigable in checking countless details. Christine McArthur saw it through to the end.

I acknowledge the assistance of the *Journal of the Society of Architectural Historians* for permission to use sections of my earlier article entitled 'The Gatehouse of the Shogun's Senior Councillor: Building Design and Status Symbolism in Japanese Architecture of the Late Edo Period' (December, 1988) in chapter eight, and to Cornell University Press for permission to use in abbreviated form in chapter seven, 'Building a New Establishment: Tokugawa Iemitsu's Consolidation of Power and the Taitokuin Mausoleum', in James L. McClain, John M. Merriman and Ugawa Kaoru (eds) *Edo and Paris: Urban Life and the State in the Early Modern Era*, Cornell University Press, 1994.

Finally, all photographs are by the author unless otherwise acknowledged.

Glossary

bakufu: literally, 'tent government'. Shogunate, first by the Minamoto at Kamakura (1185–1333), then by the Ashikaga at Muromachi in Kyoto (1333–1573), and finally by the Tokugawa at Edo (1603–1868).

bansho: guard house set to the side of the main entrance to a *nagayamon* (q.v.) in the later Edo period.

byōbu: folding screen.

chidorihafu: triangular-shaped dormer gable; literally 'plover gable' because of its resemblance to the outstretched wings of the plover bird.

chigaidana: split level shelving used beside the *tokonoma* (q.v.) in *shoin-zukuri* (q.v.).

chigi: finials placed at each end of the ridge on the roof of Shinto shrines.

daiku: general term for carpenter; master carpenter. Originally title for highest rank of artisan, meaning 'great craftsman'.

daimyō: regional lord; highest ranking members of the warrior class with a rank of at least 10,000 *koku* (q.v.); in the Edo period daimyo were divided into two main categories: *fudai daimyō*, the related or hereditary warriors of the Tokugawa, and *tozama daimyō*, who pledged allegiance to the Tokugawa after the Battle of Sekigahara in 1600.

fushin bugyō: administrator, usually of daimyo rank, in charge of organizing the engineering part of a major building project, particularly site excavation and stone wall construction.

fusuma: opaque sliding screen, usually decorated with elegant paper or paintings, used as an interior space divider.

gongen-zukuri: style of mausoleum architecture which reached maturity in the first half of the seventeenth century. The main building consists of a *haiden* (worship hall) at the front linked by an *ishinoma* (stone floored chamber) to the *honden* (main hall or inner sanctuary) at the rear.

goten: palace built in the *shoin-zukuri* style. Usually located within the *honmaru* (q.v.) or *ninomaru* (q.v.) of a castle, or in the immediate vicinity of the outer wall. The palaces served as the focus of the ceremonial and administrative activities of warrior government, as well as serving as the residences of the shogun and daimyo.

hafu: roof gable, usually ornamental. See *chidorihafu* and *karahafu*.

hinoki: Japanese cypress (*chamaecyparis obtusa*).

hiwada-buki: cypress bark shingle roofing.

hongawara-buki: orthodox terracotta tiling, consisting of concave pantiles (*hiragawara*) and convex cover tiles (*marugawara*).

honmaru: inner compound of castle complex.

ishigaki: stone wall constructed using dry-wall methods, that is, without a rigid binding medium; it provides a foundation for timberframe super-structures in castles, particularly *tenshu* (q.v.), towers and parapets.

jōkamachi: castle town; literally 'the town below the castle.'

kami: deity in Shinto belief.

karahafu: cusped gable. Most elegant form of roof ornamentation.

karajishi: mythological lion associated with Chinese legend.

katsuogi: billets placed transversely along the roof ridge of Shinto shrine.

kaya: miscanthus reed used as roof thatching.

kayaoi: eaves purlin.

ken: traditional unit of measure equivalent to 6 *shaku*, or approximately 1.82 metres.

keyaki: zelkova (*zelkova accuminita*).

kokera-buki: cypress wood shingle roofing.

koku: unit of measure equivalent to 180 litres or 5.96 bushels. A measure of status determined by the official tax on the estimated rice yield of an estate.

mon: gate, gateway, gatehouse.

nagayamon: gatehouse. Usually part of the rowhouse surrounding a daimyo palace compound.

ninomaru: second compound of a castle complex, surrounding or immediately adjacent to the *honmaru* (q.v.).

ōhiroma: principal audience chamber in *shoin-zukuri* (q.v.) palace.

onarimon: gateway reserved for exclusive ceremonial access by the shogun.

sakuji bugyō: administrator, usually of daimyo rank, in charge of organizing the architectural work at a major construction project.

shaku: traditional unit of measure equivalent to 10 *sun*, or approximately 30.3 centimetres.

shikidai: chamber for official greetings in *shoin-zukuri* (q.v.) palace.

shikinen sengū: periodic rebuilding or renewal of a Shinto shrine, a practice observed most consistently at Ise Shrine.

shinden-zukuri: style of mansion architecture developed during the Heian period (794–1185) for members of the aristocratic class in the city of Heian (Kyoto).

shoin-zukuri: style of residential architecture which reached maturity at the end of the sixteenth century. Characterized by asymmetrical grouping of buildings in landscaped setting, with interior chambers furnished with *tsuke-shoin* (q.v.), *tatami* mats (q.v.), *tokonoma* (q.v.) and *chigaidana* (q.v.).

shōji: translucent sliding screen.

sugi: Japanese cedar (*cryptomeria japonica*).

tatami: woven straw mat used as floor covering. Approximately 180 x 90 centimetres in size, its dimensions varied according to region and period. Became the module for interior design by the seventeenth century.

tenshu: principal tower of a castle complex; the *tenshu* was used for a variety of symbolic, ceremonial, residential and military functions. It was similar in function to the keep of European fortifications but fundamentally different in construction methods.

tokonoma: alcove used in *shoin-zukuri* (q.v.) for display of works of art and as hierarchical focus of chamber.

torii: open gateway, consisting of two pillars and architrave, found along the approach path to a Shinto shrine.

tōzamurai: anterooms or waiting rooms for receiving visitors in a *shoin-zukuri* (q.v.) palace.

tsuke-shoin: study in the form of a bay window with writing shelf located to the side of the *tokonoma* (q.v.) in *shoin-zukuri* (q.v.) and projecting onto the veranda.

Introduction

Architecture is one of the most inspired and inspiring manifestations of Japanese civilization, a pillar of both its traditional society and the modern state. This book had its origins in a course of lectures and tutorials presented at the Oriental Institute of the University of Oxford in the Michaelmas terms of 1989 and 1991. The course was designed to immerse undergraduates studying Japanese language in Japanese history and culture through its architectural manifestations. A detailed study of carefully selected buildings was designed to provide deeper understanding of the motive forces at work in Japanese civilization.

These lectures have here been expanded into a series of essays on the theme of the relationship between architecture and authority. The resulting book is not planned as a general survey of architecture in Japan although the essays are arranged in chronological order. Neither is it intended as a comprehensive survey of Japanese history and its cultural, political and religious institutions. Rather it is a book about architecture and its power to influence, coerce and legitimise. It draws on the findings of research on Japanese architecture by specialists over the last generation, including my own work on monumental gateways, building regulations and customary architectural practice. This is the first time an attempt has been made to draw together the relationship between buildings and the political and religious institutions they house from early times to the present day in Japan. Each chapter concentrates on a different aspect of this complex theme through detailed description and analysis of a particular building or set of buildings and their religious and political significance. The focus remains on architecture and is directed to a general audience of those interested in Japan and the dynamic relationship between beliefs and buildings. Because of the wide time-span, encompassing some 1,500 years from the pre-Buddhist age to the modern era, and the short eight-week Oxford term for which the lectures were prepared, it was at times necessary to traverse unashamedly whole eras with rapidly constructed generalisations and brief reference to built and institutional forms. At other times, however, the audience will find itself suspended at a particular moment in time, hovering over the structural or decorative detail of a particular building. This is not prompted by intellectual narcissism. The non-specialist will discover that seemingly unimportant architectural detail often yields the richest information about a particular historical situation. Care has been taken to limit this detail to that which is deemed essential to bring out historical meaning and to ensure that technical material is presented in explicable form for the non-specialist. The experience of teaching at Oxford confirmed my conviction that an attentive audience not only readily understands the need and nature of such detail but soon comes to delight in discerning its significance.

The element common to all the chapters is the focus on buildings, but the varied circumstances surrounding their construction and later fate demanded some flexibility in preparing each study. In reworking the teaching materials the special historical sources and methods used in each chapter are explained, particularly the problem of buildings which no longer survive but which are too important to ignore. In preparing the course the intention had been to focus on a single work of architecture considered to be at the heart of the contemporary circumstances of political and religious authority. In practice it was necessary to consider more than one building because few works of historical architecture survive in their original condition and only rarely does one selected building reflect the total religious and political tenor of its times. In most chapters it proved more useful to concentrate attention on two or three building complexes in order to compare different facets of the architectural expression of authority manifest at the time or to explain different phases in its evolution. Many of the great architectural statements of authority no longer survive, but recourse to archaeological, pictorial and written sources facilitated reconstruction of their architectural style. The most difficult section from this point of view was the chapter covering the Heian, Kamakura and Muromachi periods from which only a handful of buildings remain. This epoch was dealt with only in passing in the Oxford lectures, while a concurrent course of lectures delivered by Professor Jeffrey Mass, based on written documents from the period, guided the undergraduates through the institutional complexities of the era. To provide continuity between the examination of ancient and late medieval architecture and authority in this book I have expanded the brief account of the architecture of the age made during the Oxford course into a separate chapter.

An important feature of this study is the inclusion of a chapter discussing the modern era. This places modern trends into a broader historical matrix. It is particularly difficult to write about recent developments due to the plethora of information and lack of temporal perspective, but those who would leave Japanese history in the nineteenth century are condemning history to the past and missing its important meaning for the present and future.

Some of the buildings included in the study are well known to tourists and those familiar with general cultural surveys, but their full significance has rarely been enlarged upon or appreciated. Other buildings are introduced and analysed in detail in a Western language for the first time. These include the Daigokuden of the Nara Imperial Palace, Azuchi Castle, Tokyo Station and the New Tokyo Metropolitan Government Headquarters. They are all buildings of seminal importance to the meaning and interpretation of their times. It is particularly surprising that so well-known and centrally located a monument as Tokyo Station has been largely overlooked by art and architectural historians alike.

Due to the inevitable strictures placed on teaching time in a single term, the focus in the course was upon individual buildings rather than upon cities and was consciously directed to monuments of church and state rather than to privately created vernacular housing. Some 130 separate building complexes distributed throughout Japan are registered by the Japanese Government as 'National Treasures' and this list does not include a number of significant buildings such as Ise Shrine and Tokyo Station because of the circumstances of their ownership. Only a few of the most significant so listed could be included for the purposes of the exploration of authority. Most of the remaining buildings are worthy of sustained analysis in their own right.

It is important to clarify certain aspects of usage observed in this book. Japanese names are written in conventional Japanese order, with family name first. Proper nouns are not usually italicised. Building height follows Japanese (and American) usage, with the initial or lowest storey or floor referred to as 'first storey', rather than 'ground floor' as is common in British usage. With regard to the actual geographical location of cities and building sites mentioned in the test, many reliable maps of Japan such as Teikoku's *Complete Atlas of Japan* (Tokyo, Teikoku Shoin, 1979) are readily available. For the purposes of this book it is sufficient to bear in mind that the most important buildings discussed are situated in clusters around the ancient capital city of Nara in the Yamato Basin in mid-Japan and the imperial city of Kyoto to its north. In the east, Tokyo, the modern capital, and Nikkō in the mountains of Tochigi prefecture, are also of significance. Further than that and for more serious topographical study, the reader is referred to the several excellent *rekishi chimei jiten* (dictionaries of historical geography) which now exist, as well as to the 1 : 50,000 topographical surveys published by *Kokudo chiriin*.

Authority in Architecture 1

Container and Contained

The soaring silhouette of Himeji Castle, the graceful roof-lines of the Nara Buddhist temples and the ebullient decorated forms of the Tokugawa mausolea at Nikkō are all examples of consummate artistic inspiration harnessed to building technology in the service of authority (Figure 1.1). This book examines Japanese architecture as the visible framework or container of authority and the processes by which authority is contained in and moulded by architectural form. For this purpose 'authority' may be defined as encompassing influence and power, dignity and legitimacy, status and hierarchy, religion and belief, and tradition and continuity, all of which play a role, but not all necessarily at the same time or in equal measure. How this varies will become clear as we study specific buildings and the circumstances of their creation.

The terms which are used for 'authority' in Japanese offer an important key to understanding the relationship between architecture and authority. *Ken'i*, combining the characters for 'authority' and 'dignity', and *kenryoku*, using the characters for 'authority' and 'power', provide some insight into the meaning of the term. It is also illuminating to study the nomenclature of authority as used in its various historical contexts because these reveal a heavy reliance on architectural reference. From as early as the Nara period (710–794) the emperor or empress has been referred to as the *mikado* or

Fig 1.1
Himeji Castle,
Hyōgo
prefecture.
View of
Tenshu
complex

1

'honourable gateway', or by the title *heika*, meaning literally 'below the palace steps', the place from which petitions were customarily offered. From the Heian period (794–1185) it became customary for persons of high court rank and political influence to be described as *kenmon* or 'gateway of power' because of the impressive gateways which guarded the entrances to their palaces in Kyoto. In the medieval era the term was extended to refer to the leaders of the powerful new warrior clans.[1] *Kenmon* and *heika* were adopted from Chinese usage, indicating a similar equation in ancient China between important people and impressive architecture, but *mikado* appears to have been of Japanese origin. In other words architectural metonymy was a standard way of referring to persons and institutions of authority and influence and this is itself indicative of a powerful association between what we see and what we believe.

If seeing is believing, then by implication seeing an impressive building is more than halfway to believing what its creators would have us believe, whether it be the dignity of the law, the all-pervasiveness of government, the inescapability of death. At some time in our lives we have all experienced the profound impact of a stately building – the solid masonry mass of a medieval castle or a court-room with panels of darkened oak, or it may have been the soaring vaults of a Gothic cathedral which lifts the spirits as it stuns the senses. As John Ruskin trenchantly observed more than a century ago, 'great architecture makes us believe what we would not otherwise have believed.[2]

The atmosphere created by certain buildings may be carefully calculated to elicit a particular reaction from the observer, or it may be the inevitable consequence of the process and materials employed in its construction. Whichever is the case, the interaction between buildings and the people whose lives and activities are contained in them has profound implications for how authority is perceived. The exterior of a symmetrical building may serve as a soothing simile for balance and harmony in a political system. The interior layout of a building can communicate highly specific information about status and responsibility. In Washington and Whitehall, government officials learn to identify authority by office size and location, and to measure influence by the number of windows and amount of sunshine enjoyed in midwinter. In Tokyo, the desk arrangement in the open-plan offices of government ministries and major corporations like Mitsubishi and Sumitomo serves as a mandala from which may be divined the status and responsibilities of their occupants, the lowliest clerk placed next to the entrance door, far removed from the division chief ensconced near the window and the newspaper rack.

Japanese castle towns founded in the sixteenth century were laid out in zones according to these same principles of status, with the castle of the local lord or *daimyō* at the focus and the mansions of his highest ranking retainers ranged close by. Physical separation from the locus of power was equated with distance in status from the daimyo. Yoshida Kenkō (1283–1350), the celebrated poet, court official, monk and philosopher, expressed a universally accepted truth when he wrote that 'the appearance of a house is in some sort an index to the character of its occupant.'[3] Similar sentiments were expounded by Leon Battista Alberti (1404–1472) in the prologue to *On the Art of Building in Ten Books*, his seminal exposition of Renaissance architectural philosophy:

Who would not boast of having built something? . . . When you erect a wall or
portico of great elegance and adorn it with a door, columns, or roof, good citizens approve and express joy for their own sake, as well as yours, because they
realise that you have used your wealth to increase greatly not only your own honour
and glory, but also that of your friends, your descendants, and the whole city.[4]

Statements of such diverse origins make it obvious that in both Europe and
Asia architecture has been a common vehicle for the expression of authority.
It serves as an ideal medium for creating convincing metaphors. Institutions
espousing democratic principles of government throughout history have
chosen the Doric, Ionic and Corinthian orders of architecture because of their
abiding association with the ideals of Classical Antiquity. Gothic arches have
reinforced the authority of the Venetian city state and the intellectual authority
of great centres of learning such as Oxford, as well as the spiritual meaning
of Christianity. A jaded, secular world-view should not blind us to the sacramental significance of a great cathedral and its manifestation of divine presence
for the medieval believer. As John James explains:

In our day we call the church the House of God, for His presence occupies it. But
the thirteenth century was less circumspect. They had the audacity to believe that
they were constructing a slice of eternity itself, and the simplicity to trust that God's
Essence would be made manifest in something they built from the materials found
on earth.[5]

In the Japanese context the same might well have been written of the shrines
at Ise, that sublime expression of communion between the gods and this
world, or of the Yōmeimon, the ethereal gateway to the Tokugawa mausoleum
at Nikkō.

The relationship between architecture and authority, therefore, goes beyond
signs and symbols. In manifesting authority, architecture can serve as a potent
tool for political or social engineering or for profoundly affecting religious
belief. We may readily acknowledge the power that a work of art of ineffable
beauty has to move us, but what of the power of a work of architecture of
sublime proportions to convince us? A beautiful building can move, inspire,
and beguile its beholders with the visual language of architectural form in
the same way as a charismatic orator can move, inspire and beguile an audience with words.

Buildings, therefore, afford more than mere lip-service to authority: they
are an intrinsic part of authority itself. One can neither be conceived nor
apprehended without the other. The container and the contained are an
organic whole. War and architecture were the twin preoccupations of much
traditional authority, and when states and their leaders were not engaging in
the former, they were indulging in the latter. As shelter is essential to life, so
architecture is essential to the projection of authority. It would be impossible
to understand Pericles without the Athenian Acropolis or Augustus Caesar
without Rome, the city he inherited as brick and bequeathed as marble. The
political power and religious piety of Philip II of Spain are inseparable from
the Escorial palace monastery, and the Venetian doges took their formal
authority from the dignity of their Palace and the rituals performed in the
Basilica in the Piazza San Marco. The glory of the 'Sun-King' Louis XIV

would be diminished without Versailles, Peter the Great without St Petersburg, the Ming and Qing Dynasties without the palace city of Beijing.

From its character as an .attribute of authority flows the role of architecture as an activity of that authority. Ancient rulers built their empires by constructing temples and palaces as well as by building armies and destroying enemies. Modern government is still preoccupied with architecture as an expression of civic responsibility as well as a tool for economic stimulus. Since time immemorial the equation between architecture and authority has been established through the power of building. Some of the earliest written documents of human civilization, inscribed in cuneiform script on the clay cylinders of Sumer, describe the energetic temple building programme of the prince Gudea, who ruled over southern Mesopotamia *ca* 2150 BC. Stone sculpture excavated from the ancient Fertile Crescent depict rulers as builders: kings carry baskets of bricks on their heads; Gudea sits with the plans of a temple on his knees.[6] It was no coincidence or passing whim which made the process of building a vital prerogative of governing authority. To rule was to build, and to build was to rule.

Architecture both as an attribute and an activity of authority has also had definitive implications for the operation of authority as a political, religious and social force. Architecture affects thoughts and actions, both as a tangible expression of ideas and as a tool for ordering the places where human activity and interaction occur. One illustration of this is the way people feel and act differently in square as opposed to rectangular buildings because of the absence of a dominant direction. A square plan generally affords greater opportunity for human interaction, whereas a rectangular plan automatically creates a spatial hierarchy which can be articulated to serve the ends of authority. The difference between square and rectangular plans was to have profound implications historically for the design of ritual spaces. For example, the rectangular plan of medieval churches and cathedrals emphasised the remoteness of the divine at the east end from the mortal plane stretching towards the west end of the building. This contrasted strongly with Renaissance churches which generally had square plans to express the humanist concern with the centrality of the rational person.[7] Similarly, square classrooms offer more flexibility for open seating arrangements of students, whereas the dominant direction of the rectangular classroom establishes a hierarchy based on distance from the teacher at the front – a characteristic exploited by nineteenth-century educational reformers in England, with students ranked from the front to the back according to performance.[8] A round plan has even more dramatic impact on behaviour, a fact Jeremy Bentham utilised in *Panopticon* for the reform of prison buildings through centralised control.

The architectural profession may have been long aware of its power to influence the human condition, for better or for worse, through determining the configuration and juxtapositions of structure and space, but it was not until recently that the behavioural sciences turned their attention to this phenomenon. In a pioneering study in 1965, B.W.P. Wells established empirically through what he described as 'socio-metric analysis' the ways in which the design of an office building may both facilitate and hinder interpersonal communication. He concluded that:

... common entrances to different departments mean that there are many more opportunities for inter-departmental contacts than if there were separate ones ... the size of the rooms themselves also sets the limit and range of working, and therefore, social intercourse. Another consequence of room size may follow from the introduction of very large clerical areas which would seem to offer the chances for the introduction of more autocratic measures in supervision and management.[9]

By the 1970s, work by Christopher Alexander, Rudolf Arnheim and Joseph Rykwert had broadened the interpretation of buildings and human behaviour into a more comprehensive understanding of the interaction of person and place.[10] Such seemingly inconsequential factors as the height of tables, the direction of lighting, the shape of a room, the height of its ceiling, the colour of the walls, the positioning of doors, and the aesthetic character of the materials, all contribute towards building the mind as well as housing the body. They can be manipulated to lessen crime, as O. Newman found in his studies of urban housing in New York,[11] to increase commercial power by enticing people into retail shopping spaces,[12] or they can be used to serve the ends of political or religious authority. However, the implications of this for the study of the history of authority have been overlooked. 'Traditional history', with its emphasis on written documents as sources, has not encompassed methodology for examining phenomena that are rarely recorded in written word. Architecture, as both a record of and active participant in the past, offers the opportunity to bridge the disciplines of history and the behavioural sciences for a better understanding of political and religious institutions. Wells' recognition that buildings may perform 'autocratic' functions is particularly intriguing in the context of this historical study of the use of architecture by elites to represent and reinforce authority. Clearly the tangible effects of architectural form on human behaviour have had practical implications for the exercise of power. Inseparable from the notion of authority itself is the role of 'power to influence the conduct and action of others'.[13] Such influence is generally perceived as ranging from absolutist assertion to persuasion reinforced by prestige. If power is the assertion of authority, buildings serve as a tectonic means of affecting power by every means possible, from overt physical coercion to subliminal psychological persuasion. Like power itself, buildings may simply overwhelm with the magnitude of their physical presence, or they may attempt to persuade by lending visual prestige to their sponsors.

The means of communication may vary from literal to abstract, the culturally relative to the universally relevant, but the homology between authority and architecture has a constant bearing on the power to influence the conduct and actions of others. Power sets apart even as it unites. A work of architecture manipulates human relations in like manner: walls divide, roofs unite. Buildings give tangible structure to the relationships inherent in authority; they signify and separate ruler and ruled, superior and subordinate, sacred and profane, by the calculated use of walls and gateways, courtyards and corridors, and different levels of seating.

Hierarchy is essential to the ordering of authority; it is intrinsic to differences in the splendour or height of two buildings, or implied in any procession between chambers of greater or lesser magnificence. Use of buildings as the stage for ceremonial, be it religious rite or secular pageant, translates the

Fig 1.2
'Propping Up
the Edifice'.
Pancho, *The
Washington
Post*, 1992
(Courtesy of
*The Washington
Post*)

EDITORIAL

Propping Up The Edifice

structural and spatial dynamics of built forms into vestments of authority. Authority is magnified by ceremonial, which as Baldwin Smith explains, 'reinforced many social and political relationships'.[14] Churches and palaces had an enlarged presence and a consequent sense of occasion and authority when used for religious rites or court ceremony. The music and pageantry of medieval church liturgy performed within the physical context of a cathedral created a powerful sense of God's presence by communicating with the participants at sensory as well as psychological levels. In a more sinister manner, Hitler's use of monolithic stadium buildings at Nuremberg for his carefully orchestrated mass rallies vastly reinforced Nazi authority.

Architecture, therefore, serves as a container for authority but inevitably the container helps shape the contained because the relations of power are essentially fluid. Buildings serve as a mould or matrix into which the fluid forms of authority are poured, thereby taking a definite shape. This architectural form to authority is reflected in the very language frequently adopted to express ideas of authority. For instance, many institutions carried metonymic names based on readily recognisable architectural features. 'The White House' is the most ubiquitous way of referring to the Presidency and its concomitant power in the United States. Architectural phrases like 'structure of power', 'pillar of the establishment', 'laying the foundations for policy' and 'building a consensus' permeate the parlance of political discourse. The image of an edifice collapsing or being propped up is often invoked as a metaphor for the fall of a government (Figure 1.2). The phrase 'architects of power' refers to those outstanding statesmen generally credited with founding independent nations and building empires. Law as an instrument of authority is commonly likened to a building:

> The house of law is the home of all mankind. It is contemporary, yet coeval with man himself. It has sheltered society since the human race began and still performs its ancient task. Standing four-square, it can only be partly comprehended from any one fixed point.'[15]

This type of analogy between architecture and law was a result of their shared attribute of a desire to structure and organise, and, with the move towards codification of jurisprudence, becomes a familiar theme in eighteenth-century thought. As Peter Stein notes, 'if the stock analogy for jurisprudence in the seventeenth century was geometry, in the eighteenth century it was architecture'.[16]

In the same way, use of architectural references pervades the Japanese language of authority. In recent history this has in part been a result of assimilating Western theories and practices of government, law and administration. Today Japanese foreign policy is often referred to as having 'three pillars' – a phrase seen as an acceptable policy description although an improbable structure for any building. However, use of architectural vocabulary for authority is not simply a recent imported phenomenon; as noted earlier it is deeply entrenched in traditional Japanese thought patterns. The birth of a new political faction is customarily greeted by newspaper headlines which proclaim that its ridge-pole has been hoisted into position (*sōseikai o muneage shita*), a term originally associated with long-established Shinto building rites marking the completion of the structural framing. The examples of *mikado* for emperor and *denka* for crown prince have already been remarked upon. Another revealing example is provided by Yoshida Shōin (1830–1859), the imperial loyalist and scholar who so profoundly influenced his generation of young, disaffected samurai that his former students held major positions of authority in the Meiji governments of the later nineteenth century. Shōin described the crisis facing Japan with the intrusion of the West in the final days of Tokugawa shogunal control in architectural terms:

> The world of today is like an old, decaying house. . . . I believe that if this house were blown down by a great wind, and we were to rebuild it by replacing the rotten pillars, discarding worn-out rafters, and adding new wood, it would become a beautiful building. . . . But because of this [the need for major renovation] it will not be easy to put into effect the doctrines of *sonnō-joi*.[17]

These examples of architectural metonymy may be of Japanese origin but they are also in keeping with the usage of other ancient and medieval civilizations such as the title 'pharaoh', which meant literally 'great house' in ancient Egypt, and 'palace' to refer to the royal family in England. These linguistic associations were a result of the visual association between important people and impressive buildings, the homology between architectural form and the structure of ruling authority, and the central role of the process of building in the process of ruling.

It may be seen from the preceding discussion that the title of this book, *Architecture and Authority in Japan*, poses the fundamental question, 'how are architecture and authority linked?'. The question may be answered in terms of the universal ability of buildings to communicate, to convince and even to coerce. Since antiquity the links between architecture and authority have been the object of some attention by scholars and philosophers but the subject of more sustained study since the publication of John Ruskin's *The Seven Lamps of Architecture* in 1849.[18] There have been numerous studies of architecture and art as propaganda.[19] It is now inconceivable in scholarly terms to turn to the politics of the Renaissance Papacy and Italian city-states without giving due consideration to the role of their architectural and artistic preoccupations in definition of self and state authority.[20] Victorian society is recognised to have been profoundly influenced by new building types, especially the prison, the factory, the school, the hospital and the railway station.[21] Certain building forms, such as the Palladian villa, are acknowledged for their special contribution to political ideology and state formation.[22] Similarly, buildings are seen as performing an important political role in the American experience from the Revolution to the present.[23] There are also readily accessible studies of the expansion of the British Empire and the way in which heavy reliance was placed on buildings for the social and political engineering of its international dominion.[24]

Despite the importance of this subject, there is no systematic study available in either Western or Japanese languages which recognises the centrality of the architectonic impulse to the development of Japanese ideas and institutions over the course of documented history. An examination of Japanese buildings may be recognised as having a proper place in the history of architecture and technology, but these same buildings have equally as much to offer the historians of societies and states which have been housed within them. They display the aspirations of their patrons, the skills of their builders and the broader intellectual, political, religious and economic milieu which they both reflect and helped to fashion.

Scholars consistently underestimate the role played by official building projects in the institutional consolidation of Nara imperial or Tokugawa shogunal authority because institutional historians have seldom scrutinised architecture as a primary source for understanding political processes. This is sometimes simply because few buildings from the period have survived to the present day. As in the case of ancient Sumer, however, the absence of extant buildings for some phases of political or religious development in Japan does not indicate that a relationship between architecture and authority did not exist. On the contrary, architectural research in Japan, using written, pictorial and archaeological sources, is now reaching a more sophisticated understanding of destroyed buildings, which together with extant architecture, affords rich opportunities to pursue this relationship further.

Here, as we address the methodological problem of dealing with destroyed buildings, we also encounter one of the abiding intellectual concerns in the study of architecture and authority; in short, what was the role of concepts of permanence and monumentality in the architectural expression of authority in Japan? It is a generally accepted axiom that Japanese civilization as a whole reflects a profound philosophical, spiritual and aesthetic preoccupation with the impermanence of all things. The sombre warning in the opening lines of the *Tale of Heike* that 'all is vanity and evanescence' seems to offer an important clue in our search for meaning in the architecture of authority. After all, Japanese architecture often uses ephemeral materials and may be unassuming in its physical presence. Yet the problem of frequent destruction of significant architectural evidence may have helped create a misapprehension about the nature of the role of architecture in expressing authority. Could it be that the destruction of so many buildings has distorted our ability to arrive at a fully informed understanding of the range of built expression assumed by authority? To what extent is the prevailing notion of ephemeral and fragile an appropriate characterisation of Japanese architecture, and to what extent is it a stereotype requiring modification as a result of a more informed awareness of the relationship between authority and architecture? It is to such questions as these that we address ourselves in this study.

It is precisely the strength and complexity of the links between architecture and authority which may explain the vitality of the Japanese architectural tradition. It is the ageless ambitions of powerful patrons which renders explicable the grandeur of the great temples and palaces of Nara and Edo, far removed in spirit as they are from the self-effacing intimacy of tea-houses and princely retreats upon which Western scholarship has so fondly dwelt. John Ruskin, writing 150 years ago, has a timely message for Japanese historical studies today:

> There are but two strong conquerors of the forgetfulness of men, Poetry and Architecture; and the latter in some sort includes the former, and is mightier in its reality: it is well to have, not only what men have thought and felt, but what their hands have handled, and their strength wrought, and their eyes beheld, all the days of their life.[25]

Accordingly, it is time to allow the architectural conquest of the forgetfulness of scholars of Japan, and to examine the theme of authority in the shrines of ancient Shinto and the temples of state Buddhism; in the courtly metropolis of Nara; in the palaces, castles and mausolea of the warrior governments of the medieval and early modern eras; in the monumental high-technology structures of late twentieth-century Tokyo. In viewing these built forms both as context and content, we are breaking new intellectual ground in Asia at the same time as we follow a tradition long established in Europe. In seeing what hands have handled, strength wrought and eyes beheld, we may attain a different perspective on the dynamics of architectural form and new insights into authority in Japanese history.

It is vital, therefore, to analyse the ways in which architecture represents and communicates authority in Japan. An essential element in this analytical task is to identify the vocabulary of authority with which buildings communicate. The prerequisite for this is systematic observation of actual buildings. Second-hand experience of a building through drawings of photographs is equivalent to reliance on secondary sources for writing history, although in some circumstances, such as loss by destruction, it may be unavoidable. A number of questions may be posed as a basis for the necessary disciplined looking: What is the initial impact of the building on the viewer in both intellectual and emotional terms? What is the nature of the site and the placement of the building? Does the setting impart any special qualities to the building? What are the main parts of the building? What stands out and why? What is the sense of scale and proportional relationship between the parts? What is the structure? Are the walls load-bearing and, if not, what opportunities for decoration does this create? What is the relationship between mass and void? What types of spaces are enclosed within the building? What materials are used for the different parts of the building and why? Does decoration play a significant role in the overall impact of the building? What is the role of colour, surface, and texture? Is the decoration representational or abstract?

In seeking the answers to such questions it is important to view the building from various angles, to see it under different light and seasonal conditions, to experience it when it is stiflingly hot as well as refreshingly cool. A foreground of pristine snow or a backdrop of glowing autumnal hues may work a miraculous transformation upon a building's appearance and emotional impact. Monet's numerous studies of the single façade of Rouen cathedral at differing times of day has forever increased awareness of the transience of certain visual effects.

Beyond observing the formal characteristics of a building and experiencing it as an artistic entity lies the world of the construction process. A building may have an existence as a work of art but it belongs equally in the domain of applied science. It is essential to understand the human and technological infrastructure which supported the construction of the building. What may be gleaned from finely finished timbers or roughly hewn stones about the craftsmen who created it? What sorts of trades and professions were involved in the building process? What types of tools would have been needed for measuring and calculating, and for cutting and smoothing? What were the most difficult tasks in the construction process, challenging the technology of the day, the skill of the builders, and the resources of the patron? One cannot help but marvel at the Herculean achievements of the builders of Tōdaiji or Himeji Castle, for some of the most simple mechanical operations of today such as spanning great spaces were then the source of considerable perplexity and were achieved only by the most insistent authority.

After questions of architectural form and construction processes have been considered, the next step is to place the building in its historical context. Contemporary written documents can help establish the identity of the builders and the purpose of the patron in sponsoring the project. Sometimes records survive of the costs and administration of the construction process. It is useful to consider such information in the more general historical context, the tenor of the times, the preoccupations of society, government, religion and the arts. Contemporary reactions to a building may also prove useful, as will comparison with other buildings constructed at the same time. These issues lead naturally to a broader consideration of the ways in which the building in its parts and as a whole served the ends of its sponsors. Symbols of high status, great wealth, and overarching authority become apparent. It is then possible to identify the architectural vocabulary of authority and follow its evolution as time and circumstances themselves changed.

While benefiting from the tradition of awareness of the relationship between architecture and authority in the West, we should at the same time be cautious in using contemporary Western standards of judgement as the measuring-rod for Japanese historical architecture. Inevitably we reflect our contemporary intellectual concerns and methodologies, which have included, in no particular order, such things as semiotics, Postmodernism, 'history from below', Deconstructionism and the 'New Humanities'. While arguing for appropriate attention to be paid to the issues of the common man and woman which flow from these preoccupations there is a myopia inherent in our thinking when it comes to what is described as 'High Civilization', of which 'elite architecture' is part. 'Elite architecture' may be unfashionable precisely because it is elite, yet by definition a study of the architecture of authority is very much concerned with the architecture of the elite. Contemporary thinking should not blind us to the fundamental role of 'elite architecture' as a building-block for civilization both high and low. Nor should we overlook the broad impact of 'elite' projects in shaping society generally, in engaging the labour and inspiring the creative and spiritual impulses of men and women of every estate. Common man built uncommon buildings. In Japan it was the inter-action between the elite and the vernacular traditions in building which was a fundamental dynamic in the creation of built form. To understand fully what the buildings tell us of their day and circumstance it is essential to set aside our own intellectual predispositions and view the architecture of Japanese authority within the social, cultural and intellectual milieu of its own time. The architectural assertion of authority may be a universal attribute of the human psyche, the expression of a desire to dominate or a certain phase of kingship, but it is equally an historical and culturally conditioned phenom-enon. Buildings communicate on several levels and unless we are aware of these different levels of meaning their messages will be misunderstood. There is at once a universal language of architectural symbolism and a more care-fully and deliberately coded language of specific time and place, social class or power group, occasion or event.

Luis Frois, the intrepid Jesuit missionary to Japan in the late sixteenth century, had little difficulty in understanding the message of authority of Azuchi Castle, for it communicated across cultural boundaries in a universal language of authority. In a letter back to Rome he wrote:

> On the top of the hill in the middle of the city Nobunaga built his palace and castle, which as regards architecture, strength, wealth and grandeur may well be compared with the greatest buildings of Europe. Its strong and well-constructed walls of stone are over 60 spans in height [approximately 14 metres] and even higher in many places. . . . And in the middle there is a sort of tower they call *tenshu* and it indeed has a far more noble and splendid appearance than our towers. It consists of seven floors all of which both inside and out have been fashioned to a wonderful architectural design . . . inside the walls are decorated with designs richly painted in gold and different colours, while the outside of each of these stories is painted in various colours. . . . This *tenshu* and all the other houses are covered with bluish tiles which are stronger and lovelier than those we use in Europe; the corners of the gables are rounded and gilded, while the roofs have fine spouts of very noble and clever design. In a word the whole edifice is beautiful, excellent and brilliant. As the castle is situated on high ground and is itself very lofty, it looks as if it reaches to the clouds and it can be seen from afar for many leagues.[26]

For the European visitor to sixteenth-century Japan, Azuchi Castle articulated authority with a universal language of height, strength, technical sophistica-tion and beauty (see Figure 5.1, p. 108). Bombast may make a strong initial impression, but Frois demonstrates it is also in the realm of beauty that power resides. However, it is with beauty that the greatest of scholarly caution must be exercised in interpreting buildings. A thing of beauty may be a joy for ever, but it does not necessarily follow that it can be appreciated everywhere. We should remember that beauty lies in the eye of the beholder and the interpretation of the architecture of authority may be relative in time and place as often as it is universal in its communication of meaning. Assumptions about beauty may even undermine objective analysis of Japanese buildings. Each generation, proudly reserving its traditional right to rewrite history, may fall into the error of allowing taste from another time and place to distort its interpretation of the aesthetics of authority. We would be well advised 'to define beauty not in the most abstract, but in the most concrete terms possible', as Walter Pater urged over a century ago.[27] In the case of Japanese architecture, 'concrete terms' could be interpreted to mean the tangible evidence of timber-frame form and the contemporary reactions to it as documented in written and pictorial sources.

Taste is intrinsic to the interpretation of architecture, but it must be carefully gauged when assessing the impact of a building on the viewer. We must 'read' a building in its own language as well as according to universal standards, in the same way that we need to read written primary sources in their original language to savour their full meaning. Japanese architecture requires an observer who is literate in the special meaning of motifs and forms, and mindful of the distinction between similar and the same. Left and right seem to be universally accepted as absolute indications of direction, but in the Chinese capitals of Chang'an and Luoyang, and the Japanese cities of Nara and Heian, directional thinking was dictated by the view from the seat of authority at the north and centre. As we look at the plans of these ancient cities today, we find that the left of the city viewed from the north, is in fact the right-hand-side according to our planning conventions. It may have been an honour to sit on the right hand of God, but what if God had been left-handed, as some would contend?

The Tokugawa mausolea at Nikkō provide a useful demonstration of the relativity of judgement and the misunderstanding of the architecture of authority which may result. The Nikkō Tōshōgū has been lambasted with scorn by almost every twentieth-century architect and Japan specialist from Bruno Taut to Paul Varley. Taut for instance wrote in 1937, at the height of the Modern Movement in architecture, that Nikkō was 'barbaric, overloaded Baroque.'[28] Baroque may no longer be seen as primitive exhibitionism, but something of that prejudice still lingers in the Western disregard for Nikkō. Taut also criticised the *karamon* – the cusped gable gateways which adorned the entrances of great palaces of state in the later sixteenth and seventeenth centuries – for their 'swinging curve in the gable and all the added ornamental trifles which satisfy people of primitive artistic sense'.[29] As we shall see, it was precisely these features which made the gateways the supreme statement of authority in the Edo period. By contrast, Victorian taste would have had no such difficulty in appreciating the language of architectural authority as expressed at Nikkō. Ruskin firmly asserts that:

> There is not, as far as I am aware, in Europe, any monument of a truly noble school which has not been either painted all over, or vigorously touched with paint, mosaic, and gilding in the prominent parts.[30]

Fig 1.3
Tōshōgū,
Nikkō. Detail
of decoration
of Yōmeimon

To Ruskin, the Nikkō Tōshōgū would have been as intelligible and admirable
as his beloved Doge's Palace in Venice (Figure 1.3). His reactions may well
have been similar to those of Edward Morse, who visited Nikkō some 20
years after Ruskin made his comments on ornamentation:

> I must confess the utter inability of doing the slightest justice to the temples and
> tombs, so wonderful are they, so elaborate, so vast and magnificent. In two hours
> I became completely exhausted. I have little photographs of them, but these do
> the scantiest justice to the minute ornamentation, the intricate wood carving, the
> bronzes, wrought-brass work, brilliant colouring, and the thousand details that
> cannot be recorded.[31]

When clarifying what is culturally explicit it is helpful to establish that,
throughout much of Japanese history, authority moves in two powerful
currents – the imperial and the shogunal. Although strictly speaking shogunal
authority derived its legitimacy from the imperial, each current of authority
flowed from a different source; the imperial from a courtly, aristocratic and
civil power and the shogunal from a warrior ethos and military power. These
two streams of authority were to intermingle, and in time each assumed something of the character of the other. This was particularly true after the shogunal
authority adopted many of the forms and manifestations of the imperial during
the Muromachi rapprochement between court and *bakufu* in the fourteenth
and fifteenth centuries.

It is important to recognise that both the imperial and shogunal traditions
of authority have each a religious and secular dimension. Imperial authority
was based on notions of unity of church and state shared by most systems
of ancient kinship. Shogunal authority, for its part, was at times extraordinarily sophisticated in invoking sacerdotal authority to enhance its status. This

13

overlapping and interweaving of authority raises the possibility that a common language of architectural form should exist in Japan, shared by the secular and the religious, the imperial and the shogunal. In the course of this study we should determine what elements are shared, and identify the means by which, at the same time, distinctions were maintained.

Here again we must be mindful of the ease with which our contemporary world-view may distort our perceptions, in this case of the relationship between sacred and secular in the architecture of authority. Since the Industrial Revolution the secularisation of world-view in the West has led to a stricter separation of religious from secular authority than had generally prevailed in the past. George Steiner concluded in *Real Presences* that 'where God's presence is no longer a tenable supposition and where His absence is no longer a felt, indeed overwhelming weight, certain dimensions of thought and creativity are no longer attainable'.[32] Today we routinely separate secular from sacred architecture, though much of the architecture of authority is held in common by both the secular and sacerdotal dominions. This applies equally to the case of Europe under the Holy Roman Empire as it does to Japan of the Nara period. 'Romanesque' was as much the architecture of castles and palaces as it was of the monasteries and chapels of the Cistercian Order. Indeed art, including architecture, draws the secular and the religious together. This is evident in the thinking of the English Aesthetes, including most notably Ruskin himself, and the whole mid-nineteenth century ambience of High Church Anglicanism and the Oxford Movement, which expressed the spiritual through the medium of ritual and art. The 'religion of art', which Richard Aldington points out 'so naturally followed art as part of religion',[33] belongs to that fruitful and creative interaction between spheres which we now separate as a matter of course. Perhaps it was a heightened spiritual as well as aesthetic awareness which led Ruskin to discern in certain types of architecture an authority transcending the secular and profane. This awareness came about at a special moment of coincidence in social, political, spiritual, intellectual and artistic forces in late nineteenth-century England. It produced, along with much richly self-indulgent language, a peculiar clarity of vision which may usefully be applied to the case of architecture and authority in Japan, where the concomitant social, political, religious, intellectual and aesthetic conditions have frequently spawned works of architecture as assertively authoritative as the buildings which commanded Ruskin's attention.

The artificial separation of secular and sacred has had a direct consequence for the interpretation of Japanese architecture. Since the later nineteenth century there has been a propensity for both Western scholars and Japanese specialists to divide scholarly study into religious and secular domains.[34] The result has been to emphasise the former at the expense of the latter in research in the period up to the sixteenth century, and the latter at the expense of the former in studies developed in subsequent periods. In reality, the locus of architectural energy and innovation was not so sharply divided, and the patterns of patronage and authority tended to ignore the distinctions which latter-day preoccupations have made statutory. Insight into the dynamics of architectural authority have been hindered by this obfuscation.

The fine texture of the interweaving of the imperial and the shogunal, the universal and the culturally specific, the sacred and the secular, are all evident in the rich tapestry of Japanese architectural history which will unfold in this study.

2 The Grand Shrines of Ise and Izumo

The Appropriation of Vernacular Architecture by Early Ruling Authority

The Grand Shrine of Ise (Ise Jingū) and the Great Shrine of Izumo (Izumo Taisha) are the two most venerable shrines of Shinto in Japan. Located in remote, awe-inspiring natural settings, the architecture of both Ise and Izumo is an expression of Shinto, the animistically based indigenous belief of Japan, and the symbiotic relationship enjoyed with ruling authority since time immemorial.

The Ise shrine complex is located on the eastern side of the Kii peninsula to the southeast of the ancient centres of government in the Yamato basin. It basks on a coastal plain warmed by the Pacific ocean currents and bathed in bright sunshine even in mid-winter. It is an ideal setting for the worship of Amaterasu, the Sun Goddess and legendary ancestress of the imperial family, and Toyouke, a local agricultural deity of grains and the harvest. The Izumo shrine complex, by contrast, is situated in Shimane prefecture, an inhospitable region of frequent storms and fierce elemental forces on the rugged Sea of Japan coast facing towards the mainland of Asia. Appropriately the name 'Izumo' means the place 'from whence the clouds come'. It was originally known as 'Yakumo tatsu' ('where the eight clouds rise').[1] The shrine is dedicated to Okuninushi, the deity of fishing, sericulture, good fortune and fertility. In Japan's creation myths Okuninushi is the son of the tempestuous Storm God Susano-o, the elder brother of Amaterasu. Thus from the time of the age of myths, Ise and Izumo have been locked in the uneasy embrace of supernatural familial rivalry. This reflects their portentous role in the consummation of governing authority in Japanese history, for whatever the religious significance of the shrines as the expression of Shinto belief, their meaning is ultimately as much political as sacred. Historically they served as the centres of worship for two powerful clans which were engaged in a fierce political and ideological struggle for national hegemony in the late bronze and early iron ages, a process which culminated in the supremacy of the Yamato clan associated with Ise.

From the sixth century the shrines at Ise were to play a critical role in transforming local power into national governmental authority based on the institution of the imperial family. Their architecture, appropriated from the form of vernacular storehouses and granaries long the focus of village festivals and animistic worship in praise of the gods of creation and the harvest, was to become an enduring tradition in Japanese civilization, as pervasive in physical form and deep in cultural meaning as Classical architecture in the

Mediterranean world.[2] Like the columns and architraves of the temples of ancient Greek temples, the raised-floor timbered structure with thatched roof and rafters crossing over the ridge-pole became synonymous with both worship and authority in Japanese tradition.

Izumo Shrine as an institution shared the same political, religious and architectural strategies as Ise, employing an architectural idiom based on early elite residences and differing from the granary prototype of Ise in detail only. However the defeat of its patrons in the struggle for national hegemony relegated its architecture to a less illustrious fate as a regional shrine, its myths and legends to a place of derision in the official mythology of the nation, and its clan leaders to disgruntled provincial obscurity. This fate was sealed, as we shall see, by a series of spectacular structural failures of the main shrine building in the eleventh and twelfth centuries.

The architectural forms of Ise and Izumo thus manifested and, in turn, influenced the respective success and failure of their local patrons in the struggle for national hegemony. They attest to the power of authority in politicising architectural form, particularly by the appropriation of vernacular building types into the high culture, and their consequent evolution from the functional into the abstract and the secular into the religious. At the same time these shrines bear testimony to the indispensable role of architecture in the definition and enforcement of ruling authority, fundamental to its power and prestige, dignity and legitimacy, its status and hierarchy, and its tradition and continuity. One of the most ancient and jealously guarded prerogatives of ruling authority was sponsorship of the periodic rebuilding of these shrines, a process at first required by the ephemeral nature of the materials used, but as time passed, dictated more by power and prestige.

The two shrine complexes thereby reveal the way in which certain buildings do more than act as mere symbols: how they become part of the very fabric of authority and its institutional processes, in turn exerting their own powerful influence on the way that authority is defined, enacted and enforced. In so doing they facilitate exploration of one of the most pervasive and poignant of all themes in the study of Japanese authority, namely the struggle between the impermanence of materials used in creating buildings on the one hand, and the ambition to establish an enduring expression of authority on the other. Monumentality, or the power of buildings 'to impress and endure',[3] is customarily expressed in large and visually imposing structures of solid and seemingly immutable character. Such is the timeless quality of the great cathedrals of Europe, their massive masonry forms an affirmation of belief in the immortality of God. Ise and Izumo, we shall establish, shed light on the meaning of monumentality to Japanese authority and its relationship to the pervasive counter-concept of the impermanence of all things.

Ruling Authority and Religious Practice at Ise and Izumo

In common with the architecture of authority in the ancient and medieval Mediterranean world, in which the pillar and capital, arch and vault were held in common by the sacred and secular dominions,[4] the architecture of Ise and

Izumo transcended the realms of religious conviction and political certitude. Their buildings represented an authority which drew no necessary distinction between the rites of worship and the right to rule. Along with the other provincial centres of early Japan, the leadership of Ise and Izumo sought to broaden the basis of their respective ruling authority by architectonic methods. Authority stemmed from ritual, in which the ruler served as intermediary between the world of gods and the world of human beings. Effective power derived from association with the supernatural, control over craft industries and the organisation of wet-rice agriculture, and from some military force. The contemporary term used for 'government', *matsurigoto,* meant performing rites in honour of the gods, but was used interchangeably to describe procedural matters of religion and everyday administration.[5] The elite of each clan built a hierarchy of status and title, and wove from fact and fiction elaborate mythologies establishing their own divine ancestries. They also used shrines as a setting for demonstrating their power prerogatives. It was the direct patronage of an elite preoccupied by such ambitions which elevated the vernacular forms of the secular storehouse and raised-floor residence to the level of sacred architecture, creating buildings which became the most pervasive icons of Shinto and the most compelling demonstration of their right to rule. For them, as for the kings of ancient Mesopotamia, to rule was to build and to build was to rule.

Ise and Izumo in History

As a result of their profound importance to the process of consolidation of national governing authority, an enormous body of written documents and interpretation has accumulated over the centuries pertaining to every aspect of religious practice, political role and architectural forms of Ise and Izumo. This in itself indicates the importance which has been placed on the elevation of the authority of Ise and the relegation of Izumo to inferior status throughout recorded history. Inevitably the written record has been decisively shaped by the victors in any confrontation so that much that claims to be historical record is intrinsically polemical and can be used only within the limitations so imposed.

Study of Ise Shrine in particular is further complicated by the transitory nature of the architecture of the building complex itself. The Ise shrine buildings have been completely rebuilt at intervals of 20 years since the late seventh century, with one major interruption only, lasting 123 years, caused by the protracted civil war of the later fifteenth and sixteenth centuries. The last rebuilding process of the twentieth century was completed in 1993, replacing the structures which had been finished in 1973. At Izumo reconstruction has been carried out far less systematically, but the main buildings are still comparative newcomers in historical terms, dating only to the mid-eighteenth century.

It is conventional to begin the study of Japanese architecture with the Ise and Izumo shrines because of their close association with the formation of early elite architecture in Japan. Strictly speaking, the buildings which occupy the sacred sites at Ise and Izumo today are of far less consequence as historical artefacts than the architectural and religious traditions they represent, dating as they do to rebuildings completed in 1993 and 1744 respectively. Many of their technical and stylistic characteristics are a fascinating indication of building and ritual practices under constant refinement since antiquity, and reflect the changing circumstances of authority over the entire span of Japanese history, not simply those of the early state. However, it is valid to begin this study with these two institutions because they form enduring traditions of architecture and authority, and we need to identify the nexus between early rule and early shrine buildings as the point of origin for their associated traditions. Immediately we begin this exercise we discover that the Ise shrine buildings were originally far less impressive architecturally and less important politically than were those of Izumo. The Ise shrine buildings were modest in scale and unassuming in architectural form until at least the ninth century.[6] The architectural priority for the chieftains of the early clans had been the construction of monumental, stone-faced key-hole-shaped tombs or *kofun* in which they themselves were to be buried. The largest tomb, that of the fourth-century emperor Nintoku, has the same base dimensions as the largest of the Egyptian pyramids and was surrounded by two water-filled moats crossed by a great causeway. These tombs were the most dramatic statements of authority in the period from about 190 AD, when the semi-legendary priestess and ruler Himiko is said to have held sway over much of western Japan, until well into the sixth century when the arrival of new architectural forms and the practice of cremation from the kingdoms of the Korean peninsula and China ended tomb construction.

In the seventh and eighth centuries the consolidation of institutions of a centralised, bureaucratic and imperial state on the Chinese model prompted the formal redefinition of the rituals of the Ise shrines in terms of the imperial institution, as well as stimulating efforts to give it a more substantial architectural presence. Chinese concepts of monumental construction and planning, order and hierarchy, were superimposed on the Ise and Izumo sites and formally differentiated compounds were adopted to signify the inner sanctuaries instead of simple straw ropes and white pebbles. The orientation of the Ise sites was shifted from east–west, the trajectory of the sun and an axis appropriate in direction to worship of the Sun-Goddess, to a north–south orientation, in conformity with Chinese practice.[7] The official histories compiled at the Nara imperial court, the *Kojiki* completed in 712, and the *Nihon shoki* in 720, consolidated into written form the imperial mythology concerning the origins of the imperial family with Amaterasu as Sun-Goddess. At the same time, in a sustained campaign to discredit mythologically based claims to authority emanating from Izumo, they poured scorn on Susano-o, father of Okuninushi enshrined at Izumo.

Izumo was able to stake a counter-claim for greater political and religious prominence through energetic rebuilding of the Grand Shrine in the later Heian period and again in the later sixteenth and early seventeenth centuries, periods characterised by weakened central authority. Ise, for its part, was to enjoy renewed importance at the expense of Izumo during the Edo period with the growth of a popular cult associated with the Outer Shrine dedicated to Toyouke, while the revival of 'National Learning' later in the period, in the eighteenth and nineteenth centuries, laid the intellectual basis for a dramatic increase in the role of the Inner Shrine as part of the philosophy of the Imperial Restoration movement. The scholar and physician ·Motoori Norinaga (1730–1801) wrote exhaustive commentaries on the *Kojiki* which profoundly influenced the interpretation of Shinto as 'the Way of the Gods'[8] as part of this revival of nationalist sentiment. Motoori, in stressing the status of the successive generations of the imperial family as *kami* or gods, conferred additional authority on Ise as their ancestral shrine. With the re-establishment of imperial government in 1868 and the creation of State Shinto came enthusiastic state sponsorship for rebuilding and enlargement of the imperial shrine.

During the Pacific War Japan's military expansion was justified as a holy cause centred on the emperor. His association with the Shinto gods became the basis of militarist ideology to sustain the war effort and justify death as noble sacrifice.[9] After the Allied victory over Japan in 1945 this manipulation of the authority of Ise as a means of justifying military expansion drew upon it the wrath of the conquering powers. The Occupation-imposed constitution officially separated church and state based on the American model, relegating Ise, at least in Occupation thinking, to the status of a private religious foundation with no state support. The separation of the religious from the secular has been encouraged by the general political and intellectual climate of postwar Japan although it is still a source of considerable controversy. However, at the funeral of the Emperor Shōwa in 1989, a carefully drawn official distinction was made between the private Shinto rites of the imperial family, for which a *torii* gateway was erected, and the public ceremonies conducted by the constitutionally separate state, for which the *torii* was removed. The separation of church and state has swept away the official support for Ise as an institution and for the funding of the essential periodic rebuilding. This disestablishment is, in effect, the same fate which Izumo suffered early in its history. Ise Shrine must now function in the same manner as any private religious institution and the funding for its regular renewal is raised by public subscription. Ise does not have access even to the national and local government subsidies allocated for the repair of important cultural properties and national treasures, with which, ironically, periodic maintenance of Izumo is undertaken.

It is important to bear this complex historical background in mind when analysing the architecture of the two shrines. The fact that they have been so consistently a source of inspiration as well as controversy in Japanese history is evidence of their special importance. In this study, however, the emphasis is directed to an examination of extant buildings, their stylistic origins and siting, style, materials and meaning, rather than to a detailed discussion of each historical phase.

Ise Jingū

Character of the Site and Buildings

The generic term 'Ise' or 'Ise Shrine' refers to a large institution consisting of numerous shrines and lesser sanctuaries distributed around a narrow, verdant, coastal plain on the east coast of the Kii peninsula in Mie prefecture. The area is blessed by warm sunshine even in mid-winter, and crossed by the fast-flowing Isuzu River. A visitor gazing over the landscape shrouded in the mists of early morning could well be persuaded to believe in the presence of benign deities. The shrine dedicated to Amaterasu is known officially as the *Kō daijingū* or 'Imperial Shrine' but from the Heian period has been referred to generally as the Naikū ('Inner Shrine'). The other principal shrine, dedicated to Toyouke, is officially called the *Toyouke daijingū* or the Gekū ('Outer Shrine'). The Inner Shrine is situated well inland from the coast, while the Outer Shrine is some five kilometres to the northwest and closer to the sea. Originally the two shrines were unrelated, the Toyouke shrine being of more ancient foundation than that dedicated to Amaterasu, but, together with a number of other local shrines, they were incorporated into a unified institution in the ninth century.[10] In addition to the two main shrine complexes, Ise now encompasses close to 120 separate shrines including a number of tiny sanctuaries dedicated to the spirit of a single rock or the deity of some clear bubbling spring.

Only after a reasonable acquaintance with the buildings and the layout of the shrine sites is it possible to appreciate the role of the Inner Shrine at Ise in the history of authority. It is especially important to understand the way in which the Inner Shrine communicates with the visitor and worshipper as an integrated built and natural environment. It is laid out on a site which slopes gently upwards from the rapidly running water of the Isuzu River towards the low hills which in turn ascend abruptly out of the edge of the coastal plain (Figure 2.1). It is approached across a great bridge constructed from fragrantly scented cypress wood (*hinoki*). At each end of the bridge is a large *torii*, the open gateway which is the universal symbol of a Shinto sanctuary in Japan, with principal pillars measuring almost one metre in diameter. The visitor proceeds from the bridge to the right or southwards along a broad avenue strewn with gravel and flanked by carefully tended gardens. Some 200 metres further on another great *torii* is encountered, and beyond it there is the large stone basin for ritual purification of mouth and hands, a feature common to all Shinto shrines. From this point cedars (*sugi*) some 80 metres in height, and an occasional zelkova elm (*keyaki*), close in around the visitor, creating a sense of primal force and majesty. The approach path, now surfaced with small grey pebbles, swings around in an easterly direction through another *torii*. Thick moss covers the aged rocks beside the path. In these rocks and trees the native *kami* or spirits are traditionally thought to dwell. This is a living sanctuary of animistic belief.

One hundred metres from the last *torii* the path snakes around to the south and then back to the north, bringing the visitor to an enclosed compound 100 metres north–south and 60 metres east–west. This is the inner sanctuary itself. The most immediately notable feature of the compound is the way in which it is elevated some 4 to 5 metres above the level of the approach path. This is accomplished by assembling two layers of large rocks into a retaining wall, much in the manner of medieval castle foundations, so that the final approach is made by mounting 21 stone steps to an outer fence of horizontal boards (Figure 2.2). Beyond lies another small fence guarded by a timber-frame gatehouse with a thatched roof of moss-encrusted river reed (*kaya*). A fine silk curtain hangs across the entrance to the gate, marking the point of intersection between the profane and the sacred, beyond which traditionally only members of the imperial family and priests of the shrine may proceed. Here the visitor may make obeisances and offer prayers, and glimpse something of the sacred precinct beyond as it rises gently away to disappear from sight behind a second gateway which affords access to the inner sanctum. Grey pebbles cover the surface of the compound, with white rocks forming the path leading the way to the sanctuary buildings. The ridge of the main sanctuary building, or Shōden, may be glimpsed from this vantage point, rising above the protecting gateway and surmounted by towering forked finials known as *chigi*. Some 4 to 5 metres in length and sheathed in gilded bronze, these *chigi* gleam in the sunlight like a portent of the presence of the Sun Goddess herself.

The inner sanctum, which is hidden from view, contains three separate structures organised axially north–south (Figure 2.3). At the centre is the

Fig 2.1
Map of Inner
Shrine of Ise
(1985–93
rebuilding)
(Courtesy of
Ise Jingū)

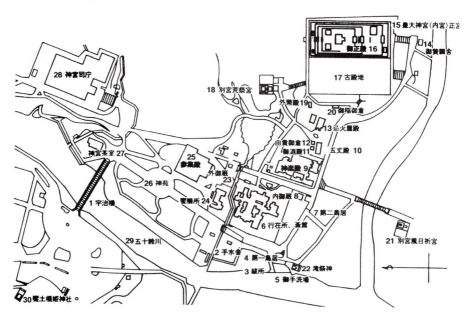

1. Uji Bridge (Main Entry into Naikū)
2. Font for Ablutions prior to Worship
3. Haraedo (Place for Purification)
4. Daiichi Torii (First Sacred Gateway)
5. Site for Ablutions by the Isuzu River
6. Saikan (Purification Hall)
7. Daini Torii (Second Sacred Gateway)
8. Inner Stall for Sacred Horse
9. Kaguraden (Hall of Sacred Music and Dance)
10. Gojōden
11. Misakadono
12. Yukinomikura
13. Imibiyaden (Hall of Pure Fire)
14. Minie Chōsha (Sacred Foods Ceremonial Preparation Hall)
15. Kōdaijingū Shōgū (Main Sanctuary)
16. (Go)shōden (Main Sanctuary Building)
17. Kodenchi (Alternate Site of Sanctuary)
18. Auxiliary Sanctuary Aramatsurinomiya
19. Geheiden (Outer Treasury)
20. Mishinenomikura (Rice Storehouse)
21. Auxiliary Sanctuary Kazahinominomiya
22. Lesser Sanctuary of Takimatsurinokami
23. Outer Stall for Sacred Horse
24. Kyōzensho
25. Sanshūden (Rest Area for Worshippers)
26. Sacred Garden
27. Jingū Chashitsu (Jingū Teahouse)
28. Jingū Shichō (Jingū Administration)
29. Isuzu River
30. Lesser Sanctuary Aedohashihime Jinja

Fig 2.2
Approach to
the sanctuary,
Inner Shrine,
Ise (1965–73
rebuilding)

Shōden, and behind it, to either side of the axis, are two smaller sanctuary buildings. The pillars and walls are made of Japanese cypress and the straight gable roofs are thatched with *kaya*. The ridge-poles are lined with cylindrical wooden billets known as *katsuogi* ('bonito fish timbers'), a name which refers to their distinctive bonito-like shape, and are surmounted by the projecting finials. At each end of the buildings are external pillars which rise from the ground to support the ridge-poles. All of the pillars are sunk deeply into the

23

Fig 2.3   Sanctuary of Inner Shrine, Ise, showing sacred fences,
Shōden and smaller sanctuary building (1985–93 rebuilding)
(Courtesy of Ise Jingū)

earth. The Shōden is 15 metres long, 10 metres wide and 9.7 metres in
height measured to the top of the ridge course (Figure 2.4). A wooden staircase at the front is covered by a simple gabled roof in the same style as the
main roof itself.

Set beside the inner compound and covered with white pebbles is the
Alternate Site where the main buildings will be erected during the next periodic renewal of the shrine (Figure 2.5). At the centre is a small wooden hut
erected to protect the heart pillar (*shin no mihashira*) over which the Shōden
of the new shrine will be raised in the next rebuilding.

The rebuilding process, known as *shikinen sengū* ('the transfer of the god-
body to a new shrine in a special festival year'), spans eight years and consumes
approximately 13,600 cypress trees yielding some 10,000 cubic metres of
timber. Originally these trees were available in plentiful supply in the
surrounding region but since the thirteenth century forests have become seriously depleted and the requisite supplies of timber have had to been procured
from the more distant mountains of the Japan Alps in the province of Kiso.
The Kiso River, flowing into Ise Bay, provided a ready means of transport
for the logs which skilled loggers floated down the river through its hazardous
gorges and rapids.

The rebuilding of Ise involves a protracted succession of 32 major ceremonies. It commences with the *Yamaguchi-sai*, or expiatory prayers offered

Fig 2.4
Shōden of
Inner Shrine,
Ise (1985–93
rebuilding)
(Courtesy of
Ise Jingū)

to the *kami* of the mountain where the sacred trees selected for the reconstruction are to be felled, and culminates with the ritual transferral of the
sacred mirror from the old to the new precinct, after which the superseded
buildings are dismantled.

The Outer Shrine is located five kilometres to the northwest of the Inner
Shrine. The layout of the site and architecture of the buildings are similar in

Fig 2.5
Aerial view of
main sanctuary,
Inner Shrine,
Ise (1985–93
rebuilding)
(Courtesy of
Ise Jingū)

Fig 2.6
Shōden of
Outer Shrine,
Ise (1985–93
rebuilding)
(Courtesy of
Ise Jingū)

most respects to those of the Inner Shrine, as is the importance of the inner compound and the provision of an Alternate Site for periodic rebuilding (Figure 2.6). There are, however, certain subtle variations in the siting and characteristics of the buildings arising from deliberate distinctions in authority

Fig 2.7
Approach to
sanctuary of
Outer Shrine,
Ise (1965–73
rebuilding)

drawn architecturally between the Inner and Outer Shrines. For example, the Outer Shrine is approached across a sacred bridge but the sentinel *torii* are little more than half the height of those marking the entry to the Inner Shrine. *Torii* are also set at strategic points along the approaches to the main compound, but the approach itself is different in character to that of the Inner Shrine: the way is flat and more direct, the trees less imposing and physically encroaching, the atmosphere not so awe-inspiring as at the Inner Shrine. The compound itself is approximately the same size as the Inner Shrine and also aligned axially north–south. However, it is set on the same level as the approach path, not elevated by stone-faced embankments (Figure 2.7). The buildings contained therein are thus more readily visible to the casual observer.

Architectonics of Imperial Authority at Ise

How, then, is authority expressed and defined in this complicated shrine precinct with its distinctive buildings and elaborate process of periodic renewal?

The impression created by the Inner Shrine is powerful and elemental, the unpainted timbers and the thatched roofs affirming close affinity with the natural world. There is no apparent distinction between authority imperial and authority spiritual, between the powers of the natural world and the powers of imperial governance. All are organically interrelated, each aspect reinforcing the other in a relationship which has been refined to a high degree of visual expression and stylistic abstraction over the centuries.

The *Nihon shoki* records that it was at this place that Amaterasu first came to earth, having proclaimed that 'the province of Ise, of the divine wind, is the land whither repair the waves from the eternal world, the successive waves. It is a secluded and pleasant land. In this land I wish to dwell.' The account then continues by stating explicitly that 'in compliance with the instruction of the Great Goddess, a shrine was erected to her in the province of Ise. . . . It was here that Amaterasu first descended from Heaven'.[11]

It is a deeply seated Japanese belief that the *kami* select certain places where they will descend to earth, thereby rendering them holy. People come to these sacred sites, generation after generation, to commune with the gods, to make offerings of the harvest of mountain and sea to them, and to give thanks. In early Shinto practice the places where the particular gods had their abode were not necessarily marked by buildings or special structures; the *kami* could establish their dwelling places in trees, rocks or waterfalls. Sometimes a simple building was constructed as the gods' temporary home as a sign of gratitude for their presence. At Ise the role of the Inner Shrine buildings has been to house Amaterasu in the form of the sacred bronze mirror, which, together with the curved jewel and sacred sword, comprise the three imperial regalia. Throughout the countries of ancient Asia the mirror was regarded as one of the most important symbols of authority, closely associated with the worship of the sun whose light its burnished bronze surface reflected so brightly. At Ise we find the persistence of this association, with the enshrined mirror serving as the physical manifestation of Amaterasu.[12] Accordingly, the Inner Shrine has served as the locus for the multitude of ceremonies of oblation,

Fig 2.8 Emperor Shōwa arrives for formal visit to Ise Shrine following the completion of his Enthronement Ceremonies in Kyoto (November 10–15, 1928)
(Source: Official publication, *Shōwa tairei shashinchō*, Tokyo, Ōtsuka kōgeisha, 1930)

thanksgiving, purification and offering necessary for her propitiation. It was not until the late seventh century that the association of the Ise site with Amaterasu and the imperial family was formalised. Thereafter it was to serve as the focus for the religious rites of the imperial institution. To the present day, important events, such as coming of age and weddings of members of the imperial family, and above all the death of an emperor and the enthronement of his successor, are reported to the ancestral spirit at the shrine with due solemnity and ceremony (Figure 2.8).

Pragmatic methods have been employed to achieve inspired effects to express the religious and ruling authority of Ise. Once explained they lose something of that mystery essential to their purpose. Authority is established by recourse to a dual strategy of spatial segregation and partial revelation. The inner compound is separated from the plane of mortal beings in a hierarchy of spatial transitions. The first of these is accomplished by means of the elevation of the compound high above the level of the approach path. It is no accident that the final approach is up a series of steeply rising steps. Here the mortal plane is permitted to rise to meet the gods, in studied contra-distinction to the use of a completely flat site for the inner compound of the Outer Shrine.

A series of wooden fences and gateways removes the inner sanctum, in which Amaterasu resides, into the unapproachable distance, with the Shōden hidden from view apart from the merest glimpse of the top of its finials. The singular significance of what lies within is emphasised by the arbitrary denial of entry; the partial revelation of the roofs of the buildings grants the beholder a glimpse of the world beyond while making clear that the ultimate truths are reserved for those privileged to enter the inner sanctum. The privilege to enter this sanctum and act as intermediary between this world and the world of the gods of creation and nature was traditionally confined to the members of the imperial institution. Access to the inner sanctum has thereby become one of the most important rights and acts of authority in Japanese civilization.

Hierarchy in authority is enacted through a finely calibrated hierarchy of access through gateways of obeisance. At first the series of open *torii* along the approach path signify the accessibility of that which lies immediately beyond to all who proceed along the way, while making it clear that a place of great authority is drawing closer. Folk-belief also confers on these gateways the role of perches for the large sacred fowls who arrive as messengers of the gods at daybreak.

At the inner sanctuary there are four separate ritual spaces reserved for obeisances (*sampai*) performed by worshippers. These spaces are ranked hierarchically by status and defined physically by the four fences and gateways surrounding the main sanctuary building (Figure 2.9). An imposing *torii* allows all visitors to pass through the outer fence or Itagaki to make obeisances at the eaves of the roofed gateway which guards entry through the second fence or Outer Tamagaki (see Figure 2.2, p. 23). Passage through this gateway is reserved for members of the imperial family and, in modern practice, for the Prime Minister and elected representatives of the people at national, prefectural and local level. Local mayors and members of assemblies worship at the inner eaves of the Outer Tamagaki, while the representatives of prefectural government, as well as 'living national treasures' stand at the *torii* half-way towards the Inner Tamagaki. The Prime Minister worships directly in front of this gateway while the imperial family progresses further up the gentle slope of the compound to make obeisances under the outer eaves of the gateway through the Inner Tamagaki. The crown prince and crown princess, as heirs to the throne, customarily proceed through the Inner Tamagaki to pray at the eaves of the Mizugakimon, the gateway set into the innermost fence surrounding the Shōden. A special dispensation to proceed through the innermost gateway in order to worship directly in front of the steps of the Shōden is given on the occasion of the marriage of the crown prince and crown princess. Under normal circumstances, however, the privilege of entering the innermost space of the shrines is reserved for the reigning emperor and empress and the Chief Priestess (*Saishu*) of the shrine. The emperor and empress make their obeisances separately and successively at the foot of the steps of the Shōden. Immediately after the enthronement ceremonies, however, they are each permitted to climb the steps to worship on the verandah of the Shōden in front of the main door. In this way passage through a hierarchically ordered sequence of gateways becomes a carefully calibrated enactment of ritual order within the hierarchy of authority.[13]

The use of a series of fences to protect the inner compound reflects the early Japanese practice of constructing a succession of fences around centres of local power. A typical example is the use of multiple palisades around the

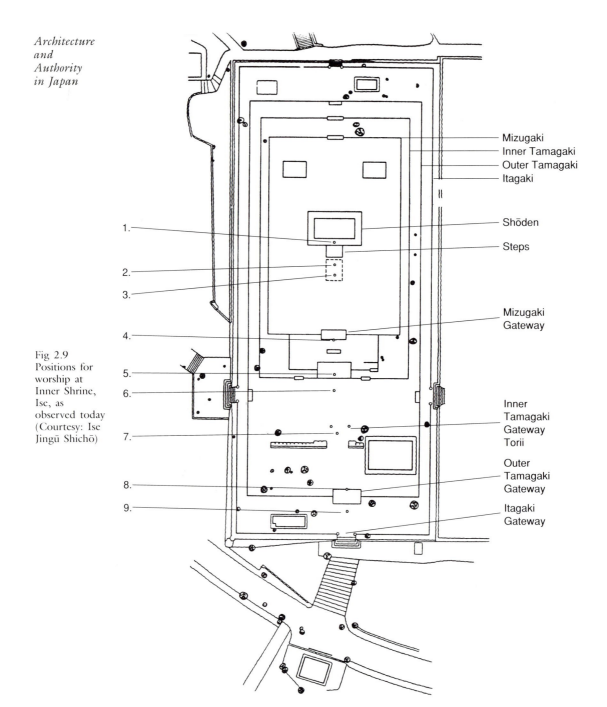

Fig 2.9
Positions for
worship at
Inner Shrine,
Ise, as
observed today
(Courtesy: Ise
Jingū Shichō)

Mizugaki
Inner Tamagaki
Outer Tamagaki
Itagaki

Shōden

Steps

Mizugaki
Gateway

Inner
Tamagaki
Gateway
Torii

Outer
Tamagaki
Gateway

Itagaki
Gateway

1.
2.
3.
4.
5.
6.
7.
8.
9.

eighth-century fortification of Tagajō, located to the immediate northeast of the modern city of Sendai. The Inner Shrine of Ise today employs a total of four fences but historically the number of fences changed in response to the circumstances of authority. According to the *Kō daijingū gishiki-chō* of 804 AD, which records details of the rebuilding of the shrines following arson which destroyed much of the complex in 791, there was a total of five fences around the compound in the ninth century. In the fourteenth century, during the imperial succession struggles known as the Nambokuchō (1318–92), the three outer fences were lost, and despite subsequent attempts to reinstate the missing fences, there were only two fences around the compound for much of the eighteenth and nineteenth centuries. Obeisances were made standing under the eaves of the gateway of what is now known as the Inner Tamagaki. In the periodic rebuilding completed in 1869, a year after the restoration of imperial government, the Itagaki and Outer Tamagaki, the two outer fences, were rebuilt to restore the site to its pre-1318 configuration. This had the effect of enhancing the dignity of the emperor by further distancing the inner sanctum of Ise from the outside world, at the same time as creating a special place for obeisances by the Prime Minister as official representative of the new government at the Inner Tamagaki. This can only be described as an interesting exercise in political fence-mending.[14]

Gateway architecture at Ise may owe much to Chinese precedent, with the gatehouses guarding the inner sanctum being structurally identical to those protecting temple and palace compounds in Nara, but the Shōden, with its two flanking treasuries and the smaller halls used for daily offerings of food and drink, developed directly from Japanese vernacular architecture of the pre-Buddhist age. The special character of these buildings is explicable only in terms of the origins of this architectural style in vernacular building forms, and by the process by which these were transformed under the patronage of state authority over many generations of renewal at the same site.

The form of the principal Ise buildings is derived from the unadorned raised-floor structures in use from proto-historical times for storing rice throughout the wet-rice agricultural regions of Asia (Figure 2.10).[15] Archaeological excavations in Japan, along with unsophisticated depictions of buildings incised into cast bronze bells, prove that buildings of this type, with sunken pillars, raised floors, plank walls interlocked in the manner of a log cabin, and thatched roofs with rafters projecting at each end and lashed together for strength, were accorded special significance. The main buildings of both shrines

1. Reigning Emperor and Empress following the Enthronement Ceremonies
2. Reigning Emperor and Empress on all other occasions
3. Crown Prince and Crown Princess on the occasion of their marriage
4. Crown Prince and Crown Princess on all other occasions
5. Other members of the Imperial Family
6. Prime Minister, members of both Houses of the Diet and other senior elected officials such as prefectural governors
7. Elected members of prefectural governments and mayors of cities, Living National Treasures and Officials of Ise Shrine
8. Elected officials of local governments, including mayors of towns and villages
9. General public

Fig 2.10
Reconstruction
of raised-floor
granary, Toro
archaeological
site, Shizuoka
prefecture

are based on this vernacular form, with their raised floors protecting their important spiritual contents in the way that village granaries protected the harvested rice from moisture and rodents. The covered wooden steps at the centre front of the Shōden were originally necessary as a way of carrying the harvested rice into and out of the granary (see Figures 2.4 and 2.12).

In early agrarian Japanese society it was inevitable that the importance of the granary should be deeply embedded in community consciousness. It was

32

the focal point for festivals, particularly the autumn harvest celebrations. It was then only a short step to transferring belief in the beneficence of the gods to the specific buildings which housed the grain of life. Grain represented the product of the forces of nature – rain and water, and above all the miracle of growth and regeneration. Moreover, in any traditional village community the raised-floor storehouse was the sturdiest, most impressive and carefully constructed building.

For all these reasons it was natural and logical that the Yamato court should make the raised-floor storehouse the abode for Amaterasu. It is not surprising, therefore, that recent archaeological excavations have established that the use of the raised-floor building type at Ise for religious purposes was the rule rather than the exception in early Japan. Such buildings were geographically widespread throughout the populated regions and an intrinsic part of the festivals of local ruling authority. They were typically erected inside ceremonial enclosures within the palisaded headquarters of the most powerful chieftains. There are other significant indications of widespread observance in proto-historical times of ritual practices similar to those followed at Ise. For example, stone pebbles like those employed at Ise to signify a sacred area were used to cover the ceremonial enclosure containing a raised-floor building at the fifth-century Mitsudera I site, near Takasaki, Gumma prefecture, on the western periphery of the Kantō Plain.[16] Similarly, the Makimuku II and III phase sites, at the foot of Mount Miwa in Nara prefecture, near present-day Sakurai city, included a raised-floor building 4.4 by 5.3 metres in plan with pillars approximately 20 centimetres in diameter. It was orientated east–west, in keeping with the theory that this was the principal axis employed in the site planning of early Shinto sanctuaries, and not north–south. Moreover it included the same structurally fossilised ridge-pole pillar and central pillar as are used at Ise. The building was enclosed by a fence and was almost certainly flanked by two smaller raised-floor structures.[17] With the single exception of orientation it is difficult to envisage a more precise correlation in structure, style and site layout with the inner compounds of the Ise Shrine.

One of the most intriguing features of the Shōden of both the Inner and Outer Shrines is their ridge decoration (Figure 2.11). Much of the visual impact of the buildings is derived from the forked finials and cylindrical billets set on the ridges because of their visibility from beyond the compound fences. The finials are abstracted representations of the projecting tips of the gable-end rafters used in early thatched roofs. The ridge billets are a similar reference to pre-Buddhist architecture. The clay *haniwa* model houses, which were placed on the outer surfaces of the burial mounds of clan chieftains of the Tumulus period, show how heavy wooden cylinders were placed along the ridges of larger buildings to weigh down the peak of the gable and seal it against rain or prevent strong winds blowing the roof apart. By the sixth century, written records establish that these billets had become symbols of status, and government regulations restricted their use to homes of high-ranking members of the ruling class.[18]

The ten billets on the ridge of the Shōden of the Inner Shrine and the nine used on the same structure of the Outer Shrine were thus indications of high status, with the former clearly ranked more highly than the latter

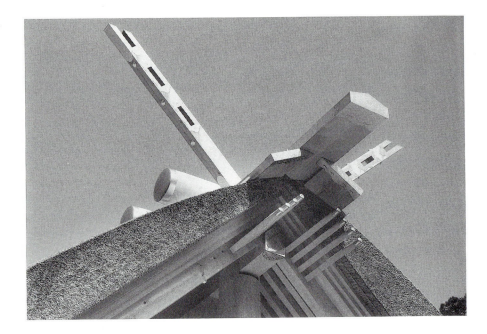

Fig 2.11
Ridge decoration of Shōden
of Inner
Shrine, Ise:
Forked finials
(*chigi*) (top)
and cylindrical
billets
(*katsuogi*)
(bottom)
(1985–93
rebuilding)
(Courtesy of
Ise Jingū)

(Figures 2.12 and 2.13). They may also represent elemental folk belief concerning gender, so important in early Shinto and reinforced by Chinese *yin-yang* principles introduced at a later date. There could be some correlation between even numbers and female gender and odd numbers and male gender. In the final analysis Ise does consist of two main shrines, one dedicated to a female god and the other to a male deity. In the amalgamation of the two institutions mythological gender may have played a more important role in their symbolism than has heretofore been acknowledged.

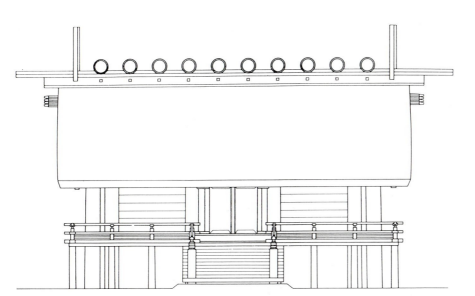

Fig 2.12
Shōden, Inner
Shrine, Ise.
Front elevation
(1985–93
rebuilding)
(Courtesy of
Ise Jingū)

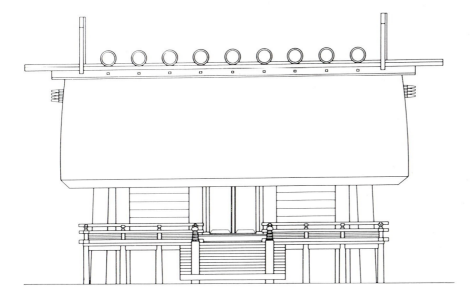

Fig 2.13
Shōden, Outer
Shrine, Ise.
Front elevation
(1985–93
rebuilding)
(Courtesy of
Ise Jingū)

Despite every effort to maintain the physical form of the Ise Shrine through each rebuilding process, there was a slow mutation of the architectural style from the functional to the abstract. Nishina Shimmeigū, in Omachi, Nagano prefecture, the oldest extant shrine built in this style, reflects the simpler functional logic of the earlier Ise building style. It was last rebuilt in 1636, as part of the nationwide observance of the cult of Amaterasu, under the patronage of the local daimyo of Matsumoto. With its single, large ridge-pole, finials made up of the projecting ends of the principal rafters and absence of gilded bronze ornament, this exquisite small shrine hints at the elemental quality of earlier Ise.[19]

35

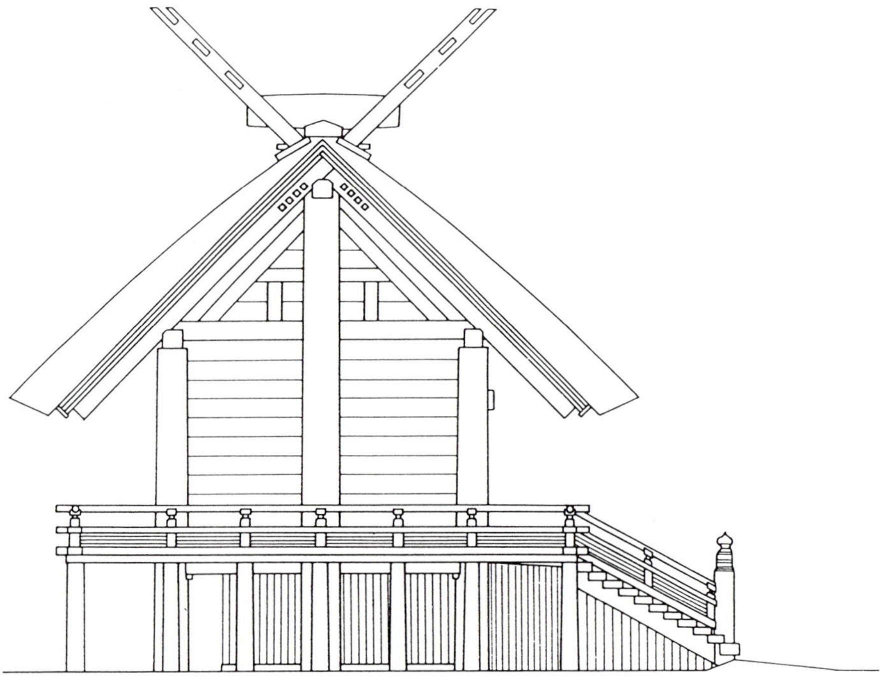

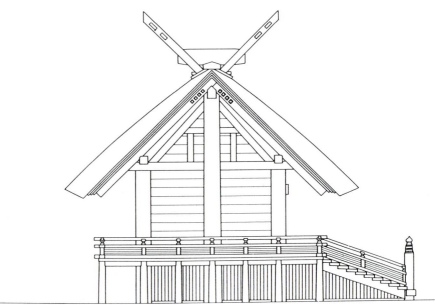

Fig 2.14
Shōden, Inner
Shrine, Ise.
Side elevation
(1985–93
rebuilding)
(Courtesy of
Ise Jingū)

Fig 2.15
Shōden, Outer
Shrine, Ise.
Side elevation
(1985–93
rebuilding)
(Courtesy of
Ise Jingū)

Another example of the increasing abstraction of architectural form at Ise is
to be found in the small Halls of Daily Offering (*Mikeiden*). The joinery which
links the timbers of the walls in these two buildings consists of interlocking tenons which recall the robust 'log-cabin' construction (*azekura-zukuri*)
used for the walls of early Japanese storehouses and the buildings of Ise probably until medieval times.[20] These tenons are now no longer structural but

are retained in fossilised form as part of the official iconography of the Ise style.

The architectural form of the Outer Shrine, being less important politically, has consequently been subject to less attention and less rigorous renewal practices. Its Shōden has a more elementary arrangement of pillars and beams supporting the rafters of the roof than has the Inner Shrine, and longitudinal head-ties are placed directly on top of the principal cross beams (Figures 2.14 and 2.15). This is a simpler method of construction than that employed for the Inner Shrine, where the longitudinal tie-beams are set beneath the cross beams, requiring complex joinery and calculation of dimensions. The intention may have been to make the slope of the roof of the Inner Shrine steeper and more impressive.

Periodic Renewal and Authority

Whatever the status symbolism of different parts of the Ise buildings and the role of the integrated architectural strategy in representing authority through hierarchical distinctions, periodic rebuilding of the entire shrine complex has added a special dimension to the relationship between architecture and authority at Ise (Figure 2.16). Periodic renewal sustained through most of recorded history has not only ensured the survival of its physical form but does much to explain its religious and political significance.

There are three reasons for this seemingly extraordinary commitment of energy and resources to the periodic rebuilding of a religious edifice. The first is architectural, the second religious and the third political. In the eighth century, during the period of consolidation of state authority, the original architectural and religious reasons were to be overwhelmed by a powerful political imperative.

Fig 2.16 Aerial view of Inner Shrine, Ise, showing old and new shrines side by side in 1992 prior to the dismantling of the structures built in 1965–73 (Courtesy of Ise Jingū)

The first, architectural reason is, quite simply, the ephemeral nature of many of the materials used for the construction of the shrine buildings. These buildings have been subject to the same inexorable process of deterioration as is experienced by any farmhouse made from similar exposed timbers and thatch. The reed thatch of the roofs, although carefully shaped and manicured to the dictates of its elite patrons, still rots in the same manner as any ordinary roof composed of reed, straw, or wooden shingles (Figure 2.17). Similarly, the practice of inserting the pillars directly into the ground renders them ready victims to rotting and white ants. In the tightly-knit communities of the Bronze and early-Iron Age where these construction practices originated, cooperative rebuilding of individual structures including community storehouses took place in the course of each generation.

The second reason for the periodic renewal of Ise flows logically from the first: the process of decay and renewal inherent in its architectural forms was seen as an affirmation of the cycles of nature which are central to Shinto belief. The rebuilding process became a metaphor for the cycle of growth, decay, death and rebirth to be found in every aspect of the physical universe, ranging from agriculture to life itself. The rebuilding of Ise, together with early Shinto buildings generally, became a form of existential affirmation. It also constituted ritual purification: cleanliness was indeed next to godliness in Shinto, for uncleanliness and decay represented defilement. This belief was reflected in the early Japanese practice of abandoning the palace headquarters upon the death of the ruler in order to avoid defilement, and the subsequent creation of a new, specially purified palace as the seat of authority. Likewise, the pure, clean image of the buildings in Shinto architecture is essential to the preservation of the sanctity of the site for the gods. Purity was to be achieved through ritual, and it transformed the practical need to replace decaying building materials into a high spiritual obligation to renew shrine architecture as a place suitable for the habitation of the gods.

The periodic rebuilding of the Grand Shrine of Ise is the supreme example of architectural process transformed into religious ritual, the sanctification of an architectural rationale of replacement. Correct ritual ensures the protection of the *kami*. This character is evident in each of the 32 principal rituals and ceremonies which are performed during the eight years of the rebuilding operation. These ceremonies are faithfully re-enacted at each rebuilding in the form standardised by the early tenth century. Many are described in detail in the *Engi-shiki*, one of the earliest extant written records of imperial court etiquette compiled in the Engi era (901–922) and itself based on the earlier *Kō daijingū gishiki-chō* ('record of ceremonial procedures for exchanging shrines') of AD 804.[21]

However the religious meaning of renewal goes far beyond the formal ceremonies and rituals. At Ise the actual practices of rebuilding take on the essence of sacred ritual. The pragmatic acts of the reconstruction process become an offering or oblation to the gods. Each stroke of an adze and every cut of a saw is presided over by master carpenters who have been specially purified for their sacred task, while many of the rituals of renewal are ceremonial enactments of carpentry practices (Figure 2.18). In other words, building practice at Ise is more than a mere extended metaphor for religious belief; it has become a religious act in its own right. The cutting of the wood and the planing of its surfaces are performed with something of the sacramental nature of the breaking of bread and the drinking of wine in Christian practice. The practical and the common in each instance is elevated by commitment and faith to the level of the highest spiritual ritual. The building process is seen as a perfect oblation for the imperfection and impurities of the physical world – virtually a 'rite by which supernatural grace is imparted' – the definition of a 'sacrament' in Christian belief. The power of any building made by such transcendental means to influence the conduct and actions of others, central to the definition of authority, is all the mightier as a consequence. Indeed, it is absolute in the religious sense.

This brings us to the third or political reason for periodic renewal of Ise. It is here at Ise that we find the point of departure from other sites sacred to Shinto belief and practice. The association of the state with the periodic renewal of Ise, a process initially necessitated by the impermanence of the building materials and sanctioned by Shinto theology, was indispensable to the consolidation and ultimately the character of imperial authority. It was this political imperative which was to subsume the architectural and religious rationale.

That familiar mixture of politics and piety is apparent even in the circumstances of the official recognition of Ise as the shrine to Amaterasu. An imperial succession struggle broke out in 672, and the eventual victor in the armed conflict, who subsequently became the Emperor Temmu in the next year, is reported to have worshipped and made obeisance in the direction of the Ise site as he rode out to the decisive battle.[22] Regular rebuilding of Ise was formalised as a state responsibility during Temmu's reign (673–686). From 685 onwards this emperor began the systematic centralisation of state

Fig 2.18 Ceremonial enactment of carpentry practice. The 'Pillar Erection Ceremony' (*Ritchū-sai*) for the Shōden of the Inner Shrine, March 31, 1992
(Courtesy of Ise Jingū)

authority, a process in which architecture played an important role. Under Temmu the government took over responsibility for sponsoring and supervising the periodic rebuilding of Ise, the first state-sponsored rebuilding being completed in 690, four years after his death. A century later it was to be the authority of the Emperor Kammu (r. 781–806) which completed the first comprehensive formalisation of Shinto rites, including the rites of renewal of Ise, as part of state administration. It was also Kammu's vision of a systematically ordered ruling authority, with officially prescribed ceremonies and close associations with both Buddhism and Shinto, which was responsible for the bureaucratic consolidation of Ise and its rites within the practices of the imperial state. In 792, a fire caused, it is thought, by robbers, destroyed much of the Inner Shrine and offered a convenient opportunity for the government to regulate its rebuilding practices. The *Kō daijingū gishiki-chō* was the result, to be followed a century later by further formulation as part of the *Engi-shiki*.[23] In every detail of construction and consecration recorded in these official manuals a sense of order is apparent. The attention to detail, down to the last beam and metal stud, was more than the familiar manifestation of religious zeal for strict compliance with intricate liturgy. It is evidence of a powerful political determination to reinstate the Shinto *kami* alongside Buddhist deities by the provision of copious ritual. With these formal codifications the practice of Shinto rites, including the ritual renewal of the Ise buildings, became part of the official practices of government. Moreover, as a result of the ritual rebuilding, Ise became part of the definition and revelation of imperial authority, and by its Shinto character, evidence of a determination to confer a stronger indigenous character on government after a period of powerful Chinese influence.

It was from this carefully formulated and officially imposed position at the heart of eighth- and ninth-century government that the architectural forms and building practices of Ise were to be transformed into a representation of the sacerdotal authority which sanctioned the imperial order and to become the intermediaries between this order and the natural and supernatural world. By reason of this insistent pressure maintained by ruling authority, the periodic rebuilding of Ise was performed more frequently and comprehensively than architectural necessity alone dictated. Only the rethatching of roofs is essential every 20 to 25 years in this region of Japan. The timbers are quite another matter. The cypress wood used for all the structures is one of the most durable of all building materials. The surfaces are polished to a dull gleam by the action of the planing knives used in traditional carpentry so that water actually beads on the surface of the wood instead of being absorbed by the timber. A structure made of such superlative material and with such dedicated technique would easily last twice the officially designated span of 20 years. Moreover, in the eleventh century the principal pillars of the Shōden were 80 centimetres in diameter and a contemporary account boasts that these would normally be expected to last 'one hundred years without rotting'.[24]

The sustained and regular re-creation of Ise over the course of many generations attests to the authority of two particular traditions: the multiple-stranded craft tradition, which has effected the physical task of rebuilding, and the patronage of the imperial institution. Physically the periodic renewal has been made possible by the hereditary infrastructure of carpenters, thatchers, metalworkers, weavers and dyers, ceremonial saddle-makers, sculptors, lacquer experts and tool smiths. The continuity of the many and varied craft traditions

41

necessary to maintain and renew the myriad buildings of Ise has been vital to the survival of the shrine as an architectural entity. However the key reason for this architectural survival has been the special financial, political and ideological support of the imperial institution. The 20-year renewal observed at Ise was certainly not the exception in Shinto institutions. As already noted, physical decay of materials and the need for religious purity were universal facts. Regular 20-year rebuilding programmes were observed in a large number of institutions. Sumiyoshi Taisha in Osaka carried out systematic rebuilding over a period of more than 500 years from 928 until 1434, and subsequently at less regular intervals until 1810. At Kasuga Taisha in Nara, rebuilding at intervals of from 5 to 33 years has occurred 46 times between 1099 and the present day. The Kamo shrines in Kyoto also observed periodic renewal until 1864, although the intervals were more irregular, a variation of a mere 3 years to 144 years being recorded by local documents.[25]

It is not the observance of the rebuilding process *per se*, but the authority of the imperial institution, which has maintained the tradition of periodic rebuilding far more consistently than that of any other shrine complex in Japan, which sets Ise apart from other shrines. There was a switch from completing the rebuilding in the 20th year, as laid down in the *Engi-shiki*, to completing the rebuilding after 20 years from 1343 onwards, but the only protracted break in that long continuity occurred as a result of the complete breakdown of authority during the period of civil war following the outbreak of the Ōnin Rebellion in 1467. The buildings completed in 1462 were to stand, slowly rotting to point of collapse for 123 years. The rebuilding cycle was revived to suit the political ends of Toyotomi Hideyoshi and then the Tokugawa, reaffirming the indispensability of Ise to ruling authority in Japan.[26]

Izumo Taisha

Turning our attention to a study of Izumo Taisha may seem something of an anti-climax after the high drama of architecture and authority at Ise, but that is precisely what the Nara court and its heirs and successors would have had us believe. While Emperor Kammu and his officials were working assiduously to incorporate the rituals of Ise into the very fabric of the centralised bureaucratic state, Kammu was attacking the residual regional authority of Izumo by attempting to isolate the members of the local aristocracy of Izumo from their Great Shrine. They were chastised for performing their religious functions at the shrine to the neglect of their administrative duties, and prohibited from holding the civil office of provincial governor as a consequence.[27] This was nothing short of an attempt to separate church from state at Izumo, the same tactic which was more recently employed by the Allied Occupation authorities in post-Second World War Japan. For Kammu it was the natural corollary to increasing the status and authority of Ise in national government. It mattered not at all that the same accusations of neglecting administration for the sake of religion could have been laid against Kammu and his court had the positions been reversed. Such is the arbitrary nature of authority, and in this case it was decidedly at the expense of the Izumo establishment.

Despite the Nara court's obfuscation of the written record, historical evidence makes it abundantly clear that the Great Shrine of Izumo was as venerable a centre of Shinto worship as was Ise, and probably at times equally important as a centre of power.[28] It is accorded respect in legend as the oldest shrine in Japan and was long thought to be the place where not one god came to earth, as in the case of Ise, but where the eight million gods of the entire universe assembled on one special occasion each year, a belief still celebrated in the grand festival at Izumo every October. Despite the appeal of the legends of Amaterasu, the presiding deity of Izumo, Okuninushi, has enjoyed abiding prestige as the *kami* in Shinto belief responsible for fishing, sericulture and good fortune. He has wider appeal in folk belief in which he is enshrined and revered as Daikoku, the god of wealth, fortune and the five cereals. In folk custom the *Daikoku-bashira* is the central pillar upon which the structure of a traditional building rests, affording the occupants protection against collapse or other calamity. There is, accordingly, a large and imposing pillar representing this deity placed at the centre of the Honden of Izumo Taisha. Ironically, such a pillar also rests beneath the Shōden of Ise. Given more favourable historical circumstances it is conceivable that the chieftains of Izumo would have exploited the political potential of architectural metonymy to interpret their role as the central pillar of the state.

Izumo was the religious centre of a major regional power-base facing Korea across the Sea of Japan. This proximity to the Korean peninsula made it a long-established point of cultural and technological intercourse with the Asian mainland. This contact enhanced its prestige and power. At the turn of the fourth century the consolidation of power by the Yamato around their home province in the centre of the Kii peninsula was a result of a combination of cunning political manoeuvring and expedient alliance-forming, especially through intermarriage and some degree of military power. The claim to national hegemony by both regional powers was also promoted through ideology, in which the divine associations of the clan leaders and sponsorship of the local shrines played an important part. As we have seen, Izumo's political status was greatly diminished by the successful strategies of the leadership of the Yamato region which culminated in the consolidation of their authority at the imperial court at Nara in the eighth century. As part of this process the myths and legends of Izumo were relegated to secondary status within the official histories of the Nara court. Susano-o, father of Okuninushi, is reviled in the *Nihon shoki*:

Amaterasu [the Heaven-Shining Deity] had made august rice fields of Heavenly narrow rice fields and Heavenly long rice fields. Then Susano-o, when the seed was sown in spring, broke down the divisions between the plots of rice and in autumn let loose the Heavenly piebald colts, and made them lie down in the midst of the rice fields. Again, when he saw that Amaterasu was about to celebrate the feast of first-fruits, he secretly voided excrement in the New Palace. Moreover, when he saw that Amaterasu was in her sacred weaving hall, engaged in weaving garments of the Gods, he flayed a piebald colt of Heaven, and breaking a hole in the roof-tiles of the hall, flung it in.[29]

Such activities as breaking down the dykes in paddy fields and defiling the palace where an important Shinto ritual was to be performed were a heinous attack on the very fabric of good social order and a desecration of sacred and political authority. This is a case of myth and legend coming together using all the principal characters of Izumo legends but with changed emphasis and interpretation to suit the ends of the Nara court. According to the *Kojiki*, Susano-o was expelled from heaven for his misbehaviour and thereupon descended to earth to settle in the land of Izumo.[30]

As in the case of Ise, there is a close correlation at Izumo between the vicissitudes of political and religious fortune and changes in the architecture and organisation of the shrine site. A visit to the Izumo shrine site is like entering a world of architectural authority complementary and alternate to that of Ise, a world in which there is an underlying tension between great ambitions and muted achievements. The declining national authority of Izumo is clearly reflected in the diminished splendour of its architecture, and in the absence today of ritual renewal, the dynamic of which was central to the continuity of authority at Ise.

Izumo Taisha occupies an area of approximately 80,000 square metres, on a flat site to the southwest of a low hill just inland from the coast of the stormy Sea of Japan – a locality very different in ambience from the benign physical environment of Ise. The heart of the complex is a rectangular compound 80 metres north–south and 70 metres east–west, only slightly smaller than the compounds of the Ise Inner and Outer Shrines (Figure 2.19). Set within this compound is the inner precinct, containing the main building or Honden dedicated to Okuninushi (Figure 2.20). The enclosure is guarded by a two-storey gatehouse and a simple paling fence covered by a bark shingle roof. The outer compound, its perimeter defined by another paling fence and a single-storey gateway, is the setting for three smaller shrine buildings dedicated to Okuninushi's mythological consort and two princesses.

The compound rests at the same modest level as the approach path, in the subdued manner of the Outer Shrine at Ise and, like the Outer Shrine, very different in dramatic effect from the Inner Shrine with its elevated sanctum. Most significantly there are only two fences surrounding the Izumo compound, the buildings within being readily visible from outside through the spaces between the fence palings. The deity of Izumo is therefore more proximate to the mortal plane and access, while restricted historically to the clan leadership, is not imbued with the spatial and symbolic intensity as is found at Ise.

It is curious to note, given the inordinate emphasis upon layers of separation used at Ise, that so important a shrine as Izumo has two fences only. The great political and religious authority of Izumo before the Yamato ascendancy suggests that there were more fences surrounding the inner sanctum than are found today. No archaeological excavations have been carried out at the site to test this hypothesis, but an important clue is provided in the *Kojiki*. In the description of the role of Susano-o in killing a serpent which had devoured all but one of the eight daughters of the Earth Deity, particular emphasis is placed on the number eight. Quite apart from the fact of eight daughters, Susano-o kills the serpent with 'eight-fold refined sake

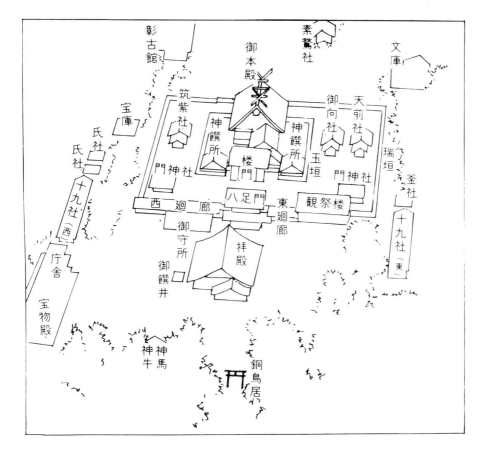

彰古館　素鵞社　文庫

御本殿

宝庫　筑紫社　御向社　天前社

氏社　神饌所　神饌所　瑞垣

氏社　玉垣　釜社

十九社（西）　門神社　楼門　門神社　十九社（東）

庁舎　西廻廊　八足門　東廻廊　観祭楼

宝物殿　御守所　御饌井　拝殿

神馬　神牛　銅鳥居

Fig 2.19
Map of Main
Sanctuary
Compound,
Izumo Shrine
(Courtesy of
Izumo Taisha)

placed in eight vats upon eight platforms built at eight gates.'[31] The *Kojiki*
records that Susano-o then 'sought in the land of Izumo for a place where
he might build a palace', and eventually found an appropriate site at Suga,
in the vicinity of the present shrine. When he first built the palace of Suga,
clouds rose up thence, and then he made an august song. That song said:

> Eight Clouds arise. The eight-fold fence of Izumo makes an eight-fold fence for
> the spouses to retire [within] Oh! that eight-fold fence.[32]

Complete with eight fences and eight gateways, Susano-o's palace must have
been spectacular indeed. We can but speculate about the actual number of
fences and gateways around the shrine at Izumo dedicated to his son, but
the two fences which enclose it today appear a little too modest by any standards for the symbolism for which they are required.

The Honden of Izumo Taisha is similar in general form to the main sanctuaries of the Ise shrines – with the same distinctive raised-floor structure,
and a roof covered in the same cypress-bark shingles (*hiwada-buki*) as were
used for the roofs of Ise until medieval times.[33] However there is no dearth
of architectural detail which sets Izumo apart from Ise. Both feature a covered
entrance with ample wooden steps leading up to the main structure, but at

45

Fig 2.20
Honden of
Izumo Shrine.
Rebuilding
completed in
1744
(Courtesy of
Kodansha)

Izumo the entrance leads to the narrow end of the building in the style of the early residences of the elite as depicted in *haniwa* models (see Figure 2.20). Such side entrances were designed to ensure greater privacy and protection against the elements than was possible with entrances situated at the centre of the main wall. As has been noted in the case of Ise, central doors were the preferred arrangement for granaries because they allowed easier access to the interior for the purposes of storage and removal of rice. The reason why a residence rather than a granary was chosen as the vernacular prototype for Izumo Taisha is shrouded in the mists of antiquity, but undoubtedly it was related to a commendable desire to honour the gods worthily with an august temporal abode. After all, this structure was nothing less than a palace intended to accommodate the coming to earth of Okuninushi himself, so a building similar to the palaces of the local elite was highly appropriate.

There are other, more subtle differences between the architecture of the two great shrines which may readily be explained by referring once more to the differing circumstances of authority. The ornamentation of the ridge of the Izumo Honden is striking evidence of the shrine's reduced status in religious and political terms: unlike the ten-ridge billets of the Inner Shrine at Ise and the nine billets of the Outer Shrine, the Izumo building has three billets only. Even more illuminating is the absence of any Alternate Site beside the main compound, though periodic renewal was carried out at Izumo until the middle of the Edo period. It was last performed in 1744 during the reign of the eighth Tokugawa shogun Yoshimune (1648–1751) when the present Honden was completed. It is interesting to note that a rebuilding was carried out as early as 659 AD, some decades before the earliest state-sponsored rebuilding at Ise.[34]

Although the interval between the periodic renewals varies considerably, the existence of a systematic rebuilding process at Izumo is unquestionable. Examination of the reasons for the differences in timing opens up another fascinating chapter in the dynamics of architecture and authority. The rebuildings were least frequent during the Nara period, with no rebuilding recorded for the period between 659 and 822. Even allowing for some deficiency in records this clearly indicates that some disruption to ritual authority, as enacted through periodic shrine renewal, occurred as a result of the waning of the political fortunes of Izumo during the Nara centralisation of state power.

In contrast to the situation during the Nara period, there were systematic attempts at periodical renewal from the late tenth century until 1744. Rebuilding at Izumo was maintained even throughout the period of civil wars in the later fifteenth and sixteenth centuries, a record that not even Ise could match. There were some six rebuildings between 1467 and 1609, at intervals ranging from 19 to 33 years. A strong political imperative may be identified behind these rebuildings, namely an exercise in the promotion of local authority by the Mōri, the daimyo family controlling much of western Honshu at the end of the sixteenth century. Mōri Terumoto, who succeeded his grandfather as domainal lord in 1571, and whose estimated wealth of 1,205,000 koku[35] was second only to that of the Tokugawa, was responsible for a major reconstruction completed about 1580.[36]

After vanquishing the Mōri at the Battle of Sekigahara in 1600 the Tokugawa commissioned an extensive rebuilding of the Izumo Shrine. This was carried out between 1605 and 1609, with Tokugawa Ieyasu, now officially designated shogun, himself donating some of the timbers used in the rebuilding.[37] The Mōri rebuildings had been an active assertion of one of the ancient prerogatives of rule, the tradition of patronage by regional lords of their local tutelary shrine. The Tokugawa rebuilding appropriated that prerogative as part of its national strategy of using architecture to extend central authority. For this reason it comes as no surprise to learn that the Tokugawa shogunal government sponsored the rebuilding of Ise at the same time as it was supporting the renewal at Izumo.[38] By the later seventeenth century, however, the Tokugawa no longer felt compelled to sponsor the periodic rebuilding of either shrine complex because their own ideology was by then firmly focused on the Tōshōgū at Nikkō. There was to be one final rebuilding of Izumo under Tokugawa patronage, namely the eighteenth-century construction of the Honden which still graces the site. It was part of a mid-Edo period programme which also included the rebuilding of the main halls of Tōdaiji in Nara and Zenkōji in Nagano.

The Heian-period rebuilding projects, five centuries before these events occurred, are equally fascinating for what they disclose about the preoccupation of local authority with monumental building. The later Heian period was an era marked by gradual decline in the central power of the court, and the rise of regional warrior power. At Izumo from 1067 until 1115 the Honden was to be rebuilt with ever-increasing frequency and on a progressively larger scale, coinciding with the beginning of the decline of central authority. Research by Fukuyama Toshio has established that, during the 200 years from the middle of the Heian period until the beginning of the Kamakura period, the Honden was rebuilt no fewer than six times. By the time of the rebuilding which was completed in 1115, it was a massive structure, 48 metres (16 *jō*) in height (Figure 2.21). It was approached by a giant staircase 109 metres long, rising to the level of the floor of the Honden in a latter-day Japanese version of Jacob's Ladder.[39] This ramp provided the means of raising the timbers for the walls and roof. This Honden, therefore, was some two and a half times the height of the extant, mid-Edo period building. In fact it was comparable in that respect to the Great Buddha Hall of Tōdaiji, one of the tallest buildings in preindustrial Japan. Shrine tradition maintains that, during the Heian period, an even taller structure may have been erected, rising to a height of nearly 100 metres (32 *jō*). There is evidence to confirm the construction of a 48-metre Honden but a building twice that height seems unlikely.[40] Archaeological excavations confirm that as early as the fourth century, in the Tottori region close to Izumo, a number of raised-floor buildings of considerable height were constructed. One such building had what appears to be a staircase at the front and post holes as large as 2 to 3 metres in diameter, suggesting a building of considerable height.[41] This archaeological evidence is corroborated by an account of early large-scale construction

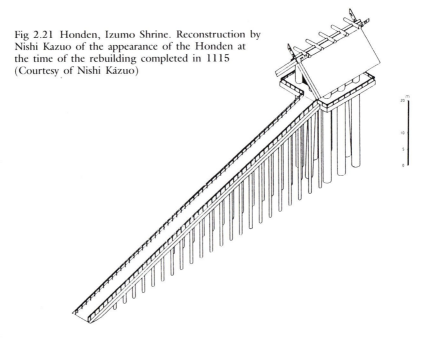

Fig 2.21 Honden, Izumo Shrine. Reconstruction by Nishi Kazuo of the appearance of the Honden at the time of the rebuilding completed in 1115 (Courtesy of Nishi Kazuo)

in the vicinity of Izumo contained in the eighth-century *Izumo fudoki*. The
entry for the Community of Takagishi states that:

> Ajisuki Takahiko, a son of the Lord of the Great Land, cried loudly day and night.
> His father constructed a high building for Ajisuki to live in. The Lord of the Great
> Land attached a long ladder to the building so that his son could climb up and
> down as he wished. Thus he reared and consoled Ajisuki. (This building was likened
> to a high cliff.) This is how the community came to be known as Takagishi, meaning
> 'high cliff'.[42]

Further evidence of the grand scale of the Heian-period Izumo Honden is
furnished by a plan preserved in the collection of the hereditary chief priests
of the shrine. The *Kanawa no zōeizu*, an Edo-period copy of an earlier Heian-
period document, suggests that the principal pillars of the Honden were bound
together with large iron hoops in clusters of three in order to form massive
piers with a diameter of approximately 3.6 metres. Another Edo-period document states that no fewer than 100 great trunks of cypress trees were brought
to Izumo by sea for use in the 1115 Honden reconstruction.[43] It is claimed
that the largest of these had been brought from Tottori and was supposedly
45 metres in length and over 4.5 metres in diameter. We can see from the
Kanawa no zōeizu how such mighty timbers might have been strapped
together to support the Honden. A similar technique was to be used in the
eighteenth-century Tokugawa-sponsored rebuilding of the Great Buddha Hall
of Tōdaiji.

Although the Edo-period sources purporting to represent earlier records
must be treated with caution, a fascinating picture of large-scale construction
at Izumo emerges from them which is consistent with the archaeological and
early written records. Such construction demanded considerable resources.
The modern construction company, Ōbayashi-gumi, using advanced computer-
aided design technology which it employs as part of its building practice, has
estimated that the 1115 reconstruction of Izumo would have required 8,533
cubic metres, of timber and 50 tonnes of iron for the metal hoops holding
together the pillar clusters, and a total budget expressed in 1989 terms would
have been 12.1 billion *yen* or approximately the same cost as the construction of a high-rise office building in Tokyo.[44]

In the search for architectural form appropriate to the authority of Izumo
the master carpenters of the great shrine were pushing at the very frontiers
of building technology. In the course of this quest they created a structure
which was unstable, with disastrous consequences. The *Nihon kiryaku* states
that in 1031 the Honden 'collapsed without reason'.[45] Neither earthquake,
typhoon wind nor other natural disaster was responsible. The shrine was quickly
rebuilt, a project completed in 1036, only to collapse again 25 years later in
1061. Once again the contemporary records establish that the reason for the
collapse was a great mystery. The pattern repeated itself yet again in 1108
when the rebuilt shrine collapsed the third time, to be reconstructed using
the giant pillars from Tottori that we have discussed above. Such disasters
were to occur again in 1141, 1172 and 63 years later in 1235, making a
total of six occasions when the main building was reduced to a pile of jumbled
timbers by inexplicable forces. Given that each rebuilding took between four

and six years to complete, Izumo was under reconstruction almost as long as it was standing during the later Heian period, particularly as periodic renewal was also carried out on two occasions (completed in 1096 and 1190 respectively) in the brief respite between structural failures. Recent research by structural engineers indicates that the reason for the recurrent collapses was a lack of understanding of elementary structural dynamics: the great pillars were not bedded into the earth sufficiently deeply to support the superstructure. It is also possible that the region's high snowfall may have contributed a 'live load' which further destabilised the building.[46]

The 1744 Honden now standing on the site, although half the size of the Heian-period building, is still the largest shrine building in Japan. It rises an impressive 19.7 metres from ground level to the ridge-pole, and nearly 24 metres to the tip of the forked finials. Even at this reduced height it is twice that of the main buildings at Ise.

There is scope for further research into the motivation for this prodigious building effort at Heian-period Izumo, but unquestionably the construction work was driven by a combination of religious piety and political pragmatism. Rebuilding took place during a period of declining influence of the central government, thereby providing an excellent opportunity for renewed expression of local identity and authority which had been eclipsed by Ise in the Nara period. It was perhaps inevitable that, with a building perceived as the expression of their very polity, local ambition should have exceeded the limits of material technology.

Monumentality and the Meaning of Ise and Izumo

The shrines at Ise and Izumo, as they stand today and as revealed in the historical and archaeological record, provide dramatic evidence of the special role of architecture in the projection of religious and ruling authority in Japan. They both appropriated vernacular building forms for higher religious and political purposes, and subsequently used these building types to project, define and reinforce the authority of their respective sponsors. At Ise architectonic strategies were more fully elaborated than at Izumo, particularly in the inner compound of the Inner Shrine, by virtue of the sustained patronage of state and the imperial institution. However, the most telling difference between Ise and Izumo is to be found not in details of siting and architectural form, nor even in the different fortunes of their patrons. What sets them apart is a different approach to monumentality. At Izumo the quest for monumentality was pursued in terms of the monolithic, that is, imposing size and permanence, a quest which reached its most ambitious expression in the Heian period. The massive pillars, bound together in clusters to create a structure as large as any built in the course of Japanese civilization, tell of an ageless ambition to reach for the heavens and defy the forces of gravity, even time itself. Although at Izumo the roofing materials required periodic maintenance, given the remarkable durability of Japanese cypress the structural timbers could certainly have lasted a millennium had other structural problems been resolved. At Izumo, therefore, the role of renewal was subordinated to an inordinate ambition to create an architectural testimonial to eternity, which inevitably brought about its own destruction. This search for monumentality through physical size and permanence parallels the ambitions of the cathedral builders of medieval Europe, who pursued a similar quest for architectural form transcending temporal constraints and whose buildings on occasion met a similar fate.

Ise represents a very different approach to monumentality from that of Izumo. Its buildings were ultimately to prove more enduring by virtue of a fundamental paradox: despite the rustic, self-effacing nature of the buildings, Ise has achieved permanence as an abiding presence in the national ethos of Japan. This has been accomplished by virtue of the continuing patronage of the imperial institution and by the hereditary infrastructure of craft and belief associated with the shrine. Buildings which have self-consciously glorified in the transience of the material have found in this sublimation of physical frailty a tradition which has both impressed and endured. Izumo, by virtue of its faltering political sponsorship and its structurally unsustainable architectural ambitions, concedes greater power to the monumentality of Ise, and the ultimate efficacy of the principle of dynamic renewal over the monolithic.

3   Great Halls of Religion and State

Architecture and the Creation of the Nara Imperial Order

As both a city and a centre for national government, Nara was based on an architectonic vision of the human order embracing a symbiotic relationship between imperial authority and the built environment. There was a special relationship between place and purpose at Nara, with a concerted policy by the political leadership to apply Chinese planning and architectural principles to Japanese political needs. The emperor may have been robed with the mantle of the mandate of heaven, derived from Chinese concepts of imperial authority, and the organisation of Nara government may have aspired to the balanced and symmetrical order of the Tang dynasty governmental model, but equally important to the creation and character of authority, emperor and government were accommodated in a monumental palace and city where ritual and ceremony provided tangible evidence of the ideological assertion of that authority.

For most of the eighth century in Japan the planned capital city known as Nara was the focus of church and state, culture and technology.[1] Nara was officially established in AD 710 as the 'capital city of peace'. Here the scale of urban planning and architectural construction undertaken by the Japanese state was to reach new and unprecedented proportions as it strove to emulate in its institutions and their physical setting the example of its illustrious contemporary, the Tang dynasty, then at the height of its power and glory in China. Nara was the locus of imperial government based upon the Tang-inspired penal and administrative codes (the *Taihō ritsuryō* codes), the centre of state religion and the matrix of a classical court culture. It was equally the cradle of new technologies, particularly in city planning and in the creation of monumental architecture, exemplified by the Daigokuden (Imperial Audience Hall) at the palace and the Daibutsuden (Great Buddha Hall) of Tōdaiji which, although later reconstructed on a more modest scale, is still reputed to be the largest timber-frame building in the world.

Little of the original eighth-century city stands today. Scholarly attention has therefore been concentrated on the painstaking archaeological task of re-establishing the physical form of the city and of its architecture from beneath the mud of the paddy fields which spread over the ruins of once proud portals and halls of state after the capital was moved to a new site in 784.[2] Nara studies have been the province of the archaeologist and historian specialising in interpreting the official history of the era, the *Shoku Nihongi*, covering the years 697–792. Second only to the *Nihon shoki* in the *Rikkokushi* or 'Six

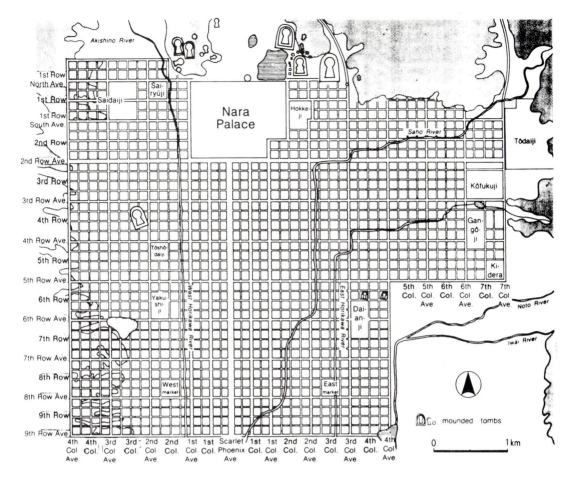

Fig 3.1 Plan of the city of Nara (Heijō-kyō) in the eighth century (Scale: 1:450,000)
(Source: Tsuboi Kiyotari and Tanaka Migaku, *The Historic City of Nara. An Archaeological Approach*)

National Histories', it is more reliable as an historical source because it largely dispenses with mythology and concentrates on contemporary events, recording decisions of the day and activities of the court.[3]

Considerable progress has been made in archaeological endeavour and documentary analysis, but the fruits of these endeavours have not as yet been integrated in order to recreate the entirety of place and purpose which is the focus of this study. It is particularly important that this integrated approach should be applied to Nara because place and purpose were not related simply by coincidence: there was a deliberate, concerted and sustained government policy to link the two as an organic whole. Central to our historical perspective on the entire Nara period is an understanding of the relationship between the principles and processes of government on the one hand, and the principles and processes of city building on the other. Two important questions must be addressed. Firstly, what was the relationship between Nara as a place and Nara as the centre of imperial government? And secondly, how did government policy and concepts of authority dictate the form of the city and its architecture of state?

53

The Relationship between Place and Political Purpose at Nara

The relationship between architecture and authority has special importance in the case of cities planned primarily as government capitals. Throughout history cities have expressed the power of ruling classes or factions. The careful structuring of a built environment according to an overall conception of human relations has definitive psychological and behavioural effects on a community. This makes cities effective tools for social engineering, especially through class-determined zoning of the populace, and by regulation of architectural style according to status. Cities have also acted as unrivalled symbols of authority, partly as a result of the opportunity they afford to give physical expression to an all-encompassing vision of the human order, partly because of their functional efficacy as organisational tools, and finally as a consequence of the symbolism of the architecture itself.

The city of Nara exemplifies all these characteristics of the wilfully ordained built environment. Its creation was the consummation of the process of remodelling Japanese institutions of government and society on the Chinese Tang dynasty model of a symmetrically ordered, centralised, bureaucratic state, focused on a virtuous emperor reigning with the mandate of heaven. The *Taihō ritsuryō* codes of 701–702 were created to form the basis of government administration, while the city and architecture of Nara were to become the immediate physical matrix of the new order.

The *Shoku Nihongi* declares that in the second month of 707 Emperor Mommu announced to the assembly of the highest ranking courtiers his intention to abandon Fujiwara-kyō, the short-lived predecessor to Nara established in 694, and move the capital to Nara.[4] The Fujiwara-kyō site had proven too confined to accommodate the ambitious scale of the new institutions of government and court. Within three years the new capital was fully operational. Within a decade it had so grown in size and sophistication that it had become a city of international standing in East Asia. Construction and maintenance of the myriad palace buildings, from the most spectacular ceremonial structure to the most mundane latrine, were the responsibility of the Timber Construction Department (*Mokkōryō*) within the Imperial Family Ministry (*Kunai-shō*).[5] This department was charged with the daunting responsibility of obtaining the high-quality lumber, particularly Japanese cypress (*hinoki*), needed for the official building work.[6] Other government departments were responsible for the decoration of buildings, and for special building projects as the need arose. The most significant of these was the Bureau for the Construction of Tōdaiji (*Zōtōdaijishi*), the construction of which preoccupied the Nara state throughout the middle decades of the eighth century. By mid-century, also, the task of maintaining the hundreds of different palace buildings necessitated the establishment of a new department solely responsible for repairs. Elsewhere in the city, temple construction was proceeding apace under the auspices of the six major Buddhist sects, while the aristocracy and court officials busied themselves with creating mansions and gardens befitting the dignity of their status, on sites granted to them in accordance with their court rank. Not a few of the religious and residential structures were transported to Nara from their original locations at Fujiwara or elsewhere in the Asuka region and re-erected at sites in the new city, a process which saved time, cost and timber.[7]

Nara ranks in the history of civilization with other planned cities of the ancient world such as Ionian Miletus, Nineveh in Mesopotamia and the Tang capital of Chang'an. All three utilised an orthogonal grid plan which, as an urban planning device, is singularly arbitrary and prescriptive, making it well-suited to the purpose of imposing order by government. The Nara grid consisted of carefully standardised blocks (*jōbō*), defined physically by a system of major avenues (*jō*) running east–west and north–south (*bō*) (Figure 3.1). The city was 4.8 kilometres north–south and 5.7 kilometres east–west, making it four times larger than its immediate predecessor Fujiwara-kyō. The plan was characterised by a north–south axis composed of the grand Suzaku Avenue, 74 metres in width, which ran from the towering south gatehouse of the city, the Rajōmon, to the Suzakumon, the two-storey gatehouse guarding the principal entrance to the imperial palace complex at the central north.

The palace was virtually a city in its own right, measuring some 1,000 metres north–south and 1,200 metres east–west. It was enclosed by a wall 3 metres thick and guarded by gateways of imposing character. Within the palace were several precincts. The State Halls Compound included the offices of the eight government ministries and the two supreme government organs instituted under the *Taihō ritsuryō* code, namely the Council of State (Dajōkan) and the Department of Religion (Jingikan), which was responsible for the Shinto rites and observances of the emperor and court. To its immediate north in a separate compound were ceremonial halls used for state occasions, of which the Daigokuden, the 'Imperial Audience Hall' or 'Great Hall of State', was the most important. The imperial residence was housed within its own compound, probably to the east of the State Halls Compound in the early Nara period, and to the immediate north by the late Nara period (Figure 3.2).[8]

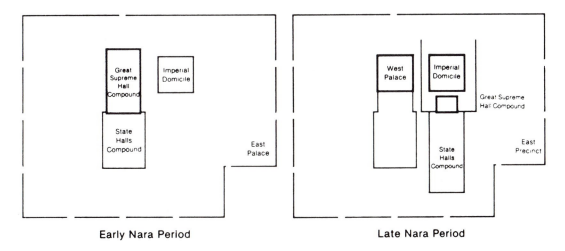

Early Nara Period   **Late Nara Period**

Fig 3.2 Conjectural plan of the Nara Palace compounds in the early and late eighth century (Source: Tsuboi Kiyotari and Tanaka Migaku, *The Historic City of Nara. An Archaeological Approach*)

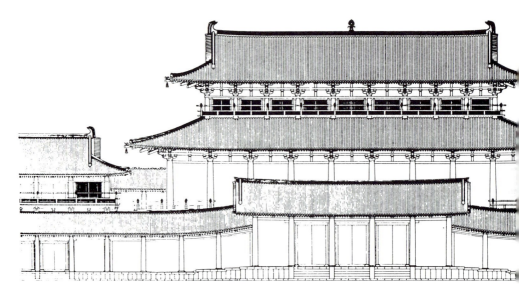

As a result of recent archaeological excavations the architectural form of the Daigokuden of the western precinct has been reconstructed (Figures 3.3–3.5). Referred to in the archaeological reports as the 'First Daigokuden',[9] it was a long, narrow, two-storey building set on a high stone podium and orientated east–west across the main axis of the palace site. The structure was nine bays east–west and four bays north–south, with an impressive span of slightly more than 5 metres between the pillars. This gave it a total width of 51.48 metres and a depth of 21.20 metres. The first floor of the building above the podium was open at the front to provide a good view into and from the interior and was entered via three formal stone staircases. The Daigokuden was a building of overpowering size, approaching the dimensions of the Daibutsuden of Tōdaiji in width and height, although considerably narrower. It would have been a commanding presence in the palace compound, befitting its role as the formal centre of imperial authority and court ritual.

The *Shoku Nihongi* establishes that the Daigokuden and the State Halls Compound were the focus for New Year ceremonies, horse races and mounted archery contests, as well as for the official reception of ambassadors and their retinues from the Korean kingdoms.[10] The court records also reveal that imperial edicts were delivered by the emperor while standing on the podium of the Daigokuden above the central stairs.[11] The most important ceremony of all, that of imperial accession (*Sokui-no-shikiten*), was also performed at the Daigokuden, when, as on other important state occasions, the entire court assembled in front of the emperor, who was seated on the imperial throne (*takami-kura*) placed above the central stairs facing south. The emperor and the immediate imperial retinue were separated from the rest of the court by the southern wall of the Daigokuden compound. Ministers would pay obeisance to the emperor by approaching the entrance to the Kōmon, the gateway separating the southerly compound from the Daigokuden compound, and there bowing deeply. However at the time of the accession ceremonies, the highest-ranking courtiers and officials were permitted to enter the courtyard

Fig 3.3 Daigokuden (Imperial Audience Hall) of Nara Palace. Front elevation of the main hall and flanking towers as seen from the south. The Kōmon and enclosing cloisters are situated at the front. Reconstruction drawing by the Nara National Cultural Properties Research Institute
(Source: Nara National Cultural Properties Research Institute)

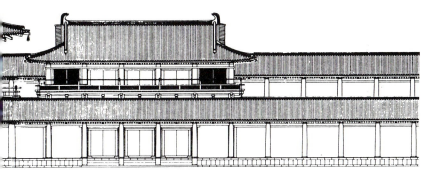

itself directly in front of the Daigokuden. When Emperor Shōmu ascended the throne in 724, seven temporary flag-poles were erected transversely across the Daigokuden compound and the senior courtiers and ministers, ranked in lines behind them, paid their obeisance.[12] At other times the emperor or empress advanced to the Kōmon to view activities such as musical performances presented in the State Halls Compound.[13] Later in the Nara period, the Daigokuden compound became smaller but the scale of the building increased in size so that the emperor or empress could see the events in the State Halls Compound 'without leaving his (or her) seat in the Great Supreme Hall (Daigokuden)'.[14] Tsuboi observes that 'these developments surely reflect a change in the emperor's status'.

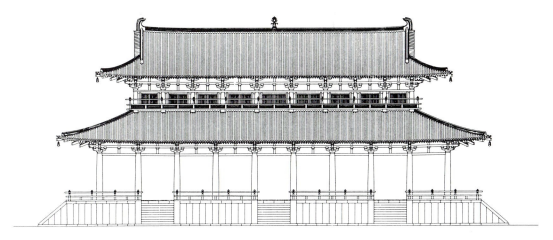

Fig 3.4 Daigokuden (Imperial Audience Hall) of Nara Palace. Front elevation. Reconstruction drawing by the Nara National Cultural Properties Research Institute. (Source: Nara National Cultural Properties Research Institute)

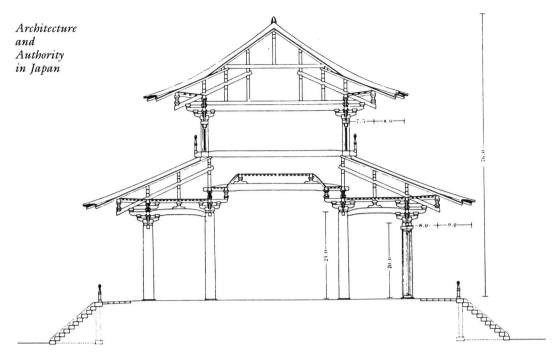

Fig 3.5 Daigokuden (Imperial Audience Hall) of Nara Palace. Transverse section. Reconstruction drawing by the Nara National Cultural Properties Research Institute
(Source: Nara National Cultural Properties Research Institute)

Notwithstanding its lofty ceremonial functions, the Daigokuden was similar in architectural form to the lecture halls of the great Buddhist monasteries of Nara and its environs, such as the Daikōdō of Hōryūji, which was added to the main western precinct of the temple in the ninth century. Although the Daigokuden was a two-storey structure and the Kōdō of Hōryūji single storey only, both buildings were long and narrow in plan, orientated east–west across the main north–south axis of their respective sites, and mounted on a stone-faced podium (Figure 3.6). At Hōryūji the chief abbot stood at the top of the central steps of the Kōdō to address the monks assembled in the fore-court, in much the same manner as the courtiers would have gathered in the forecourt to the Daigokuden and the adjacent administrative precinct for imperial audiences. The Hōryūji building shows how the Nara palace hall would have framed the focal ceremonial figure during these rituals, providing a dramatic setting to enhance his or her authority (Figure 3.7). A shared architectural strategy for both religious and governmental authority at Nara is hardly surprising in view of the theocratic pretensions of the court. Shared architectural form was also to be found in the castles and cathedrals of medieval Europe, where Gothic vaults sanctified the authority of kings as well as crowned the majesty of the church.

From such evidence of urban planning and palace architecture at Nara it is clear that the built environment was more than just an incidental setting for the character and conduct of government. It was part of the very nature

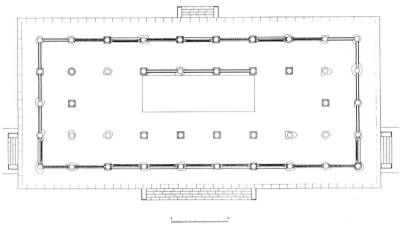

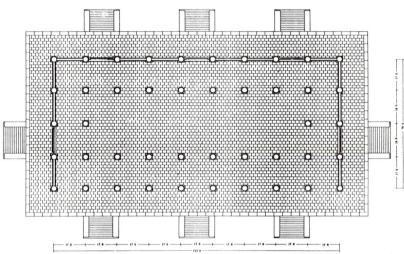

Fig 3.6 Plans of Daikōdō (Great Lecture Hall) of Hōryūji (top) and Daigokuden of Nara
Palace (bottom)
(Source: Bunka-chō, *Kokuhō jūyō bunkazai [kenzōbutsu] jissoku zushū* and Nara National
Cultural Properties Research Institute)

Fig 3.7 Daikōdō (Great Lecture Hall) Hōryūji. Front elevation
(Source: Bunka-chō, *Kokuhō jūyō bunkazai [kenzōbutsu] jissoku zushū*)

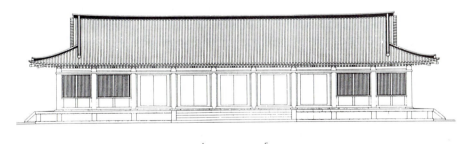

of government, inherent and indispensable to the definition of authority and the exercise of power.

The Adoption of Tang City Planning and Architectural Principles

A mainstream issue in Japanese historical enquiry is the relationship between foreign ideas and technology, and indigenous institutions and culture. The striking scale and sophistication of the city and palace of Nara are evidence of a deliberate and concerted attempt to apply Chinese planning principles and architectural practice to the perceived needs of the Japanese state. Two questions claim our attention at this point: how effective was the Nara government in implementing the Chinese ideal of a planned city with monumental buildings? What was the effect of deliberate adoption or even imposition of foreign models of state and civilization on indigenous traditions of government, building and belief?

City Planning

The Nara plan conformed with general principles of Chinese planning as propounded in Confucian philosophical writings and understood by the scholars of the Nara court in the eighth century. This of necessity was based on an ideal concept. As a tangible model of this ideal form, the Tang dynastic capital of Chang'an exerted a powerful influence. Our understanding of the extent of Nara's specific indebtedness to Tang Chang'an is hampered by limitations in understanding Chang'an itself. Exactly the same scholarly contretemps pertains to the study of Chang'an as to the study of Nara; at both sites there has been vigorous archaeological exploration but little systematic synthesis with documentary sources.[15] Moreover, early Chinese city planning was inconsistent with theory so that there was not a single authoritative urban realisation of Chinese conceptions of place and purpose.[16] Tang dynasty Chang'an itself lost its symmetrical perfection when the Daming Palace was located as a trapezoidal accretion at the northeast corner of the urban grid (Figure 3.8).

Whatever the realities of balancing unanticipated growth with an inflexible planning device like the grid pattern, or the limitations of our understanding of Tang Chang'an, it is universally accepted that the architectural philosophy of Chinese cities was based on the principle of correspondence between the terrestrial and the celestial orders, a correspondence which permeates the classical Confucian texts formulated in the Zhou dynasty, particularly the *Book of Documents* (*Shu Jing*) and the *Book of Rites* (*Li ji*).[17] Acceptance of the importance of this principle led to the adoption at Nara of the generic morphological features of Chinese cities, especially the north–south grid plan governed by axial symmetry and a spatial hierarchy coinciding with the status hierarchy of the court. This planning strategy was similar to the one which had been employed at Chang'an. Similarly, the seat of government and the residence of the emperor at Nara stood at the centre north, while an axial processional avenue bisected the city in the manner of the grand avenue at the centre of Chang'an.

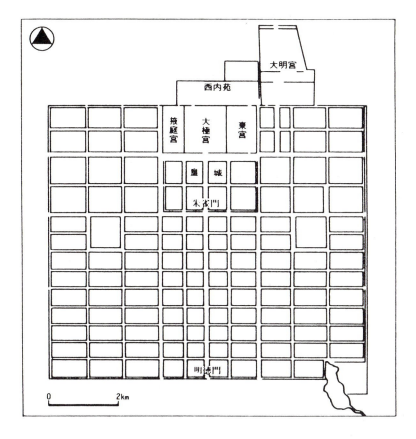

大明宮

西内苑

掖庭宮　大極宮　東宮

皇　城

朱雀門

明徳門

0　　　2km

Fig 3.8
City Plan of
Chang'an
during Tang
Dynasty
(Source:
Okayama
Shigehiro (ed.)
*Tojō to kokufu,
Fukugen Nihon
taikan*, vol. 3)

Chinese influence is also clear in the siting of Nara. The site selected for the city satisfied geomantic criteria similar to those which permeate Chinese civilization. Specifically this meant having high ground to the north and east of the area of human habitation, to protect against the flow of the malevolent forces in the universe and the cold northerly winds, and low ground and water to the south of the site, coinciding with the direction of the benevolent forces and the sun, an eminently practical arrangement for locations in the northern hemisphere. The confluence of ancient geomancy with formally articulated Confucian philosophy interposed the palace of the ruler between the malevolent forces of the north and the habitations of people in the south over whom benevolent rule was to be exercised. The Chinese geomantic doctrine of the Four Deities was also applied in part to the plan of the city of Nara. The well-preserved seventh-century Takamatsuzuka tomb, richly decorated with paintings of the Scarlet Phoenix, Black Warrior, White Tiger and Green Dragon on its four walls, establishes beyond doubt that this doctrine was already understood in Japan by the time of the building of Nara.[18] However, of the Four Deities, only the Scarlet Phoenix (*suzaku*) is actually employed at Nara, revealed in the name of the Suzakumon, the two-storey scarlet-lacquered gatehouse guarding the entrance to the Nara Palace. The comprehensive application of all the Four Deities to city planning had to await the building of Heian-kyō, or Kyoto as it is now known, at the end of the eighth century.

The Official Architectural Style

The architectural form of the first Daigokuden at Nara Palace is another example of the close conformity in general style and specific system of mensuration with Chang'an palace architecture, in this case the Hanyuan Dian or main hall used for state ceremonies at the Daming Palace of Chang'an. Archaeological work carried out on the site in the late 1950s established that the hall had been a spectacular structure with red timbers, white walls and gold ornaments. The hall itself was flanked by towers.[19] It has been possible for archaeologists to reconstruct accurately the plan of both the Hanyuan Dian and that of the first Daigokuden. Comparison of the two buildings shows that the Japanese building was four bays shorter and two bays narrower (or 15.85 metres by 8.00 metres smaller) than was the hall of the Chang'an building, but pillar placement and the length of intercolumnial span were identical.[20] The two plans may be transposed upon one another, so similar is the structural organisation and the measurements of the two buildings.[21] We may conclude, therefore, that the Daigokuden at Nara was modelled directly on the Hanyuan Dian in both style and scale. Flanking towers were even added in the 720s to complete the re-creation of the architectural form of the Chang'an palace.

Precise numerical correspondence between the two buildings highlights the lengths to which the Nara government was prepared to go to standardise Japanese measurements on the basis of Tang mensuration. A major responsibility of government is to impose order by regulating the spatial quiddity of a society. As in both ancient Rome and medieval Europe, early Japanese measurements were subject to considerable variation as a result of different workshop traditions. Such diversity presented serious problems to a government intent on extending control over the whole nation, conducting international trade, and building a new capital city rapidly and efficiently. Close coordination through use of standardised measurements was essential for the veritable army of surveyors and builders coopted into government construction service from many different regional traditions including the famous master carpenters of Hida province.

The *Taihō ritsuryō* codes officially adopted the long-established Chinese system of a 'short foot' (*shōjaku*) and 'long foot' (*taijaku*) as part of the comprehensive attempt to remodel the Japanese governmental system along the lines of the Tang administrative and legal system. The larger measure was approximately 1.2 times greater in size than the smaller unit and is generally thought by mensuration specialists to have been the same length as the *Komajaku*. This 'Korean foot' was 35.45 centimetres in length, and had been in widespread use in Japan for building the funeral mounds of the fourth to sixth centuries when influence from the Korean kingdoms was strong.[22] In the final analysis Korean usage was based upon Chinese practice because of the general Chinese influence in the Korean kingdoms, largely as a result of the presence of Han commandaries in the north of the peninsula.

The increased tempo of capital city construction, first at Fujiwara-kyō, and then at Nara itself, necessitated immediate modification to official mensuration policy. In 702, the year after the Taihō Code, the government announced that the long foot would be used exclusively for land surveys and the short foot for all other purposes.[23] This important modification to the Tang-inspired standard was made under Emperor Mommu in response, no doubt, to specific but now undocumented problems encountered during building operations at Fujiwara-kyō.

Detailed information about government regulation of measurements during the first stage of the building of Nara was obtained from the excavations carried out in the 1970s at the site of the western Chōdōin precinct. This proves that the modified system of two different foot measures was still in operation when the palace was built between 708 and 712. On the one hand the Taihō long foot is used as the land survey unit for determining the dimensions of the excavated precinct and for positioning the buildings within it. These measurements are all rounded out to the nearest long foot units, an expedient which made surveying more simple. On the other hand in the Daigokuden building a short foot measure of 29.45 is used.[24] Like the land survey long foot, it is used as a rounded unit for simplicity and speed, particularly important as customary building practice seldom relied on detailed working drawings. From this archaeological evidence we may conclude that for the first decade of its rule, the Nara government was effective in bringing order to measurements on the basis of applying Tang principles modified in the light of Japanese experience at Fujiwara-kyō.

This Tang dual system of measurement proved cumbersome in operation and further rationalisation of building standards became necessary for the orderly coordination of work being carried out simultaneously at construction sites throughout the city. Builders no doubt found two standard measurements confusing, doubling the number of measuring rods and marking ropes required to no advantage other than to satisfy some arbitrary rule of government for reasons of modernity on the Chinese pattern. Accordingly in 713, the year after the first Daigokuden was completed, an edict was issued which stated that henceforth 'each and every government ministry shall use the short foot for all purposes'.[25] A short foot approximately 29.5 centimitres in length now became the official standard. This is a further indication of the niceties of government policy bowing before the practical demands of large-scale construction.

The case of mensuration reveals a familiar pattern of initial conformity with Tang principles yielding to the pressure of actual building practice in Japan. A similar conclusion may be reached regarding the stylistic features of some of the important buildings constructed by the Nara establishment, by comparing written documents with archaeological and architectural evidence. The *Shoku Nihongi* records a request made from the Dajōkan to Emperor Shōmu shortly after his accession to the throne in 724:

> . . . the capital is where the emperor lives and every province comes to court but it does not possess the magnificence needed to express virtue (*toku*). Its wooden shingled roofs and thatched dwellings are relics of the past. They are difficult to build and easily destroyed, exhausting the people's resources. It is requested that an order be issued that aristocrats of the Fifth Rank and above, and those commoners able to do so, should build tiled-roof houses and paint them red and white.[26]

Fig 3.9
Terracotta tiles
being laid on
temple roof
(Enryakuji
restoration,
1980)

Although couched in the circumspect language of supplication to the emperor, this document is nevertheless a statement of official policy for the Nara political order formulated by the emperor in consultation with his chief Dajōkan officials.[27] It reveals the adoption of an official architectural vocabulary based on Tang usage, and makes an equation between government by virtue, a fundamental Confucian tenet, and appropriate physical form. It is the same type of equation that we accept exists between democratic governments and Greek Classical architecture. In the Japanese case this equation would be realised through tiled roofs and polychrome decoration. Terracotta tiling is one of the most durable of all building materials and its adoption indicates a dramatic change from reliance on different types of thatch and wooden shingles for roofing purposes (Figure 3.9). The Daigokuden excavations show that in the year of promulgation of the Dajōkan document the official architectural vocabulary was used for the most important ceremonial building of the palace complex. Here the excavations of the site have uncovered monumental stone foundations, traces of brightly painted timber-framing and triple-glazed terracotta tiled roofs.

The most tangible evidence of architectural form within Nara Palace is the Higashi Chōshūden, or Eastern Morning Waiting Hall, of the State Halls Compound. This is the only extant building of the Nara Palace and is one of a pair originally erected on either side of the north–south axis of the State Halls Compound of the palace site after rebuilding in 747. These two buildings, located in a small courtyard to the immediate south of the main State Halls precinct, served as the place where courtiers and other visitors awaited their morning audiences with government officials.

Fig 3.10
Higashi Chōshūden
(Eastern Morning
Audience Hall) of
Nara Palace (above).
Reconstruction
drawing by Nara
National Cultural
Properties Research
Institute. Kōdō
(Lecture Hall) of
Tōshōdaiji (below)
(Source: Okayama
Shigehiro (ed.) *Tojō
to kokufu, Fukugen
Nihon taikan*, vol. 3)

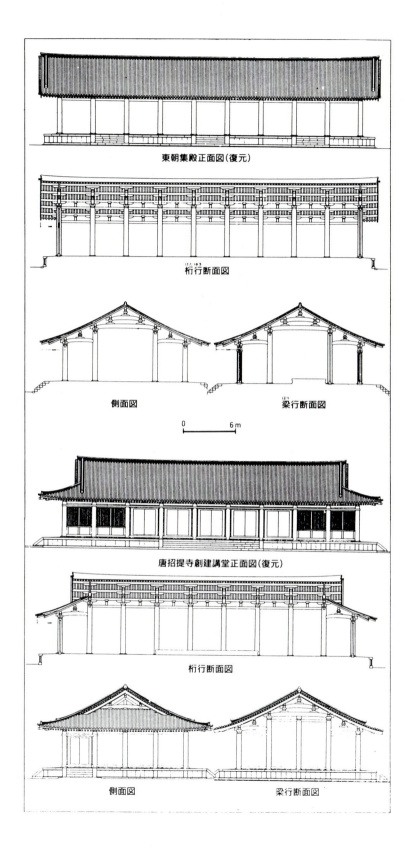

東朝集殿正面図（復元）

桁行断面図

側面図　　　　　　　　梁行断面図

0 ⊢——⊣ 6m

唐招提寺創建講堂正面図（復元）

桁行断面図

側面図　　　　　　　　梁行断面図

The survival of the Higashi Chōshūden is fortuitous for the historical record, but it also highlights some of the difficulties associated with the use of buildings as historical evidence because it has been rebuilt on a new site. The building now serves as the Kōdō (Lecture Hall) of Tōshōdaiji, the temple founded by the Chinese monk Ganjin (Jian Zhen) (Figure 3.10). Ganjin had reached Japan from China in 754 after five unsuccessful attempts to complete the journey. He was brought to Japan by the government for the purpose of conducting ordination rites and thereby legitimising the Japanese Buddhist priesthood in the international Buddhist order. Five years later, in 759, he was granted by imperial decree a site on which to found the Tōshōdaiji. Eighth- and ninth-century temple records note that one of the Chōshūden buildings from the palace was donated to the temple.[28] At the time extensive rebuilding was being carried out at the Heijō Palace, so extensive in fact that, according to the *Shoku Nihongi*, no New Year ceremonies were held for the year 761. The waiting hall structure probably became redundant as a result of these rebuilding activities. The foundation of the new temple provided a perfect opportunity to demonstrate imperial largesse and, at the same time, dispose of a surplus structure. Archaeological excavation of the Higashi Chōshūden site and examination of the Kōdō of Tōshōdaiji have confirmed unquestionably that the extant temple building was the former Higashi Chōshūden of the palace. The base dimensions are identical. Moreover the pillars, beams and truss of the Kōdō still carry the identifying numbers and letters (*bansuke*) inscribed on them at the palace prior to the structure being dismantled and reassembled at its new home.[29]

The present-day Kōdō of Tōshōdaiji is a single-storey structure nine bays wide and four bays deep surmounted by a hip-gable terracotta tiled roof. It is some 27 metres long and 12 metres wide and is similar in plan to the Daigokuden, although significantly smaller in size. The palace excavations disclose that, like the Daigokuden, it had three sets of stone steps at the front and was open there to entry and egress. The truss which supports the roof of the extant building has the gracefully curved pairs of tie-beams typical of the High Tang style in China. However, analysis of framing of the extant hip-gable roof has established that it was originally a simple gable form, a style used for less important buildings at the Nara Palace and, one would think, unsuitable for the important new temple. When the building was re-erected at Tōshōdaiji a lattice ceiling was suspended from the roof, altering the spatial dynamics of the interior, while, in the Kamakura period, straight penetrating tie-beams were added to strengthen the structure.[30] The original red paint of the pillars and beams has now worn away, leaving the timber exposed in its natural state. The roof was originally covered with exotic triple-glazed green, white and brown tiles in the Tang mode favoured for important political buildings, lending it an elegance and decorative brilliance far removed from the present sombre hue of its grey tiles. We may deduce something of its original visual impact from a description after its removal to Tōshōdaiji: 'It was magnificent with gold, silver, vermilion and jewels, and, so to speak, like a heavenly palace, but with the passing of years it became dilapidated . . .'.[31]

The extant Tōshōdaiji hall, therefore, supplemented by archaeological evidence and written records, allows us to recreate the appearance of official

Nara buildings. It illustrates the type of building specified in the 724 Dajōkan document as essential to the state order, and provides additional information about the use of curved tie-beams and glazed tiles as part of that visual order. These features would have added significantly to the powerful impression created by the building on all who viewed and visited it.

Divergence from the Tang Model

Thus far we have been concentrating on the way much of the city plan and the official buildings of Nara reflected Chinese planning and architectural principles but significant differences were also indicated when the mensuration of the first Daigokuden was considered. In fact by the middle of the eighth century there seems to have been a complete breakdown of authority over length measures despite the early efforts of the government. Twenty-six *shaku* rulers are preserved in the Shōsōin where personal treasures of Emperor Shōmu were collected after his death in 756. Among them there are no fewer than 13 different lengths, ranging from 29.42 centimetres to 31.21 centimetres.[32] It is clear that official control over builder workshop practice had been lost once the frantic rush to establish the new city was past.

As the Nara period progressed we find there are other significant departures from the principles of Tang imperial architecture. Even at the outset, for example, the plan of the first Nara Palace buildings did not adhere to the strict axial alignment evident at the Chang'an palaces, although some rebuilding in the middle of the eighth century did bring them closer in organisation to the Chinese pattern. Nara lacked impressive city walls like those of Chang'an and other important Chinese cities, although the palace complex was set apart from the rest of the city by tiled-roof walls in the Chinese manner. There is much speculation as to why the Japanese never developed a tradition of walled cities. It may have been a result of the absence of outside threat coupled with the need to impress those living within the city with the authority emanating from the palace, or simply that the Japanese desired the closer communion with nature afforded by an uninterrupted view of fields, trees and mountains.

More important than these differences in detail was a mid-century crisis of confidence in the Chinese ideal of a monumental and enduring capital – the rationale for the very founding of Nara – precipitated by factional struggles at the Nara court. Power politics impinged upon the definition of authority expressed by the creation of a monumental city. This resulted in a brief revival of the indigenous Japanese notion of the impermanence of all things, not least the capital city itself. There had been no fewer than 17 movements of palace and capital from one site to another in Japan from the time of the Empress Suiko, who ascended the throne in 592,[33] until the establishment of Nara in 710. This practice had its basis in both religious belief and political pragmatism. It was carried out to satisfy Shinto requirements for ritual purification of a site following defilement caused by death. Equally important, however, it addressed the pragmatic needs of court politics by allowing a new ruler to be housed in a fresh architectural setting, dissociated from the visible accomplishments of the preceding ruler and, more often than not, at a site deep in the heartland of his or her own local power base.

In sharp contrast to this tradition, the principle underlying the founding of Nara was the creation of a city which would both impress and endure, to borrow again J.J. Coulton's definition of the monumental. Tension between the Chinese notions of a permanent capital and the Japanese custom of establishing a new palace and government headquarters at the death of each emperor culminated in a remarkable interregnum in the Nara period when Nara itself was completely abandoned as the capital. At the end of 740, a mere 30 years after its official foundation, when the Herculean tasks of construction were barely completed, the capital was moved to Kuni, a site some 20 kilometres to the northeast on the Kizu River. That great edifice, the Daigokuden, together with its flanking cloisters, was dismantled and transported to Kuni for re-erection at the site of the new capital.[34] The *Shoku Nihongi* notes that it took four years to complete the rebuilding of the Daigokuden and its corridors.[35] Shortly afterwards Kuni itself was abandoned in favour of a new capital at Naniwa. By the end of the same year, 744, large-scale construction work had begun on a temple at Shigaraki, 35 kilometres to the northeast of Nara. The idea of moving the capital to Shigaraki seems to have taken firm root because the New Year Ceremonies for the year 745 were held there. At the very time the possibility of moving the capital to Shigaraki was being considered, however, an inauspicious earthquake devastated the region. The ministers of the Dajōkan voted unanimously to 'move back to Nara'. After some vacillation by Emperor Shōmu the capital was re-established at Nara.[36] The versatile Daigokuden, however, was left behind at Kuni: the court had learnt from painful experience that it was easier to build a new one than move the old.

This reversion to what can only be described as the peripatetic palace syndrome was precipitated by the powerful Tachibana clan employing the ancient expedient of trying to break the power of a rival, in this case the House of Fujiwara, by disrupting its power base through moving the entire capital. The movement of the capital to Naniwa and eventually back to Nara itself was the Fujiwara response and a successful strategy to reassert their authority.[37]

Inconsistencies are evident not only in the application of Chinese city planning to Japanese circumstances: similar tensions between foreign and indigenous ways can be seen in the style of the buildings constructed in Nara. There was, for example, an important difference in the style and materials used in the construction of the most important gatehouses which protected the entrances to the palace compounds in the two cities. Excavations of the Chengtian Men, at the main palace entrance of Chang'an, revealed that the lower storey was of brick and masonry construction with three arched entrances, similar to the monumental barbicans of later Beijing and Nanjing but very different from the more modestly proportioned timber frame Suzakumon of Nara. This gatehouse may have observed the official architectural style as prescribed in the 724 proclamation, but it would have been strikingly different in appearance from the Chengtian Men of Chang'an.[38]

The most dramatic evidence of inconsistency between stated policy objectives and actual architectural practice is to be found in Nara Palace itself. The Dajōkan document of 724, it will be recalled, criticised indigenous building

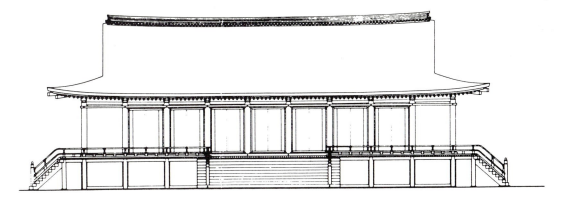

practices as outmoded, wasteful and inappropriate for the architecture of imperial order. It referred specifically to the practice of covering roofs with straw or reed thatch, or with wooden shingles. By implication it also criticised strongly the long-established practice of erecting buildings with unpainted pillars set directly in the ground, exactly the same method of construction we have seen was employed for the shrines at Ise and Izumo.

Despite the official pronouncements and the enthusiastic application of Tang principles to buildings such as the Daigokuden and Higashi Chōshūden, the archaeological record tells a very different story about the authority of foreign models. The chemical composition of the paddy fields which later covered the abandoned Nara Palace site preserved the lower section of most of the pillars of its buildings. Excavations show conclusively that most of the buildings of the palace complex had pillars set directly into the ground in conformity with native custom. Further, the Imperial Residence itself was an elegant version of the raised-floor timber dwellings of the earlier era criticised in the 724 document, not the polychrome and tiled-roof structure set on stone foundations sanctioned in the official document (Figure 3.11). Although the residence was rebuilt at least three times during the Nara period, archaeologists have found no evidence whatsoever at the site of the use of terracotta tiles, the most durable of all building materials. Moreover the excavated pillars were unpainted and were set directly into the earth in the long-preferred Japanese manner.[39]

Thus the emperor continued to live in a building of the very style that the government was proscribing as unsuited to the dignity of the imperial capital. It may have been deemed necessary to adopt foreign architectural forms for some of the most visible buildings used for government business and ceremony, including the largest of them all, the Daigokuden. When it came to satisfying the requirements of daily life the authority of indigenous custom remained preeminent, even for the residence of the emperor under whose rule virtue was to be expressed through appropriate physical form. If the commitment to a permanent capital was not firm in practice, as we have seen, then the continued use of sunken pillars with a life-span equivalent to that of most imperial reigns is not surprising. The same may have been the case in regard to the ephemeral thatch and shingle roofs but for these another practical reason dictated continued use: they were quieter than tile under which to sleep during the heavy rains of the wet season and typhoons. No-one enjoys sleep disturbed by the cacophony of rain drumming on hard baked-clay surfaces.

Fig 3.11
Seiden (Main Hall) of Dairi (Imperial Residence) of Nara Palace. Front elevation. Reconstruction drawing by the Nara National Cultural Properties Research Institute (Source: Nara National Cultural Properties Research Institute)

It would have been like trying to sleep during the furious storm under the great tiled roof of the gatehouse featured in Kurosawa's film *Rashōmon*. And the unpainted timbers, in the pristine purity in which they were undoubtably used for the palace buildings, would have struck that deep note of resonance with nature and the world of indigenous belief that was still at the heart of the Japanese sense of self and purpose, despite all the public and official posturing to the contrary.

Nara Palace is not an isolated example of the continuing indigenous preference for cypress shingles in aristocratic architecture at Nara. The Denpōdō of the Eastern Precinct of Hōryūji was originally a residential structure built in the early 730s for the powerful Tachibana family. It was donated to Hōryūji in 739 and substantially altered to suit its new role as a sacred structure, a situation similar to that of the Higashi Chōshūden at Tōshōdaiji.[40] It originally had a cypress shingle roof which was replaced with tiles when the building was moved to the temple, the heavier tiling requiring strengthening of the roof truss.[41] The villa built for Fujiwara no Toyonari at Shigaraki in 743–44 also had a wooden shingle roof. In the 740s Toyonari was the most powerful member of the Fujiwara family during the struggle for dominance against the Tachibana, rising to the office of Minister of the Right under Tachibana no Moroe in 749.[42] Reconstruction of the appearance of the villa shows the untroubled persistence of indigenous building modes at a site which was then being considered for a new capital. The villa had a shingled roof, pillars which were sunk into the ground, and a raised timber floor built in the manner of the *haniwa* house models of the pre-Buddhist period.[43] It was far-removed ideologically from the kind of architecture sanctioned in the Dajōkan edict of less than two decades earlier.

The urban and architectural records also proffer special insight into the uncertainties of direction experienced mid-way through the process of adoption of foreign models. The adoption and adaptation, as well as the rejection, of some of these foreign forms of city planning and architectural order – from style to mensuration – parallel a similar accommodation of the adopted *ritsuryō* system to Japanese circumstances, notably in the insertion of the Jingikan on equal standing with the Dajōkan at the top of the bureaucratic structure of government. This amounted to nothing short of a collision between the new authority of foreign models of government, social order and their built environment, and the old authority of long-established custom in government and building.

Religious Piety and Political Power: Tōdaiji and the Unity of Church and State

During the second half of the Nara period the authority of the state was projected with renewed vigour and certainty through the creation of Tōdaiji. Tōdaiji was a vast cathedral of state religion, acting as the headquarters for the *kokubunji*, the nation-wide system of regional monasteries and nunneries.[44] These religious foundations extended the central authority of Nara to each and every province using the vehicle of sophisticated buildings in the official style. As well as serving as an enduring reminder of central authority, these

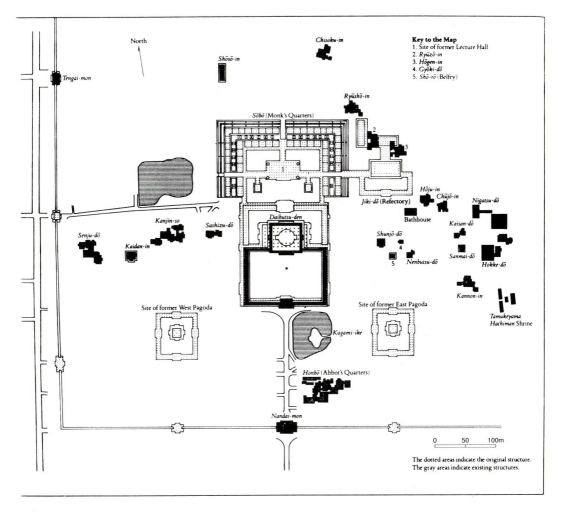

The following labels appear on the plan:

North

Tengai-mon

Shōsō-in

Chisoku-in

Key to the Map
1. Site of former Lecture Hall
2. Ryūzō-in
3. Hōgen-in
4. Gyōki-dō
5. Shō-rō (Belfry)

Ryūshō-in

Sōbō (Monk's Quarters)

Hōju-in   Chūjō-in   Nigatsu-dō

Jiki-dō (Refectory)   Bathhouse

Kaisan-dō

Kanjin-so   Sashizu-dō

Senju-dō

Kaidan-in

Shunjō-dō

Sanmai-dō

Nenbutsu-dō   Hokke-dō

Daibutsu-den

Kannon-in

Site of former West Pagoda

Site of former East Pagoda

Tamukeyama
Hachiman Shrine

Kagami-ike

Honbō (Abbot's Quarters)

Nandai-mon

0   50   100m

The dotted areas indicate the original structure.
The gray areas indicate existing structures.

temples and religious houses became the source for advanced building technologies and sophisticated capital culture in even the most remote regions.

Ranked chronologically, Tōdaiji was the second major building project of the Nara period after Nara Palace itself. The construction of the 'Eastern Great Temple', with a Great Buddha or *Daibutsu* as its spiritual and spatial focus, directly paralleled the establishment of Nara Palace with the Great Audience Hall or Daigokuden at its centre. Tōdaiji was conceived under the direct patronage of Emperor Shōmu and its construction preoccupied the highest levels of government during the middle decades of the eighth century after the return from the uneasy experimentation with other capitals in 745. Tōdaiji therefore reveals as much about the political priorities as the spiritual concerns of national government at Nara.

Tōdaiji has lost most of its original buildings to natural disasters and to the civil wars of the twelfth and sixteenth centuries, but archaeological investigation and early descriptions and maps have established beyond doubt that the present layout of buildings reflects the original eighth-century plan (Figure 3.12). The generously scaled site, some 900 metres east–west and 800 metres

Fig 3.12 Plan of Tōdaiji (Courtesy: Chicago Art Institute. Source: John M. Rosenfield *et al., The Great Eastern Temples. Treasures of Japanese Buddhist Art from Tōdai-ji*)

Fig 3.13
Daibutsuden,
Tōdaiji, Nara.
As recon-
structed
1688–1707

north–south, is level on the western side but on the eastern side rises 50 metres up the slopes of Mount Wakakusa in a series of terraces. The disposition of the temple buildings on this site shows the same considerations of axiality, order and monumentality as does Nara Palace. The temple is oriented approximately north–south along a central axis, in the best continental tradition, delineated by the approach avenue running from the Great South Gate (Nandaimon) towards the main precinct 230 metres away. The main precinct is enclosed by a covered cloister 110 metres north–south and 170 metres east–west. Entry is via the Inner Gate, Chūmon, and the enclosed area is dominated by the Daibutsuden, much in the way the Daigokuden dominated the inner precinct of Nara Palace (Figure 3.13). In the eighth century there were two smaller compounds immediately south of the Daibutsuden precinct, enclosing a pair of matching pagodas, each over 100 metres in height (Figure 3.14). These towering build-

Fig 3.14
Tōdaiji. Model
by Amanuma
Shun'ichi
reconstructing
the appearance
of the Nara-
period
buildings
(property of
Tōdaiji)

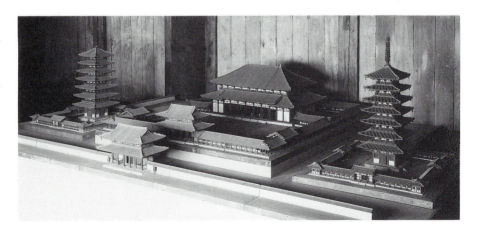

Fig 3.15
Daibutsuden,
Tōdaiji.
Interior of
extant building
showing Great
Buddha

ings, capped by their bronze finials, were amongst the tallest structures built
in ancient East Asia. The symmetrical east–west placement of a pair of pagodas across the primary south–north axis of the temple is based on customary
Chinese temple planning practice at the zenith of the Tang dynasty in the
eighth century. Finally, like Nara Palace, the entire Tōdaiji complex was
enclosed on the south and west sides by walls, each with three gateways.

Tōdaiji served as the setting for the grandest religious ceremonies of the Nara state, as befitting its exalted role as the centre of state Buddhism. On such occasions high-ranking members of the court and government officials approached the monastery from the south. After passing through the imposing Great South Gate, they would proceed down the long pathway to the more modest Inner Gate, and thence to the vast open courtyard of the inner precinct. There they confronted the Daibutsuden, with its soaring grey-tiled roofs and cinnabar-red pillars and beams from which an aura of enormous power and serene confidence emanated. Inside the hall stood the statue of Vairocana, symbolic core of the monastery, soaring high in the darkened, incense-laden space. The colossal gilt-bronze image, framed by the geometry of great timber pillars and beams, shimmered in the light of flickering candles. The form of the Daibutsuden was closely determined by its function as a setting for the Great Buddha. Its interior was planned around the central bronze figure and even today it dominates the space of the interior (Figure 3.15). The surrounding bays of the building permit worshippers to view the sculpture from all four sides. Originally the plan was rectangular, with an additional two bays on each side of the main figure to house the attendant bodhisattva sculptures. In both the original plan and the present-day version, therefore, the interior of the Daibutsuden was designed to create a focus on a sculptural core.

Eighth-century records and archaeological evidence have together permitted reconstruction of the appearance of the original Nara-period building (Figure 3.16).[45] The original Daibutsuden differed from the present-day building in several important ways. It was over 30 per cent wider than today's building, measuring 86.1 metres across as compared with the 57.1 metres of the extant building. More significantly, this made the Daibutsuden almost one-third wider than the Daigokuden, which maintained a width of approximately 50 metres throughout the Nara period. The first storey was divided into twelve bays, three more than were used in the Daigokuden, and the lower roof of the original building was stepped up over the central seven bays of the façade both for visual emphasis and for relief from the sense of massive and over-powering weight generated by the heavy grey roof-tiles. The Nara-period Daibutsuden was imbued with a much stronger sense of harmonic proportion than is found in the current building, whose ungainly upper storey is a mere five bays wide in contrast to nine bays in the original structure.

The present Daibutsuden is, in fact, the fourth structure to be built on this same site. Completed in 1707, it is 47 metres high, 57 metres long and 52 metres wide and is still reputed to be the largest timber-framed building in the world, indicating the immense scale of construction of which the Japanese were capable in the eighth century. The statue has suffered considerable damage, like the building around it, but its massive 10.82 metres indicates the monumentality of conception of sculpture and building alike. Their scale rivals in size and splendour many of the most impressive works of monumental architecture and sculpture in the known world. They may be placed with confidence beside not only the great Tang monuments but also the Colossus of Rhodes and Phidias' Olympus.

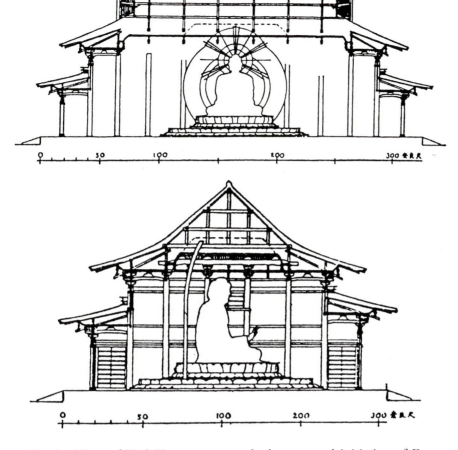

Fig 3.16
Daibutsuden,
Tōdaiji.
Reconstruction
drawings of
Nara-period
building by
Fukuyama
Toshio
(Source:
Tōdaiji
Daibutsuden
Shōwa daishūri
iinkai (ed.)
*Kokuhō Tōdaiji
Kondō
[Daibutsuden]
shūri kōji
hōkokusho*)

The building of Tōdaiji was very much the personal initiative of Emperor Shōmu, particularly after his earlier plans to build a Great Buddha and Hall first at Kawachi (740), then at Shigaraki (743) and finally at Kōga (744), were thwarted by the insistence of the court under Fujiwara dominance to return to Nara, as already discussed. In 743 Shōmu announced to his court the reasons for the founding of a great temple dedicated to the Vairocana Buddha of the Kegon sect:

> Our fervent desire is that under the aegis of the Three Treasures,[46] the benefits of peace may be brought to all in heaven and on earth, even animals and plants sharing in its fruits, for all time to come. . . . We take this occasion to proclaim Our great vow for erecting an image of Locana Buddha [Vairocana] in gold and copper. We wish to make the utmost use of the nation's resources of metal in the casting of this image, and also to level off the high hill on which the great edifice is to be raised, so that the entire land may be joined with Us in the fellowship of Buddhism and enjoy in common the advantages which this undertaking affords of the attainment of Buddhahood.[47]

The pious language of Shōmu's proclamation masked reasoning which was unmistakably political, namely sponsorship of the Kegon sect and its focal

75

deity, the Vairocana Buddha. It was a strategy adopted by Shōmu to assert his personal control in the arena of factional feuding within the court. The Kegon Sect, at that time only a recent arrival in Japan, was based on the *Avataṁsaka Sūtra* or 'Flower Garland Sutra'.[48] It had been translated from Sanskrit into Chinese as recently as 695–99 under the sponsorship of the Empress Wu (655–705).[49] Its textual complexity and convenient ambiguity gave Shōmu ample scope to construe its spiritual message of a centralising spiritual force in the universe into an expedient religious justification for tightening imperial authority. This was based on the precedent furnished by Empress Wu herself. In order to strengthen her authority she sponsored Buddhism in general and the Huayan (Kegon) sect in particular. Buddhism with its equitable view of women rulers, and the Huayan sutra with its principal notion of a centralising deity, provided powerful religious underpinnings for her position in the Tang court, dominated as it was by male-orientated Confucian and Daoist ideology.[50] In 691 under Empress Wu, Buddhism was officially ranked above Daoism. She was patron of the monk Fa Zang who systematised the doctrine of the Huayan sect, and she herself acted as a copyist in the daunting task of translation from the Sanskrit of the Flower Garland Sutra. Empress Wu sponsored the creation of at least 380 Buddhist images at the cave temples of Longmen, near the second Tang capital of Luoyang, more than twice the total number of such images produced at these cave sites during the other 240 years of the Tang dynasty.[51] The most dramatic of these images was a massive figure of Vairocana, the central deity of the Flower Garland Sutra, carved out of the sheer rock face and flanked by guardian kings and bodhisattvas of almost equal size and expressive power. Today this Great Buddha, some 13.37 metres in height, and its monumental attendants, stand exposed to the elements. Deep mortise holes cut neatly into the cliff face behind the sculptures show where sturdy wooden beams were once anchored in the wall to help support the great hall which enclosed the sacred figures.

The construction at Nara of the Great Buddha, complete with its attendants and housed within a vast hall, was in conscious emulation of the architectonic strategy employed by Empress Wu to consolidate her imperial authority in the Tang dynasty. In a broader sense, the creation of Tōdaiji amounted to the physical consummation of an ideology of state which reiterated, in new theological guise, the placement of government under the aegis of Buddhism as formulated in Prince Shōtoku's Seventeen Article Constitution of 604. However there can be little doubt that Shōmu was also appropriating temporal power when we read the conclusion to his announcement concerning the founding of Tōdaiji: 'It is We who possess the wealth of the land; it is We who possess all power in the land. With this wealth and power at Our command, We have resolved to create this venerable object of worship'.[52] By the expedient of patronage of the recently arrived Kegon sect, with its convenient theology of a centralised universe and great capacity for grandiose representation in sculpture and architecture, the attention and energies of the court were diverted, and the potential of monumental architecture used in concert with monumental sculpture to proclaim authority was fully exploited.

The overt affirmation of the importance of Buddhism to the state was accompanied by a pragmatic accommodation with Shinto. All the public avowals of the importance of Buddhism, and the specific benefits which the Three Treasures offered to high and low alike, did not negate the importance of Shinto to the authority of the imperial institution. In fact, the institutionalisation of Shinto in the Nara state, in which the Ise shrines and their periodic rebuilding were placed under formal imperial protection, assigned the foreign gods to the protection of the native ones. It was the Shinto deity Hachiman whose divine aid allowed the construction of the Daibutsu to be completed against all adversity, thereby helping to consolidate the imperial significance of Shinto.[53] The *Shoku Nihongi* takes pains to explain the important role played by Hachiman in travelling to Tōdaiji from his home at the Usa Shrine in Kyushu in order to worship before the Great Buddha.[54] In so doing Hachiman became the guardian or tutelary deity of Tōdaiji. Thereafter a Hachiman shrine was established at each *kokubunji* throughout the country to provide similar protection to the Buddhist gods.[55]

The enormity of the Tōdaiji building enterprise is a measure of the seriousness of its political purpose. Its construction paralleled in scale and complexity that of Nara Palace itself and was supervised by an administrative apparatus of the state. Construction was under the control of a specially created government department presided over by a senior monk, as well as by high-ranking officials of Shōmu's court. The government department was divided into nine separate sections, each responsible for a different part of the project. A timber collection section dispatched lumbermen west to Harima on the Inland Sea to obtain the 48 principal pillars, each 30 metres long and 1.5 metres in diameter, needed for the Daibutsuden. The forested mountains around Lake Biwa, north of Nara, provided the smaller timbers necessary to complete that hall and the many other worship and residential structures in the temple complex. A transportation section floated the timbers from the mountain forests to collection points along local rivers, while the building section was responsible for the prefabrication and assembly of all the structures. This was, of course, the most labour-intensive aspect of the entire project, employing 227 site supervisors, 917 master builders and 1,483 labourers. At peak periods in the construction, over 1,000 cooks prepared meals for craftsmen and labourers employed at the site. This undertaking would have exceeded in scale that of the construction work for Nara Palace.

The most ambitious and arduous section of the Tōdaiji construction project is the least visible to the eye today. This was the excavation and landscaping of the western slopes of Mount Wakakusa to a depth equivalent to the height of the upper eaves of the present Daibutsuden. This project had been announced as part of Shōmu's proclamation of 743. Commencing in 745, half the side of the mountain over a distance of 700 metres was excavated to a depth of 10 to 30 metres, transforming the slope into four terraces. The most westerly terrace held the Ordination Hall and West Pagoda. On the second terrace, some 10 metres higher and immediately to the east, was the main precinct, containing the Daibutsuden. On the third terrace, 15 metres further up the site, was the East Pagoda, while on the highest and easternmost level stood the Sangatsudō and a number of other buildings. Even close scrutiny of the temple site today gives little indication of how radically it was landscaped in the eighth century.

Preparation of this site was followed by the casting of the 16-metre high Great Buddha. Now considered to have been the largest bronze casting project undertaken in the ancient world, it was a difficult trial and error process. It involved possibly as many as seven separate smelting furnaces.[56] The great hall was then erected around it. Meanwhile work was proceeding on the myriad of other buildings which were an essential part of the temple complex in its role both as a religious centre and a living community. This work was to continue for more than a decade after the completion and dedication of the Daibutsu itself.

The building of the temple may have been an official state project but ultimately the cost proved too great a strain on government finances seriously depleted by the abortive and costly movements of the capital in the early 740s. Shōmu may have declared in 743 that he wished to make the 'utmost use of the nation's resources of metal in the casting of this image'. This did not necessarily mean that he expected the cost to be so great, however, and it was only the timely discovery of gold in 749 for the first time in Japan, in the remote northern province of Mutsu, that permitted the completion of the gilding of the Great Buddha.[57] This fortuitous coincidence, construed at the time as nothing short of miraculous, only added to Shōmu's prestige and authority. Ultimately, the general financing of the project took the form of what would, in modern terms, be described as 'public subscription'. Significant support was generated by the ardent nationwide fund-raising efforts of the monk Gyōki who had been appointed chief solicitor for Tōdaiji. Temple tradition holds that Gyōki elicited contributions of timber for construction from 50,000 people, received donations of gold coins, copper goods, and other valuable objects from 370,000 others, and mobilised as many as 1.6 million volunteer labourers over the course of the project. A vast army of administrators, site supervisors, skilled master builders and labourers participated in the construction process.

This prodigious expenditure of wealth and energy in the service of the centralised imperial state was consummated at the official completion ceremony for the Great Buddha, the 'Eye-Opening Ceremony'. This lavish and spectacular rite was conducted in the fourth month of 752 under the direction of the Indian monk Bodhisena before a vast host of courtiers, monks and foreign envoys. The elaborate ceremonies involved in this rite were performed on special stages erected in the expansive grassed courtyard in front of the Daibutsu which still stood starkly exposed to the elements prior to erection of the great hall planned to house it. Over 10,000 monks, arranged in groups around the courtyard, joined in the solemn chants of Buddhist sutras. Four thousand court musicians performed Bugaku music accompanied by dancers dressed in flowing saffron and gold-threaded robes and wearing masks of the divine countenance of the Buddha. The consecration of the new cathedral of Salisbury in 1258, attended by Henry III of England and his court, as well as the Archbishop of Canterbury, bishops, clergy and a vast congregation, would have been a ceremonial occasion of like grandeur and spiritual and political significance in the western world. Protracted feasting, performances of court dance and music, and the Eye-Opening Ceremony itself, when the hoods covering the Buddha's eyes were pulled away by means of long ropes held by all members of the congregation, may have been of avowed religious purpose. In reality they were remarkably like many of the ceremonies performed in the courtyard of the State Halls Compound of the palace whose configuration was similar. These great ceremonies, with their pageantry and ritual, pomp and circumstance, transcended the boundaries of sacred and secular, highlighting the authority of their sponsors.

Tōdaiji, like Nara Palace, is the manifestation of the symbiosis between architecture and authority, each essential to the other and mutually sustaining. In the case of Nara Palace, the establishment was dominated by the ideology and rituals of an emperor whose power was based equally on secular prerogatives and divine association, architectural style and technology being the shared province of both. At Tōdaiji a similar situation prevailed, but in reverse. It came into existence as a great religious establishment intended to further the ends of the state while pursuing the goals of religious fulfilment with a rare zeal and vision. Conceived at a crucial moment in the power struggle for dominance at court which had already led to the undignified and abortive attempts to establish new capitals between 740 and 745, Tōdaiji achieved its political purpose for several decades. It provided a bulwark for Shōmu's personal authority, and through the *kokubunji* system, furthered the end of projecting capital influence in the regions of Japan.

Ironically it was to be the very strength of this association of the state with Buddhism which precipitated the sudden demise of Nara as the national capital. At Nara the peculiar dynamism of the new urban environment became an arena for competing interests of church and state, a conflict focused on the influence of the clergy on the imperial court, and of the priest Dōkyō on the empress. Dōkyō, a handsome monk and brilliant political tactician, was in highest favour with the Empress Shōtoku. Warning bells sounded about the Buddhist church's challenge to the power of the state when the empress issued two edicts in 764 and 766 respectively, naming Dōkyō Chief Minister and Ruler of the Law. It was rumoured Dōkyō had aspirations to the very throne itself. The aristocratic families at court, moving to protect their own power, had the Dajōkan forbid further female accession to the throne pleading its vulnerability to such intrusion. There had been four female sovereigns during the Nara period and Shōtoku had reigned previously (749–758) under the Empress Kōken.

The ultimate solution was a reversion to those long-established peripatetic and historically acceptable practices – to abandon the city as a centre of government and build a new capital. After one false start the site of Kyoto, some 40 kilometres to the north, was selected and named optimistically as Heian-kyō, 'Capital of Peace and Tranquillity'. The logic of this decision was impeccable. It was designed to separate church from state physically by excluding the major Buddhist temples from within the boundaries of the new city precincts, except for the controlled presence of an East Temple and a West Temple. This solution is a further demonstration of the homology between authority and the architecturally created environment.

The architecture, archaeological and written records together demonstrate that Nara was a seething vortex of instability despite the pretensions to stability and order of its public buildings. The factionalism of the court and tensions between church and state were directly reflected in the built environment even as political will sought unequivocal expression in monumental architecture and city plans.

Heian Palaces and Kamakura Temples

4

The Changing Countenances of Aristocratic and Warrior Power

The 700 years from the establishment of a new capital city of Heian in 794 to the outbreak of the Ōnin War in 1467, which destroyed much of the city, was an epoch of profound change in both authority and architecture. It covers the three historical periods of Heian (794–1185), Kamakura (1185–1333) and Muromachi (1333–1467). The general historical framework of these periods is well known and need be mentioned only briefly here. The Heian period saw the flourishing of indigenous forms of government and culture under the civil aristocracy in the Heian capital, now generally referred to by its modern name of Kyoto. The centralised authority of aristocratic government based in Kyoto was eroded by the growth of private land holdings in the provinces, and by the creation of warrior bands to protect and promote these landed interests. Political and military turbulence reached its culmination with the defeat of the Taira forces by those of the Minamoto in 1185 and the establishment of a warrior government at Kamakura. Minamoto Yoritomo assumed the court title of shogun, setting the precedent of using this imperially conferred office to sanction *de facto* warrior power as *de jure* government. The succeeding period witnessed an uneasy balance between the civil power of the court in Kyoto and the military power of the warrior class at Kamakura.[1] By the end of the fourteenth century the balance had shifted decisively towards the military. The overthrow of the Kamakura shogunate by a coalition of disaffected warrior and aristocratic interests under the leadership of the Ashikaga family saw the destruction of the city of Kamakura, and the establishment of warrior government in Kyoto itself. The warrior class was gradually absorbed into the cultural milieu of the old capital. The confluence of warrior and aristocratic culture transformed the high culture to create many of the characteristic features for which Japanese civilization was henceforth known in architecture, theatre, religion, literature and painting. The authority of the Ashikaga shogunate, however, was still vested in the formal authority of the imperial institution. The Ashikaga presided over a loosely controlled system of national and regional government in which the regional was once again to triumph over the central. The eventual breakdown of Ashikaga control over regional lords at the time of the outbreak of the Ōnin War in 1467 precipitated nearly a century and a half of civil wars which devastated the cities, ruined the economy but, paradoxically, stimulated religious and artistic expression.

These seven centuries were characterised by religious movements of lasting importance to Japanese civilization. The relocation of the capital to Kyoto broke the dominance of the Nara Buddhist sects over court government. The esoteric sects of Shingon and Tendai became a powerful religious and cultural force, while popular forms of Buddhism, particularly of the worship of the Buddha Amida, offered an easier form of personal salvation and gained a strong following with the Heian aristocracy. The establishment of warrior government at Kamakura in 1185 broadly coincided with the arrival of new forms of Buddhism from China, particularly that of Chan or Zen Buddhism as it became known in Japan. Zen flourished amongst the warrior leadership under the charismatic guidance of Chinese emigré monks and Japanese who had studied in China, of whom the monks Eisai (1141–1215) and Dōgen (1200–1253) had the most enduring influence. At the same time Shinto took on a more militant form in association with the cult of Hachiman, which we have seen had flourished under the sponsorship of the Nara court.

This was unmistakably an epoch of profound consequence for political and religious authority and the exercise of power at all levels. It was equally an epoch in which there was constant architectural activity directed at housing new institutions of government and religion, and expressing changing nuances of power, belief and daily life. The Heian period saw the creation of a new form of palace and mansion architecture now known as *shinden-zukuri*. By the Kamakura period there was a fresh wave of architectural influence from Song China, coinciding with the arrival of Zen Buddhism. There were also important innovations in design methods, particularly in the use of square roots to describe the pronounced curves of roofs and framing, one of the direct and distinctive results of Song architectural influence.[2]

Despite the obvious importance of developments in both architecture and authority in the period lasting from the ninth to the fifteenth century, it is difficult to probe the intricacies of this interaction in detail. Documentation of authority, particularly in the Heian period, is diffuse and sometimes obscure in meaning. Some of the written records, from the Kamakura period and beyond, comprise *ex post facto* justification of the meritorious actions of the victorious, and condemnation of the dastardly deeds of the defeated. With all the ingredients for fine romantic ballads including love, war, hate, jealousy, treachery and valour, it is no wonder that these accounts are a rich contribution to the world of literature but unreliable for use as historical sources. The position is even more difficult in the case of architecture. Few buildings survive from these 700 years. Those that do remain date mostly from the very beginning or the very end of this epoch, the notable exceptions being the Byōdōin at Uji to the south of Kyoto, and the Chūsonji at Hiraizumi in north-eastern Honshu.[3]

Because of these difficulties there is, of necessity, more generalised description and greater speculation in this section of this study. The focus will be on the palaces and villas of the Heian capital in the first half of the eleventh century and the Zen temples of the late thirteenth century associated with the sphere of Kamakura influence: the former saw the apogee of Fujiwara power at the Heian court and the latter the flourishing of architectural patronage by the Hōjō. Each has sufficient primary evidence of architectural and political activity to allow general characterisation and tentative conclusions to be drawn concerning the relationship between the two.

Shinden-zukuri and the Power of the Fujiwara

Shinden-zukuri is the name now given to the form of residential and palatial architecture which evolved for the comfort and pleasure of the aristocracy in the city of Heian. As we saw in the preceding chapter, Nara was abandoned in order to remove government from the influence of the Buddhist sects. After an abortive attempt to establish a new capital at Nagaoka, another larger and more suitable site further to the north was selected for the new city. This new city was 5.2 kilometres north–south and 4.5 kilometres east–west, considerably larger in dimensions than Nara had been but it was laid out on a similar grid plan with the imperial palace at the centre-north, and observed the same principles of symmetry, axiality, and hierarchy.

Shinden-zukuri reached its maturity in the eleventh century under the patronage of the Fujiwara family. It evolved in the rarefied atmosphere of the court during centuries of indigenous cultural flowering following the decision to break all communication with China in 898 AD as the Tang Dynasty slid into self-destruction. *Shinden-zukuri* was the architectural style of a small elite, estimated to number no more than a few thousand persons, whose influence in terms of political power was to decline dramatically after the eleventh century with the rise to power of the samurai. Its architectural and cultural importance, however, was to transcend the limitations of time and space of this numerically small group. It was to become no less than the well-spring of the Japanese residential architectural tradition.

The single term *shinden-zukuri*[4] in reality encompasses three different types of building complexes in the Heian capital. The first type consisted of imperial palaces, including the Imperial Palace or official centre of the court and emperor, the palaces of retired emperors, as well as imperial villas situated in the pleasant countryside around the capital. The second category was that of 'detached palaces' (*rikyū*) which were used as centres of clan and familial government by powerful members of the court aristocratic families. The third type of *shinden-zukuri* refers to the private residential mansions of aristocrats in Heian-kyō.

All three *shinden* types shared a common style, although with variations occasioned by differing needs for ritual space. As an aristocratic architecture, *shinden-zukuri* continued distinctively Japanese building traditions which had been eclipsed by Chinese building styles in the Nara period. It translated vernacular practices into an aristocratic milieu and gave formal expression to native preferences in materials, design and decoration. Features of Chinese monumental architecture used at Nara for official buildings, particularly tiled roofs, bracket sets, stone foundations, and polychrome decoration, made way in the official architecture of the Heian capital for the unpainted timbers, raised-wood floors and shingle roofs which had been retained at Nara only for private residences. *Shinden-zukuri*, therefore, represents the re-emergence of a self-assured, native building tradition in the high culture which, while benefiting

from the stimulus of international contacts, had reached a stage of confidence in its own identity. In this way *shinden-zukuri* was a product of two dynamic processes: the indigenous response to the architectural traditions of the Asian mainland on the one hand, and the establishment of status distinctions between the architectural styles of different classes on the other. The former was a tacit rejection of the authority of foreign architectural models, while the latter gave rise to expression of ruling authority through a new hierarchical language of built form.

The depiction of the Sanjō Palace in the *Heiji monogatari emaki* is one of the most vivid records of *shinden* architecture (Figures 4.1 and 4.2).[5] This scene from the illustrated hand scrolls showing the struggle between the Taira and their mortal military adversaries, the Minamoto, affords a tantalising glimpse of a palace complex at the moment of its destruction by fire. Even as the buildings are enveloped in flame the painting allows us to examine the two processes of indigenous response to Chinese influence and social stratification in more detail. The *Heiji monogatari emaki* was originally a large set of handscrolls of which only three now survive intact together with a small number of fragments of the remainder.[6] Painted in the second half of the thirteenth century, they depict the civil disorder in the Heian capital at the

Fig 4.1
*Heiji mono-
gatari emaki*,
handscroll,
second half of
thirteenth
century. Night
attack on the
Sanjō Palace.
Detail
(Courtesy of
Museum of
Fine Arts,
Boston.
Fenollosa-Weld
Collection)

end of the year 1159, one of the incidents from which the Taira, under their leader Kiyomori, were to emerge as the dominant military force in capital politics.

The section of the scroll in the Museum of Fine Arts, Boston, depicting a night attack on the Sanjō Palace by the Minamoto, is one of the most dramatic scenes in all Japanese art. It vividly illustrates the fate of both architecture and authority in the Heian period. The Sanjō Palace was the residence of the emperor Go Shirakawa, who resorted to using the Taira for military support against the Minamoto. In this scene the attacking Minamoto warriors are shown rampaging through the *shinden-zukuri* buildings of the palace. The blood of the supporters of the retired emperor flows freely as sword and spear do their worst. The palace itself is completely enveloped in smoke and flame and it is easy to imagine the savagery and confusion of the actual incident.

These scenes were painted some 100 years after the events they depict, the artist relying on imagination and contemporary buildings as a source of reference to recreate the appearance of the destroyed Sanjō Palace. Despite the dating problem, we can see clearly the features of *shinden-zukuri* which distinguish it from the official architecture of the Nara period. The buildings are linked by long corridors which open on to wooden verandas. The roofs are

85

dark brown in colour, indicating a covering with thin layers of cypress bark – a type of roofing known as *hiwada-buki* (see Figures 4.2–4.3). The ridges of the roof are crowned with layers of terracotta tiles. All the timbers of the structural framing, floors and doors are unpainted, very different in effect from the brightly painted and lacquered Chinese style adopted at Nara. The floors of the buildings are elevated above the ground, continuing the practice established in pre-Buddhist times. There is a notable absence of bracket sets supporting the eaves; the lighter cypress-bark shingles required less elaborate support under the eaves, and by the middle of the Heian period the Japanese had developed a sophisticated method of inserting cantilevers inside the roof to carry the weight of its framing hidden from view. Details of the walls are also discernible. Those in the foreground of the composition have sections which have been filled in with lath or plaster, with barred windows set high up under the eaves. Other parts of the walls have been left open, covered with black-lacquered reticulated shutters known as *shitomido*. The lower shutters are set like removable half walls while the upper shutters hinge outwards under the eaves. The distinctive bamboo blinds with green brocade fringes, now known as *sudare*, screen the interior of the building from outside view.

This scene highlights the use of cypress-shingle roofs and exterior gateways as status symbols in the Heian palaces. They became features of authority in the same way that forked finials and ridge billets had become symbols of authority in Shinto architecture, that is, by a process of cooption from vernacular architecture. The state had insisted on the use of terracotta tiling for government buildings in the city of Nara, a policy we have seen officially articulated in the court memorandum of the year 724. We also noted how

Fig 4.3
Cypress-bark
shingle roofing
(*hiwada-buki*).
Detail of roof
restoration at
Enryakuji,
1981

shingles of cypress bark remained an important part of Japanese architectural practice despite government policy. In the Heian period there was to be a reversal of this policy of state insistence on terracotta over shingles for buildings of the aristocracy. In the year 1030 the court issued an edict stating explicitly that cypress-bark shingles were not to be used by aristocrats of and below the sixth court rank in status.[8] This marks a fascinating *volte face* from the memorandum of 724. The law in effect completed the process of elevating cypress shingles to the level of conscious aristocratic privilege. Simultaneously with this elevation within indigenous practice, there was also confluence with the adopted Chinese building tradition. The Sanjō Palace scene discloses that, while shingles are used for the main covering of the roof, terracotta tiles were used to cover the ridge courses. Japanese experience had established that tiling, rather than lighter bamboo and thatch binding, was better able to resist the force of wind and rain at the vulnerable apex of a roof. The Japanese showed no xenophobic compunctions about employing the Chinese system if it meant a more efficient way of keeping out the rain.

Status considerations affected more than roof covering methods only. During the Heian period status distinctions were carefully established and regulated by means of sumptuary laws. The most important target for this legislation was gateway architecture, which as a result became the key exterior indicator of high court rank to the outside world (Figure 4.4). For example, an edict dating to the Kōnin era (810–824) declared that 'those of the Third Court Rank and above, and also *sangi* [senior Dajōkan officials of the Fourth Court Rank], must have permission to build gateways on the main avenues. All others of the Fourth Rank and persons of a Fifth Rank should not build them'.[9] The gateway thereby became a badge of rank, built with pride along

Fig 4.4
Heiji mono-gatari emaki, handscroll, second half thirteenth century. Night attack on the Sanjō Palace. Detail showing gateway to the Sanjō Palace (Courtesy of Museum of Fine Arts, Boston. Fenollosa-Weld Collection)

the main avenues by those entitled by customary court practice to do so, and probably regarded jealously by those excluded from the practice.

Status and its prerogatives was also intrinsic to the rationale for the siting of palaces in the Heian capital. The blocks in the city in closest proximity to the emperor's palace were reserved by the city planners for persons of highest court rank, as had been the practice in Nara. Courtiers of high rank were allocated larger blocks while those lower in the aristocratic hierarchy were given smaller sub-divisions within main blocks. There were also differences in design between the *shinden-zukuri* of persons of different rank.[10] Symmetry in the arrangement of wings was reserved for the palaces and mansions of members of the imperial household and of the most important aristocrats. In contrast, palaces used by lower levels of the aristocracy, together with the country retreats of the elite, had a less formal arrangement of buildings. The lower the status, the further distanced from Chinese practice.

As so often in Japanese history, study of Heian city architecture is made more difficult by the frequent occurrence of fires which obliterated all trace of many buildings from the visual record. Tragically, not a single Heian period *shinden* palace survives as direct testimony of the style of architecture of the age. The Imperial Palace in Kyoto, or Kyōto Gosho, as it is known today, has been rebuilt on innumerable occasions and now occupies an entirely different site from that of the original Heian-period palace. The Gosho as it stands today is a 1950s reconstruction of a mid-nineteenth century recon-struction, itself based on problematic pictorial sources. In lieu of actual buildings, the most useful procedure is to study paintings and the records of archaeological research to re-establish the architectural practices of the Heian period capital. However, paintings themselves must be used with caution despite their apparent wealth of beguiling detail. Many works, including the

Heiji monogatari emaki, were painted well after the events depicted and corroboration from other sources is essential for scholarly analysis. Those Heian-period *emakimono* which do survive, including the famed *Genji monogatari emaki*, were painted by artists whose interests appear to have been focused more on the courtiers and their romances than with architectural realism. Fortunately, some attention was paid to architectural details, such as the framing and the organisation of interior space, and these scenes are generally helpful in recreating the internal appearance of the lost buildings. Other paintings such as the *Nenjū gyōji emaki*, which purport to depict Heian-period customs and rituals, are available only in Edo-period copies and also require care in use as historical resources.

It is only since 1979 that significant progress has been made in comparing detailed descriptions of *shinden* architecture in contemporary accounts with the results of new archaeological discoveries.[11] As a result the Tsuchimikado-dono of Fujiwara Michinaga emerges as the most important example of a *shinden-zukuri* palace for purposes of examining the relationship between architecture and authority in this era. Here we have the most powerful court figure of the late tenth and the first decades of the eleventh century, together with the most magnificent palace of the age. Through intermarriage with the imperial family and the skilful manipulation of the office of regent,[12] the Fujiwara family had become the most powerful force in the government and politics of the Heian court. So strong was Fujiwara Michinaga's position between 995–1027 that the anonymous writer of the *Ōkagami*, the tales of Michinaga's life and times compiled at the turn of the twelfth century, wrote: 'The regency has never left his house, and we may assume that it never will.'[13] Michinaga himself became father-in-law to three emperors. Three more emperors were to be his grandsons and he became uncle to two more. His power reached a zenith in 1016 when he assumed the office of regent in order to rule on behalf of his nephew, the Emperor Go Ichijō. The following year Michinaga became Grand Minister of State, the highest government office.

Tsuchimikado-dono was Michinaga's principal palace and residence during these years of unrivalled power. The palace occupied two entire blocks in the north-east section of the city, each some 90 metres by 100 metres. It faced onto Tsuchimikado Ōji, one of the principal east–west avenues of the capital from which it took its name, and Higashi no Tōin Ōji, an avenue running north–south. Michinaga inherited this prime site from his father-in-law, Minamoto Masanobu, who had been Minister of the Left (Sadaijin), the senior minister in the court government.[14]

The main buildings of the palace were placed to the direct north of an extensive garden boasting an artificial lake and island. This was a special feature of *shinden-zukuri* and required a significant modification of the Chinese planning canon of a southerly approach to buildings of importance. The lake was now in the way of an approach from the south, and as a consequence the main gateways to this palace, as well as to most *shinden* palaces, were moved to the east and west compound walls. This entirely changed the flow of ritual space as well as practical usage of Heian palaces and mansions.

To the north of the main buildings of the Tsuchimikado-dono, numerous service buildings such as kitchens, storehouses and accommodation for servants were located. Their precise placement and size is not known. A riding ground 200 metres in length, running north–south to the east of the palace buildings, was set up as Michinaga was a particularly keen horseman and enjoyed both riding and watching races.[15]

The years from 991 to 1027, when Tsuchimikado-dono served as Michinaga's palace and government headquarters, were decades of extraordinary cultural vitality. Murasaki Shikibu's *Tale of Genji* belongs to this era and it is not inconceivable that Michinaga himself was the model for Prince Genji. Whatever the historical truth in this epic tale, we are given tantalising glimpses of how the *shinden-zukuri* palaces such as Tsuchimikado-dono were used for daily life and court ritual – a sliding door here, a half-rolled blind there. The narrative scrolls illustrating the *Tale of Genji*, dating from about a century later, also show scenes of the daily life of the courtiers. We can see the early use of *tatami* mats for seating purposes on wooden floors, bamboo screens (*sudare*) hanging from the eaves for shade and privacy, and sliding screens (*fusuma*) acting as flexible interior-space dividers. The aristocratic world of the Heian *shinden* residence was one in which the building was an organic part of a garden landscape. There were few fixed walls between exterior and interior, allowing the garden and the sense of nature to flow inside to the world of the private preoccupations of the aristocrats. The paintings on the *fusuma* depicted themes from nature and showed the same concerns with the passage of human life mirroring the passing of the seasons as are to be found in the *Tale of Genji*.

The creation of the spacious and sumptuous palace of Tsuchimikado-dono was a direct response to a significant shift in the nature of political power in the middle of the Heian period, the ceding of actual power from reigning emperors to the Fujiwara. The first century of Heian government had been dominated by politically active emperors, starting with Emperor Kammu who had taken the decision to abandon Nara in order to break the nexus on power of the Buddhist sects. After the death of the third emperor to reign from Kyoto, the Emperor Saga (r. 809–823), the Fujiwara exerted greater influence at the court, a process which reached its culmination with Michinaga. This shift in power from direct imperial rule to rule by the Fujiwara as regents was reflected in the pattern of palace-construction activity. In the initial era of imperial power the palaces and mansions of the imperial family were, predictably, the most magnificent buildings in the capital. The most important was the Daidairi, or main imperial palace and the ceremonial and administrative focus of government. With the ascendancy of the Fujiwara by the turn of the eleventh century, palace construction by the imperial household ceased completely. Instead, the Fujiwara became the patrons for virtually all new palace and mansion construction of consequence. There was precise correspondence between actual power and building activity. In the era of their dominance in the eleventh century, the Fujiwara were to be responsible for the building of some twenty new palaces and mansions. During the same years the imperial family built none. Michinaga himself had eight palaces and mansions in addition to the grand Tsuchimikado-dono. These included Higashi Sanjō-dono, Biwa-dono, Ichijō-dono and Nijō-dono.[16]

The private palaces of the Fujiwara became the *de facto* centres of government as power moved away from the formally constituted institutions of imperial authority founded in the Nara period to a more familial form of authority based upon the power of the Fujiwara. Their dominance reached a point where, after the accession to the throne of Michinaga's nephew Go Ichijō in 1016, the new emperor resided at Tsuchimikado-dono for a period of six months.[17] Go Ichijō had been driven away from the Imperial Palace in 1016 after fire had destroyed it, and his uncle Michinaga was best placed to offer appropriate alternative arrangement for housing the emperor. Go Ichijō was not the only emperor by any means to use a Fujiwara mansion as his palace.[18] This practice reached a climax with Tsuchimikado-dono, for it was here that actual government was conducted. Tsuchimikado-dono became the *de facto* Imperial Palace, in the same way that Michinaga was *de facto* emperor. Three emperors were to be born at Tsuchimikado-dono and it was within its precincts that Fujiwara daughters were betrothed to emperors. The gossamer curtains and blinds which surrounded its chambers delineated the real corridors of power. The official Imperial Palace, some 500 metres away to the west, was little more than an empty shell. Fire and typhoon winds ruthlessly claimed its buildings in relentless succession in the eleventh and twelfth centuries. The loss of authority sapped the will to rebuild the palace and gradually the Imperial Palace site became an open field populated not by the tall poppies of the court but by more modest wild flowers. It was finally abandoned as the Imperial Palace in the early thirteenth century and the Tsuchimikado-dono site was designated for future use as the Imperial Palace. This serves today as the site of the much rebuilt Kyoto Gosho.[19]

Towards the end of the eleventh century the locus of political power again shifted, with the reassertion of the political power of the emperors by the expedient of early retirement from office.[20] This enabled them to exercise power over young emperors and to conduct government from the position of their ostensible retirement, unencumbered by official duties, protracted court rituals or by the limelight of reigning emperor status. The practice of government by retired emperor (*insei*) was instituted by Emperor Shirakawa in 1086. He was to be followed in this practice by the Emperors Toba and Go Shirakawa.

The change in power structure once more had a concomitant effect on architecture, in the same way that the earlier pattern of palace construction and usage had reflected the Fujiwara political ascendancy. It now became necessary to build mansions and palaces from which to pursue the new forms of government by retired emperors. These 'retirement palaces' became the centres of power in the late Heian period but, in keeping with their more private role, their buildings were less formally organised and used for fewer ceremonial occasions than had been the *shinden-zukuri* of the early and middle Heian period. Formal court ritual depended upon formal symmetry in building design in order to facilitate ceremonies for hierarchically stratified participants, in which rank was equated with position in ceremonies on the official left or right. This was reflected in court titles such as 'Minister of the Left' and 'Minister of the Right'. Typical of the new generation of palaces were Shirakawa-in and Toba-dono,[21] which abandoned the symmetrical wings and connecting corridors common to the earlier Heian *shinden* because the rituals themselves were no longer conducted at these 'retirement' palaces.[22] This represented a profoundly important shift away from the Chinese-inspired symmetry in palace and other public buildings in the later Heian period, and a significant step towards general use of asymmetrical plans in the evolution of Japanese residential architecture.

The shift of power to the retired or cloistered emperors effectively ended Fujiwara domination of the court. The effect on architecture was also marked. The ossification of Fujiwara power led to the fossilisation of their palaces. Tsuchimikado-dono and Kōyō-in, beloved by Michinaga and Yorimichi respectively, continued to be ravaged by fires and to be rebuilt in progressively less and less ostentatious and inspiring form. By the end of the Heian period, the Fujiwara had shifted the venue for their ceremonial and ritual activities to the Higashi Sanjō-dono simply because, by the twelfth century, it remained the only example of a symmetrically designed *shinden-zukuri* mansion in existence in the capital, and this formal organisation was essential for the conduct of the formal rites of the seasons demanded by court ceremony.[23] By this stage the Fujiwara rituals were also removed from the realities of power.

Reference has been made to the frequency of fire in the Heian capital. Fire was unquestionably nothing less than a catalyst for the enactment of change in architecture and authority in the Heian period. Fire systematically and periodically swept clean the palace sites of the capital, compelling rebuilding but also offering the opportunity to reassess architectural design according to changing political imperatives. Change was not, however, always the result of conscious political decisions. As we have seen, the impact of fire was at times incremental: the decision to abandon a site as important as that of the Imperial Palace itself was reached as a result of a sequence of natural disasters coinciding with the cumulative effect of a drift of power away from the emperor.

Our attention is once again directed to the Sanjō Palace fire and the searing destruction of the flames depicted in that immortal scene. The inherent flammability of the materials employed in the building of the *shinden* mansions meant that they were in constant danger of destruction by fire. The indigenous preference for roofs of cypress-bark shingle, and for interiors illuminated by oil lamps and divided by papered screens and flowing silk curtains, was a sure formula for disaster. In the twelfth century the tendency towards conflagration of *shinden-zukuri* palaces and mansions was exacerbated by civil disorder in the capital. The Heiji scroll scene showing the burning of the Sanjō Palace may be spectacular but it was by no means an isolated incident. Tsuchimikado-dono itself was consumed by fire three times. After its initial construction in 991 it was destroyed by fire in 1016, the same year as the Imperial Palace was also destroyed by fire, to be rebuilt by Michinaga over the next two years. In 1031, four years after Michinaga's death, it was again destroyed by fire, to be rebuilt by his son, Yorimichi. History repeated itself with another fire in 1040 after which Yorimichi steadfastly rebuilt the palace. When fire destroyed the palace again in 1064 the passion to rebuild could not be rekindled. Instead Yorimichi chose to live in his own detached villa at Uji, the Kōyō-in, well clear of the capital and its conflagrations.[24]

Fire and its inescapable association with the architecture of authority in the Heian period profoundly influenced Japanese attitudes towards permanence. It poignantly reinforced Shinto notions of inevitable decline and decay as exemplified in nature, as well as Buddhist precepts of the cycle of birth and rebirth and the transitory nature of existence. The immortal and haunting words at the beginning of The *Tale of the Heike* echo this heightened awareness:

> The Bell of the Gion Temple tolls into every man's heart to warn him that all is vanity and evanescence. The fading flowers of the sāla trees by the Buddha's death-bed bear witness to the truth that all who flourish are destined to decay. Yes, pride must have its fall, for it is as unsubstantial as a dream on a spring night.[25]

These sombre words seem to apply equally to the buildings which represented authority in the Heian capital. The Sanjō Palace and Michinaga's Tsuchimikado-dono were a case of pride having its inevitable fall, for they proved to be as 'unsubstantial as a dream on a spring night'. Those who are born to rule also have an affinity, it would seem, with buildings which are made to be destroyed.

Architecture and the Contemplative Counterpoise to Warrior Authority

In the Kamakura period (1185–1333), authority takes on a more aggressive countenance with the usurpation of the power of the court aristocracy by regional warrior bands. The process culminated with the victory of the Minamoto over the Taira in 1185 and the establishment of a military headquarters or shogunate at Kamakura, the local power base of the Minamoto. The complex nature of authority in the Kamakura period is frequently described by the term 'diarchy' or dual authority, for in reality there were two governments, the old civilian government of the Heian court and the new 'tent government' or *bakufu* of the Kamakura warriors.[26] After the demise of the founding Kamakura shogun Minamoto Yoritomo, the family of Hōjō Masako, his formidable wife, was to govern as regents to a series of titular shogun until its overthrow in 1333. Thus we have a situation in which the Hōjō were exercising power in the name of a figurehead shogun, who himself derived title and claim to legitimacy from the authority of the emperor. The governmental structure of Kamakura operated on the basis of a fine interweaving of feudal-type loyalties in a multi-layered hierarchy of lords and vassals. Kamakura control extended into the regions through a system of *jitō* and *shugo*, or estate stewards and provincial governors.

Central to the conventional interpretation of authority in Japanese medieval history has been our understanding that the title *sei-i-tai shōgun* or 'barbarian subduing generalissimo' was conferred upon Minamoto Yoritomo by the imperial throne as legitimising his position as military hegemon. It is equally well known that this title was assumed only in 1192, some seven years after the defeat of the Taira forces at Dan no Ura in 1185. It is far more significant for our present discussion to recognise that this title was of little contemporary significance during the early stages of Yoritomo's eminence, and that the emphasis upon the shogunal title comes from interpretations of later history. In the fluid political situation following the Minamoto victory of 1185, several titles were in fact used for Yoritomo, only one of which was *shōgun*. For example, Jeffrey Mass notes that *shōgun* was used as a title for some documents emanating from the new administration in Kamakura but that 'the office of shogun was neither retained by Yoritomo until his death [in 1199], nor bequeathed to his son and successor Yoriie.'[27] Yoritomo instead made personal use of his earlier court title of *utaisho*, a position of commander in the inner palace guards, while being referred to commonly by his own vassals as *tono*.[28] The lack of standardisation of titular reference reveals uncertainty about the appropriate way of signifying new authority and the coexistence of different functional roles, but the point of reference is frequently architectural. *Tono* meant both 'palace' and 'lord'. The character occurs as a suffix to palace names in the Heian period, as in Michinaga's Tsuchimikado-dono. It had been used in the *Man'yōshū* to designate the buildings of the aristocracy, which it distinguished from *ya* or plebeian housing. As lords lived in palaces, the association was inevitable.

Another title used by Yoritomo was *buke no tōryō*, which means literally 'the ridge-pole of the warrior house'. An example of this usage is to be found in the *Heiji monogatari*, which notes that Yoritomo was already *buke no tōryō* when he received the title of *sei-i-tai shōgun* from the retired emperor.[29] *Tōryō* is a supreme example of architectural metonymy. The ridge-pole is the apex of the roof of any building and its insertion at the intersection of the roof planes is marked by religious ceremony and celebration. For any person at the top of a hierarchical structure, such as a warrior house or a household of craftsmen, it was an obvious and immediately comprehensible role description. The title was used in the Nara court to refer to the head of an aristocratic clan but came into common parlance from the late tenth century to designate the leaders of the bands of warriors which were becoming an increasingly significant element in local and national affairs.[30] Later its usage contracted to refer only to the chief master builder at a traditional construction site but at Kamakura it constitutes an architectonic definition of warrior authority.

The warrior government was based at Kamakura but, as was the case with the city of Heian before it, virtually nothing remains of the thirteenth-century city and its architecture. It was consumed in the jealous fires ignited by the Ashikaga warriors as they violently overthrew the Kamakura *bakufu* in 1333. Although the lack of extant buildings makes interpretation difficult, the dearth of thirteenth-century buildings today is not simply a result of fire and other misfortune. The Kamakura shogunate did not regard the creation of an impressive built environment for its governmental headquarters as an important priority in the consolidation of its power. Although observing the urban convention of a grid plan with a central avenue, which still bisects the city today, Kamakura as a city was basically a regional warrior camp over which was laid the functional architectural matrix for governmental administration. The lack of an extensive building programme in Kamakura is not surprising. After all, for whose benefit would great monuments have been built? The authority of Kamakura rule was at best equivocal, shared with that of imperial Kyoto. As a result, its architecture was also equivocal. The Hōjō exercised power under the authority of a shogun, himself deriving legitimacy from the authority of the imperial institution in Kyoto and often, in the later stages of the government, himself also a member of the court. The nature of authority was further complicated by an ever-shifting balance of power within the aristocratic factions of the Heian imperial court and tensions between the Kamakura shogunate and local warrior power throughout the land. There was a constantly changing pattern of local allegiance, and frequent need for arbitrated settlement of disputes over land between warriors, and between warriors and courtiers.

Kamakura rule was equally unemphatic architecturally when it came to patronage of religious institutions. For much of the thirteenth century, the temples and shrines sponsored by the warriors were of the nature of private institutions. The cult of Hachiman occupied a strong place in the official beliefs and religious practices of the new government. The Minamoto adopted this protector of the state in the Shinto pantheon as their family tutelary deity and Yoritomo moved a shrine to Hachiman to a site beside his residence in Kamakura, as early as 1180. The Tsurugaoka Hachimangū became, in effect, the establishment shrine of the Kamakura government, with the vassals of the Minamoto obliged to participate in its upkeep and rituals. However its size and style was subdued, far removed from the trumpeting official presence of Tōdaiji at Nara.[31]

From its inception, the commitment of Kamakura government to both a rule of written law and a rule of religious propriety is impressive, as is the absence of bombast from its own architecture during its first half century. The civil code of 1232, formulated by Hōjō Yasutoki, starts with injunctions to keep the shrines of the gods, along with temples and pagodas, in good repair and for services to be 'diligently celebrated', but this should not be interpreted as a statement of architectural ambition.[32] Perhaps the violent experience of their rise to power had also given warriors different architectural priorities from those who preceded them. Of all those who exercised power in medieval Japan, none knew better than the warriors of Kamakura how little effort was needed to destroy buildings constructed with such enormous effort and expense.

An architecture of authority in the sense that we have been exploring is in evidence only at the beginning and towards the end of Kamakura rule. The first architectural projects of Kamakura grew naturally out of the Minamoto military victory over the Taira. Sponsorship of the rebuilding of Tōdaiji and Kōfukuji in Nara by the Minamoto was a timely and effective statement of their desire for legitimacy. Both temples had been largely destroyed by fire started by their Taira adversaries in 1180, so Minamoto sponsorship of their rebuilding gave a parallel architectural dimension to their military victory. More importantly, patronage of Nara temples long associated with the imperial court was nothing less than a statement of *lèse-majesté* by the newly established warrior regime. Such a resort to architectural projects as a method of buttressing the authority of a new regime is a common strategy and, in employing this well-tried strategy, the Kamakura warriors did much to stake their claim to moral authority in the heartland of traditional authority at the expense of the Taira.

After the brief excursion into architectural endeavours in Nara, there was to be a hiatus of a generation before the Kamakura shogunate again embarked upon monumental construction. The serious commitment of warrior government to building projects in the city of Kamakura itself was belated, dating from the 1250s. For the first half-century of Kamakura rule there was a deep preoccupation with the mechanisms of government, formulation of legal codes and judicial settlement of disputes over land and succession. The exception to this rule was the building of a Great Buddha of Kamakura and the surrounding hall in emulation of the Daibutsuden of Tōdaiji. Planned first in 1238, the statue was completed in 1252. It was a formidable 11.36 metres in height and 29 metres in circumference around its base, making it larger than the Tōdaiji Great Buddha which had been rebuilt under Kamakura patronage some 60 years earlier. Although much repaired it still stands today, now exposed to the elements since the Great Hall which housed it was destroyed in 1495.[33] Despite its impressive size, the Kamakura Daibutsu had a religious purpose very different from that of its Nara counterpart. This was no Vairocana, representing the centralising force in the universe and the controlling power of government. Instead, the central deity was the Amida Buddha, dedicated to a personal form of salvation of greater meaning to a warrior class living on the sword's edge between life and death in the service of their lords. The Amida cult had grown rapidly in popularity amongst the Kamakura warriors caught up in the movement led by the charismatic Buddhist saint, Hōnen. Piety, more than propaganda, was the motive behind this monumental creation: in Nara the reverse was the case.

The shift to a more deliberate architecture of authority was occasioned by three significant developments: a decisive shift in the balance of power between court and warriors in favour of Kamakura following the abortive attempt to restore imperial power by the retired Emperor Go Toba (1219–21), the Hōjō success in checking the power of military rivals, and the defeat of the Mongols.

The military threat posed by the grandiose territorial ambitions of the Mongols, dating from the year 1266 until the failure of the second invasion in 1281, completely absorbed the energies and resources of the warrior class. It was only after the destruction of Kublai Khan's second fleet that the Hōjō, under Tokimune as regent, turned their attention and resources to creating civic and religious monuments which would be comparable in scale and sophistication with the architecture of Nara and Kyoto.[34]

This era saw the establishment of the great Rinzai Zen sect monasteries in Kamakura, including Kenchōji and Engakuji. The founding of the warrior government at Kamakura had coincided with the penetration of new influences from China, particularly from the architectural and cultural attainments of the Song Dynasty, and the discovery of Chan Buddhism by the Japanese. This form of meditative Buddhism, which became known as Zen in Japan, was eventually adopted with enthusiasm by leading members of the warrior class. In Zen the warriors found a form of introspective discipline and self-discovery which was the perfect spiritual complement to the loyalty and self-sacrifice demanded of them in their service to their lords. It was to be in the more contemplative authority of Zen monastic institutions that the Kamakura rulers found a contemplative counterpoise to their military power. However this personal appeal of Zen to individual warriors was, historically, secondary to its institutional importance to the Kamakura shogunate. With its strong association with Song power and culture, Zen initially satisfied the yearning for political and cultural legitimacy of the warrior elite. It was only later that it addressed the spiritual yearnings of the ordinary warrior.[35] Zen monasteries were established around the city of Kamakura under the patronage of the government in a system of five official monasteries (*Gozan*). The most important Zen sect was Rinzai, founded by the monk Eisai together with a number of Chinese monks who had been exiled to Japan after the collapse of the Song Dynasty in 1279, towards the end of Kamakura rule.

Of the Zen temples founded at Kamakura itself, Engakuji is one of the most important to survive. Unfortunately, the buildings now standing at the temple site are not the original structures and cannot be used for the purposes of this study to investigate the relationship between Kamakura-period architecture and authority. Over the centuries fire ravaged the temple several times, most particularly in 1563 when the Shariden was burnt to the ground.[36] The present Shariden is a Kamakura-period building, but not originally from Engakuji itself. It was constructed as the Buddha Hall (*Butsuden*) of Taiheiji, one of the Kamakura nunneries, and was moved to its present location after a fire in the 1560s as a substitute for the earlier building.[37] It may be of Kamakura vintage and style but it is a lesser architectural work than its predecessors, equipped with a crude reed thatch roof added at a later date which destroys the harmony of its proportions.

Hōjō Tokiyori and the Jizōdō of Shōfukuji

To find a building which provides an accurate picture of the official architecture of Kamakura, it is necessary to travel to the hinterland of the Kantō Plain along the Kamakura Kaidō, that major artery of travel, communication and commerce which linked Kamakura, through the provinces of the Japan Alps, to the capital of Kyoto in the east. The highway also acted as a vehicle for the diffusion of culture and building technology from Kamakura into the inland provinces. A branch temple of the Rinzai Zen sect, Shōfukuji, was founded *ca* 1270 at a post-town in the vicinity of modern Higashi Murayama. A small Jizōdō, or Hall of Jizō, the guardian deity of children, stands to the left of the main temple buildings. Although physically removed from the centre of Kamakura authority and repaired extensively in 1407,[38] this modestly scaled building, the size of a two-storey house, is nevertheless the most direct evidence of architecture associated with Kamakura authority to survive to the present day (Figure 4.5).

According to the temple records the hall was built as the result of the patronage of Hōjō Tokiyori, who fell ill during a hunting expedition in these remoter regions of the Musashi Plain in the year 1278.[39] Cared for and cured by a priest of the recently founded Shōfukuji, Tokiyori, according to temple tradition, commissioned master builders from Kamakura to build a hall dedicated to the bodhisattva Jizō. It was this Jizō that Tokiyori believed had been

Fig 4.5
Jizōdō,
Shōfukuji,
Higashi
Murayama,
Tokyo. Front
view

responsible – through the person of an aged monk of the temple – for his recovery. Like many temple records, this document should not be taken at face value, particularly as Tokiyori died in 1263, 15 years before the incident is reported to have taken place. However there is no reason to reject the probability of a relationship between the Jizōdō and the master builders of Kamakura: Tokiyori is known as the first of the Hōjō regents to have become a serious disciple of Zen and to sponsor construction of Zen temples.[40]

Fig 4.6
Jizōdō,
Shōfukuji.
Front elevation
(Source:
Bunka-chō,
*Kokuhō jūyō
bunkazai
[kenzōbutsu]
jissoku zushū*)

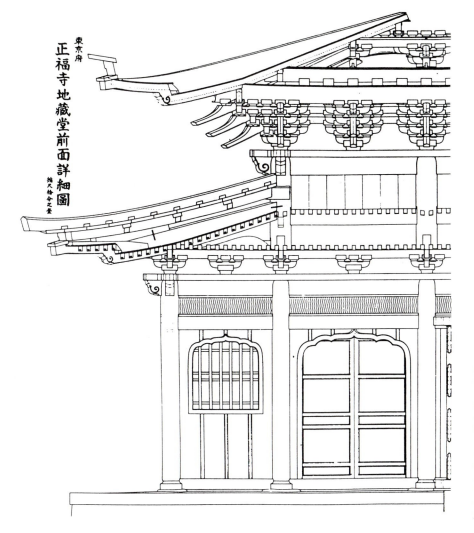

Fig 4.7
Jizōdō,
Shōfukuji.
Detail of front
elevation and
longitudinal
section
(Source:
Bunka-chō,
Kokuhō jūyō bunkazai [kenzōbutsu] jissoku zushū)

The Jizōdō is a small structure with an upper hip-gabled roof of cypress-wood shingles (*kokera-buki*), and a lower pent roof covered with copper sheet tiles (Figure 4.6).[41] From the exterior it appears to be a two-storey building, but the interior is open, rising through a series of corbelled bracket arms and cantilevers to the plain flat ceiling (Figure 4.7). Together with the gracefully attenuated timber-frame structure and the curved doors and window frames, it is a faithful expression of the Song-influenced style of building which became the architectural orthodoxy of Kamakura. The building is structurally far more sophisticated than temple halls of earlier times in Japan, employing horizontal tie beams which penetrate the pillars (Figure 4.7). This technique, utilising the sharper-edged, laminated, steel chisels developed in the Kamakura period, gave structural strength and resistance to the torsion experienced during earthquakes without resorting to the heavy, external 'wrap-around' bracing which had been the standard structural system of both religious and secular monumental architecture from the Nara period. The stylistic result was a building

99

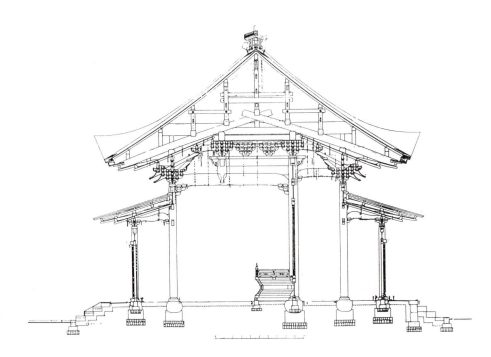

Fig 4.8
Jizōdō,
Shōfukuji.
Transverse
section
(Source:
Bunka-chō,
Kokuhō jūyō
bunkazai
[kenzōbutsu]
jissoku zushū)

framework imbued with a grace and lightness entirely different in character from that of earlier architecture.

As the Jizōdō reveals, the new Kamakura style had a flowing rhythm which extends from the framing into every detail. The pillars are gracefully tapered at top and bottom, while the spaces between the transoms are animated by serpentine struts. The frames of the doors and windows resemble the flamboyant tracery of Gothic cathedrals, rolling in an undulating cusped curve to rise to a point at the centre. The rafters of the upper roof radiate outwards in a series of increasingly acute angles from the mid-point of the roof, at the same time performing the acrobatic feat of rising to a gentle point at the gable intersections. The profusion of bracketing detail on the upper storey, an assemblage of bracket block and bearing arm, cantilever and other crafted detail, all flow in curvilinear patterns to delight the eye and inspire the spirit. The hip roof is the most remarkable feature of the entire building, curving upwards and outwards with a grace that seems to defy the force of gravity (see Figure 4.5). Herein lies the greatest achievement of the master builders of this age for, in shaping Zen temple roofs, the Kamakura builders devised a way of going beyond Chinese architectural conventions. The upper rafters, mostly hidden from view by the lower level of decorative rafters, operate as cantilevers to carry the eaves, while the bracket sets in the upper level, intricate in detail, are almost entirely decorative in function. They are designed to attract attention and to proclaim the supreme skills of their builders, whatever the more pious intentions of the patron. The real work is done by large, self-effacing cantilevers hidden within the shell of the roof (Figure 4.8).

The curvature of the roof of the Jizōdō is remarkably strong in expressive power, an aesthetic effect achieved technically by clever use of the *kayaoi*, the horizontal member which helps hold together the rafters at the eaves. At the Jizōdō the original timbers at the eaves' edge are in place and reveal an important technical innovation by the Japanese which creates this special aesthetic effect (see Figure 4.5). Unlike the eaves' edges of buildings of similar type in China and Korea, the *kayaoi* at Zen sect temples in Japan thrusts forward on the horizontal plane rather than being held back by anchoring joints. The result is that the roof curves both upwards and outwards like an inverted bow. This is an extraordinary technical accomplishment, requiring sophisticated understanding of proportions, curvature and tangents, and structural dynamics in determining the organisation of the splayed rafters and end elements of the roofs. In the Japanese case it has been made possible by the remarkable elasticity of native Japanese cypress. The Chinese and the Koreans suffered from a lack of such a building material with its superlative tensile properties.

The building is an architectural masterpiece, the result of one of those sublime moments which combine creativity and religious conviction to transcend particular technique. It is justifiably designated a 'National Treasure' as it sits today in its solitary and frequently wind-swept splendour on the treeless Musashi Plain, its soaring roof-lines an encapsulation of all that was dignified and beautiful in Kamakura Buddhist architecture under the stimulus of the Hōjō patronage. Whatever the precise details of its construction at the end of the Kamakura period, and the extensive repairs and rebuilding work carried out in 1407, the Jizōdō is a work of metropolitan culture, constructed by or under the direct supervision of master builders of great skill and vast experience.

The diffusion of Kamakura influence along the highways into the provinces, of which this building was a part, is an important characteristic of medieval culture. New temples of Zen and Pure Land Buddhism were established in remote regions, to spread the latest building techniques and forms of religious art along with doctrine, in the same way that the Nara *kokubunji* had disseminated culture as well as control from Nara in the eighth century. In fact the only remaining example of a three-storey pagoda in the Song-influenced style of Kamakura is to be found in the Japan Alps province of Shinano further along the same Kamakura highway from Shōfukuji. The octagonal three-storey pagoda of Anrakuji, tucked away at the edge of the Shiodaira Plain near Ueda, is the result of metropolitan master carpenters working under Hōjō patronage, the same combination of talent and resources which created the Jizōdō of Shōfukuji. In the Kamakura period, lineal descendants of the Hōjō family had occupied the stronghold of Shioda Castle and sponsored temple construction at nearby Shiodaira. The Zen monk Shōkoku Isen was invited to open Anrakuji as a Zen temple to coincide with a visit of Hōjō Yoshimasa to Shioda in 1277, the year before the problematic posthumous visit to the Shōfukuji by his father. The pagoda built for the new temple conformed to the most sophisticated stylistic precepts of Zen architecture also evident at the Jizōdō, including the more extraordinary design and technical virtuosity demonstrated in the octagonal curved roofs and radial raftering beneath (Figure 4.9).[42] The Jizōdō at Shōfukuji is, therefore, not alone as an example of the diffusion of Kamakura building style and techniques along

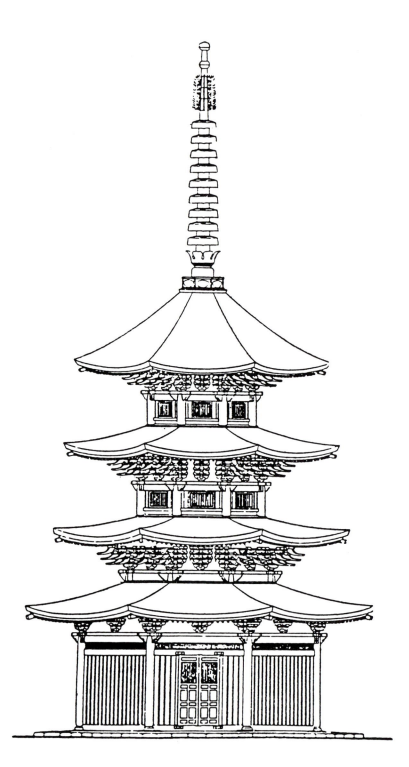

Fig 4.9
Pagoda of
Anrakuji,
Nagano prefec-
ture. Elevation
(Source:
Nagano-ken
kyōiku iinkai
(ed.), *Kokuhō
Anrakuji
sanjūnotō shūri
kōji hōkokusho*)

the transportation routes of the day as part of the osmosis of central culture into the regions.

Given the character of its authority and the violence of its fall, it is not surprising that the Kamakura shogunate bequeathed so few architectural monuments to posterity, particularly in the city of Kamakura itself. The Jizōdō at Shōfukuji, despite its isolation and scale, reveals this with clarity and conviction. It is to buildings dispersed along the hinterland and highways of the Kamakura sphere of influence that we need to travel in order to discover the contemplative counterpoise to warrior power.

5 Castles

The Symbol and Substance of Momoyama and Early Edo Authority

The age of castles (1576–1639) was a period strictly circumscribed by the circumstances of power. It was also a period indelibly stamped with the authority of the three great national unifiers: Oda Nobunaga (1534–1582), Toyotomi Hideyoshi (1536–1598) and Tokugawa Ieyasu (1542–1616). During the civil wars of the sixteenth century, these daimyo rose by diverse means to become the heads of regional power blocs. Then, as the scale of conflict spread and power coalesced, they launched their bid for national hegemony.

Nobunaga, Hideyoshi and Ieyasu were by no means the only remarkable regional leaders in this century of divisive civil war but, in historical hindsight, they stand out as having made the most visible political and architectural contributions. Nobunaga, the lord of Owari, succeeded by brutal means to break the power of the great Buddhist sects, and then to extend his military rule over most of central Japan. Hideyoshi, one of his vassals and a great organisational genius, achieved the national unification to which Nobunaga had aspired but not reached, and added an increasingly imperial dimension to his authority. Ieyasu, a minor domainal lord and vassal under Hideyoshi, founded by military means and political strategies an enduring shogunal dynasty which ruled Japan until 1868. The authority and power of the three unifiers summoned forth the great castles of this era. Nobunaga was responsible for Azuchi, Hideyoshi for castles at Osaka, Fushimi and Jurakudai (amongst others), and Ieyasu for the greatest castle of all, at Edo.

Fortifications in Japan have a long history but the castle had only a brief period of full technical and stylistic maturity. This was the period of 62 years beginning in 1576 with the construction of Azuchi, which inaugurated the age, and ending with the reconstruction of the keep of Edo Castle in 1638. Before 1576 castles were simple fortifications. After 1638 castle construction virtually ceased following the effective imposition of sanctions by the Tokugawa *bakufu* as part of the institutionalisation of its nationwide authority.

In the later sixteenth century and first half of the seventeenth century, the character of castle construction corresponds closely with the evolution of the power of ruling authority. This process may be divided into three clearly identifiable phases, each closely related to a particular stage in castle construction. The first dates from 1576 and the establishment of Azuchi, and lasts until 1600, the period now referred to by historians as the Momoyama period. This was the period of most intense national struggle towards unification, first under Nobunaga, and after his death in 1582, under Hideyoshi.

The second period lasts from 1600 to 1615, a period confusingly referred to by historians as either the late Momoyama or the early Edo period As this ambivalence of nomenclature suggests, it was a transitional era following the military victory of the Tokugawa forces over the Toyotomi and their allies at the Battle of Sekigahara in 1600. It was an uneasy time, an era of false peace in which both the Tokugawa and the Toyotomi, in anticipation of a final showdown, buttressed their authority with massive building programmes. As inevitably as night follows day the final confrontation between these two great powers came with two sieges by Tokugawa forces against the Toyotomi headquarters at Osaka Castle, the first during the winter of 1614–1615, and the second in the summer of 1615. The sieges ended with the annihilation of the Toyotomi and the destruction of their castle with an enthusiasm recalling that of the Roman destruction of Carthage, lacking only the salt.

The third phase of castle construction was of similar duration, lasting from 1615 to 1638. Immediately upon the defeat of the Toyotomi in 1615, the Tokugawa moved to consolidate their power by the implementation of various sanctions, of which two were important measures directly affecting castles. The first of these, imposed in the seventh month of 1615, was a law restricting all daimyo to 'one castle per province'. Implementation of this law in effect required the systematic demolition of all but the actual castle residence of each domainal lord. It was followed a few days later by the inclusion of a ban on new castle construction explicitly set out in the *Buke shohatto*, the basic code for the warrior class:

> Whenever it is intended to make repairs on a castle of one of the feudal domains, the [shogunate] authorities should be notified. The construction of any new castles is to be halted and stringently prohibited. 'Big castles are a danger to the state'. Walls and moats are the cause of great disorders.[1]

Castle prohibition, complete with invocation of Confucian precedent, was thereby built into the fundamental code of Tokugawa rule. The ban meant that in this third phase of castle history, that of Tokugawa consolidation, new castle construction was in practice confined strictly to Tokugawa projects designed to assist in the institutionalisation of *bakufu* authority. By the 1650s, however, with the completion of this process, castle keeps, walls and moats were to become a dispensable tool of authority, empty of military meaning and lacking political purpose.

The castle of this period of 62 years, a mere two generations, was as much the child of politics as it was the progeny of warfare, and as much the product of human ambition as it was the creation of material technology and military engineering. The castle as an institution became the focal point of the age as the symbol and substance of authority. As the symbol of authority it was the most visible statement of the accomplishments and power of the warrior class, particularly the *tenshu*, the soaring keep which commanded attention as the nucleus of the physical and political order of its patron. The castle was also the palatial residence of regional and national rulers, and the centre for court observances and patronage of the arts, its glittering array of buildings and endless entertainment activities a constant reminder of the power and authority of its patrons.

105

As the substance of authority, the castle was by definition a bastion of military might, but its substantive role was far more varied. Castle construction was the major activity of the age, requiring massive mobilisation of labour and building materials. As the struggle for national unification reached a climax, castle-building reached its architectural apogee: architecture and authority beat with the same accelerated pulse of power. Between 1596 and 1615 alone, almost 100 major castles were built, many of them on an unprecedented scale. These included the castles at Himeji, Nagoya, Osaka and Fushimi which equalled or exceeded in size the largest castles built in medieval Europe, including the great Crusader fortresses of the Middle East.

Castles also provided substance to authority by serving as the physical seat of government, the centre of civil administration for domains which in a period of national integration were increasing in size and complexity. Around these seats of government developed towns or *jōkamachi*, a further substantive dimension to authority as hierarchically ordered representations of status within the political order as well as centres of commerce, culture, communications and, of course, of population. Many of Japan's modern cities were founded as castle towns in this era, including Kanazawa, Nagoya, Sendai, Shizuoka, Hiroshima, Okayama, Kōchi, and the largest of them all, Edo – which was to become today's capital, Tokyo.

This chapter concentrates attention on three examples of the castles constructed in this era, one drawn from each of the three phases of authority: Azuchi, which marks the beginning of the first phase; Himeji, which belongs to the second phase following the Tokugawa victory of 1600; and Edo, which dominated the third phase, that of Tokugawa consolidation. The discussion establishes the circumstances of power which spawned each castle, the way each acted as the symbol and the substance of the authority of its sponsors, and the ways in which castle design and construction responded to the demands of authority.

Azuchi Castle and the Establishment of Nobunaga's Authority

The first castle of the new age was Nobunaga's Azuchi. Built between 1576 and 1579, it established the architectural form and governmental role for all later castles. It was built as the embodiment of Nobunaga's personal power, and became his visible countenance, his public face, as well as the revelation of the inner workings of his ambition.

Nobunaga's national ambitions are first revealed in his plans for his earlier headquarters at Gifu, which served as his power-base during the years before he wrested power from the shogunal house of Ashikaga. In 1575, the year before work began at Azuchi, the intrepid Jesuit priest Luis Frois (1532–1597) remarked ecstatically of Nobunaga's Gifu palace, set at the foot of his mountain fastness:

> I wish I were a skilled architect or had the gifts of describing places well, because I sincerely assure you that of all the palaces and houses I have seen in Portugal, India

and Japan, there has been nothing to compare with this as regards luxury, wealth and cleanliness . . . in order to display his magnificence and enjoy his pleasures to the full, he [Nobunaga] decided to build for himself at enormous cost this his earthly paradise (for the Mino people call it *Gokuraku*, the Paradise of Nobunaga)'.[2]

Nobunaga may have built an impregnable stronghold on the summit of a local mountain, but the magnificent palace he created at its foot is a sure indication of his desire to assert a courtly as well as military authority.

After driving what was to prove the last Ashikaga shogun from Kyoto by military force in 1573, and assuming prestigious court titles and vestigial imperial authority,[3] Nobunaga set about creating a new castle centre to serve as the symbol and the substance of his authority. For his grand purpose Nobunaga chose a site on a low hill on the eastern shore of Lake Biwa. This in itself marked a bold departure from the accepted practices of castle-building. Prior to this, for over a millennium, castles had been simple fortifications set atop steep hills and mountains. Many consisted of little more than boulders piled up to form defensive parapets, with palisades of sturdy timber erected on top for protection and watch-towers for observing enemy movements in the valley floors way below. This was the standard pattern of fortifications from the time of the rise of the warrior class in the later Heian period until well into the period of civil wars in the sixteenth century. Even Gifu Castle, built by Nobunaga in the early 1570s, conformed to this pattern. Such fortifications were intended for military service during times of conflict but, because of the very inaccessibility which afforded them protection against attack, they were entirely unsuitable for prolonged habitation or purposes of civil administration. Instead, the residence of the local warrior leader was located at the foot of the mountain or hill upon which the fort was built, and it was from here that the civil affairs of the domain were conducted. These residences were usually protected by moats and walls but they were far removed in character from the later castles.

During the civil wars of the sixteenth century, mountain-top fortifications became more sophisticated, with terracotta tiled roofs, sturdy timber frames and plastered walls, and more carefully constructed stone walls. However it was Azuchi Castle that marked the watershed between medieval fortifications and the mature castle. The scale and sophistication of its stone walls, barbican gatehouses, corner towers and central keep was unprecedented. At the same time the siting of the castle on a small hill commanding a plain, not on a remote mountain-top far above it, was a radical departure from previous building practice. This hill commanded a view of the three highways from eastern Japan as they converged upon the imperial capital of Kyoto: the main highway running down from the regions bordering the Sea of Japan, the Tōkaidō or Pacific coast highway from the eastern provinces, and the Nakasendō, the inland route from the Kantō Plain traversing the Japan Alps to Kyoto.

At the foot of the hill Nobunaga laid out a new urban centre, one of the first consciously created castle-towns of the era, with an orderly street system, including a central north–south avenue, and zoning organised according to status.[4] Artisans and merchants were encouraged by financial incentives to move to Azuchi and settle in the sectors of the town reserved for their respective

Fig 5.1
Tenshu of
Azuchi Castle.
Reconstruction
drawing by
Naitō Akira
© Naitō Akira

trades. The Jesuits founded a church and theological seminary within the town boundaries.

The Architectural Form of Azuchi Castle

Today only massive stone walls remain at this site, for Azuchi was sacked and burned within days of the assassination of Nobunaga in 1582. However it is clear from contemporary records that the architecture of its gold-bedecked keep was a dramatic departure from that of earlier castles. Despite its sad destruction there is a considerable body of evidence available from which to reconstruct its physical form and symbolic meaning. The most comprehensive written source is a section describing the appearance of the *tenshu* included in the *Shinchō kōki*, the biography of Nobunaga compiled and edited from earlier sources by Ōta Gyūichi early in the Edo period. There are several versions of the biography, but research has established that the descriptions of the *tenshu* are based upon a record of a visit to the castle in 1579. The information contained in the different versions is generally consistent, although there are discrepancies in some of the details of the decoration of the upper two levels of the building.[5] According to this source the stone wall at the base of the *tenshu* was over 12 *ken* (approx. 22 metres) in height. The building itself rose from the basement set deep within the stone walls through seven interior levels. The area on top of these walls was 20 *ken* wide (approx.

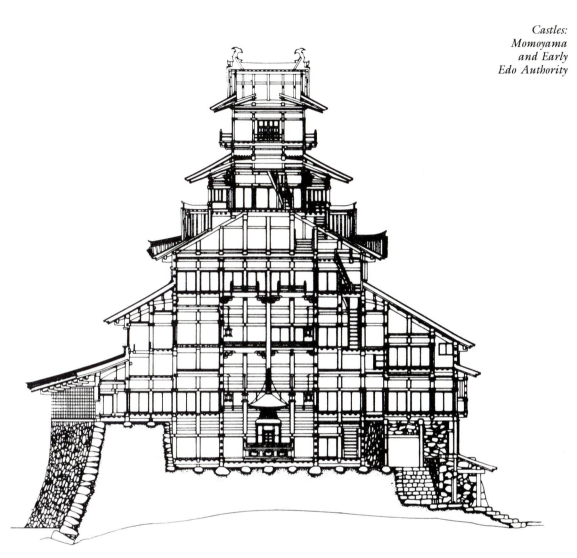

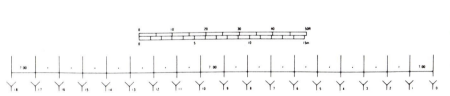

Fig 5.2
Tenshu of
Azuchi Castle.
Reconstruction
of east–west
section by
Naitō Akira
© Naitō Akira

36 metres) north–south and 17 *ken* (approx. 31 metres) east–west.[6] This gave
the *tenshu* dimensions similar to those of Hideyoshi's Osaka Castle, one of
the largest *tenshu* ever built, and height equal to that monumental expression of state authority in the Nara period, the Daibutsuden of Tōdaiji.

The most significant developments in this process of reconstruction have
taken place since 1976 when Naitō Akira, then Professor of Architecture at

109

Nagoya Institute of Technology, published a comprehensive set of scaled technical drawings and renderings to reconstruct the appearance of Nobunaga's castle (see Figures 5.1–5.2).[7] These drawings were based upon a document entitled *Tenshu sashizu* or 'Specifications of the Tenshu', which had been preserved in the Seikadō archives in Tokyo. This single scroll is a 1766 copy of a document originally compiled in 1670 by Ikegami Uhei, Official Master Builder to the Maeda family, daimyo of the Province of Kaga. The copied document contained plans for the *tenshu* of an unidentified castle, showing architectural details of a building with seven interior floors, each annotated with the names of chambers contained therein and the subject-matter of the wall and screen paintings. The plans also showed the position of the pillars and staircases and the shape of the roofs, including the complex configuration of decorative gables.

Naitō carefully compared these drawings with the archaeological evidence from the *tenshu* site and the several extant versions of the *Shinchō kōki*, concluding that the *Tenshu sashizu* represented the plans and specifications of the long destroyed *tenshu* of Azuchi. According to Naitō there was an exact correlation between the carpenter's specifications, the archaeological site and the written descriptions, down to such particulars as the irregular octagonal shape of the ground floor of the *tenshu*, a result of the uneven topography of the hill-top site.

From this research the *tenshu* emerged as a structure some 46 metres in height with five exterior levels and seven interior floors, including the basement. The floor immediately above the basement level, called the 'first level' in the plans and in Ōta's account, contained an entrance hall, waiting rooms and an audience chamber. The main audience hall (*hiroma*), was set on the second level while Nobunaga's personal suite and service areas were allocated to the third and fourth levels. These levels were all located within a single large timber-frame structure. This was crowned by a two-storey belvedere, consisting of a gilded, octagonal chamber which, in turn, was surmounted by a room three bays square.

Naitō's reconstruction suggested that the castle keep had some unusual features, including an interior organised around an atrium rising from the basement level to the ceiling of the fourth floor. According to Naitō, in one corner of the second level a stage supported by cantilevers projected out over the atrium for performances of music and dance, including Nobunaga's beloved Nō, as part of the ritual of entertainment enacted in the main audience chamber located on the same level. Naitō suggested that this atrium was influenced by the ideas of interior space of European cathedrals, described to Nobunaga by the Jesuits. Naitō also postulated that a *hōtō*, a Buddhist stupa or reliquary pagoda dedicated to Tahō Nyōrai (Sanskrit: *Prabhutaratna*), was given pride of place at the centre of the basement where it could be overlooked from each of the three floors opening onto the atrium (see Figure 5.2). Naitō speculated that, as the Tahō Nyōrai shared theological preeminence with Sakyamuni according to the Lotus Sutra, it symbolised the nucleus of creation in Buddhist cosmology, and suggests that Nobunaga's authority included pretensions to the divine.

Naitō's interpretation of the stupa caused some debate,[8] while his reconstruction of Azuchi Castle sparked one of the liveliest controversies in over a century in Japanese architectural history. Less than a year later another architectural historian, Miyakami Shigetaka, published a broad challenge to its reliability in the same prestigious journal.[9] Miyakami presented his own comprehensive drawings reconstructing the castle keep, along with an equally exhaustive documentary analysis. He questioned the validity of the *Tenshu sashizu* on the grounds that it was a copy of an earlier document. He maintained that, rather than substantiating the descriptions in the *Shinchō kōki* as Naitō had claimed, the *Tenshu sashizu* was actually based upon it. After all, it was a mid-eighteenth-century copy of an original document itself dating to a period nearly 100 years after the building of Azuchi.

The controversy over the reconstructions of Azuchi remains to this day, although Naito's version is widely used in publications and was the basis for a reconstruction of the upper stories displayed at the Japan Pavilion at the 1992 World Exposition in Seville.[10]

Whatever the finer points of argument over Azuchi, the work by Naitō and Miyakami clearly project the general appearance of the destroyed *tenshu* – whatever the disagreement about details of its interior organisation. The controversy has succeeded in focusing attention on Azuchi as the seminal castle of the Momoyama period, and it remains for us to consider it more fully in the context of architecture and authority.

Azuchi as an Expression of Authority

We need not depend on reconstruction drawings or written records alone to consider the authority of the architecture of Azuchi Castle. Many of the walls, including the base of the *tenshu* and the foundations of several gateways and barbicans, still stand on Azuchi Hill. These walls, of roughly hewn boulders carefully assembled using dry-wall techniques, bespeak enormous labour and vaunting ambition. The appearance of the *tenshu* which crowned these walls in magnificent display is captured dramatically in the writings of Luis Frois, quoted earlier. The presence of a European Jesuit at the court of Nobunaga should come as no surprise; it is a useful reminder of the international character of sixteenth-century Japan, in tandem with the expansion of the Portuguese, Dutch, Spanish and English empires into Asia seeking trade and territory, and translating the internal wars of Europe into an Asian power struggle. Frois's fulsome praise of the 'architecture, strength, wealth and grandeur' of Azuchi, particularly the way the seven floors of the *tenshu* 'both inside and out are fashioned to a wonderful architectural design', helps us see the way the castle articulated authority with a universal language of height, technical sophistication, strength and beauty. Frois's description makes clear those architectural features which readily cross the boundaries of culture: height, for Azuchi was an edifice which 'looks as if it reaches to the clouds'; the method of construction, in the 'strong and well constructed walls'; and the hypnotic beauty of the *tenshu*, with its 'noble and splendid appearance', sumptuous materials, bright colours and strong contrasts between white plaster and black lacquer.

While these features have successfully communicated authority across cultural boundaries, Frois's judgement is also informed by comparison with the architecture of his own cultural milieu. His comment, for example, that the tower or *tenshu* at the centre of the castle complex was 'far more splendid and noble in appearance than our towers', indicates that height, while perhaps the most universal of all the attributes of architectural authority, is also relative to individual experience. The language actually used to describe such phenomena is also culturally conditioned: Frois's comment that Azuchi looked 'as if it reaches to the clouds' recalls Shakespeare's 'towers which buss the clouds'. To the European mind of the sixteenth century, the measure of impressive height was fixed by the height of the clouds. The notion is still encompassed in the term 'skyscraper'.

Despite these cultural influences in points of comparison and linguistic nuance, there is a universal equation between high buildings and high authority evident in Frois's reaction to Azuchi. A tall building expresses superordination and infers subordination, whether it be European or Japanese. High buildings exemplify the role of architecture as metaphor interpreted by Rudolph Arnheim's in the following terms:

> all genuine metaphors derive from expressive shapes and actions in the physical world. We speak of 'high hopes' and 'deep thoughts' and it is only by analogy to such elemental qualities of the perceivable world that we can understand and describe nonphysical properties.[11]

This principle permeates the tightly structured world of protocol, offering formal expression to authority by providing strictly segregated spatial relationships, especially those based on height. It has obvious application in Japan. Basil Hall Chamberlain, doubtless having in mind the fate of the unfortunate Mr Richardson cut down by the bodyguards of the daimyo of Satsuma in 1862, noted that:

> a point of etiquette which foreigners should bear in mind, is that neither the Emperor himself, nor any member of the Imperial Family must ever be looked down on. Should an Imperial procession pass by, do not stand at an upper window or on any commanding height. The occasional infraction of this rule has given great offence, and produced disagreeable results.[12]

Until recently there was genteel observance of the same principle for the height of buildings surrounding the Imperial Palace and environs in Tokyo.

The idea of 'commanding height' is central to any interpretation of the architecture of Azuchi. The term *tenshu* is itself rich with the authority of height. When referring to his creation in letters, Nobunaga uses the characters for 'Protector of Heaven' and 'Lord of Heaven', both of which are read *tenshu*[13] and, though we may be unsure about the precise characters to be used, his political intent is unequivocal: for Nobunaga and for all who viewed it, this building was the residence of the ruler of the world below and the heavens above. The use of the term *tenshu* itself probably echoes the Christian concept of the 'Lord of Heaven' to which Nobunaga was introduced by the Jesuits. It more than hints at a desire to lift secular power to a sacred plane, to legitimise the temporal by means of the religious.

Nobunaga's appropriation of religious terminology at Azuchi was part of his concerted strategy to break the power of Buddhist sects in the Kansai. In 1571, in one of the most infamous episodes in his rise to national power, Nobunaga had burned to the ground the 3,000 buildings of Enryakuji, the headquarters of the militant Tendai sect on Mount Hiei, and put all the monks, young and old, to the sword. Five years later, during the years when Azuchi Castle was being constructed, he was again locked in a bitter struggle against a powerful Buddhist sect, this time the Ishiyama Honganji Ikkō sect. Terms such as 'Lord of Heaven' directly challenged the fanatical allegiance of the Ikkō sect to the Amida Buddha. It would seem that Nobunaga took his pretensions to a divine status a significant stage further by placing a Buddhist stupa in the centre of the *tenshu*. Whatever the theological interpretation of Nobunaga's use of the *hōtō*, it was unmistakably part of a campaign to forge deliberate religious associations with a secular ruler, following that familiar pattern of authority displayed in Japanese society from the historically shrouded times of the institutionalisation of the shrines at Ise and Izumo.

The impressive beauty of Azuchi conveyed by Frois's account is corroborated by a screen painting showing Hideyoshi's Jurakudai, which was completed in 1587. Although Jurakudai was later dismantled, this contemporary painting (now in the collection of the Mitsui family) encapsulates its character and reveals its magnificence as if we were viewing the castle as it was first created. The debt of Jurakudai to Azuchi is unmistakable, so much so that Frois's description of Azuchi could well be mistaken for a description of Jurakudai. Here again is a castle 'fashioned to a wonderful architectural design' with soaring *tenshu* and gilded ridge and eaves' end tiles. Sitting astride the ridge are large sculptures of mythological aquatic creatures known as *shachi*, with the heads of tigers and bodies of dolphins. They are fashioned in terracotta and covered in gold to sparkle in the sunshine and magnify the gentler illumination of moonlight. Like Azuchi, Hideyoshi's castle had both a civil and a military character as symbol and substance of authority. The sturdiness of the stone walls and the formidable defensive power of the gatehouses guarding the castle are unmistakable, while windows lower in the castle keep are open to provide good fire positions for defence against enemy attack.

To return again to a contemplation of the glories of Azuchi, the spatial arrangement and decoration of the interior of its *tenshu* were carefully calculated for maximum rhetorical effect. It served as the palace and court for Nobunaga and was decorated accordingly with powerful paintings as monumental in style and symbolism as the exterior of the building in which they were housed. The Azuchi *tenshu* was a vast, multilevel palace with audience chambers and private suites. The biography of Nobunaga, *Shinchō koki*, although unreliable in some of its details, nevertheless furnishes a clear impression of the magnificent nature of these interiors. We learn, for example, that:

> the chambers on the fourth floor included an eight mat room on the west side of the building which was decorated with a battle of dragons and tigers . . . the seventh and upper level is three bays square. Both the interior and exterior of this chamber are entirely gold . . . dragons ascend and descend on the four corner pillars and on the walls are the Three Emperors, the Five Rulers, the Ten Disciples of Confucius, the Four Wise Men of Shang Shan and the Seven Sages of the Bamboo Grove.[14]

Here again a universal vocabulary of authority is evident – gold indicating power, supernatural beasts implying a realm of mystical associations for Nobunaga, and legendary sages invoking the sanction of the wise and beneficent governing rulers of ancient China. In much the same way had the Romans appropriated Greek iconography for their own political ends. Meanwhile Nobunaga was keeping his iconographic options open. The walls of the octagonal floor immediately below the veritable Confucian chapel on the top of the *tenshu* were reminiscent of a Buddhist hall, lavishly decorated as they were with a scene of the historical Buddha Sakyamuni preaching to his disciples, reinforcing the religious associations established by the stupa at the basement level.

It is also apparent from the *Shinchō kōki* and the various reconstruction drawings that in the *tenshu* there was strict segregation of interior spaces according to function. The ceremonial chambers where audience was held were decorated with paintings in the Kano style, with bold, two-dimensional trees, graceful birds and flowers, set on gold leaf with only the occasional hint of other background detail. The semi-private areas for administration and special council were decorated with more intimate, didactic images of Chinese sages, no doubt as a reminder of the importance of wise government. The walls of the private residential rooms were embellished with animated scenes of everyday life, with less gold leaf, creating a more relaxed atmosphere.[15]

The paintings ornamenting the entire interior of the *tenshu* were supervised by Kano Eitoku (1543–1590).[16] The Kano maintained an hereditary family workshop and Eitoku was to become the quintessential court artist for both Nobunaga and Hideyoshi – in effect to the national unifiers of Japan what Raphael became to the Roman papacy. None of the paintings survived the destruction of Azuchi but later Kano paintings witness to their powerful presence. For example, the screen painting of a huge cypress tree, now in the collection of the Tokyo National Museum, bears the unmistakable influ-

Fig 5.3
Hinoki byōbu.
Eight-fold
screen. Kano
school. *ca* 1590
(Courtesy of
Tokyo National
Museum)

ence of the heroic style perfected by Eitoku in response to the dictates of Nobunaga's vision of authority and the spatial character of the castle interior of Azuchi (Figure 5.3). The gold represented authority and power, but also served the practical purpose of magnifying the light sources in the dim castle interior. As the paintings were used to decorate the spaces between the pillars and beams, their composition was invariably rectilinear with strong horizontal emphasis. For the larger audience chambers the trees and rocks had bold, two-dimensional forms set close to the picture plane with little background, giving them an immediacy and powerful presence well suited to the reinforcing of Nobunaga's authority. In fact the special lighting conditions of castle interiors, and the circumstances of formal audience, spawned an entirely new decorative painting mode, combining the strong ink-line of the Chinese-inspired black-ink painting tradition as practiced by the Kano atelier, with the strong colour and flatter decorative quality of the Yamato-e tradition of painting as it had developed in the Heian court. In other words, the painting style of the castle interiors was a fusion of existing styles, ultimately greater than the sum of the parts, called into the service of the new authority of the castle overlords. This underlines the way in which arbitrary authority has a pronounced centripetal effect on all the arts.

The Organisation of the Azuchi Building Project

The power to mobilise resources is one of the universal attributes of authority. It is important to understand the process by which Azuchi was created, because the power which Nobunaga had at his command to shift mountains of rock and earth, and to create on them structures of breathtaking beauty and overwhelming strength, is a direct index of his authority.

The construction of Azuchi was a project conducted on a scale not witnessed in Japan since the building work at Nara and Kyoto in the eighth and ninth centuries. Nobunaga coopted the labour and building materials of the entire

115

region of central Japan, from the provinces of the Kansai including the Kyoto and Nara areas, the provinces surrounding Lake Biwa, and as far away as Echizen on the Sea of Japan, to Owari, Mino and Mikawa in the east.[17] Overall supervision of the construction project was placed under the direct control of the lord of nearby Sawayama Castle, Tanba Nagahide, and work was to proceed day and night for a period of nearly three years. The task was divided into the engineering construction, involving the enormous challenge of erecting the great stone walls and digging the 100 metre wide moat between the castle and the town, and the architectural construction, especially the building of the *tenshu*. These tasks were carried out more or less simultaneously, with the framing for the buildings being prefabricated in carpenters' workshops even as the mountains of rock were dragged up the steep Azuchi slope to their eventual resting places. Each aspect provides further insight into the workings of authority under Nobunaga, particularly the way in which arbitrary authority deals with technological problems.

i. Stone wall construction The building of the stone walls was the most difficult challenge from an engineering viewpoint, and reveals much about Nobunaga's approach to managing building projects. The task of assembling the veritable mountain of rock required for the fortifications alone was herculean. There were only limited quantities of suitable stone available in the immediate vicinity: 350 specially dressed stones had to be brought from as far away as a quarry at Mabechi in northern Honshu. According to Frois, a number of the stones used for the inner defensive walls were so immense that 4–5,000 labourers were needed to haul each one up the Azuchi slope. One rock alone required an army of 6–7,000 labourers.[18]

Frois, as we have noted, was particularly impressed by these 'strong and well constructed walls'. Their painstakingly interlocked shapes and the complete absence of mortar bonding them together are still readily visible today towards the top of the ruined Azuchi hill site (Figure 5.4). Such skill at assembling rocks of different sizes into a cohesive structural whole, such expertise at bedding them securely into an earthen retaining wall with small rounded locking stones, is not produced overnight in response to the command of a ruler, no matter how powerful. Nobunaga simply appropriated into the service of warrior power the techniques of masonry construction refined in the testing ground of religious architecture. The technology of stone walls was adopted from the traditions of the master stone-masons of the village of Anō at the foot of Mount Hiei, a comfortable day's journey from Azuchi.[19]

Even today if you visit the village of Anō you will see that the stone walls flanking the narrow lanes of the village, nestling in the undulating paddy fields to the south of the township of Sakamoto, are of impressive size and strength (Figure 5.5). The Anō masons were hereditary workers in stone (*ishiku*), engaged in constructing the stone foundations and retaining walls of the numerous worship halls, pagodas and other monastic buildings of the Enryakuji, the Tendai Sect establishment which sprawled over the slopes and into the valleys of Mount Hiei. Here they had practised their exacting craft, honing their skills over many generations into a fine art as they mastered the

Fig 5.4 Azuchi Castle, Shiga prefecture.
Walls in vicinity of Honmaru

techniques of creating stable stone foundations for timber-frame buildings erected on the uneven mountain terrain.

By the sixteenth century the Anō were without peer in the region in their profession and Nobunaga simply appropriated all members of this tradition to create the massive foundation walls and fortifications of his castle. He may have burned Enryakuji in all its monastic majesty to the ground in order to break the power of its Tendai Sect, but he had no compunction about employing its hereditary master masons to build his own castle when it suited his political purposes.

Inspection of the extant walls of Azuchi reveals that they were made with the special technique, perfected by the Anō, of fitting together large unhewn boulders with smaller split rocks. These were all held securely in place against the outward pressure of earth and water, and the occasional violence of earthquake, with locking stones carefully placed between the outer rocks and the earthen embankment. In later castle walls the stones may have been more carefully dressed but it was in constructing the earlier walls at Azuchi that the stonemason was put to the greatest test; it required enormous skill and infinite patience to decide how to fit together the irregular, jigsaw-like shapes of natural rocks, and the most sophisticated understanding of engineering dynamics and a subtle awareness of aesthetics to align the interlocking corner-stones in their sweeping parabolic curves.

After their experience at Azuchi the Anō masons assumed national significance in castle construction. Members of the family were to provide the technical expertise for the stone walls of many of the most important castles built in the later sixteenth and early seventeenth centuries, including Fushimi, Nagoya, Himeji, Osaka and Kumamoto castles.

Fig 5.5 Sakamoto, Shiga prefecture. Walls by Anō stonemasons

117

ii. Architectural construction The task of designing and supervising the construction of the timber-framed buildings which stood on top of the walls, including the *tenshu*, corner towers and gatehouses, was directed by the chief master builder (*daikugashira*), identified in the *Shinchō kōki* as Okabe Mataemon. According to the official family history of the Okabe, a certain Okabe Mataemon was head master builder to the Ashikaga *bakufu* at the time of the eighth shogun, Yoshimasa.[20] These same records also establish that a second Okabe Mataemon, presumably carrying on the name of his illustrious ancestor, entered the service of Nobunaga on the day he won his first decisive battle at Okehazama in 1560. The record further notes that Okabe was subsequently active in temple construction in the Atsuta area and built a large gatehouse at the Atsuta Shrine itself. Although this was destroyed by fire at the end of World War II, prewar documents confirm that this building was eclectic in style. It combined the older Wayō mode of more rectilinear framing inspired by Nara-period temple architecture, with the gracefully curvilinear Song-influenced Zenshūyō, a fact which has important implications for the understanding of the style of Azuchi Castle architecture.

From the *Shinchō kōki* we learn that Okabe Mataemon achieved a position of considerable notoriety within Nobunaga's entourage for his building of a magnificent ship in 1573, with which Nobunaga intended eventually to control the waters of Lake Biwa. This large vessel, 59 metres long by 13 metres wide according to the records, was graced with a *tenshu*-like tower. It was completed in a mere two months using master carpenters, smiths and timber cutters from the regions of central Japan where the Okabe had their home base.

The progression from this aquatic foible, to the floating, dreamlike quality of the Azuchi *tenshu* would have been smooth and easy. Mataemon's role as its chief master builder makes comprehensible the type of building which emerges from the documentary and site record.[21] The technical details of structural framing and interior fittings would have drawn heavily upon the dual traditions of temple architecture, the Wayō and the Zenshūyō, of which Okabe and his family were traditional exponents. In fact the *tenshu* would have had something of the character of an elaborate Zen monastic residence. Its distinctive octagonal belvedere was little removed in concept from the rooms placed high in the roof of monasteries for simultaneous meditative viewing of the outer world of nature and the inner world of the spirit.

iii. Roof tiling The gilded and glazed roof tiles, which Frois described as 'stronger and lovelier than those we use in Europe', were the crowning glory of the castle and its *tenshu*. These tiles, glistening in the sunshine and glowing in the dark, would have been the ultimate statement of a worldly ruler's ability to command resources and strike awe into the hearts of those who viewed his creations. There was indeed something special about the tiling of Azuchi, for the *Shinchō kōki* states that 'the Chinese tilemaker Ikkan was commanded [to make roof tiles] and these were baked by the Nara [guild of] tilers.'[22]

Tile fragments excavated from the Azuchi site reveal the use of new technology from Ming China, confirming the existence of a Chinese master tile-maker at the Azuchi building project. Mica was used instead of hemp to prevent the wet clay adhering to the wooden mould used to shape the tiles, a practice developed in China during the Ming dynasty. The eave-end tiles were emblazoned by gold leaf pressed into the clay, a difficult technical process also new to Japan. A further innovation identifiable in the Azuchi tiling was the use of multiple glazes of deep red, vermilion and yellow to highlight the overall blue glazing noted by Frois. The use of this technique was common for the tiles on important buildings in Ming China, but had not been employed in Japan since the Nara period.[23] In other words there was a considerable advance in tiling techniques in use at Azuchi, with the master tilers of Nara making the tiles under the direction of the Ming master. These same techniques were to be employed again to great effect for the roofs of Jurakudai, Fushimi and Osaka Castles.

There was thus at Azuchi a direct equation between political, military and economic power and the ability to command the materials and labour of entire regions and to marshal the services of the most skilled artisans of the age. Many of the builders, artists and craftsmen who worked on Azuchi came from traditions long associated with Buddhist temple architecture, namely the stone-masons of Anō, the Okabe master builders, the tile-makers of Nara, and the Kano atelier, which had evolved its painting style as wall and screen artists through commissions at Zen-sect temples like Daitokuji. Such happy architectural eclecticism may have been the inevitable result of patronage by a ruler untroubled by convention and more than a little self-indulgent in the way of the *nouveau riche*, but it was in equal measure a result of the compelling technological logic of the architectural expression of authority. New building technology can rarely be created on demand in a traditional society with its complex and highly evolved infrastructure of hereditary building professions. Architecture as the art of the possible responds to its own dictates of mechanical possibility and structural viability. Castle architecture of the late sixteenth century, starting with Azuchi, was created by cooption, that is, by the expedient of adding tried and tested building blocks one on another, propelled by the urgent demands of patrons. To this was added a yearning for the exotic and foreign, and the seeking of sanctions from venerated Chinese traditions in decorative iconography and in new fashions in roof tiling.

In 1582 Nobunaga was assassinated by Akechi Mitsuhide at Honnōji in Kyoto, the master builder Okabe Mataemon reputedly dying at his side. Three days later the Akechi forces sacked Azuchi Castle, Mitsuhide dividing up its gilded treasures as rewards for his vassals. Shortly afterwards Mitsuhide also met his end in a battle with Nobunaga's forces and, in the confusion following this defeat, the castle caught fire and burnt to the ground in a fire lasting for days. The 1940 excavations uncovered the extent of the terrible devastation which left little remaining above the stone walls except ash – in which were mixed fragments of tile and ceramic ware.

It is not clear whether Azuchi was deliberately set on fire by the retreating Akechi forces, or simply caught fire accidentally in the chaos following battle. Whichever the case, it is clear that the castle died with its creator, testimony to the inseparability of man and monument.

Himeji Castle and the Consolidation of Tokugawa Authority

Himeji Castle is today the largest and best-preserved castle in Japan, with the most extensive set of outer fortifications and the most impressive of all surviving *tenshu* (Figure 5.6). The castle as it now stands belongs to the period of consolidation of political power after the Tokugawa victory at the Battle of Sekigahara in 1600, and was built under the direction of Ikeda Terumasu. The major part of the construction of the castle took place between 1601 and 1613, a period lasting four times as long as that required for the building of Azuchi Castle and indicative of the increasing sophistication and complexity of the castle-building process.

Himeji is a castle closely associated with the major political and military events of the later sixteenth and early seventeenth centuries, designed to buttress the western perimeter of the sphere of immediate Tokugawa control with a massive fortification held by a close and trusted ally. It was strategically situated on the border between the regions of Tokugawa domination in central Japan, and the domains of the daimyo vanquished at Sekigahara, particularly the Mōri.

The Himeji site dominated the Harima Plain on the inland sea coastline. This made it a natural centre for fortified residence and local administration

Fig 5.6
Himeji Castle,
Hyōgo prefec-
ture. View of
Tenshu
complex
(Courtesy of
Ministry of
Foreign
Affairs)

from the fourteenth century. Major transportation routes moved westward across the Harima Plain from the direction of Kyoto some 150 kilometres to the east, and it was situated a mere 6 kilometres from the busy shipping channels of the Inland Sea. Hideyoshi, transferred by Nobunaga to this castle site in 1577, duly completed a three-storey *tenshu* there in 1581. It was from Himeji that he subsequently launched his counter-attack on the assassins of Nobunaga in 1582, a move which eventually led to his own national hegemony. Little is known of the structure of Hideyoshi's original castle, as it was completely subsumed by the later Ikeda castle construction, commenced after the military victory of 1600.

Ikeda Terumasu was transferred to the Himeji fief immediately after the Battle of Sekigahara and began a major rebuilding project there the following year. The *tenshu* complex was built during 1608 and 1609. It comprised the Great Tenshu and three subsidiary *tenshu* grouped on a square plan and linked by connecting parapets (Figure 5.7). This was one of the most elaborate plans for any castle keep built in Japan, thereby greatly extending its symbolic and functional capabilities. Work continued on the outer walls and other structures of the castle until Ikeda's death in 1613. His ambitious plans had

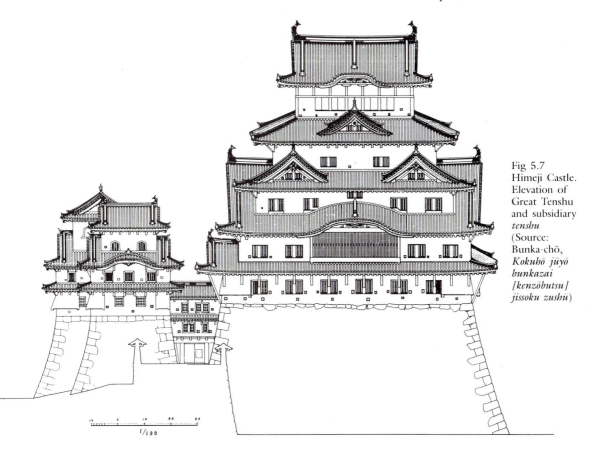

Fig 5.7 Himeji Castle. Elevation of Great Tenshu and subsidiary *tenshu* (Source: Bunka-chō, *Kokuhō jūyō bunkazai [kenzōbutsu] jissoku zushū*)

1/100

included the excavation of a canal to link Himeji Castle with the Inland Sea but this project was abandoned upon his death.[24]

The scale and character of Himeji Castle at the time of its completion under the Ikeda may be deduced from contemporary records.[25] The inner citadel or *Honmaru* was approximately 91 metres (50 *ken*) in length on each of its four sides. The outer perimeter of the fortifications was nearly 6 kilometres long, and enclosed an area 1,850 metres north–south by 1420 metres east–west.

Many of the peripheral structures and towers have since been destroyed but the greater part of the castle survives today as it stood at the time of its completion nearly 400 years ago. It occupies a total area of some 200,000 square metres. It may be the largest extant castle in Japan today, but it was to be only the fourth largest castle built in Japan, conceding greater size to the castles at Edo, Osaka and Nagoya. The Great Tenshu is 46.34 metres from the base of its stone wall to the top of the ridge capping tiles, which made it in its time approximately the same height as the *tenshu* of Azuchi. Moreover, the castle planners cleverly exploited the topography of the site (Figure 5.8). The fortifications are set on two gently sloping hills on the Harima Plain, making Himeji Castle the type of fortification known as a *hirayamajiro* or 'a castle on a hill on a plain', following the precedent established by Azuchi. The higher of the two hills, Himeyama, which rises only a modest 50 metres, serves as the site of the Inner Citadel protecting the keep complex, and a surrounding second citadel, the Ninomaru. To the west is Sagiyama or 'White Heron Hill', which acts as the site for the western citadel and its fortifications, and has given to the whole complex the popular name White Heron Castle. Along with the multiple keeps, the most impressive feature of the castle is its labyrinthine defensive system. This comprises a sequence of gateways and gatehouses organised in an irregular spiral plan sweeping around eventually to reach the site of the keep complex and the palace that was set beneath it. These gateways provide access through the towering stone walls, which reach 15 metres in height in the vicinity of the keeps. An additional defence mechanism is supplied by a series of moats. The stone walls are constructed on the same principles as those of Azuchi, not surprisingly since the Anō stone-masons were involved in the Himeji project. However, on closer examination certain technical refinements are readily identifiable. The individual rocks have been hewn into more regular shapes, simplifying the process of assembling the wall faces, and drainage outlets have been inserted at appropriate locations to allow drainage of accumulated water from behind the stone walls, which is the greatest threat to the structural viability of any such wall. Adequate supplies of suitable stone were difficult to obtain and even tombstones from nearby cemeteries and the rocks from an ancient burial mound were reused in the castle wall.

Seventeenth-century records establish that there were originally 84 gateways and gatehouses in the castle complex but only 16 remain today. Nevertheless the shrewdness of the defence they afforded is still evident: different designs are used for each gateway and gatehouse, and sudden, unexpected changes of direction are made in the approach paths and gradients in order to surprise attacking forces, guiding them inexorably into exposed positions where

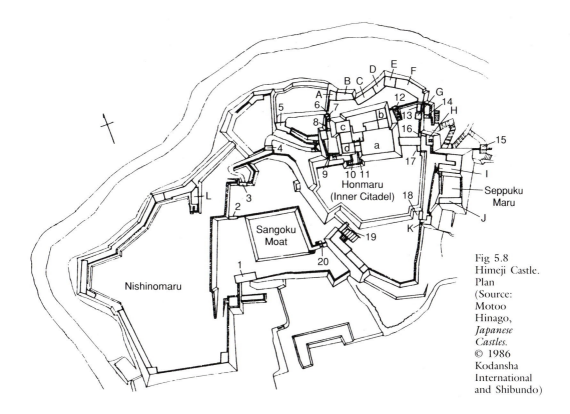

Fig 5.8
Himeji Castle.
Plan
(Source:
Motoo
Hinago,
*Japanese
Castles.*
© 1986
Kodansha
International
and Shibundo)

Gates
1. Hishi no Mon
2. I no Mon (First Gate)
3. Ro no Mon (Second Gate)
4. Ha no Mon (Third Gate)
5. Ni no Mon (Fourth Gate)
6. Ho no Mon (Fifth Gate)
7. Mizu no Ichi Mon (First Water Gate)
8. Mizu no Ni Mon (Second Water Gate)
9. Mizu no San Mon (Third Water Gate)
10. Mizu no Yon Mon (Fourth Water Gate)
11. Mizu no Go Mon (Fifth Water Gate)
12. He no Mon (Sixth Gate)
13. To no Ichi Mon (Seventh Gate Number One)
14. To no Ni Mon (Seventh Gate Number Two)
15. To no Yon Mon (Seventh Gate Number Four)
16. Chi no Mon (Eighth Gate)
17. Bizen Mon
18. Ri no Mon (Ninth Gate)
19. Nu no Mon (Tenth Gate)
20. Ru no Mon (Eleventh Gate)

Corner and Connecting Towers
A. I no Watari-yagura (First Connecting Tower)
B. Ro no Watari-yagura (Second Connecting Tower)
C. Ha no Watari-yagura (Third Connecting Tower)
D. Ni no Watari-yagura (Fourth Connecting Tower)
E. Ho no Watari-yagura (Fifth Connecting Tower)
F. He no Watari-yagura (Sixth Connecting Tower)
G. To no Watari-yagura (Seventh Connecting Tower)
H. Seikaku Yagura (Well Enclosure Tower)
I. Obi no Yagura (Obi Tower)
J. Obi-guruwa Yagura (Obi Enclosure Tower)
K. Taiko Yagura (Drum Tower)
L. Keshō Yagura (Keshō Tower)

Tenshu Complex
a. Great Tenshu
b. East Small Tenshu
c. North-west Small Tenshu
d. West Small Tenshu

Fig 5.9
Himeji Castle.
Ni no Mon
viewed from
Great Tenshu

defenders could easily concentrate arrow and musket fire. The most intriguing
of all these structures is the Ni no Mon, the fourth gate in sequence from the
outer fortifications. It is set immediately beneath the Great Tenshu and guards
a right-angled turn in the approach path (Figure 5.9). Attackers would have
been enticed into a welcoming large entrance area, but would have swiftly

discovered that the gateway closes in like a lobster trap, forcing invaders to turn abruptly at right angles and virtually crawl out of the small aperture at the exit. The complex design of the gateway demanded great skill and versatility on the part of the builders who created it. The entrance section is two storeys in height but the exit area which abuts it is located on higher ground and rises to a height of three storeys.

The defensive plan required all who entered the castle grounds to travel almost three times further than the direct distance between the outer entrance gateway and the keep complex. In part this was designed as a counter to the menace of firearms, introduced to Japan by the Portuguese in the middle of the sixteenth century. The matchlock musket (arquebus) arrived in Japan in 1543 with the first Portuguese sailors, shipwrecked on Tanegashima. The cannon followed in 1576. The musket played a decisive role in Nobunaga's victory at the Battle of Nagashino in 1575 but posed no real threat to castles built high on sturdy stone foundations. The cannon, which was instrumental in transforming the European castle into a tightly constructed bastion, was never employed effectively against the Japanese castle due to low levels of casting and gunnery skill available in Japan at the time. As may be seen at Himeji, there was some strengthening of walls, extension of the outworks, and the addition of iron plating to the wooden doors of gateways for protection against musket fire, but the overall effect on castle design itself was minimal. The combined forces of siege and artillery were never brought to bear fully against the Japanese castle. If they had been, the exuberant, flamboyant forms of castles like Himeji would have been transformed into the smooth-walled, hunched shapes of later European castles. The Japanese castle remained an extravert, a seeming flight of physical fancy matched in Europe only by such whimsical castellated palaces as the nineteenth-century Neuschwanstein.

The keep complex of Himeji Castle shows how the full range of existing technology was brought together to give physical expression to the needs and the ambitions of the Tokugawa channelled through the hands of the Ikeda. The degree of sophistication of the building techniques is evident not only in the provision of three smaller keeps to increase the spectacle and efficacy of the Great Tenshu, but also in the internal structure of the Great Tenshu itself. As with the stone walls, the timber-framing techniques employed to create this soaring edifice are more sophisticated than those which must have been employed at Azuchi Castle and other early castles such as Okayama and Inuyama. This structure was not contrived by adding a belvedere to a large timber-framed building, as had been the practice. The entire structure is unitary in form, held together from basement to the upper storey, the seventh interior floor, by two massive pillars which pass through and lock together each level of the building (Figure 5.10). During the restoration work carried out spasmodically over a 20-year period because of the war, and completed in 1959, it was discovered that the east pillar was a single trunk of silver fir (*momi*) reaching 24.8 metres in length. The west pillar was created by tenoning two tree trunks together, the upper part of hemlock (*tsuga*) and the lower of silver fir.[26] The understanding of the mechanical properties of high-rise structures demonstrated at Himeji, and the sureness and strength of the numerous joints fashioned to splice and tenon this frame together, are staggering even in the light of our knowledge of modern building technology. The only precedent for such skills in the Japanese experience was to be found in the multi-storeyed Buddhist pagoda tradition. Buildings of similar size to the Himeji keep complex had been constructed as part of the monumental architecture of the Nara period. Himeji Castle, and its predecessor at Azuchi, are comfortable technical and stylistic companions of the Daigokuden and Daibutsuden of the eighth century. They are also technologically indebted to structures such as the twin pagodas, each reaching over 100 metres in height, which flanked the approach path to Tōdaiji. As in the case of the stonemasons and castle walls, the master carpenters of Himeji adapted the techniques of pagoda construction to their particular needs.[27] In order to stabilise pagodas against earthquake shock they were equipped with a tall, mast-like pillar at the centre known as the *shinbashira*, or 'heart pillar', which runs from the foundation podium through each storey and culminates in the bronze finial (Figure 5.11). The designers of the Himeji Great Tenshu equipped the framework with two such pillars to stabilise the structure and brace it against both lateral and vertical earthquake movement. Here is further evidence of the general trend in castle technology of the age observed initially

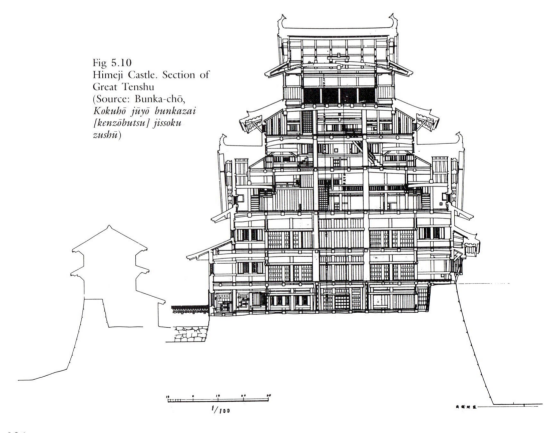

Fig 5.10
Himeji Castle. Section of
Great Tenshu
(Source: Bunka-chō,
*Kokuhō jūyō bunkazai
[kenzōbutsu] jissoku
zushū*)

1/100

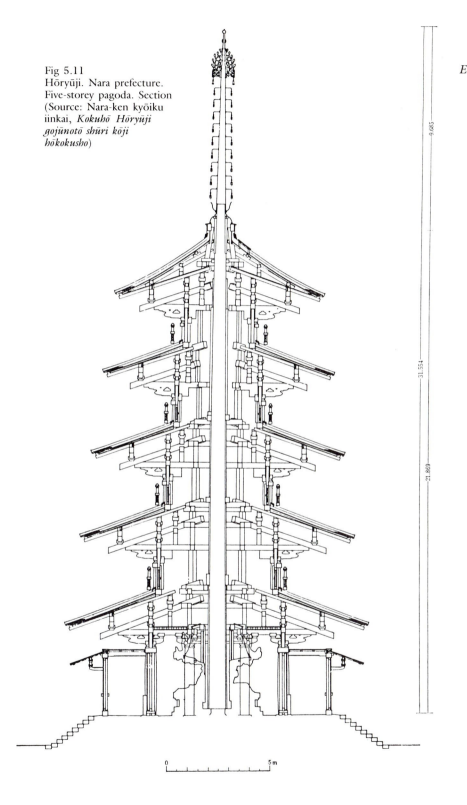

Fig 5.11
Hōryūji. Nara prefecture.
Five-storey pagoda. Section
(Source: Nara-ken kyōiku
iinkai, *Kokuhō Hōryūji*
gojūnotō shūri kōji
hōkokusho)

0   5 m

Fig 5.12
Himeji Castle.
View of Great
Tenshu

in the case of Azuchi in which the techniques of religious building were
conscripted to serve the ends of secular authority.

   When viewed from the exterior, the most impressive and seductive part of
the Great Tenshu and its subsidiary towers are undoubtedly the different
roofs. These roofs are covered with grey tiles embellished with white plaster
in order to secure them against high wind while at the same time providing
dramatic decorative emphasis. On the main ridges are the *shachi* whose frolicking forms from the time of Azuchi Castle became a ubiquitous presence

on all castle roofs. Finally the carefully orchestrated syncopation of gables, alternating between sharp triangular shapes and the flaring gables or *kara-hafu*, gave dramatic emphasis to the keep buildings.

The beauty of the exterior of the castle fulfilled the ambition of its patron to create a symbol of authority, but the effectiveness of Himeji as a fortified centre is undeniable – both in the labyrinthine defences and in the variety of technical devices utilised for the superstructures. These included the projecting apertures at the corners of the keeps and towers which allowed defenders to drop boulders and even more unpleasant items upon any attackers attempting to scale the stone walls beneath (Figure 5.12). These *ishiotoshimado*, or 'stone-dropping windows', have their equivalent in devices employed in European castle architecture as defence against attackers.

Himeji Castle accordingly continued the tradition established at Azuchi of the castle which served both as a military installation and as a centre of civil authority. Himeji makes manifest on the one hand the enormous commitment of the warrior class to the castle as the nucleus of its authority, and on the other the centripetal effect of castle construction on building technology, especially in drawing together the expertise of the venerable traditions of monumental temple construction to serve the ends of newly established warrior authority.

Edo Castle and the Tokugawa Order

The genius and achievements of the age of castles culminated in the construction of Edo Castle, the supreme bastion of the Tokugawa order established at the heart of the shogunal metropolis. This edifice marked the third phase in the evolution of the castle from the time of Azuchi, while its completion to all intents and purposes ended the age of castles. The growth of the city of Edo with the castle as its focus is closely related to the circumstances of authority and played a key role in defining the new Tokugawa order. The castle *tenshu* dominated the city as its highest structure, while the stone walls and moats which snaked out from the centre defined the spatial configuration of the urban development and the hierarchical zoning of its inhabitants.

After a long history of sporadic settlement Edo experienced its most significant development as a Tokugawa centre. In 1590, following the defeat of the Hōjō family, Hideyoshi transferred his vassal Tokugawa Ieyasu to the Eight Provinces of the Kantō, which included the territory of the defeated Hōjō. The move was designed to disadvantage the Tokugawa in any further bid for power by separating them from their home-base in the province of Mikawa. It confronted Ieyasu with the challenge of a site for his new headquarters which was low-lying and in many parts swamp and marsh. To address this problem an energetic programme of hydraulic engineering was immediately embarked upon. Canals and moats were excavated to drain the marshes and to create a defence system for the castle. However the physical fragmentation of the site made the orderly arrangement of city blocks on a plan such as that of Nara and Kyoto next to impossible. Moreover, in 1594 the rapid expansion of the new city was slowed when Hideyoshi, keen to restrain the

129

eager plans of aggrandisement of the Tokugawa, ordered Ieyasu to participate in the rebuilding of Fushimi Castle, his own headquarters to the south
of Kyoto. The consequence was that, until after 1600, Edo remained a castle
town without a castle keep.

The Tokugawa military victory at Sekigahara of 1600 cleared the way for
the construction of the central part of the castle at Edo. In fact the Tokugawa
victory and the subsequent formal establishment of the Tokugawa *bakufu* in
1603 marked a watershed in the evolution of authority with palpable implications for official architecture and the city of Edo itself. The city entered a period
of explosive growth, at a rate rarely exceeded in world history. By the 1720s
it had a population of at least 1.2 million, making it one of the most populous
cities of the contemporary world. The policies of the Tokugawa were the prime
impetus behind this remarkable growth, and they gave the city its distinctive
architectural character (see Figure 5.13). Some 60 per cent of urban land was
occupied by the palaces and mansions of the daimyo, who were required to
create permanent establishments in the Tokugawa headquarters under the system of obligatory part-time residence known as the *sankin kōtai* system. Their
principal palaces, constructed on land allocated by the *bakufu* in the immediate vicinity of the castle, were built on a lavish scale with extensive facilities for
formal audiences and ritual entertainment, especially for Nō drama. We shall
return to these begilded corridors of power later. Here it is pertinent to note
their placement proximate to the castle. The three Tokugawa collateral houses
of Owari, Mito and Kii were positioned on the high ground to the immediate north of the castle grounds. Other *fudai* or vassal daimyo had similar
favourable locations to the north and east. The *tozama daimyō*, whose loyalty
to the Tokugawa had been enforced through military sanctions, were situated
to the west and south of the castle, in a belt of land sweeping down the hill
from what is now Kasumigaseki, through Hibiya into present-day Marunouchi.
The lower lying and reclaimed land beside Edo Bay became the crowded site
for the homes and shops of the merchant and artisan classes, offering a striking contrast to the space and luxury of the daimyo zones of the city centre.
Excavation of moats and the reinforcing of their walls with massive quantities
of rock proceeded alongside the work on daimyo palaces and the Edo *tenshu*.
The moat extended outwards to create a spiral through the heart of Edo.[28]
The spiral itself was irregular in shape; there were many parts of the city, such
as the environs of the Akasaka barbican, where the marshes demanded a pragmatic rather than doctrinaire response to siting conditions.

The actual process of constructing the moats and stone walls of the castle
was used by the Tokugawa as a mechanism to eviscerate daimyo resources. The
Tokugawa required the daimyo to undertake the most onerous engineering
and architectural tasks necessary for the urban development. The excavation
of the moats was a deliberately herculean burden designed to drain their
energies and preclude their political ambitions. The outer moat of the castle,
completed in 1636, was 15.7 kilometres long, over 50 metres wide and almost
as deep. This compared with the 6 kilometres of moats excavated for Himeji
Castle, itself a remarkable achievement. The moat may have made the inner
city and the castle virtually impregnable, but it conveniently and deliberately
depleted the resources of the daimyo responsible for its construction.[29]

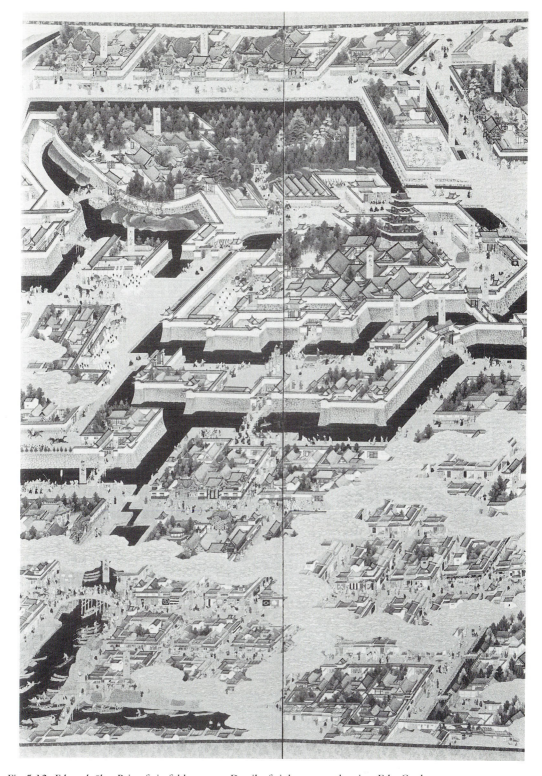

Fig 5.13 *Edozu byōbu*. Pair of six-fold screens. Detail of right screen showing Edo Castle at right with palaces of daimyo in immediate vicinity
(Courtesy of National Museum of Japanese History, Sakura)

The provision of stone for the castle walls was also a task carefully calculated for maximum effect in asserting Tokugawa authority. It was distributed among the daimyo according to the size of their officially assessed rice tax, a crippling burden for some due to the lack of any good stone deposits on the alluvial Kantō Plain. The boulders had to be quarried from the distant Izu mountains and transported by ship across Sagami Bay to the construction site at Edo. The city and its castle walls were therefore built on the backs of the daimyo through the cunning conscription of regional resources both of manpower and materials to serve the ends of the new central authority.

Building and Rebuilding the Tenshu of Edo Castle

The *tenshu* of Edo Castle was the ultimate focus of architecture and authority in the first half of the seventeenth century. The construction of, and as it transpired, the frequent rebuilding of this *tenshu*, serve as an architectural index of the state of authority under the first three Tokugawa shogun. The *tenshu* of Edo Castle was an eloquent, even verbose, architectural proclamation of temporal mastery. Like that of Azuchi before it, the keep of Edo Castle did not long outlive those who created it, falling victim to the changed political circumstances of the middle of the seventeenth century. Although destroyed by fire in 1657, and never rebuilt for reasons to be discussed later, the details of this grand edifice can be recreated by paintings, carpenters' drawings and references in literature. The *tenshu* was the largest ever constructed in Japan in terms of height, standing 58.4 metres from the base of the stone wall to the ridge-capping tiles – some 30 percent higher than the Great Tenshu of Himeji Castle. Unlike Himeji, however, Edo Castle had only a single keep as a result of changing political circumstances. At Azuchi we saw that castle and palace were combined in the same towering structure. At Himeji it was necessary to increase the interior space in response to the expanding spatial needs of civil administration and government by creating a system of multiple keeps. Although this approach was tried in several other castles of the period, when it came to building Edojō there was a parting of the ways between the *tenshu* and the palace. The centre of ritual and administration shifted from the castle keep to the palaces erected within the castle walls at the base of the *tenshu*, a new form of palace architecture discussed in the next chapter. At this point in our discussion the focus is upon the lingering power of that high-rise structure, the castle keep.

The most vivid record available for recreating the appearance of the Edo *tenshu* is a pair of six-fold screens in the collection of the National Museum of Japanese History at Sakura (Figure 5.13). Known as the *Edozu byōbu*, these screens contain an incomparable wealth of detail about the architecture of Edo prior to the Great Meireki Fire of 1657 which destroyed as much as 80 per cent of the city. Caution must be exercised in relying on these screens however. Although they depict Edo prior to the 1657 fire, they were painted as much as a generation later, and the architectural content is itself internally inconsistent.[30] It is essential to cross-check the information it contains with other sources, such as written descriptions. The sumptuous nature of the materials and excellent condition of the screens suggest a date of origin not

Fig 5.14
Edozu byōbu.
Detail showing
tenshu of Edo
Castle
(Courtesy of
National
Museum of
Japanese
History,
Sakura)

later than the turn of the eighteenth century. The artist, assisted to some
degree by imagination, recreated the pre-1657 city as an architectural collage
based on earlier drawings, paintings and maps.

The castle is featured on the right-hand panels of the left screen, at the
heart of the city and at the centre of the composition of the painting (Figure
5.14). We look down upon the great castle and are struck, in the same way
as the inhabitants of Edo would have been, with its grandeur and dignity.

133

It was delicately sculpturesque in appearance, with multiple gables and rich gold-leaf decoration highlighting the eave ends and the ridge in a manner strongly reminiscent of Azuchi Castle. The stone base, the only part of the castle keep to survive today, is made from finely finished granite. The principles of construction are the same as for the Azuchi walls but the quality of finish is entirely different, each massive block of granite being neatly squared off at right angles and aligned with its neighbours. The timber-framed superstructure rose five levels above the base and was crowned by gilded *shachigawara*. Dramatic emphasis was given to the second level by a large triangular gable (*chidorihafu*). The third level had a pair of similar but smaller gables while above these on the fourth level we see the elegantly curved gable which was such a gracious characteristic feature of Himeji Castle. To the front of the castle, set within the inner citadel, are clearly revealed a complex array of large, blue-tiled roofs, the palace buildings which were increasingly the focus of administration and ritual. Here again the roofs are bedecked in sculptural ornament covered in gold and lacquer, leaving little doubt as to the importance of the activities carried out within.

The *tenshu* may be depicted with a certain strength of conviction, and it does convey the spectacular nature of the building. Unfortunately, the details of the gables are not accurate, confirming that the painting dates from after the destruction of the keep in 1657. The actual technical drawings, used by the chief master builder to build this *tenshu*, have happily survived.[31] These are drawings by Kōra Munehiro, the master builder who was in charge of the project. They include an isometric projection similar to modern architectural drawings, with cut-away sections illustrating details of the roof truss and gables, and written inscriptions identifying the building as the Edo castle keep, the author as Kōra Munehiro and the date of the document as 1638.

The Kōra drawings differ significantly from the *Edozu byōbu* in the arrangement of the all-important triangular and curved gables, the *chidorihafu* and *karahafu* respectively. They show a logical progression of gables up the east side with a pair of triangular gables on the first-storey roof. These are crowned by a larger gable of similar style on the second storey immediately above. On the fourth level a large, flattened *karahafu*, typical of 1630s architecture, flows into the eave line. In the painting the artist has incorrectly reversed the position of the triangular gables and the *karahafu* is shown as a separate roof, spoiling the graceful effect of the whole.

If the artist strayed from reality in showing the gables on the east face of the *tenshu*, his efforts are even less satisfactory when it comes to the south side. Here he simply creates a single triangular gable on each of the first, second and third storey roofs. The Kōra drawings establish that the design was more sophisticated, complementing that of the east face with a single triangular gable on the first storey and a pair of smaller matching gables above. On this side of the *tenshu* a *karahafu* is again used to accentuate the eave line of the fourth-storey roof, a feature omitted from the screen painting.

The *tenshu* pictured in the *Edozu byōbu* and the Kōra drawing is no less than the third keep to be built at Edo Castle. The first three shogun each built a new *tenshu* to express his own authority, even, perhaps, as an atavistic gesture to the ancient ritualistic practice of building a new palace for a new emperor.

The first *tenshu* was built between 1604 and 1607, immediately after the formal establishment of the Tokugawa shogunate. The only surviving evidence of the design of this building is contained in a large plan of Edo Castle dated 1605. It consists of a Great Tenshu with a single smaller tower connected to it. The details are not clear but it would appear to have been similar in principle to the multiple connected keep design which was to be employed at Himeji Castle shortly afterwards.[32] Whatever the actual details of this first Edo *tenshu* may have been, Ieyasu's architectural and political preoccupations shifted almost immediately upon completion. This was a reflection of changing circumstances of power in Edo. In 1605 Ieyasu had officially retired as shogun in order to gain room to manoeuvre behind the scenes, and indeed behind the walls of another castle. With much pomp and ceremony he had returned to Sumpu, now the city of Shizuoka, and thrown his energies into repairing and restoring the castle there.[33] From Sumpu Ieyasu was to exercise long-distance control over national affairs for over a decade, while his son Hidetada supervised the growing shogunal bureaucracy in Edo.[34] Thus in the critical period of the new shogunate, while the era of stand-off with the Toyotomi continued, much of the decision-making process was physically separated from Edo itself. Until the death of Ieyasu in 1616, the city of Edo was the locus of state symbolism and governmental control but not the focus of real policy-making. There is an interesting analogy in terms of political behaviour between Tokugawa Edo and the separation of institutional and personal power in *insei*, or cloistered government, of the Heian period, when retired emperors exercised real authority from the separate palaces to which they removed themselves upon abdication.

Ieyasu was also preoccupied with establishing a powerful architectural presence in and around the imperial capital of Kyoto rather than with building a grandiose keep for Edo on the distant Kantō plain. By 1606 he had built a new headquarters for Tokugawa affairs in Kyoto at Nijō. Fushimi Castle, to the immediate south of Kyoto, was completely rebuilt by the Tokugawa in the same year. These two castles became the focus and the definition of shogunate authority *vis à vis* imperial authority, while Edo Castle became the power base for the Kantō. It was only after the demise of Toyotomi power in 1615 and Ieyasu's death in 1616 that Edo became the unequivocal centre of Tokugawa authority.

The circumstances of authority changed dramatically with the military victory over the Toyotomi in 1615, and on the death of Ieyasu the following year, real power passed to Hidetada. In the years 1622–1623 Hidetada had Ieyasu's *tenshu* demolished and replaced by a new building. Unlike its multiple-keep predecessor, the new structure was a single tower. This rebuilding was part of a process for greatly enlarging the inner citadel (*honmaru*) of the castle to provide more space for palace and administrative buildings. A multiple-towered keep was no longer needed to accommodate administrative offices and audience chambers, and the floor area of the keep was substantially reduced. However the *tenshu* continued to be an important landmark signalling Tokugawa authority to the surrounding city, and particularly to the many

135

daimyo fulfilling their duty of forced residence in the castle environs. The design of the tower was therefore made more elaborate than that of its predecessor by the addition of numerous triangular and cusped gables. It was built under the direction of the Nakai, a family of hereditary master builders from the celebrated temple of Hōryūji, who had worked upon Hideyoshi Osaka Castle in 1583 before entering Tokugawa service in 1588. Their family records and a painting of Edo (*Edo meishozu byōbu*), dating to this era and now preserved in the Idemitsu Art Museum, show that the keep had assumed new authority as the symbolic centre of the governing order.[35]

This *tenshu* was to last only 15 years. It was replaced at the behest of the third shogun, Iemitsu, in 1637–1638, by an even more resplendent building – the *tenshu* depicted, albeit inaccurately, in the *Edozu byōbu* and built under the hand of the Kōra master builders. The speed with which this rebuilding was accomplished and the splendour of its final form indicate the importance of this architectural structure as a symbol of authority for Iemitsu, who was at that time engaged in a process of far-reaching institutionalisation of his own power within the overall framework of *bakufu* authority. Iemitsu had emerged from the shadow of his grandfather, Ieyasu, and his immediate predecessor and father Hidetada, on the latter's death in 1632. For the next five years he enacted a series of measures designed to consolidate his personal authority, including a reformulation of the laws governing the military households in 1615; tightened control over daimyo; persecution of Christianity, and eventual prohibition of foreign contacts. The rebuilt *tenshu* was in effect Iemitsu's grand punctuation mark to signify the completion of this process of consolidation.

When most of Edo Castle, and much of the surrounding city, was destroyed in the great conflagration of 1657, the *bakufu* immediately put into action plans to rebuild the castle keep. Work proceeded apace on the rebuilding of the stone walls and palaces of the castle, with the Maeda, the most powerful of the all daimyo, given responsibility for rebuilding the wall at the base of the keep.[36] Even as this work was being completed under the direction of the assiduous Anō masons, consultations were taking place between Hoshina Masayuki, Sakai Tadakatsu and Ii Naotaka, the daimyo in whose hands shogunal government now rested. They reached the decision that 'work on the *tenshu* would be suspended because of damage throughout the city [because of the fire] which had placed a major strain upon the financial resources of the state'.[37] The circumstances of authority were dramatically different in 1657–1659 from those at the time of the creation of the third *tenshu* 20 years earlier. Iemitsu himself had died in 1651, and his son, Ietsuna, became shogun by hereditary succession. Real power, however, was now in the hands of *fudai daimyō*, over whom Iemitsu had been vigorously asserting his control in 1637–1638: it is not surprising then that the daimyo should not wish to finance the rebuilding of the *tenshu*, symbol of that control, in the new post-Iemitsu era. There was a new pragmatism in *bakufu* policies towards the built environment, partly as a result of the practical problems of rebuilding which confronted the shogunate after the fire, and partly as a result of the increased stability of the *bakufu* in institutional terms after 1651.[38] Counting the monetary cost of political monuments was a radical departure from the circumstances of authority prior to 1651 and indeed throughout most of Japanese history.

The shogunate flirted briefly, once more, with the idea of rebuilding the *tenshu* in the reign of Ienobu (1709–1713). Once the projected cost had been ascertained the idea progressed as far as the drawing-up of detailed plans but the construction process was soon abandoned. The *tenshu* had become a political anachronism.

Presence and Power: Azuchi, Himeji and Edo Castles

The three castles examined in this chapter, each representing a separate era in the creation and consolidation of authority in the sixteenth and seventeenth centuries, had an extraordinary political presence. Each castle was an expression of a particular moment within a period of rule by control of the built as well as the political environment. Each castle, too, was a direct index to the political circumstances of its time, and in two of the three cases, was destroyed once those circumstances had changed.

As has been established, castle architecture drew heavily upon long-established traditions of religious architecture in Japan. This was no accident, for in any traditional society it is a technological imperative to build upon existing technology. However the castle was far more than the result of technological determinism: it stood on the boundary of the secular and the sacred, expressing the aspirations towards the eternal and the divine of those who were so bold as to reach towards the heavens with their earthly abodes. Such was the ambition of their military sponsors and the skill of their builders that this period of castle-building was one of the great ages of construction in world history. The frenetic fortifying of the state with castles parallels the building programmes of Imperial Rome under Augustus, the era of church and castle construction by the Normans after the Conquest of Britain in 1066, and the cathedral and church building in the Paris region around the year 1200, during which, as John James has written, 'a frantic and insatiable urge to construct consumed the riches of France'.[39] Japan was beset by a similar frantic and insatiable urge to build castles for a mere two generations around the turn of the seventeenth century. It was equally a frantic but fleeting moment when the concentrated energy, inspiration, technology, artistic talents and materials of the nation were brought to bear on the physical realisation of authority in the architecture of the castle. It was an era in which the master builders and other master craftsmen, at the head of vast armies of labourers mobilised in the cause of castle-building, became the professional peers of the architects and artists who served imperial Rome, Norman conquerors and medieval bishops. The majesty of the Japanese castle, its formidable strength, the grandeur of its spectacle, the infinite subtlety of its crafted decoration, created monuments as ageless as ambition itself.

6 Nijō Castle and the Psychology of Architectural Intimidation

Nijō Castle was the alpha and omega of formally constituted Tokugawa rule. At this sumptuous, fortified palace in Kyoto, Tokugawa Ieyasu first presided over the daimyo as newly appointed shogun in 1603. It was within the same stone walls in the Ninomaru Goten (Palace of the Second Compound) that the last Tokugawa shogun, Yoshinobu, officially returned ruling power to the imperial institution in 1867. Between 1603 and 1867 Nijō Castle was to serve as the headquarters of the Tokugawa shogunate in the imperial capital, as the location for its administration of the Kansai region, the base for a military garrison, and as the place where the shogun resided while conducting business with the imperial court and local daimyo.

Nijō Castle was a large and elaborate complex, in keeping with its important and diverse role. It is conventionally known as a 'castle' – as in its official title 'Nijōjō'. In reality it was more a fortified palace than a palatial castle. It consisted of several palaces and administrative buildings set within two compounds, each protected by walls and moats in the manner of castles of this period (Figure 6.1). Within its Second Compound today stands the best

Fig 6.1 Nijō Castle, Kyoto. Aerial view from south showing Palace of the Second Compound (Courtesy of Nijōjō)

Fig 6.2
Nijō Castle.
Palace of the
Second
Compound.
Front view

preserved example of a Tokugawa palace. This 'Palace of the Second Compound' survives to offer an incomparable opportunity for understanding the equation between artistic form and political order in the high culture of seventeenth-century Japan (Figure 6.2).[1] Here we can still examine *in situ* the buildings in which Tokugawa officials worked and where some of the most important ritual audiences of the shogunal state were conducted, including its official termination. Artistic media ranging from architecture to landscaping, painting to filigree ornament, sculpture to lacquer work, are brilliantly orchestrated in a concert of effects, greater than the simple sum of the parts, to achieve a finely tuned expression of authority. When viewed today, some of the distinctions in design and material, painting style and iconography, may seem self-indulgent or even unimportant, but it is essential to remember that these palace chambers were designed to accommodate highly informed observers, well schooled in interpreting the visual vocabulary of architectural form and applied ornament. It was the shogun, if not God, who was present in the detail, and we too should look for political significance in small details because these chambers were to play a vital role in defining the status and standing of those who used them. The Palace of the Second Compound at Nijō Castle allows us a rare opportunity to examine a Tokugawa palace in the light of findings by the behavioural sciences concerning the influence of buildings on human behaviour. In particular we shall seek evidence that buildings may perform what Wells termed 'autocratic functions'.[2] When applied to Tokugawa official architecture this raises some obvious questions which must be addressed: how, for instance, did the Tokugawa use architecture to define and enforce their authority? What artistic devices were used to achieve homology between the autocracy of authority and the autocracy of the buildings? How did the physical spaces created between individuals, and between groups, establish or reinforce the perception of relative status in the Tokugawa order?

Built Environment and Tokugawa Authority

We have seen how the bountiful resources of the shogunal state of the Tokugawa were mobilised to build a new physical establishment at Edo to house and manifest a new political order. In the first half of the seventeenth century there was a fundamental congruence between the process of state formation and the process of creating the built environment of a planned city. The Tokugawa set out to solidify a fluid political situation by pouring society into a new physical mould. This is a perfect illustration of the theory of container and contained. Inevitably at Edo the contained, that is Tokugawa government and its officially sanctioned socio-political order, acquired much of the character and many of the formal configurations of the container, the city of Edo and its officially sponsored or imposed building projects. The state became a work of art and art became a work of state, to borrow Jacob Burckhardt's classic characterisation of the Italian Renaissance. The first three Tokugawa shogun, Ieyasu (1542–1616), Hidetada (1579–1632) and Iemitsu (1604–1651) proved remarkably adept at translating their political ambitions into physical forms, sharing that universal ambition of rulers throughout the ages to create palpable manifestations of authority.

This raises one further question of great significance – how was authority defined during this period of consolidation? Here the limitations of relying on written sources alone become apparent. The official ideology of Tokugawa government is generally held to have been Neo-Confucianism, based on the synthesis and commentary on the Confucian classics undertaken by the Song-dynasty philosopher Zhu Xi (1130–1200), and reinterpreted in Japan by the Hayashi school of philosophers beginning with Fujiwara Seika (1561–1619) and Hayashi Razan (1583–1657).[3] Zhu Xi's philosophical reordering was sweeping in scope and it is not hard to find some textual justification for the Tokugawa emphasis on the physical forms of authority amongst the texts he emphasised and his own commentaries. In *Principle and Material Force*, for example, we find the pronouncement that:

> in the universe there has never been any material-force [*ch'i*] without principle [*li*] or principle without material-force . . . . Throughout the universe there are both principle and material force. Principle refers to the Way [Tao], which is above the realm of corporeality and is the source from which all things are produced. Material-force refers to material objects, which are within the realm of corporeality; it is the instrument by which things are produced. . . . There is principle before there can be material-force. But it is only when there is material-force that principle finds a place to settle. This is the process by which all things are produced, whether large as Heaven and earth or small as ants.[4]

'Material-force', as here defined, may be construed to have been given effect by the Tokugawa in the city of Edo and its architectural splendours, but it would be misleading to attribute a Neo-Confucian interpretation to the built environment of Edo during the first generations of Tokugawa shogunal rule. In fact, the first official Zhu Xi academy was not founded by the *bakufu* until 1630, and systematic propagation of Neo-Confucian tenets in education was initiated only in the later seventeenth century.[5] There was no special imperative, either explicit or implicit, towards building great monuments in Zhu Xi's writings, and certainly no recognition of the role the built environment may perform in actively shaping conduct. Zhu Xi simply affirms the basic Sino-Confucian principle that the material world, including the socio-political order, is part of the order of the cosmos, a principle which had been applied in the Tang capitals and found its way into the planning of the cities of Nara and Kyoto in the eighth and ninth centuries respectively. It is significant that Zhu Xi relies on the Daoist notion of the Way as well as the Confucian concept of harmony between things seen and unseen.

When in 1600 the House of Tokugawa achieved national military supremacy at the Battle of Sekigahara, it turned increasingly to buildings, as 'things seen', to establish a working definition of authority unseen. The Tokugawa order was created in a protracted process of accommodation with, and eventually assertion over, the authority of the imperial institution above and the power of the daimyo below.[6] Much of this accommodation was architecturally achieved. The authority of the Tokugawa shogunate was structured by its specially created architectural setting; the Tokugawa built environment defined spatially the crucial relationships between the shogunate, the imperial court and the regional lords. It achieved this in terms of spatial juxtaposition to establish hierarchy, physical access to equate with political importance, and the use of architecture as the officially sanctioned image of authority both to influence and intimidate.

Architecturally, the consolidation of Tokugawa rule was effected through the transition from an age of castles to an age of palaces. This was marked in building design by a shift from an age of vertical emphasis to an age of horizontal emphasis, from a period of preoccupation with the symbolism of towering castle *tenshu* and massive masonry walls, to an age of single-storey palaces. Their rhetorical effect was accomplished through gilded gateways and intimidating interiors carefully organised for maximum polemic impact during the ceremonies of obeisance by the daimyo to the shogun. The initial shift to horizontally organised palaces may have been motivated by the inconvenience, not to mention the potential danger, of having to ascend and descend the steep, ladder-like stairs of *tenshu* in full court regalia, complete with wide silken trousers up to a metre longer than the legs they clothed. However, the political potential of a horizontal sequence of spaces was soon realised. These palaces were built in a style now referred to as *shoin-zukuri*, the style of the Japanese residence characterised by a loose grouping of buildings in a landscaped setting with interiors organised spatially on the module of the *tatami* mat.

Shoin architecture had its origins in *shinden-zukuri*, the mansions and palaces of aristocratic authority we encountered in the Heian period. Following the warrior usurpation of civil authority in the twelfth century, features of the shinden style – such as their special garden settings, open-plan interiors, sliding screens and *tatami* mats – were adopted by the warrior class as well as the ecclesiastical hierarchy for their residences. The use of *tatami* was extended to become the module for interior space, and equipment and furnishings were suitably adapted from the residences and studies of Zen monks. This included the *tsuke-shoin*, or bay window with writing shelf, from which the style takes its name, the *tokonoma* or alcove for the display of *objets d'art*, and *chigaidana*, or split-level ornamental shelving. These and other features from the same

141

context found a natural second home in the buildings of the warrior establishment of Muromachi Kyoto in the fourteenth and fifteenth centuries, as the Ashikaga *bakufu* and its vassals consciously acquired the appurtenances of scholarly accomplishment and religious discipline. The newly appropriated features immeasurably enhanced the overall effect created by the chambers designed for receiving subordinates and entertaining distinguished guests, in much the same way as many politicians today resort to impressively book-lined offices to create the verisimilitude of wisdom. The *shoin* style was to reach its rhetorical culmination in the first part of the seventeenth century. Today it is the awe-inspiring palace at Nijō Castle which bears most eloquent testimony to the success of architecture in defining the Tokugawa order in relation to the authority of the imperial institution and the power of the daimyo.

The Construction of Nijō Castle

Nijō Castle was built in the city of Kyoto in a rectangular compound some 400 metres north–south and 500 metres east–west, flanked by Horikawa Avenue on the eastern side and Nijō Avenue on the north. Unlike the palatial castles constructed at the height of the struggles for unification under Nobunaga and Hideyoshi, its palatial character reveals the transition to an age of more subtle civil sanctions by ruler over the ruled. The first Tokugawa building work at the Nijō site was carried out from 1602 to 1603, the period following the victory over the Toyotomi-led forces at the Battle of Sekigahara. The new complex was built on the site of Nobunaga's earlier Kyoto palace. It was created by the same process as was to prove so effective in the building of the city of Edo, namely 'obliging' the daimyo of the Kansai region to build the new moats and stone walls.[7] The original ditch and earthen embankments surrounding the palace compound were widened to a distance of 4 metres, above which imposing walls of finely hewn granite were assembled. A towering two-storey gatehouse today demonstrates to the assembled phalanxes of tourist coaches and their passengers the greatness which was once Tokugawa power. The gatehouse was erected at the main entrance on the east side. Its massive beams and sturdy wooden doors, plated with iron for protection against assault by sword or musket, are evidence of the military character of Nijō Castle during those uncertain years between the Battle of Sekigahara and the annihilation of the Toyotomi in 1615.

However, the Tokugawa were quick to incorporate the more courtly refinements of a palace into these impressive fortifications for the ritual enforcement of their authority. Here, on the twenty-fifth day of the third month of 1603, Ieyasu required the daimyo to present themselves in order to congratulate him formally on the imperial conferral of the title of *sei-i-tai-shōgun*.[8] He may have already received the sword of shogunal office the preceding month in a ceremony at the Imperial Palace in Kyoto, followed by reception of the official imperial envoy in audience at his castle headquarters at Fushimi,[9] but it was at the newly rebuilt Nijō Castle that Ieyasu was to receive congratulations and enforce daimyo subservience through ceremony.

Only scanty written records remain of these events and the buildings which housed them. It is to the structures, rebuilt some 20 years later, that we must turn for extant buildings and more comprehensive documentary records. This Nijō Castle, which survives essentially intact, was built for a formal visit of state upon the shogun by the Emperor Go Mizunoo in 1626. Its architectural character is an unmistakable statement of the subtler psychological sanctions brought to bear on emperor and daimyo alike as the Tokugawa asserted their authority as national rulers.

The construction of extensive new palace buildings in the Second Compound of the precincts of Nijō Castle was not an isolated architectural event. Rather it was part of a concerted *bakufu* strategy to place its indelible architectural stamp on the imperial capital, which included the rebuilding of important temples such as Kiyomizudera, Nanzenji and Chion'in. This strategy conveniently eclipsed the glory of the vanquished Toyotomi still persisting in the many buildings they had sponsored in the preceding generation.[10] The architectural policies of the Tokugawa in Kyoto, however, were most pointedly directed towards redefining relations with the imperial court. This policy, part of the process of establishing a working definition of the Tokugawa order in relation to the authority of the imperial institution, purposely included *bakufu* financing and rebuilding of the Kyoto Gosho, the Imperial Palace and residence. It is difficult to imagine a more explicit way of showing who had the ascendancy in the relationship than did the rebuilding of the emperor's inner sanctum. It may seem presumptuous for an imperially appointed shogun to rebuild the emperor's own house, but in the context of political realities of the first half of the seventeenth century it could be construed favourably – as constituting an example of their responsibilities as emergent national rulers, *noblesse oblige* rather than *lèse majesté*.[11] In terms of *realpolitik*, the Gosho rebuilding was an unambiguous measure which put the emperor in his place, in exactly the same way as each class in the socio-political order was set in its place in the city plan of Edo.

Nijō Castle furthered the same ends by legitimising the *bakufu* through the creation of a visible presence near the Gosho. It dominated the northwestern sector of the city, acting as a counterpoise to the courtly dignity of the Imperial Palace, while its five-storey *tenshu*, gracing the east corner of the Inner Compound until destroyed by lightning in 1750, rivalled the soaring five-storey pagoda of Tōji on the sky-line of the city.

Nijō Castle was more than simply a visual spectacle in the cause of asserting Tokugawa authority over the court, because here the Tokugawa were to employ the same architectural strategies in relation to the emperor as were proving so effective in Edo against the daimyo, the practice of official visitation. In this case, however, the practice was cunningly reversed, for the Tokugawa rebuilt much of Nijō Castle, particularly the Second Compound, to receive the 'favour' of visitation by the emperor in 1626. The practice of receiving the emperor in an official visit, known as *miyuki* or *gokyō,* had been used to good effect by Hideyoshi to help invest his authority in Kyoto with the trappings of imperial legitimacy. In theory, the favour of imperial visitation was bestowed by the emperor on a subject, but in Momoyama and subsequent Tokugawa practice, the ultimate purpose was to enhance the

143

authority of the theoretical subordinate: the emperor was seen publicly to respond to, and acquiesce in, the invitation of a subject, and to be received in courtly manner within the host's own built environment especially prepared for the occasion.[12]

The facilities provided for the imperial visit were extensive, comprising a palace building set to each side of a garden, and an ornamental lake in the Second Compound of the redesigned fortifications. The records of the Nakai, master builders for the project, show that work on the castle moats and walls and the collection of building materials began in the seventh month of 1624. Architectural construction was carried out from the beginning of 1625 and continued until the sixth month of 1626, when Hidetada arrived from Edo to supervise final preparations.[13] The palace for receiving and accommodating the emperor during the five days of festivities, the Gokyō Goten, was situated to the southwest of the lake. Only plans of the buildings survive, held in the archives of the Nakai family. These show that the palace was small in scale and private in character. It consisted of a single *shoin* building for accommodation and audience facing north, flanked by kitchen and service facilities on the west, and on the east side, by a covered gallery projecting northwards to provide seating for viewing Nō drama at a stage erected especially for the occasion. It was approached via a ceremonial gateway with sweeping *kara-hafu* set into the fore and rear eaves.

The significance of this imperial visitation takes on somewhat of another dimension when it is noted that Go Mizunoo, through cunning use of inter-marriage by the Tokugawa, had become the son-in-law of the retired shogun Hidetada and the brother-in-law of the third shogun Iemitsu. The reception of Go Mizunoo in his temporary palace within the Nijōjō palace, from the sixth to the tenth day of the ninth month of 1626, was anything but a public occasion, with just the three intermarried protagonists present at the drinking of the ceremonial cups of sake. The form of ceremony and architecture was based directly on the precedents established by the Ashikaga *bakufu* in the Muromachi period (1333–1467).[14]

The Palace of the Second Compound: Organisation and Function

The Palace of the Second Compound was built at the same time as the Gokyō Goten on the other side of the ornamental lake. The siting of these two palace complexes in relation to each other is itself indicative of Tokugawa political motives. Not only did the emperor's palace face north, which was undesirable in solar terms and undignified geomantically, but the shogunal palace was set to the northeast of the lake and the imperial palace to the southwest, the most hostile and most benevolent directions respectively. The Tokugawa thereby protected the emperor from the flow of evil forces in the universe, employing a strategy similar to that in force in Edo where the Kan'eiji was placed to the northeast of Edo Castle for geomantic insurance purposes.

The role of the Gokyō Goten was circumscribed ceremonially and limited to that one occasion. The buildings were eventually dismantled and dispersed.

The shogunal palace, by contrast, was more varied in function and its role continued until the end of the Tokugawa *bakufu* itself. As the focus for the conduct of *bakufu* administrative affairs in Kyoto it housed offices for shogunal officials, and a residence at the rear was provided for the shogun when he was in Kyoto. However, the most visible parts of the palace, a series of chambers which admitted the daimyo to formal shogunal presence according to their status, were designed specifically to enact shogunal mastery over the daimyo.

The extant palace complex, built as part of the 1624–1626 project sponsored by Iemitsu, replaced an earlier palace built on the same site at the time of Ieyasu. Although it retained the basic *shoin* pattern, it was built on a much larger and more lavish scale. As may be seen today, it consists of five *shoin*-style buildings, each with *tatami* rooms connected by highly polished wooden corridors (Figure 6.3). These buildings are stepped back in sequence along a receding axis. The service buildings, including bathhouse and large kitchen, are located at the rear.

A visit to the palace begins at the main gateway, a magnificent structure dominated visually by the sweeping *karahafu* set over the eaves at front and rear. The eaves and transoms are bedecked with a dazzling array of sculpture, including an enormous dragon rollicking in rough seas, phoenixes and cranes in flight, and shining lacquered pillars and filigree Tokugawa crests.[15] This gateway leads through the wall surrounding the Second Compound to the palace buildings 30 metres to the north. The first building has a large sweeping roof covered in heavy tiles embossed with Tokugawa crests (see Figure 6.2). The entry has a *karahafu* set above the main entrance, complementing the style of the roof of the nearby gateway. The large transom set over the main entrance is, like the gateway, richly decorated with polychrome sculptures of birds and flowers, while delicate openwork friezes enliven the transoms above the two side bays (Figure 6.4). Thus the points of entry to the Second Compound and the palace buildings are given dramatic emphasis by the provision of a concert of visual effects with carefully orchestrated sculptural and architectural designs.

Behind this are the sliding screens leading to Tōzamurai, the anterooms for receiving visitors (Figure 6.5). The three main interconnected *tatami* rooms on the forward-facing side of the building are decorated with screen paintings of crouching tigers and panthers, as large as life, lurking menacingly in bamboo groves (Figure 6.6). To sit and wait in such a chamber would have been an uncomfortable experience at best. It is not difficult to imagine the consequences if such an approach were employed for the waiting rooms of dental surgeries today instead of the more customary subdued tonal values and comforting landscape paintings.

Set at right angles to, and immediately abutting, the Tōzamurai, is the Shikidai, which was used for the exchange of formal greetings between visiting daimyo and *rōjū*, the daimyo who were senior councillors in the shogunal government. The main chamber is long and narrow, and of considerable size – some 45 *tatami* mats in total floor space or 73 square metres. The contrast in size with the small six- to ten-mat rooms of the Tōzamurai is deliberate, contrived for maximum psychological impact. The rear wall of the chamber

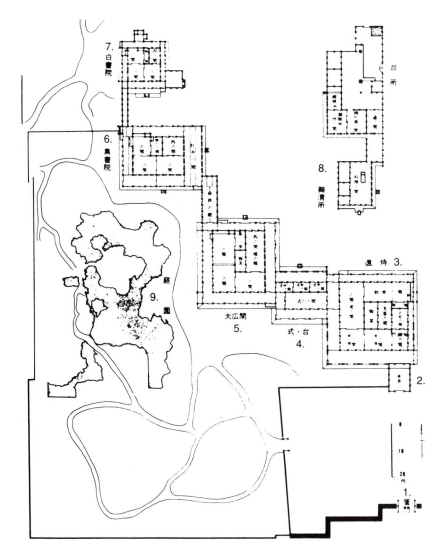

Fig 6.3
Nijō Castle.
Palace of the
Second
Compound.
Plan
(Source:
Fujioka
Michio, *Shiro
to shoin*)

1. Karamon	4. Shikidai	7. Shiroshoin
2. Entry (Kuramayose)	5. Ōhiroma	8. Service facilities
3. Tōzamurai	6. Kuroshoin	9. Garden

is dominated by a painting of two large pine trees, strong, evergreen and enduring, the pervasive pictorial symbol of perennial power in the warrior artistic vocabulary of the later sixteenth and seventeenth centuries. These two pine trees seem to defy even the structural framework of the wall itself, with their branches reaching out aggressively across pillars and beams.

Behind this chamber are three small rooms which were used as offices by the *rōjū*. Intimate in scale and detail, they are decorated with friendly scenes of wild geese feeding in river marshes, and of herons standing bravely against the blowing snow of winter, a reminder of the self-discipline and fortitude in adversity required of the warrior.

Fig 6.4
Nijō Castle.
Entry
(Kurumayose)
transom sculp-
ture of the
Palace of
the Second
Compound

The visual drama reaches a climax with the *Ōhiroma*, the great audience hall. By the time of Hideyoshi this type of audience chamber had become a standard feature of palatial castles. *Shōmei*, the official records of Hideyoshi's master builders, notes that 'during the Tenshō era [1573–1592], when Kanpaku Hideyoshi built the castle of Juraku, the *shuden* [the main hall] was made extremely wide, the reason why it is now called the hiroma [lit. 'wide room'].'[16] *Hiroma* became the standard term for the principal audience chamber in a palace and, by extension, the building which housed it. By the

Fig 6.5
Nijō Castle.
Palace of the
Second
Compound.
Transverse
section of
Kurumayose
and front
elevation of
Tōzamurai
(Source:
Kyōto-shi
moto-rikyū
Nijōjō jimusho
(ed.) *Jūyō
bunkazai
Nijōjō shūri
kōji hōkokusho*)

0   10尺

147

Fig 6.6
Nijō Castle.
Palace of the
Second
Compound.
Screen paint-
ings of the
Tōzamurai
(Courtesy of
Nijō Castle)

1620s the term *ōhiroma* or 'large *hiroma*' was in common usage for the larger
of the two audience chambers in major palaces and mansions, while *kohiroma*
or 'small hiroma' was the term adopted for the smaller chamber.[17]

There is no mistaking the importance of the building in which the *Ōhiroma*
is housed. It has the highest roof, with gables ornamented with filigree metalwork and gilded sculpture. The *Ōhiroma* within was reserved for audience

between the shogun and the *tozama daimyō* who had pledged allegiance to the Tokugawa after 1600. Here the decorative scheme of the palace reaches a crescendo with two chambers set in line and a third at right angles, all three magnificently decorated with lacquerwork, filigree, transom sculptures of birds and flowers and, predictably, large wall-paintings of pine trees set on gold leaf (Figures 6.7–6.8). These were executed under the direction of Kano Tanyū, the official artist to the Tokugawa *bakufu* who, with his family workshop, was responsible for many of the official shogunal commissions of the seventeenth century. This chamber, some 24.69 metres long and 8.6 metres wide, is divided into two separate levels, the Jōdan no ma, with a raised floor level on which the shogun and his retinue sat, and the Gedan no ma, where the *tozama daimyō* assembled for obeisance. Although the difference in elevation of the two rooms is seemingly inconsequential, a mere 67 centimetres, the psychological impact of the difference in levels would have been considerably greater for daimyo, kneeling and prostrating themselves before the figure of the shogun in the distance. The shogun would also have been seated on a single *tatami* mat raising him a further 15 centimetres. With eyes close to the floor, the distant daimyo would scarcely have been able to glimpse the figure of the shogun seated at the far end of the Jōdan no ma. Today this effect is entirely lost on the modern visitor to Nijō Castle, standing, as is the practice, amongst the visiting crowds outside these chambers and merely

Fig 6.7
Nijō Castle.
Palace of the
Second
Compound.
Ōhiroma
chambers
(Courtesy of
Nijōjō)

149

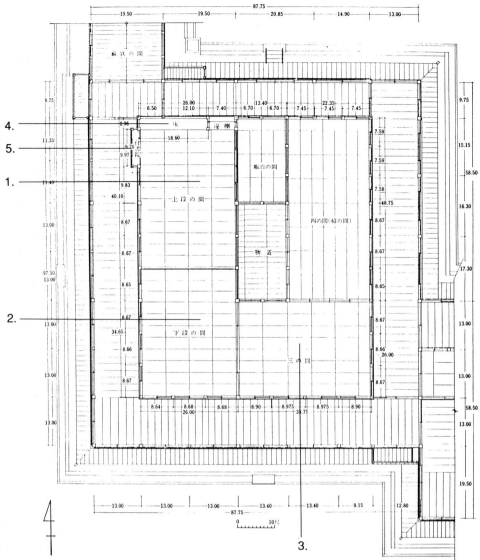

Fig 6.8
Nijō Castle.
Palace of the
Second
Compound.
Plan of
Ōhiroma
(Source: Ōta
Hirotarō *et al.*,
*Nihon
kenchikushi kiso
shiryō shūsei*)

1. Jōdan no ma ('upper chamber')   4. Tokonoma
2. Gedan no ma ('lower chamber')   5. Tsuke-shoin
3. San no ma ('third chamber')

looking in: this is an architecture of direct participation and its meaning is
largely lost on the casual observer.

At Nijō Castle the sense of the majesty of the shogun was further heightened by a panoply of special effects concentrated in the Jōdan no ma. The
shogun sat before a *tokonoma*, the rear wall of which is covered with the
heroic form of a pine tree, sharply delineated against a background of gold
leaf, its needles richly green with crushed malachite mixed in an oil paste.
Seen from the lower level of the Gedan no ma it would have subsumed the

figure of the shogun, creating an unmistakable visual equation between the personage of the Tokugawa and the everlasting power of the pine.

Other features of the audience chamber also show an appreciation of the psychological affects of architecture which modern behavioural sciences have only recently rediscovered. The ceiling of the chamber is a virtuoso exercise in lacquer and gold ornament, much of it variations on the theme of the Tokugawa crest, the gold cleverly used to emphasise the length of the chamber by highlighting the main ceiling battens. A small, double-coved and coffered ceiling is set immediately above the place where the shogun would customarily sit. With its delicate filigree metalwork of arabesques reminiscent of fine Venetian lacework, it would have heightened the perception of the importance of the person who sat beneath.

A clever use of light in the chamber intensifies the visual drama and political impact of the shogun. During formal audience the sliding doors permitting entry to the chamber from the corridor were tightly closed. The only source of natural light was through the *tsuke-shoin*, the bay to the side of the tokonoma (see Figure 6.8, No. 5). Light filters into the Jōdan no ma through its opaque white *shōji* screens and the open work transom above, a device which throws unidirectional lighting across the front wall of the raised section of the audience chamber, reflecting off the gold leaf on the walls of the tokonoma and leaving the figure of the shogun seated in front dimly lit and even mysteriously silhouetted. The intrepid Westphalian scholar and visitor to Japan, Engelbert Kaempfer (1651–1716), noticed a similar strategy employed to magnify the dignity of the shogun by minimising and concentrating the light source at Edo Castle, which he visited in 1691 and 1692. In his written account Kaempfer notes that the main audience hall of Edo Castle was open on one side to a small courtyard from which it received light. 'The Jōdan no ma', he writes,

> is narrower, deeper and one step higher than the common hall. The shogun sits at the end of this room on a floor raised by a few mats, with his legs folded under him. And it is difficult to discern his shape there, because the full light does not reach this part of the room. Also the ceremony takes place too quickly, and the visitor has to appear with lowered head and must leave again without lifting his face to look at his majesty.[18]

The shogunate thus displayed a shrewd understanding of behavioural psychology in the calculated use of light and dark for maximum dramatic effect in shogunal audience. This Tokugawa palace anticipates by many years advice given to architects today as a result of modern behavioural studies:

> the places which make effective settings are defined by light. . . . People are by nature phototropic – they move toward light, and, when stationary, they orient themselves toward the light. . . . Create alternating areas of light and dark throughout the building, in such a way that people naturally walk toward the light, whenever they are going to important places . . .[19]

The effect of the use of this lighting technique to dramatise the persona of the shogun at Nijō Castle is potent.

More special effects are utilised in the Gedan no ma to impress the daimyo at the lower end of the audience hall. The pine trees painted on the sliding

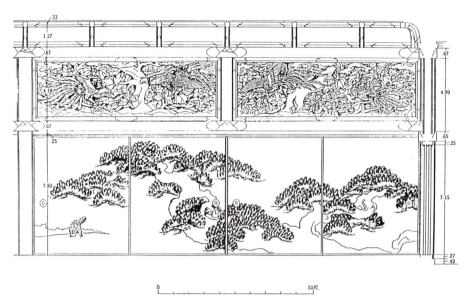

Fig 6.9
Nijō Castle.
Palace of the
Second
Compound.
Ōhiroma.
Elevation of
the east wall
of the Gedan
no ma (lower
chamber)
(Source: Ōta
Hirotarō *et al.*,
*Nihon
kenchikushi kiso
shiryō shūsei*)

screens of the inner wall are surmounted in the transom area by two of the most remarkable openwork friezes ever conceived in the whole of Japanese artistic history (Figure 6.9). They show two pairs of frolicking peacocks, tails spread in full glory, beneath the aggressively curving trunks of large pines and amidst a veritable garden of peonies. Every detail is highlighted by rich colour and gilding. These sculptural masterworks turn the upper levels of the wall into a three-dimensional paradise. Whatever the rhetorical advantage of associating the shogun with paradise, no-one present in that lower chamber could have failed to be impressed by the sheer artistic genius at the command of the *bakufu*.

The third chamber, set at right angles and off-axis to the two main rooms, allowed the shogun to view Nō drama on the stage which had been originally situated in the garden in front of the Ōhiroma building. On these occasions of more private entertainment no doubt the Ōhiroma took on a more relaxed atmosphere.[20]

The fourth building in the palace complex is the Kuroshoin. It was originally known as the Kohiroma, or 'small hiroma' to distinguish it from Ōhiroma (Figure 6.10). It was used for audiences between the shogun and the *fudai daimyō*. These daimyo were the related or hereditary vassals of the Tokugawa. In the 1620s, when the palace buildings were constructed, they were being accorded a degree of collegial courtesy which contrasted sharply with the policies towards the *tozama daimyō* and the more peremptory treatment they were to receive a decade later with the tightening of Tokugawa controls. The Kuroshoin and the Ōhiroma audience chambers are a study in contrasts. The Kuroshoin building is separated from the Ōhiroma by an enclosed cloister which emphasises in physical separation the difference in status between the trusted and the doubted. The architectural vocabulary is identical to that

of the Ōhiroma, but the artistic nuance is dramatically different, less intimidating in scale and decoration with much of the gold replaced by more restrained black lacquer surfaces. The audience chamber is 16.10 metres in length, just two-thirds the length of the Ōhiroma, but the width is approximately the same (the Jōdan no ma is 7.49 metres wide and the second chamber or Ni no ma is 9.63 metres) (Figure 6.11). The spatial dynamics of the chambers are, therefore, entirely different in character, with the *fudai daimyō* audience considerably closer to the shogun, both physically and psychologically. This effect was enhanced by the simple expedient of placing the *tatami* mats lengthways down the axis of the chamber in the Jōdan no ma, leading the eye towards the shogun and further shortening with the strong orthogonal lines of their satin edge-bindings the sense of distance between the shogun and the daimyo. In the Ōhiroma the *tatami* mats are placed sideways, each of the woven edge-bindings accentuating in linear progression the sense of separation between ruler and ruled. Moreover there is no separate coved and coffered ceiling above the normal seating position for the shogun. The Kuroshoin has no transom sculpture in the second chamber and the paintings on the gold-leafed walls are entirely different in symbolic content and emotional tenor. The end wall of the tokonoma retains a painting of the powerful pine tree, but it is less menacing in scale. It is accompanied on the flanking walls of the second

Fig 6.10 Nijō Castle. Palace of the Second Compound. Kuroshoin chambers (Courtesy of Nijōjō)

153

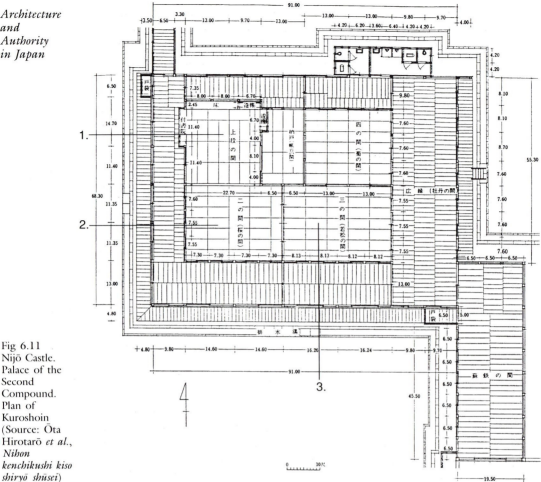

Fig 6.11
Nijō Castle.
Palace of the
Second
Compound.
Plan of
Kuroshoin
(Source: Ōta
Hirotarō *et al.,*
*Nihon
kenchikushi kiso
shiryō shūsei*)

1. Jōdan no ma ('upper chamber')
2. Ni no ma ('second chamber'). Also known as Sakura no ma ('Cherry Tree chamber')
3. San no ma ('third chamber'). Also known as Wakamatsu no ma ('Young Pine Tree chamber')

chamber, not by the starkly strong form of more pines in uncompromising stances, but by the softly optimistic double-flowered cherry trees in the magic moment of their full flowering.[21] Small swallows flit amongst the petals while pheasants sit contentedly beneath the spreading pink canopy above. All is quiet, untroubled, in this the spring-time of Tokugawa rule. The air is full of the promise of a glorious summer to come. Even the term Gedan no ma, or 'lower chamber', implying subservient status, has been studiously avoided; it is referred to merely as the 'Cherry Tree chamber' or simply 'the second chamber'. It is ironic that it was in this suite of chambers that the last Tokugawa shogun, Yoshinobu, formally announced to the emperor his return of the title of *shōgun* in 1867.[22]

To the rear of the Kuroshoin is the fifth and final building in the progression from formal audience chambers to private retreat. The Shiroshoin served as the private suite and sleeping quarters for the shogun during his periods of residence in Kyoto. While observing the basic form of *shoin* architecture, it is fundamentally different in aesthetic character from the remainder of the palace buildings. Comprising four small *tatami* rooms it is separated from the Kuroshoin by a covered corridor, in the same manner as the Kuroshoin and the Ōhiroma are also set apart physically and psychologically. The walls and sliding screens are decorated with subdued monochromatic ink paintings. Gold leaf, ubiquitous throughout rest of the palace complex, is not used, in keeping with the quieter mood. It is easy to imagine the difficulties of sleeping in a chamber with highly light-reflective, gilded walls. The scenes are predominantly of landscapes such as bamboo in the snow with swallows sleeping, feathers fluffed, on the naked branches of winter trees. Chinese-style landscapes in the Southern Song mode, with rocky outcrops and distant mountains, are peopled solely by diminutive figures of sages. This is the only part of the entire palace complex where sages appear, their didactic call for virtue and benevolence on the part of rulers kept discreetly away from the daimyo. Even the ubiquitous pine trees in these landscapes are a contented and passive part of nature, not aggressively reaching out into the domain of human relations as they do elsewhere in the palace buildings.

The Architectural Strategy of the Palace at Nijō Castle

The Palace of the Second Compound was conceived as a series of chambers each carefully designed to achieve a specific political purpose and grouped together to maximise political effect. The grouping of structurally independent buildings along a stepped receding axis is a standard design feature of *shoin* architecture. It allowed a view of the garden from at least two sides of each building. In terms of behavioural psychology it had the advantage over a symmetrical plan, favoured for the Chinese-influenced buildings of the Nara and Heian periods, of permitting a high degree of visual isolation for each building. This heightened the importance of each separate building and provided opportunity for effective use of a sequence of partial revelations for intensifying the dramatic effect of progressing through the building. It was a device which delighted in the unexpected – the corridors flanking the audience chambers turn sharply, denying any indication of what might lie in store around the next corner. This design technique afforded considerable potential for segregating different groups of visitors according to status, and created a hierarchical progression of spaces throughout the building.

This progression was dramatically emphasised by a comprehensive programme of decoration, which as we have seen, drew on all the visual arts from painting and sculpture to filigree metalwork and polished lacquer. The rhetorical use of spatial escalation, from chambers of less importance to chambers of greater significance, was in common use in palace architecture of the early Edo period. Rodrigo de Vivero y Velasco, in a detailed record of his audience with Hidetada at Edo Castle in 1609, reveals:

Next we came to the first apartment of the palace. . . . On the floor they have what is called *tatami*, a sort of beautiful matting trimmed with cloth of gold, satin and velvet, embroidered with many gold flowers. . . . The walls and ceilings are covered with wooden panelling and decorated with various paintings of hunting scenes, done in gold, silver and other colours, so that the wood itself is not visible. . . . Although in our opinion this first compartment left nothing to be desired, the second chamber was finer, while the third was even more splendid; and the further we proceeded, the greater the wealth and novelty that met our eyes.[23]

We have seen this rhetorical device used to full effect at Nijō Castle. It is not, however, a uniquely Japanese approach to the architecture of authority. Although the building design and the iconographic nuances of the paintings and sculpture are culturally specific to Japan, the way architecture and its allied arts are articulated at Nijō Castle is similar to the strategy employed in European palaces such as the Doge's Palace in Venice and Frederick the Great's beloved palace of Sans Souci near Potsdam. Like Nijō Castle, these palaces employ a hierarchical sequence of chambers, starting with a vestibule and anteroom and continuing with a series of state apartments and private apartments. The growing importance of the chambers is signalled by increasing size and by a carefully planned escalation in the level of gilded ornament. Louis XIV may have found the overall size of the palace chambers at Nijō Castle small, and perhaps been upset by the absence of mirrors, but he would surely have appreciated the gilded walls and the uncompromising bombast of the Ōhiroma. And the use of different levels of floor and seating for persons of different status is a universal feature of the rarefied world of protocol and ritual authority. At the Enthronement Ceremony for the Heisei Emperor, held on 12 November 1990, the Prime Minister stood below the level of the Emperor, although on top of the enthronement dais itself as the representative of a more democratic nation, not at the base of the steps as was the case in the Meiji ceremony. The Tokugawa and their artists would doubtless have derived satisfaction from the fact that this ceremony took place in the Pine Room of the Imperial Palace.

The palace of Nijō Castle was architecture as theatre, from the drama of the progression through the chambers to the climax in the Ōhiroma where special lighting effects emphasise the authority of the principal player, the shogun. The pine trees in the tokonoma form a backdrop painted with the boldness and power of projection of a stage set. In fact the figure of the shogun would have been set amidst a veritable forest of pine trees, raising the interesting possibility that there was a direct input from contemporary Nō drama in the staging and iconography of Nijō Castle.

The relationship of Tokugawa ritual audience to drama is as yet an unexplored field of research but the evidence for a connection is considerable. The warrior class had been enthusiastic patrons of Nō from the time of the Ashikaga shogunate. We ourselves have seen that Nobunaga made special provision for a stage in the *tenshu* of Azuchi Castle. We know that this was an age in which it was *de rigueur* for a warrior of any standing to be able to recite whole scenes from the masterpieces of Zeami.[24] Moreover, Tokugawa documents reveal that Nō provided the framework for the official *onari* visits by Iemitsu upon the daimyo from the time he became shogun in 1623, with ceremonies of fealty and obeisance organised between acts of Nō plays.[25] Plans of daimyo and shogunal palaces, including the palace at Nijō Castle at the time of its completion in 1626, show that they were invariably equipped with a Nō stage facing the ōhiroma. Looked at from the stand-point of drama it is recognised that the design of the Nō stage was formalised and largely standardised as a result of the strong patronage of the warrior establishment in the first decades of Tokugawa rule.[26] A large pine-tree painting on plain wooden panels became standard on the rear wall of the stage, symbolising the association of Nō performance with outdoor settings amongst pine trees, particularly in its early form as practiced in shrines such as Kasuga Shrine at Nara.[27] It is likely that the design of the formal entertainment chambers of palaces such as those at Nijō Castle was influenced by its association with Nō. The exterior Nō stage was as much a feature of ōhiroma design as the tokonoma was in the interior (Figure 6.12). *Shōmei*, the design treatise completed in 1609 by the Heinouchi master builders, includes the stage as part of audience hall design and even stipulates that its proportions should be the same as those of the main chamber.[28] It seems probable that the design of both stage and hiroma evolved together under a warrior patronage which placed highest importance on the architectural setting for formal entertainment. Under these circumstances Iemitsu would have naturally translated his aspirations to manifest authority in tangible terms at the palace at Nijō Castle into the same iconography of built form as used for the Nō stage, including the use of the pine tree with its deep religious connotation.

The effect of these chambers on the perception and exercise of authority is apparent in the way in which the place of audience became synonymous with status in the Tokugawa order. In official documents the daimyo were referred to by the name of the chamber in which they were received into shogunal audience at Edo Castle, such as the Teikan no ma, used for most *fudai daimyō*, and Yanagi no ma, used for *tozama daimyō* below 50,000 *koku* in rank.[29] The Tokugawa had succeeded in setting each daimyo in his appropriate place, and place therefore became the definition of person.

The Palaces at Nijō and Edo Castles: Monumental Matrix for Authority

Although physically situated in Kyoto, the Palace of the Second Compound of Nijō Castle belongs architecturally and politically alongside the palaces of Edo Castle and the *onari* palaces built by the daimyo to receive the shogun in the manner to which he was accustomed. None of the shogunal and daimyo palaces of Edo survives but they are depicted in the *Edozu byōbu* as sumptuous establishments in landscaped gardens, immediately calling to mind the palace of Nijō Castle (Figure 6.13). The main palace of Edo Castle is shown in the inner compound of the castle immediately adjacent to the *tenshu*. The buildings are depicted as having the blue-tiled roofs familiar from Azuchi Castle, and soaring rooflines are accentuated by filigree ornament and gilded sculpture. They are interconnected and are surrounded by the high stone walls of the castle. The palaces of the daimyo are also shown, aligned in

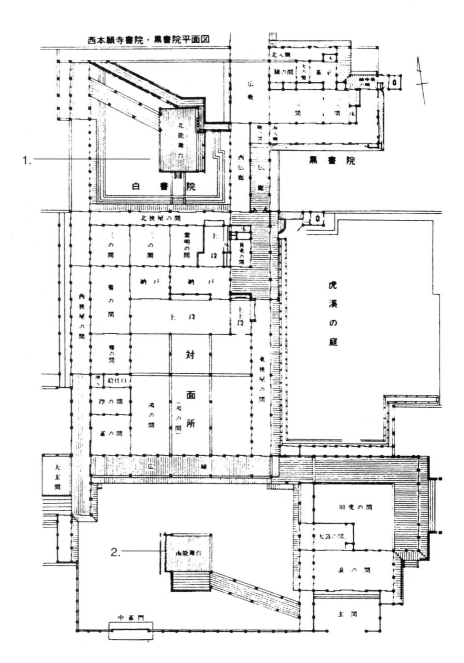

Fig 6.12
Nishi
Honganji.
Shiroshoin and
Kuroshoin.
Plan showing
location of Nō
stages
(Source:
Fujioka
Michio, *Shiro
to Shoin*)

1. Shiroshoin stage (1581. Moved to present location in 1897)
2. Kuroshoin stage (*ca.* 1632)

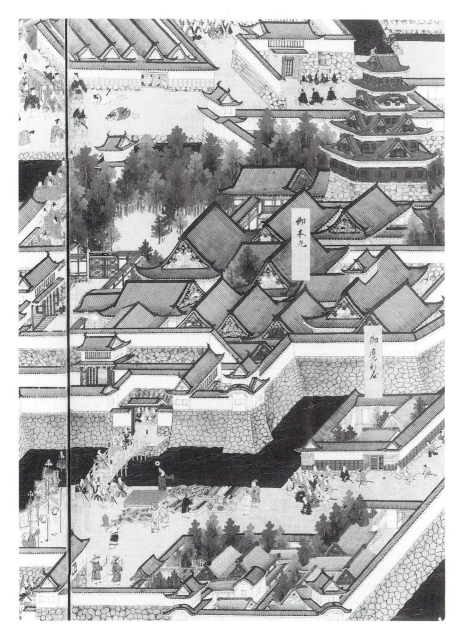

御本丸

御鷹部屋

Fig 6.13
Edozu byōbu.
Pair of six-fold
screens. Detail
of right screen
showing *tenshu*
and palace
buildings of
Edo Castle
(Courtesy of
National
Museum of
Japanese
History,
Sakura)

159

powerful array around the castle, similar in style and only slightly more modest in appearance than the palace buildings of the shogunate itself.

The Edo palaces appear to be largely identical in style to the palace of Nijō Castle. This similarity is confirmed by comparison with an important Edo-period architectural source, the *Kōra Memorandum*, the family record of the Kōra, official master builders to the *bakufu*. It was compiled by the hereditary head of the household, Kōra Munetoshi, after his retirement from active building practice in 1703. As we have seen, the Kōra became the most important family of master builders in the service of the shogunate, responsible for the rebuilding of the *tenshu* of Edo Castle in 1638.[30] The descriptions of buildings in their family records are accordingly terse, technical and detailed, clearly based on earlier written records and oral traditions.

The *Kōra Memorandum* commences with a description of the Ōhiroma of the Honmaru Palace within Edo Castle. It is described in terms which leave no doubt about its similarity to the Ōhiroma of the palace at Nijō Castle. The difference is simply one of scale, with the Ōhiroma of Edo Castle divided into three levels (*jōdan*, *chūdan* and *gedan*) rather than into the two used at the Kyoto palace.

Other details described in the Kōra document also match those of the Kyoto palace. The gateway set at the entrance of the Nijō palace compound is in the *onarimon* style, the form reserved for reception of the shogun by the daimyo in Edo. The *Kōra Memorandum* describes the typical *onarimon* as 'a large *yotsuashi* (*mon*) [gateway with two principal and four supporting 'leg' pillars] with a *karahafu* set in the front and rear eaves'.[31] The entry to the palace itself, the *kurumayose*, matches exactly the Kōra description of the entrance to the typical daimyo palace in Edo (Figure 6.14):

> The *genkan*, [which was reserved] for the daimyo and his family, was in the same style as [palaces] within [Edo] castle, with the *karahafu* in the eaves set below the front gable. The bays to the left and right [of the entrance] had *kushigata* [oval windows with cusped frames and open-work comb-pattern friezes] and the centre bay had a *karado* [panelled door mounted to swing not slide].[32]

The sequence of chambers within the palace is also identical. The entry led to the 'Tōzamurai, Shikidai, and the Ōhiroma . . . [which had a] Jōdan with *nagaoshi-ita* [the tokonoma], *tana* [*chigaidana* shelving], flanked by *chōdai* [decorated doors leading to the Jōdan] . . .'.[33] This description in fact establishes the existence of a high degree of standardisation of building organisation and interior decoration in the early Edo-period palaces as a result of the needs of formalised ritual.

The *Edozu byōbu* and the *Kōra Memorandum* therefore link Nijō Castle to the broad genre of palace architecture in Edo city, the palaces built by the shogunate within the walls of Edo Castle, and to the palaces built by the daimyo in the vicinity of the castle for the purpose of receiving the shogun on state visits or *onari*. Further evidence of this relationship is furnished by a set of preliminary paintings prepared by Kano Seisen'in (1796–1846) for the 1845 rebuilding of the Honmaru Palace. They are scaled drawings highlighted with light colour washes which show the decoration proposed for each chamber. These paintings are very similar to those of Nijō Castle, with the

Fig 6.14
Nijō Castle.
Palace of the
Second
Compound.
Entrance and
side transom
with *kushigata*
(comb-pattern)
frieze

proposed Ōhiroma decorated with pine trees, their massive trunks sprawling defiantly across the framing of the chambers in exactly the same manner as do the pine trees of the Ōhiroma at Nijō Castle.[34] These similarities should not surprise us as the official Kano artists played a powerful role in standardising the iconography and style of official *bakufu* painting.

As a result of the destruction of the Edo palaces by fire, the Palace of the Second Compound of Nijō Castle is the best-preserved example of the rhetorical style of *shoin* architecture as perfected in the political climate of seventeenth-century Edo. The Tokugawa palace at Kyoto not only represents those Edo palaces destroyed by fire; it anticipated and undoubtedly influenced the style in which the palace of Edo Castle was to be rebuilt a decade later. In 1637 Iemitsu commissioned the complete rebuilding of the Honmaru Palace, a rather simple building dating to 1604–1607, at the same time as he ordered the Kōra to rebuild the *tenshu* built for Hidetada. None of these buildings survives except in memory, but today at Nijō Castle we may still see, indeed experience, the effects of the full panoply of Tokugawa architectural devices designed to convince and coerce as well as to amaze and inspire.

At Nijō Castle, as eloquent as it seems effortless, we can find demonstrated the quintessential Tokugawa art of psychological intimidation using architecture as the tool. Simultaneously the Tokugawa were adept at avoiding any implications that might be unfortunate for their own government. While the transoms of gateway and entrance are full of didactic images of sages exercising good government, there is not a single sage visible within the formal audience chambers of the palace to invoke any awkward reminders of the responsibility of government to the governed.

Tokugawa Mausolea 7

Intimations of Immortality and the Architecture of Posthumous Authority

At the same time as the Tokugawa were establishing a working definition of their authority in relation to the power of the daimyo below and the prerogatives of the imperial institution above, they sought to elevate the temporal powers at their command to the plane of spiritual authority. This is a strategy now familiar to us from study of Emperor Shōmu with Tōdaiji and Nobunaga with Azuchi Castle. The key to this theocratic strategy was architectural, even more manifest than it was in relation to the daimyo and the court, for it is in dealing with the divine that architecture most convincingly makes tangible that which is intangible. The construction of spectacular mausolea, dedicated to their predecessors in shogunal office, offered the Tokugawa family a religious means to the secular end of enhancing the political legitimacy of its government.

Funerary monuments ranging from the Egyptian pyramids to Michelangelo's Tomb of Julius ll, and from the Ming tombs to the Tokugawa mausolea, have served both spiritual and secular ends. This is further evidence of the inappropriateness of making modern distinctions between the secular and the sacred when analysing authority. The Tokugawa were able to exploit fully the political advantage of paying pious homage to the deceased in order to sanctify the power of the living by an unprecedented programme of mausoleum construction. The Tokugawa mausolea, or *reibyō*, created an aura of divine authority around the Tokugawa shogunate, in particular the founding shogun Ieyasu who was now elevated to the status of a Shinto deity and worshipped at a special shrine dedicated to his spirit. Ieyasu's deathbed wish was that 'his remains were to be interred at Mt Kunō, the funeral rites to be offered at Zōjōji . . . and, after the passing of one full year, a small hall was to be built at Nikkō. The shogun's will is that he thus become the tutelary deity of Japan (*Yashima no chinju*).'[1] Ieyasu's last will and testament was drafted with the advice of those present at his last audience, particularly his religious advisers, Sūden, abbot of Konchiin at Nanzenji, and Tenkai, abbot of Rinnōji, the Tendai sect temple at Nikkō. However, it was not until the reign of the third shogun Iemitsu that mausoleum construction was to assume its special character and significance to the shogunate.

Two mausolea were of preeminent political importance to the apotheosis of Tokugawa authority, namely, the Taitokuin Reibyō, which inaugurated Iemitsu's personal rule, and the Nikkō Tōshōgū, with which it culminated. The Taitokuin mausoleum was dedicated to the second Tokugawa shogun

Hidetada, and built in 1632 by his successor Iemitsu at Shiba in Edo, while the Tōshōgū, dedicated to the founding shogun Ieyasu, was completely rebuilt under the direction of Iemitsu in 1634–1636. With these two projects the Tokugawa compulsion to build architectural monuments to its own authority became a magnificent obsession.

It is necessary to study the two mausolea projects in relation to each other because there was a natural progression in architectural style, building organisation and Tokugawa ideology between them. The Nikkō Tōshōgū is probably the best known but least understood work of Japanese architecture. The Modernists' dislike of ornamentation had the unfortunate scholarly consequence of academic neglect of Nikkō, while the destruction of the Taitokuin Reibyō in 1945 by Allied bombing divorced Nikkō from its true architectural lineage and political succession. The authority of the Tōshōgū emanates from the architecture and political circumstances of the Taitokuin mausoleum. It is appropriate to say *kekkō* at Nikkō only after making proper intellectual obeisance at Shiba.

The Taitokuin Mausoleum

The Taitokuin mausoleum was situated on the southeastern side of the precincts of Zōjōji, the Tokugawa family temple at Shiba. The main construction was completed in less than a year, a feat of some significance for a project of such complexity.

'Taitokuin' was the priestly name Hidetada adopted when he resigned as shogun in 1622. It is a Buddhist name meaning 'the eminence of virtue'. It suggested that henceforth he would abjure involvement in the affairs of this world, though in reality this was far from the case. After his death a decade later, Hidetada's mausoleum took his religious name.

The general architectural form and many of the decorative details of the Taitokuin mausoleum may be reconstructed from the *Edozu byōbu*, the official records compiled at the time of construction, and from a technical survey completed before the destruction of the site during World War II. In addition several of the gateways which guarded the approaches to the mausoleum are extant today, but in locations far removed in space and spirit from their original position. Each of these sources furnishes invaluable information about the lost buildings, but each has its own limitations.

The pair of six-fold screens of the *Edozu byōbu* provide a panoramic view of the site as it must have existed in the seventeenth century (Figure 7.1). The left screen shows the Taitokuin complex, in a great panoply of splendour, lying to the immediate left of the principal buildings of the Zōjōji. The main building consists of three separate but physically integrated structures: the Haiden, or worship hall at the front, linked by an enclosed chamber known as the Ainoma (the 'in-between room') or Ishinoma (because of the stone flagging originally used for the floor) to the Honden, or main hall at the rear. This complicated building mode is known as *gongen-zukuri*, a term wished upon us long after the creation of the architectural form to which it refers.[2] Structurally it was based on the Buddhist temple hall, with strong

timber-framing and multiple-arm cantilevered bracket sets supporting the eaves, but stylistically it was based on Shinto architecture. It was a shrine where Shinto rites were conducted and the arrangement of structures was based on the Hachiman shrine form which originated in the Nara period.[3] Buildings such as the Usa Hachimangū in Kyushu, an Edo-period rebuilding of a Nara-period shrine, show its features clearly, with the main hall and worship hall set parallel to each other. The Haiden was used for performance of the various ceremonies connected with the worship at the shrine. The space between the buildings covered by the roof overhead was gradually incorporated into the ritual space of the interior. The composite structure thereby created was eventually appropriated as a mausoleum building.

The Taitokuin, as depicted in the *Edozu byōbu*, unmistakably displays the characteristics of this style. The Honden is a two-roofed structure which towers over the Haiden at the front with its elaborately intersecting roof planes; the Haiden and Honden are each covered by a hip-gable roof abutting a simple gable roof over the Ishinoma. A small 'lean-to' roof (*kōhai*) is set above the main steps at the front of the Haiden to protect from the elements worshippers making simple oblations. The eaves' line is accentuated by a gracefully flowing cusped gable (*karahafu*). The walls and gables are bedecked with gold and there is a profusion of polychrome sculptural ornament beneath the upper-level eaves of the Honden. From the depiction in the *Edozu byōbu* it is clear that this was a building of such size and

Fig 7.1
Edozu byōbu. Pair of six-fold screens. Detail of left screen showing Taitokuin mausoleum (Courtesy of National Museum of Japanese History, Sakura)

165

splendour that it was rivalled in Edo only by the castle keep itself and the most important palaces at the centre of the city.

Walls and gates set the Taitokuin precincts apart from the city to the south and the Zōjōji to the east. The main southern approach is shown as guarded by a moat and high wall. A second wall of wooden palings and protective roof subdivides the grounds into two courtyards, while a delicately latticed wall with a cypress-bark roof protects the inner sanctum. Gateways, each distinct in character, stand watch at each of these walls. The gateway in the outer wall has a tiled roof with a *karahafu* set into its front eaves to greet the visitor and warn the intruder. The next gateway, providing entry through the paling wall, has a cypress-shingle roof, indicating a more private mood, but it is crowned by a ridge-pole decorated with gold-inlaid lacquer to heighten the sense of impending majesty of the inner sanctum. The third and most inner gateway, set into the latticed wall before the Haiden steps, is decorated by *karahafu* at both front and sides, a virtuoso technical performance by carpenters and roof-shinglers which provides an unprecedented rhetorical flourish to the entry to the inner precinct. Only at the Tōshōgū of Nikkō may a gateway of similar curvilinear exuberance be found.

It is clear from the disposition of walls and gateways shown in the painting that access to the mausoleum was restricted to a privileged few. Outside the main entrance sit the servants and dignitaries accompanying some shogunal visitor. The mausoleum precincts are virtually deserted except for some dozen figures in distinguished garb, surely high-ranking shogunal retainers, sitting outside the inner precinct, and four white-clad figures, presumably priestly acolytes, in attendance beside the steps of the Haiden. All that would have been visible of the mausoleum to the humble populace of Edo were the outer wall and gateway, and the upper storey of the Honden, which doubtless explains the rhetorical crescendo it reaches in the decoration of its elevated eaves and ridge. This glimpse would have been sufficient, however, to excite the imagination and sharpen the sense of status separation between shogunal plane and commoner.

On the rising ground to the left of the main complex there stands an octagonal two-storey hall with gateways and subsidiary building in front. A five-storey pagoda is located further to the left. Minor buildings are also shown in the main part of the complex while another mausoleum, similar in style but smaller in scale, is situated immediately adjacent to the east boundary wall. Altogether the Taitokuin Reibyō is strikingly similar to the Nikkō mausoleum, from the general organisation of the various precincts to the architectural character of the elaborately decorated *gongen-zukuri* buildings, including details such as the multiple *karahafu* on the inner gateway.

A report published in 1934 by the Tokyo City Government, based on a comprehensive survey of the mausoleum complex as it stood at Shiba a decade prior to its destruction,[4] is the most reliable source for evaluating the accuracy of the depiction of the Taitokuin complex in the *Edozu byōbu*. This survey includes extensive technical descriptions, photographs, site plans, and measured elevations of the main *gongen* building. It was compiled under the supervision of Tanabe Yasushi, then an Associate Professor at Waseda University.[5]

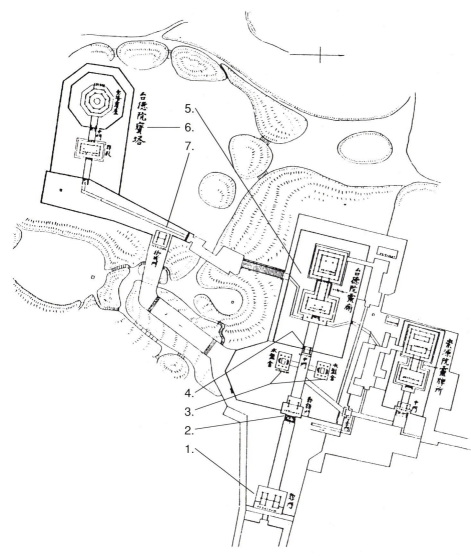

台德院寶塔

台德院霊廟

崇源院霊廟

Fig 7.2
Plan of
Taitokuin
mausoleum
prior to
destruction in
1945
(Source:
Tōkyō-fu (ed.)
*Tōkyō-fu shiseki
hozonbutsu
hōkokusho*, vol.
11)

1. Sōmon (main outer gateway)
2. Chokugakumon (second or 'imperial inscription' gateway)
3. Suibansha (sacred ablutions pavilions)
4. Chūmon (inner gateway)

5. Main building
6. Okuin (inner precinct)
7. Onarimon (gateway for shogunal visitation)

The detailed site plan in the Tanabe report clearly identifies by name the buildings shown in the painting (Figure 7.2). The gateways are identified as the Sōmon or main outer gateway, the Chokugakumon or second gateway, and the Chūmon or inner gateway. These *mon* are aligned axially and orientated eastwards. Two *suibansha*, or sacred ablution pavilions, flank the approach between the second and inner gateway. Unfortunately Tanabe's plan does not incorporate a scale but, judging by the dimensions of the main

167

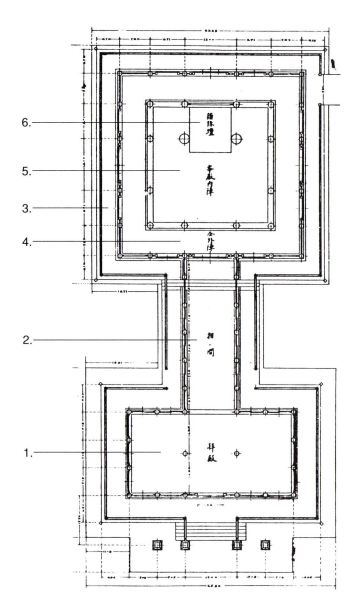

Fig 7.3
Main building
of Taitokuin
mausoleum.
Plan prior to
destruction in
1945
(Source:
Tōkyō-fu (ed.)
*Tōkyō-fu shiseki
hozonbutsu
hōkokusho*, vol.
11)

1. Haiden (worship hall)
2. Ishi no ma or Ai no ma (stone-floored chamber or intermediate chamber)
3. Honden (main hall)
4. Gejin (outer sanctuary)
5. Naijin (inner sanctuary)
6. Shumidan (altar)

building supplied in the report, the distance between the Sōmon and the Chūmon was approximately 100 metres.

The group of buildings to the south of the main complex form the Okuin, or inner precinct, in which Hidetada's remains were interred. It comprises a Hōtō or Reliquary Hall, with a Chūmon and Haiden situated in front. Tanabe's report reveals that the nearby pagoda belonged to the Zōjōji and was constructed prior to the Taitokuin Reibyō. Access to the Okuin was by a path leading from the left of the open court area in the vicinity of the *suibansha*. The Onarimon, or gateway reserved for official visits by the shogun, provided the ceremonial entrance.

There is general agreement between Tanabe's plan and the arrangement of buildings shown in the *Edozu byōbu*, although the painting shows the path to the Okuin as running directly from the main compound via a steep stairway crowned by the Onarimon. Tanabe's plan places the Onarimon on a second path which branches off near the *suibansha*.

The plan and elevation of the *gongen-zukuri* building as shown in Tanabe's report, including the masonry base, have a total length of about 132 *shaku* (approx. 40 metres – one *shaku* equalling approx. 30.3 cm), and the Honden rises to a height of some 53 *shaku* (approx. 16 metres) (Figures 7.3–7.4). The Haiden is five bays wide and three bays deep, surmounted by a hip-gable roof covered with *dōbuki-ita* or copper-sheet tiling. The Ishi no ma is one bay wide and five deep with a simple gable roof also of *dōbuki-ita*. The Honden is square in plan, five bays wide and deep. Although the exterior has the appearance of a two-storey structure because of its two roofs, as noted earlier, Tanabe's sectional drawing of the Honden reveals that the interior was a large, soaring space with corbelled roof (Figure 7.4). It was divided into an inner sanctuary (*naijin*) with the altar (*shumidan*) set against the rear wall, and an outer sanctuary (*gejin*).

This prewar record, together with other photographs held by the Cultural Affairs Agency, confirm the accuracy of the general representation of the main buildings as shown in the *Edozu byōbu*, except that a large triangular gable (*chidorihafu*) was set into the front of the Haiden roof. Combined with the cusped gable (*karahafu*) on the lean-to roof over the steps, this gave the building much stronger frontal emphasis than is indicated by the painting. Even more significantly, the artist of the *Edozu byōbu* painted the Honden sideways, with the ridge aligned with the Ishinoma instead of at right angles, as shown in the Tanabe survey (compare Figures 7.4 and 7.5). It will be recalled that the artist also had difficulty with the gables on the *tenshu* of Edo Castle.

The prewar Tanabe report also offers more detailed architectural information than does the Edo-period painting. In the photographs and elevations, important stylistic differences may be discerned between the Haiden and Ishi no ma on the one hand, and the Honden on the other (Figure 7.5). The Honden is built in the Song-inspired curvilinear style known as Zenshūyō, introduced to Japan in the Kamakura period and seen in its full glory at the Jizodō of Shōfukuji. Like this temple building the Honden has strongly curved tie-beams, chamfered pillar heads, and multiple arm bracket sets tightly clustered under the eaves. By contrast, the Ishi no ma and Haiden are predominantly Wayō in

Fig 7.4
Taitokuin
mausoleum.
Side elevation
and section of
main building
prior to
destruction in
1945 (Kōhai
and Haiden at
right, Honden
at left)
(Source:
Tōkyō-fu (ed.)
*Tōkyō-fu shiseki
hozonbutsu
hōkokusho*, vol.
11)

form, the older, more rectilinear style of Nara-period temple buildings. The wall frames are braced laterally by the external, non-penetrating ties known as *nageshi*, and the bracket sets are set directly above the pillars with the intercolumnar support provided by *kaerumata* or 'frog-leg'-shaped wooden fascias. In contrast, the Honden bracket sets have the tighter Zenshūyō profile and the corner sets are penetrated diagonally by double *odaruki* – cantilever arms which greatly enhance their load-carrying capacity. Intercolumnar support is given by additional bracket sets in the typical Zenshūyō manner. The Honden has other Zenshūyō features such as *katōmado* or cusped windows, and *sankarado*, or panelled doors which swing open. On the other hand, the Haiden is equipped with *shitomido*, the typical Wayō horizontally placed shutters, and *mairado*, or sliding doors with tightly grouped horizontal battens.

The *Edozu byōbu* is not sufficiently detailed to permit close comparisons of architectural detail with the information provided by the Tanabe Report and prewar photographs but it does serve to establish the visual impact of the decoration, particularly the colour scheme which is not, of course, indicated by the black and white photographs. The pillars of the Haiden are black with gold detailing, those of the Honden are red. The bracket sets throughout the building are shown as green, red, gold and black. The ridge-courses are a glossy black with gold detailing, assuredly dazzling all who viewed the buildings from afar on a sunny day.

The *Edozu byōbu* and the photographs contained in both the Tanabe Report and 1965 Report make it clear that the buildings were alive with an impressive profusion of applied ornament (Figure 7.5). *Karajishi*, mythological lions, are set above the pillars, and other unidentifiable creatures thrust forward as carved nosings on the cantilever arms of the multiple bracket sets of the Zenshūyō system of the Honden. Dragons frolic along the outer eaves purlin which carry the rafters, their mouths open and tongues licking viciously. In addition to this record of the appearance of the main Taitokuin buildings, three of the four gateways, or *mon*, which guarded the various precincts of the mausoleum, have survived the conflagration of the main buildings in 1945 by virtue of their physical separation. These are the two outer gateways on the

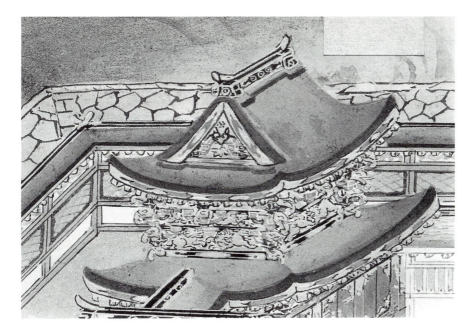

Fig 7.5
Edozu byōbu.
Pair of six-fold
screens. Detail
of left screen
showing
Taitokuin
mausoleum.
Detail of upper
eaves and roof
of Honden
(Courtesy of
National
Museum of
Japanese
History,
Sakura)

main approach, the Sōmon and the Chokugakumon, and the Onarimon which protected the inner precinct on the hill behind. In 1959 the Sōmon was moved some 100 metres east of its original site within the Zōjōji precinct, and the other two gateways, together with the Sōgen'in gateway, were dismantled in 1960 to allow for the implementation of development plans at Shiba Park. These *mon* were all reassembled as part of Fudōji, in Tokorozawa, Saitama prefecture, in 1972.

The recent discovery of a detailed scale model of the main buildings of the Taitokuin mausoleum in dismantled form in the Royal Collections, London, has provided an additional source of information about the destroyed structures. The model was commissioned for the Japan–British Exhibition of 1910 by the Municipal Government of Tokyo and reproduces in exquisite detail the architecture and decoration of the original buildings. There has not as yet been opportunity to analyse the model directly but it clearly corroborates our existing knowledge of the architecture of Taitokuin and offers significant scope for re-establishing the details of the copious wood-carvings, gilding and lacquer work which so animated the original buildings.[6]

The Edo-period screens, the prewar architectural survey, the 1910 model and the extant gateways establish beyond doubt that Zenshūyō was the style favoured for the most important building of the Taitokuin mausoleum. This showed a new preference by the shogunate under Iemitsu for the exuberantly curvilinear forms originally introduced to Japan in the Kamakura period. There was also a wealth of applied ornament, similar in subject matter and style to the decorative programmes used on the contemporary palaces and mansions of Edo, and anticipating the later Nikkō mausoleum.

The extant gateways emphasise the dramatic impact the main Taitokuin building must have had in the Edo period, combining energetically curved structural and roofing effects with exuberantly polychromed sculpture in the round. They reveal not only the subtle domination of Zenshūyō features but also close similarities with the host of magnificent ceremonial gateways which bejewelled the outer walls of shogunal and daimyo palaces in Edo.

The Builders of the Taitokuin Mausoleum

There is a common belief current about Japanese architecture that the building traditions which created it were anonymous and that the individual was subsumed within a group identity. Building forms are consequently interpreted in broad categories of style such as Wayō and Zenshūyō or as specific modes such as *gongen-zukuri*. These terms are only useful to the extent that they indicate collections of commonly held characteristics and are the accepted nomenclature of the field. Moreover they are historical afterthoughts, similar to terms such as 'Classical', 'Romanesque' and 'Gothic' in common usage for Western architecture. In recent years it has proved more useful to examine the contribution of architects as individuals or, in the case of customary building traditions, to identify the characteristic contributions of families of master artisans.

Different design traditions become clear from the analysis of the Taitokuin records and extant gateways in the preceding section. Their varying formal characteristics reflect the different hereditary skills and artistic preferences of the particular personalities of craftsmen and artists chosen by the *bakufu* to build the mausoleum. It is therefore essential for a full understanding of the architecture of Taitokuin to put faces on the architectural personalities who built it.

In 1934, when Tanabe compiled his report on the Taitokuin Reibyō, a stone stele was discovered under the floor of the Honden. On it were inscribed the names and titles of 69 principal participants in the building project, ranging from the Chief Commissioner of Construction to the master craftsmen responsible for each of the major building trades – carpenters to stone-masons, artists to lacquer specialists. This stele is an historical landmark, one of the most detailed sets of attributions in the entire history of Japanese architecture, and it supplies invaluable information about the overall organisation of the building project and the contribution of individual master craftsmen.[7]

According to the stele inscription the major participants were the *zōei sōbugyō* or 'chief commissioner of construction', and the *shimo tōryō* or 'subordinate master carpenters'. The chief commissioner of construction was the official charged with overall responsibility for the administration of the project by the *bakufu*, in modern terms the general manager. The stele states that this was 'Sakura Jijū Fujiwara Tokitomi Toshikatsu'; in other words Doi Toshikatsu (1573–1644), daimyo of Sakura domain in Shimōsa until 1633. This explains the first part of the title inscribed on the stele. The *Kansei chōshū shokafu*, a compendium of genealogies of daimyo and shogunal retainers completed in 1801, records that Doi was 'appointed chief commissioner of the construction of the mausoleum to Taitokuin at Zōjōji' in the second month of 1632, confirming the accuracy of the information given on the stele.[8] Doi was one of the most important daimyo in an official *bakufu* post. He held the position of *toshiyori*, or elder, during Hidetada's lifetime, and

became a *rōjū*, or senior councillor, when this position was created as part
of Iemitsu's reforms of the 1630s. The management of the Taitokuin construction by so important a daimyo is an immediate indication of the importance
Iemitsu attached to this project.

The *shimo tōryō* were the master carpenters who worked under the official
direction of the *onhikan daiku*, or supervising builders. They were the actual
builders of the Taitokuin Reibyō, their central role disguised by the apparatus
of shogunal titles and hierarchy. The stele records that the *shimo tōryō* were:
Kōra Bungo no Kami Munehiro, Heinouchi Echizen no Kami Masanobu,
Kōra Saemon Jō Munetsugu, Kōbō Osakabe Shōho Nobukichi, and Tenma
Izumi no Kami Munetsugu. Little is known about either Kōbō or Tenma.
Kōbō was a member of the Tsuru family workshop and probably a relative
of Osakabe Saemon Kunitsugu, noted for his work in Sendai for the Date
family. Tenma may have been from the Osaka area of the same name and
therefore a collateral branch of the Heinouchi, master builders who had served
the Toyotomi.[9]

The first three names on the list of *shimo tōryō* are Kōra Munehiro, Kōra
Munetsugu and Heinouchi Masanobu. Their involvement in the Taitokuin
building project is of utmost significance in the context of the Edo architectural establishment. In 1641 the same three master carpenters were together
responsible for the rebuilding after fire of the principal Edo palace of the
Owari daimyo family, a collateral branch of the Tokugawa. Kōra Munehiro is
credited in the records of his family with two earlier commissions for *tozama
daimyō*, the Gamō palace *onari* architecture, including its remarkable *onarimon*,
and the enormous tiger and bamboo sculpture on the service building
(*daidokoro*) of the palace of Katō Kiyomasa.[10] The Taitokuin stele establishes
that the same three members of the Kōra and Heinouchi families were the
principal on-site master builders of the Taitokuin mausoleum, indicating that
by 1632 they and their family workshops had become the major force in Edo
architecture, and had relegated the earlier master builders brought by the
Tokugawa to Edo in the 1590s to administrative and supervisory positions.
With the Taitokuin project, the Kōra and Heinouchi had moved from the
periphery of official building practice in Edo, from executing commissions
for *tozama daimyō* such as the Gamō and Katō in the 1620s, to the centre of
bakufu building practice. By 1641, as noted above, they were working on a
Tokugawa palace.

It is possible to analyse the architectural style and decoration of the Taitokuin
buildings from the pictorial and written sources to understand the building
practices of the Kōra and Heinouchi. The Kōra were Zenshūyō specialists,
while the Heinouchi, together with the Tsuru, worked in the Wayō mode.
The following specific correlation between architectural features and workshop practices becomes clear for the first time:

1 The Haiden and Ishinoma of the main building, together with the Sōmon,
  are Wayō in style, suggesting that the Heinouchi and Tsuru, practitioners
  of this mode, were responsible for their construction.[11] The Sōmon is
  extremely close in style to the *sōmon* style prescribed by the Heinouchi in
  Shōmei, the definitive design manual of their family tradition.[12]

173

Fig 7.6
Taitokuin
mausoleum,
Chokugakumon.
Relocated at
Fudōji, Saitama
prefecture in
1972

2 The Zenshūyō features of the Honden indicate strongly that it was built by the Kōra, while the Heinouchi, assisted by the Tsuru, were responsible for the Haiden and Ishinoma, built in Wayō, the preferred style of their family traditions.

The presence of the Kōra in the Taitokuin project also accounts for the notable divergence in the plan of the Honden from the bay pattern observed at the Toyotomi-related mausolea associated with the Heinouchi, such as the Kitano Tenmangū in Kyoto. The Taitokuin Honden is a square structure, five by five bays, significantly different in concept from the rectilinear five by four bay plan used for the main halls of mausolea belonging to the Toyotomi tradition. It has also been shown that the Honden was built directly on the pattern of a Zenshūyō *butsuden*. The Kōra clearly adopted the standard Zenshūyō hall type from their existing family tradition, thereby injecting a new element into the *gongen-zukuri* form. It is interesting to note that the Haiden and Ishinoma also depart from the standard Toyotomi mausoleum plan, the Haiden being narrower and the Ishinoma more elongated. Moreover the consummate mastery of the Zenshūyō idiom evident in the design of the Chokugakumon and Onarimon suggests Kōra authorship, as does the decorative sculpture under their eaves (Figures 7.6 and 7.7). The *tenjin* or heavenly being on the outer gable of the Onarimon in particular has that sureness of touch, delicate detail and grandeur of conception, of the master sculptor (Figure 7.8). In view of Munehiro's reputation as a sculptor evidenced by the bamboo tiger the Katō palace gable, it seems probable that this masterpiece is also the product of his own hand. These conclusions are based on a correlation of the formal features of the Taitokuin buildings with knowledge

Fig 7.7
Taitokuin
mausoleum,
Onarimon.
View from
approach steps.
Relocated at
Fudōji, Saitama
prefecture in
1972

Fig 7.8
Taitokuin
mausoleum,
Onarimon,
gable sculpture
of *tenjin*,
probably by
Kōra
Munehiro.
Relocated at
Fudōji, Saitama
prefecture in
1972

of the technical and stylistic practices of the different carpenters identified by the stele inscription as having been engaged in the construction project. Written evidence from the Kōra family records confirms their accuracy:

> In Kanei 9 [1632] Kasesaemon was ordered to be the chief builder [*tōryō*] of Hidetada's [Taitokuin sama] Butsuden at Zōjōji. Heinouchi Osumi was in charge of the mausoleum [*onbyō*] and Bungo Munehiro was ordered to do all the carvings.[13]

'Kasesaemon', to whom the records refer, was Kōra Munetsugu, son of Munehiro, whose name appears on the Taitokuin stele as 'Kōra Saemon Jō Munetsugu'.[14] The 'butsuden' which the shogunate ordered Munetsugu to construct was the Taitokuin Honden, which took the form of a standard Zenshūyō Buddha Hall.

The Kōra document translated above also attributes the building of a 'mausoleum' to Heinouchi Ōsumi. *Ōsumi no Kami* was the honorific title for Masanobu, head of the Heinouchi, whom the Taitokuin stele refers to as *Echizen no Kami*. The Kōra account uses the honorific 'Ōsumi no kami' which was granted to Masanobu later in his career, probably in recognition of his services at the Taitokuin project.

The 'mausoleum' referred to in the document is the tabernacle containing Hidetada's remains. The prewar photographs of the Okuin show that this Hōtō was built in Zenshūyō and was virtually identical with the Honden constructed by Kōra Munetsugu. It seems likely, therefore, that Munetsugu was also responsible for the Okuin, and that the Heinouchi made only the bronze tabernacle housed within. In fact, one of the five volumes of the Heinouchi design manual, *Shōmei*, is devoted exclusively to pagoda design and includes specifications for a reliquary pagoda which is identical in style to that shown in the photograph of the interior of the Taitokuin Hōtō.[15] Both structures have a cylindrical body set on a lotus-petal stand and capped by a pyramidal roof with nine rings on top.[16]

The final attribution in the document of 'all the carvings' to Bungo, that is, to Kōra Munehiro, is consistent with our knowledge of his remarkable career as an architectural sculptor. It also accords with the conclusion that the *tenjin* carving on the Onarimon, the dominant feature of the gateway, was the creation of a master sculptor, now demonstrated in all likelihood to have been Munehiro himself, and establishes the general importance of the decorative programmes of the extant Taitokuin gateways as representing Munehiro's style.

Munehiro's primary concern with sculpture at Taitokuin goes a long way to explain the major role played by his son in architectural work at the project. Munetsugu was the building specialist specifically responsible, under the general supervision of his father, for the architectural execution of the family commissions. Munehiro, freed from tedious on-site building responsibilities, took charge of the elaborate decorative programmes which charged these buildings with such declaratory power. On the basis of existing evidence it is thus possible to reach firm conclusions about the authorship of the three extant gateways as well as the destroyed building complex of the Taitokuin Reibyō, greatly increasing our knowledge of official architecture in the city of Edo in terms of the persons directly responsible for its construction and decoration.

Significance of the Taitokuin Project

This architectural and documentary evidence greatly enhances our understanding of the relationship between the political priorities of Tokugawa government and the internal processes of building projects, particularly of three separate but closely related aspects of the architectural institutionalisation of the Tokugawa *bakufu*.

Firstly, the Taitokuin Reibyō was of profound political importance in establishing Iemitsu's personal power as shogun. Iemitsu had become shogun in 1622 after Hidetada's retirement. However, he was unable to exercise significant prerogatives in government until Hidetada's death ten years later. Ordering the construction of the Taitokuin Reibyō was one of Iemitsu's first direct acts in government. It offered him far more than an opportunity to demonstrate familial piety to his immediate predecessor. It provided a suitable and immediate chance to create an impressive architectural monument of his own initiation in the shogunal capital. The siting, size and magnificence of the buildings speak more of vaunting ambition than they do of familial piety.

The project was to set the tone for Iemitsu's rule and his consolidation of the institutional apparatus of the Tokugawa state through a series of unprecedented measures: stronger regulation of his direct retainers, the *hatamoto*, by issuing codes regulating their conduct in 1632 and 1635; firmer control over the daimyo with the system of *ōmetsuke* (inspectors-general) in 1632; a reworked *Buke shohatto* in 1635; a stronger centralised machinery of *bakufu* government (especially through the role of senior councillors or *rōjū*, and *wakadoshiyori* or junior councillors); a dramatic increase in incidence of daimyo transfers and attainder; enforced proscription of Christianity, and the imposition of a national semi-seclusion policy in a series of measures taken from 1633 to 1639.[17] These measures further centralised Iemitsu's personal authority within the shogunate.

Architecturally, the Taitokuin Reibyō project inaugurated a succession of state building projects which were both assertively shogunal and self-consciously Edo-centric. The preceding decade had seen considerable architectural activity but many of the most spectacular projects had been concentrated in the Kansai, including the rebuilding of Osaka Castle, the Palace of the Second Compound of Nijō Castle, and the Imperial Palace, in order to balance the equation between imperial and shogunal authority in Kyoto and Osaka. Iemitsu's focus was more strictly concentrated on Edo projects. In the short space of seven years, starting with the Taitokuin Reibyō in 1632, the *bakufu* rebuilt the main structures of Zōjōji in 1634–1635 and the *tenshu* and main palaces of Edo Castle in 1637–1638. Even the reconstruction of the Tōshōgū in the mountains at Nikkō, begun in 1634, was a direct extension of the same Edo architectural policy, and built with the same techniques as the monuments physically sited in Edo such as the Tokugawa mausolea.

These few years were, therefore, an era of frenetic architectural activity, not only by the shogunate directly but also at its behest. For instance, the renewed vigour of *onari* visits by the shogun obliged the daimyo to build impressive new gateways and chambers for his formal reception at their principal palaces. The great monuments created by the well-oiled building machinery of state

177

and the harder-pressed building workshops of the daimyo, exceeded in scale and spectacle even the architectural achievements of the founding Tokugawa shogun, and of Toyotomi Hideyoshi a generation earlier at the height of the Momoyama period. Iemitsu's architectural achievements of the middle decade of the Kan'ei era (1624–1644) merit a place in history alongside those of Emperor Augustus in Rome in creating a glittering city in the image of his own authority.

A further dimension to understanding the relationship between Edo architecture and Iemitsu's building programme, his aspirations and their architectural expression, may be found in the reasoning behind the choice of the distinctive style of building and decoration displayed by the Taitokuin mausoleum. An important question should be addressed, namely what was their origin and their ultimate meaning in the context of *bakufu* power relations?

Ieyasu's first mausoleum at Nikkō certainly provided the immediate precedent for the Taitokuin Reibyō, but the practice of building spectacular mausolea to deceased warrior leaders had been established earlier by the Toyotomi. Following Hideyoshi's death in 1598, the Hōkoku Reibyō was constructed to enshrine his deified spirit, Hōkoku daimyōjin. It was built on a lavish scale on a site in the vicinity of the Hōkōji, also built by the Toyotomi, in the southeast of Kyoto.[18] The Toyotomi were likewise responsible for the rebuilding of the Kitano Tenmangū in Kyoto in 1607. Founding this shrine, dedicated to the spirit of the exiled Heian aristocrat Sugawa Michizane, was an act of piety also designed to pay handsome political dividends in the uncertain years following the Tokugawa military ascendancy at Sekigahara in 1600.

The general language of architectural authority was thus well established by the Toyotomi, but the specific stylistic vocabulary changed under Tokugawa patronage of shogunal mausolea. The Taitokuin Reibyō corresponds in general terms with the *gongen*-style buildings associated with the Toyotomi but it diverges markedly in detailed organisation of pillars and bays, overall proportions – particularly of the Ishinoma – and in the shift in emphasis away from Wayō. The growing importance of Zenshūyō as the architectural style of the Tokugawa establishment must be attributed to the ascendancy of the Kōra.

Secondly, the Taitokuin project had profound ramifications for the organisation of *bakufu* building administration. The construction of the Taitokuin Reibyō was undertaken with great expedition as a state project. The principal phase of construction was completed within six months, a remarkably short period for a project of this stylistic complexity. This entailed careful documentation of the organisation of the project, which reveals to the modern researcher in highly specific terms the administrative structure of an important facet of *bakufu* government in the 1630s.

Moreover, as a consequence of the experience of the Taitokuin project, the *bakufu* tightened upper-level administrative control over the hitherto *ad hoc* army of builders in diverse trades brought into government service at Edo, by creating three *sakuji bugyō*, or commissioners of building. This was less than four months after the main construction activities at Shiba had been completed. The *Kan'ei nikki* records that, on the third day of the tenth month of 1632, Sakuma Sanekatsu, Kanō Motokatsu and Sakai Tadatomo were appointed to the office of *sakuji bugyō* by the shogun. All three were Tokugawa household retainers, Sakuma and Kano holding the office of *shiban*, and Sakai the post of *shoin*, immediately responsible to the *toshiyori* or elders.[19] The new post of *sakuji bugyō* was ranked equally with that of *machi bugyō* and *kanjo bugyō* and other key posts in the shogunal government.

The *Kan'ei nikki* also notes that, on the same day as the three commissioners were appointed, master builders and craftsmen in 'all the [building] trades were instructed that it was the shogun's will that they were to follow the orders of the *sakuji bugyō*'.[20] The effect of this measure was to place under the control of a single office the multitude of workshops of carpenters and sawyers, shinglers and tilers, lacquer specialists and sculptors, smiths and tool-makers, needed as contractors and sub-contractors for *bakufu* building projects.[21] This measure was particularly significant because hitherto there had been no senior officials in *bakufu* service charged with ongoing administrative responsibility for architectural projects of state. Previously the post of *fushin bugyō*, or commissioner for engineering works, had been responsible for land reclamation, excavation of moats and canals, and for the collection of stone and erection of the castle walls. As a result of the experience of castle construction of the Momoyama and early Edo periods, Tokugawa architectural construction was seen as subordinate to the massive task of wall engineering, which, after all, guaranteed the security of a castle headquarters in uncertain times.

The creation under Iemitsu of the new office of *sakuji bugyō*, with ranking equal to other key officials including the *fushin bugyō* and directly responsible to the *rōjū* under Iemitsu's reorganisation, is evidence of a shift in political emphasis in state-sponsored construction in Edo from engineering to architecture. It is also a signal to historians that Iemitsu was readying his government for building projects even more grandiose than the Taitokuin mausoleum, and an indication of the shogun's determination to exercise personal direction of this new phase of architectural formation. All three of the *sakuji bugyō* had rendered loyal service either to Ieyasu or Hidetada from an early age, and were to be entrusted collectively with the administrative responsibility for the Edo Castle building projects of the later 1630s.[22]

From a broader historical viewpoint, the determined and large-scale reorganisation of state-administered construction projects under Iemitsu parallels the high priority given to the organisation of building agencies in Nara, but such bureaucratic ordering of construction through an 'Office of Public Works' or a 'Ministry of Construction' has been a common preoccupation of rulers from antiquity to the present in order to assure financial and political control, together with the effective implementation of official building policy.

The third reason for the significance of the Taitokuin project is that primary sources, particularly the stone stele recording the names of the major participants, together with analysis of the formal features of the buildings, establish the identity of the master builders responsible for the Taitokuin mausoleum. These findings are of singular importance not only for architectural but also for social and political history. Until recently there has been little cognisance of the contribution of individual artisans and artists to the creation of Japanese architecture, since commentators have conceived buildings only in stylistic terms. In the absence of effective argument to the contrary it has been acceptable to subscribe to the theory of the 'anonymous artisan'. The Taitokuin project permits the attribution of buildings to specific builders, sculpture to sculptors – in other words, to identify artistic personality in the architecture of early Tokugawa Japan, a giant step forward. Here we have the emergence of architects of authority. The Promethean artistic character of Kōra Munehiro identifies him as the leading architect and master sculptor working for the Tokugawa. On this point it is instructive to recall that it has been the scholarly research of only the last century which has led to the architectural masterpieces of the Renaissance being attributed to the hands of Alberti, Bramante and Michelangelo.

The Kōra have already been observed playing a key role in official building projects later in the 1630s, notably the rebuilding of the *tenshu* of Edo Castle for Iemitsu. In this chapter the focus of attention switches to their greatest extant work of architecture, the Tōshōgū at Nikkō. It is now one of the regrettably few surviving examples of their work but from it we may learn much of the character of Tokugawa official architecture of the 1630s.

The Nikkō Tōshōgū

In the third month of 1617 Ieyasu was elevated to the status of a Shinto deity, and had bestowed on him the posthumous title of *Tōshō daigongen*, the 'Great Avatar Illuminating the East'. This made his spirit theologically a *kami* manifestation of a Buddha, an Avatar who moves between this world and the realm of Buddha to work for the salvation of all people. Ieyasu's posthumous elevation to *kami* was itself prompted by the earlier deification of Hideyoshi as *Hōkoku daimyōjin*, the 'Great Illuminating Spirit of the Prosperous Country'. Such pretensions to divinity by rulers are not uncommon as an historical phenomenon. The 'Divine Augustus', for example, established the pattern for the elevation of his Roman successors to the status of gods. So it was to be with Tokugawa Ieyasu. In a grand ceremony in the fourth month of 1617, in accordance with his own wish that his spirit be moved to Nikkō from Mt Kunō a year after his death, Ieyasu's remains, accompanied by a great procession of warriors, priests, shrine musicians and dancers, were transferred to Nikkō where they were interred at the Okusha, or inner shrine, of the Tōshōgū complex. In the intervening period the main shrine buildings had been readied. The details of the architecture at that time are somewhat uncertain because almost all the original structures were demolished 17 years later, in 1634, for Iemitsu's rebuilding programme. Documents indicate, however, that the earlier Tōshōgū was similar in layout and style, but less lavish than the later rebuilding.[23]

In 1634 work began on the renewal of Nikkō in preparation for the twentieth anniversary of Ieyasu's death. As with the Taitokuin Reibyō, this was an act of apparent piety which at the some time furthered the political ends of Iemitsu. It demonstrated his close association with the founder of the Tokugawa *bakufu* in the same way that the Taitokuin project, undertaken

Fig 7.9
Tōshōgū,
Nikkō. View
of Inner
Sanctuary,
Karamon and
main building

two years earlier to commemorate his immediate predecessor, had also redounded to his political advantage.

As with the Taitokuin project, the Nikkō rebuilding proceeded with great expedition. Demolition of the existing structures began in the eleventh month of 1634. The major part of the project was completed by the fourth month of 1636 in time for the ceremonies marking the twentieth anniversary of Ieyasu's death, although the detailed decoration of many of the buildings continued for several more years (Figure 7.9).[24] The rebuilding was conducted on a level far exceeding that of the original project, both the speed and the scale of construction work testifying to the high level of organisation of the *bakufu* building agency following its reorganisation in 1632.

Details of the reconstruction process at Nikkō are recorded in meticulous detail in a report submitted to the *bakufu* in the ninth month of 1639. Entitled *Nikkōsan tōshō daigongen sama gozōei onmokuroku*, it was compiled by the chief commissioner of works at the site, the daimyo Akimoto Yasumoto.[25] The *Gozōeichō*, as it is generally identified, provides an itemised accounting of all phases of the project. From this it becomes clear that the Nikkō rebuilding was one of the most expensive architectural projects per square metre of building undertaken at any time in the entire Momoyama and Edo periods. Such extravagance was possible only because of the vast national resources at the command of the *bakufu*. It required 4,541,230 days of labour and 779,881 actual participants to complete the project, at a total cost of 568,000 *ryō* in gold currency and 100 *kamme* in silver (375 kilograms), as well as 1000 *koku* in rice for miscellaneous labour costs.[26] The magnitude of that investment may be appreciated when it is realised that the *bakufu* gold and silver mines had an annual production of 160,000 *ryō* at the time of Ieyasu's death and this was greatly augmented under Iemitsu. Iemitsu himself inherited approximately three million *ryō* from Hidetada.[27] Iemitsu's

181

Tōshōgū therefore absorbed the equivalent of one-fifth of his inheritance of 1632. From these figures it might well be suspected that Iemitsu had far exceeded Ieyasu's original wish that a 'small hall' be erected in his memory at Nikkō, and that the intention of the 1634–1636 rebuilding was to glorify Iemitsu more than it was to revere Ieyasu.

Building Blocks of the Gods: Funerary Funding

Popular tradition has it that the *bakufu* extracted donations in gold and silver from the daimyo to pay for the Tōshōgū, and that some daimyo were forced to contribute buildings and other special features to the project. *Nikkō meisho zue*, reflecting popular belief, states that:

> The scale of the Kan'ei [1634–1636] construction was huge and was praised as without compare before or after. Each of the lords presented *torii*, or stone lamps, or offered trees, or donated halls, pagodas or ornamental fences, or placed offerings from overseas before the gods. Truly the strength of the nation was most completely used for this meritorious achievement.[28]

If this account is to be believed this would constitute another instance of Tokugawa use of architectural projects to drain daimyo resources in order to strengthen their own shogunal position. However examination of the *Gozōeichō* proves that the popularly held view of Tōshōgū financing is in fact incorrect. The *Gozōeichō* states unequivocally that in 1635 Akimoto, the commissioner in charge of the project, withdrew approximately 568,000 *ryō* in gold and *100 kamme* in silver from the *bakufu* treasury. He also drew 1000 *koku* in rice from the *bakufu* storehouses in Edo to pay some of the builders' wages. This combined amount of gold, silver and rice accounts for the total expense of the Kan'ei project as itemised in the *Gozōeichō* and establishes conclusively that it was paid for by the *bakufu* without major contributions by any daimyo. The cryptomeria trees which line the approach to Nikkō from Edo, famous as daimyo contributions to Nikkō, were planted over a 12-year period by Matsudaira Masatsuna beginning in 1626 or 1627, a decade before reconstruction. In fact only one building was ever contributed to Iemitsu's Nikkō by a daimyo, namely the five-storey pagoda donated by Sakai Tadakatsu in 1649, 13 years after the rebuilding had been completed. Two other structures added by daimyo to the Nikkō complex are also well removed in time from the Kan'ei era project. One, the large stone *torii* on the approach path, was donated by Kuroda Nagamasa in 1618, 16 years before the starting date, and was left intact in the later project. In addition the stone lanterns along the wall beside the inner precinct were donated by different daimyo at different times but not one was contributed in the three-year period from 1634 to 1636.[29] The *Gozōeichō* establishes that ten daimyo from fiefs in the immediate vicinity were called upon to participate in the 1634–1636 rebuilding by providing unskilled labour, but the financial record shows that the *bakufu* paid for these services.

The 1634–1636 project was an assertively Tokugawa *bakufu* project, as had been the Taitokuin project, and therein lies its significance. The Tōshōgū was created by direct *bakufu* financing, a fundamentally different approach from the heavy reliance on conscripted daimyo contributions used to carry out the Edo construction projects. Nikkō was a direct investment in architecture as political capital, with the daimyo deliberately and visibly excluded from association with Tokugawa divinity. It may have been strategically expedient to require daimyo participation in the temporal establishment of Edo, but the apotheosis of Tokugawa authority at Taitokuin and Tōshōgū demanded their exclusion from the rites of architectural passage to this sacred realm.

The Kōra and the Architectural Style of the Tōshōgū

The appointment of Kōra Munehiro as the chief master builder in charge of the rebuilding of Ieyasu's mausoleum at Nikkō constituted official recognition of the supremacy of the Kōra school and its style of architectural design. This followed the dramatic success of the parts of the Taitokuin project for which the Kōra had been directly responsible, particularly the Honden and the Onarimon which stood at the entrance to the Okuin where Hidetada's remains were interred. Although there are still Wayō elements in evidence at Nikkō, the project was carried out under Munehiro's direct technical supervision and closely reflects his family tradition of Zenshūyō, as well as his personal taste and sculptural talents (Figures 7.10 and 7.11). There was some artistic accommodation with the Wayō style by the addition of external horizontal ties (*nageshi*) to the timber frames of the main Tōshōgū buildings, but the overall conception and control of the project, and the dominant stylistic characteristics, are unmistakably Kōra. In official *bakufu* building projects thereafter the hereditary exponents of the more restrained Wayō style remained active in subsidiary projects or enjoyed high rank as officials, but the commitment of the *bakufu* to a single master builder and his workshop from 1634 indicates that the contained had found its ideal container, and that each was to resonate with the authority of the other.

The debt of the Tōshōgū to the Taitokuin Reibyō was deep. There would scarcely have been time to pause for breath between the completion of the work at Shiba and the commencement of the rebuilding project at Nikkō. The carpenters and sculptors could have been forgiven for being confused about which building complex they were actually working on; during restoration of the Yōmeimon it was discovered that the principal framework and many of the parts had been prefabricated in the workshops of Edo, not made at the Nikkō sites.[30] Specialists in carving Chinese sages or lions, the experts in prefabricating timber framing for gateways and arched entrances, would have moved smoothly from one project to the other with barely a pause and little or no change in technique. The same hands, the same tools, the same talents and energies, were brought to bear on Nikkō as had been used at Shiba. The two projects shared fundamental architectural technology, artistic vision, political purpose, and building personnel. The main building at Nikkō is a clear stylistic development of its immediate forerunner at the Taitokuin mausoleum. Both were built in the typical *gongen-zukuri* form, and share specific details such as extended verandahs carried on bracket sets, and paired triangular and cusped gables at the front. The *Edozu byōbu* and prewar photographs establish that the destroyed Taitokuin buildings had a visual impact similar to that of the Nikkō Tōshōgū. The differences between the two buildings bespeak the increasing ebullience of builder and patron alike

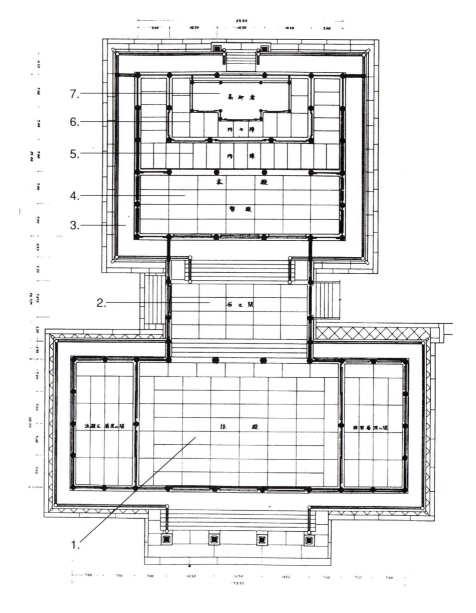

Fig 7.10
Tōshōgū,
Nikkō. Plan of
main building
(Source:
Bunka-chō,
*Kokuhō jūyō
bunkazai
[kenzōbutsu]
jissoku zushū*)

1. Haiden (worship hall)
2. Ishi no ma (stone-floored chamber)
3. Honden (main hall)
4. Gejin (outer sanctuary)

5. Naijin (inner sanctuary)
6. Inner Naijin
7. Tabernacle

as time passed. The Nikkō mausoleum is more copiously decorated and stylistically coherent. There is stylistic unity between all three parts of the *gongen-zukuri* structure which attests to the total domination of this project by a single workshop tradition, that of the Kōra. Use of Wayō and Zenshūyō

184

for the different buildings at Taitokuin has been abandoned in favour a consistent Zenshūyō throughout the Nikkō complex. The unit of intercolumniation is also more consistent at Nikkō, being further evidence of the coherence derived from a single family of builders responsible for all three parts. The bays of the three buildings use a seven *shaku* module, except for those at the front *kōhai*, which are each half as wide again to allow better access for prayer. There is considerable variation in the bay sizes of the Taitokuin buildings, indicating the presence of separate planning and execution of the parts by different carpenters' workshops (compare Figure 7.3, and Figure 7.10).[31]

The most significant difference between the Nikkō buildings and those at Shiba is the abandoning of the standard Zenshūyō hall form, with its characteristic corbelled ceiling, two principal pillars and subsidiary pent roof. The lower, single-roofed structure the Kōra designed as an alternative for the Nikkō Honden enhanced the unity of the three *gongen* buildings. At Nikkō the Kōra were given more scope to create a unified design for the Honden. The great speed with which the Shiba project had been completed, propelled by Iemitsu's urgent need to establish himself as ruler, and the competition between rival building firms, encouraged conservatism not innovation in architectural form.

A Shift in the Realm of Authority

At Nikkō there is a fresh design and the architecture reveals an innovative flow of ideas, not only within the building workshop responsible for its construction but also in official strategy in the appropriation of religious authority. There is an unmistakable shift from the Taitokuin reliance on Buddhist architectural form towards heavier emphasis on that of Shinto. Ieyasu's posthumous status as an Avatar was consciously Shinto, unlike that of Hidetada who retained his Buddhist honorific after his death. The Tōshōgū has a more insistent Shinto character architecturally, with forked finials (*chigi*) and billets (*katsuogi*) on the ridge of the Honden (Figure 7.11). These features are typical of Shinto shrines throughout Japan, as we have seen in the case

Fig 7.11
Tōshōgū,
Nikkō. Side
elevation of
main building
showing
Honden at left
and Haiden at
right
(Source:
Bunka-chō,
*Kokuhō jūyō
bunkazai
[kenzōbutsu]
jissoku zushū*)

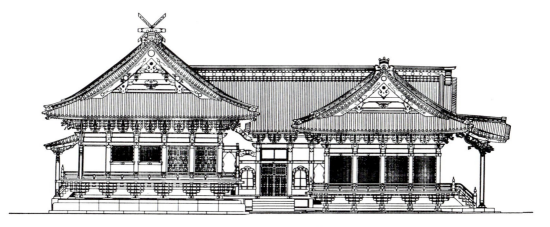

185

Fig 7.12
Tōshōgū,
Nikkō. *Torii* in
front of Inner
Sanctuary

of Ise and Izumo. Such distinctive hallmarks of the Shinto sanctuary were not employed on any earlier examples of *gongen-zukuri*, including the Taitokuin mausoleum.

The same Shinto character is evident in the disposition of the buildings at the Nikkō site, and by the provision of Shinto *torii* along the approach path. Such *torii* are absent from the Shiba mausoleum. Rather than observing the axial symmetry used at the Taitokuin mausoleum and typical of Buddhist institutions generally, at Nikkō the mausoleum is built into the steeply rising hill-side like a shrine, in a series of five levels, each level corresponding with a different part of the complex. The Shinto character of the buildings is particularly marked on the first two levels. The first level is the outer entrance area of the shrine and is marked by a large stone *torii*. The Buddhist five-storey pagoda, situated to the left of the entrance, was added at a later date. The approach path follows a general north–south orientation, but at the second level it turns sharply west to run along the contour of the hill-side before resuming its original direction through a second *torii* which frames the inner sanctuary and its guardian gatehouse in the distance (Figure 7.12). The change in direction affords more effective use of the limited space in a steeply graded site as well as easing the angle of approach for the pilgrim. Here there is a cluster of Shinto buildings, three sacred storehouses, a sacred stable, and an ablutions pavilion. One could be forgiven for thinking oneself at Ise, except for the brilliant black and red lacquer lavishly covering the wooden surfaces.

Of particular significance in the creation of a solemn spectacle of authority is the Yōmeimon, the 'sun-bright gatehouse' of almost legendary brilliance. It is set at the lip of the terrace of the fourth level of the site, above twelve steps which rise abruptly three metres from the courtyard in front (Figure 7.13). It stands at the boundary of the inner and outer sacred precincts of

Fig 7.13
Tōshōgū,
Nikkō.
Yōmeimon.
Front view

the shrine, a location corresponding to that of the Chokugakumon of the Taitokuin mausoleum, but it is infinitely more impressive as a statement of Tokugawa intentions in the definition of their authority. It was at the steps of the Yōmeimon where daimyo paid their obeisances to Ieyasu. Only the mausoleum priests and members of the Tokugawa family were permitted to pass beyond. The use of a gatehouse elevated above stone steps to exclude entry to an inner sanctum, and to serve as a place of worship, is strikingly similar to the role of the gatehouse guarding the inner sanctum of the Inner Shrine at Ise.

The Yōmeimon is wilfully ornamental, taking to a logical conclusion the decorative enthusiasm of the age, with a vivid array of polychrome effects and a profusion of applied sculptural forms animating every surface and space (Figures 7.14 and 7.15). It is a visual feast of mythological creatures and Chinese paragons. The structural framework is painted with a white lime derived from seashells, accented with gilded metalwork at the intersection of pillars and beams. The pristine surfaces of the frame stand out in dramatic contrast to the polychrome decorations of the bracket sets and eaves. The bracket arms are lacquered black with inlaid gold vine pattern, and the double tiers of rafters under the eaves are black with the interstices enlivened by green and red vine motifs also set in gold leaf (Figure 7.16). Large *karajishi*, carved in the round, thrust aggressively forward from the head of each pillar of the first floor while others prowl its main lintel. Phoenixes take flight. The large panels of the lower walls are decorated with peonies; the ceilings of the central bays are beautified by large paintings of dragons in clouds, while brightly embellished panels of *tenjin* and imaginary Birds of Paradise with human heads decorate the side bays. Dragons writhe along the lintels of the second floor or stand watch at the heads of the pillars on the upper storey.

187

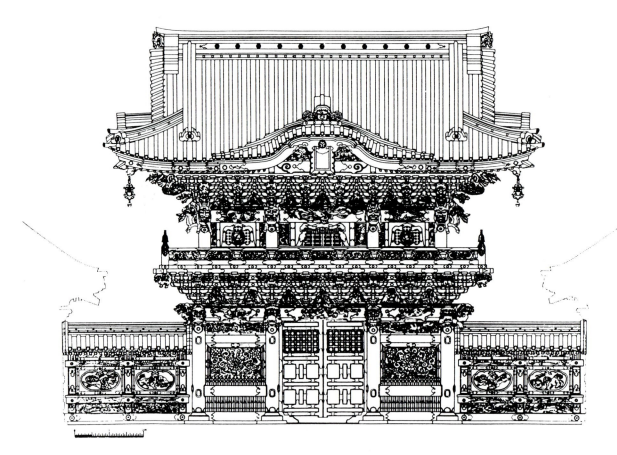

Fig 7.14
Tōshōgū,
Nikkō.
Yōmeimon.
Front elevation
(Source:
Bunka-chō,
*Kokuhō jūyō
bunkazai
[kenzōbutsu]
jissoku zushū*)

Baku, or 'dream-eating' creatures, have overrun the bracket sets which support the balcony. The open-mouthed ferocity of these creatures is startling to behold and the overall effect is of a demonic chorus screaming soundlessly in unison. The precise content and general effect created by these sculptures at Nikkō appear to be identical with the eaves decoration used for the Honden of the Taitokuin Reibyō, which was also decorated by the master artisans from the Kōra workshop. In addition there are 22 separate figural compositions depicting Chinese themes positioned between the bracket sets on the first storey (Figure 7.17). They include such subjects as the *kinki shoga*, the 'Four Accomplishments' of painting, calligraphy, music and the game of *go*, and sages and Daoist Immortals. A sculpture of Zhou Gong Dan, the 'Duke of Zhou' used by Confucius as the paragon of the virtuous ruler, is set directly over the front entrance bay.

There is a close relationship between the decorative programme of the Yōmeimon and the general meaning of the Tōshōgū. Use of a sinicised vocabulary for the applied sculpture lent the powerful sanction of Chinese tradition to Tokugawa authority, a strategy we saw employed to great effect two generations earlier at Azuchi Castle. The diversity of ornament, ranging from ferocious beasts to benign rulers, from wizened sages to young children, indicates the dual intent of the Tokugawa polemicists: on the one hand to engage

and edify the viewer with the exotic and the heroic, and on the other to
caution and teach with Confucian allegory – to present tangible and
compelling reminders of the principles of socio-political order which provided
the rationale for Tokugawa rule, by showing rulers and sages engaged in
virtuous acts.

Despite the profusion of sinicised iconography and this invocation of a
Confucian cosmos, there are subtle but unmistakable Shinto elements in this
gateway. Shinto guardian figures (*zuijin*) are seated in solemn splendour at each
side of the entrance. Further, the basic style of the gateway is Shinto, not
Buddhist. It is a two-storey gatehouse with a hip-gabled roof originally of
cypress-bark shingles, and a balcony above the first floor (see Figures 7.14 and
7.15). This style of gateway, known as a *rōmon*, was a Japanese adaptation of
the Chinese double-roof gatehouse introduced to Japan with Buddhist temple
architecture a millennium earlier. In the late Heian period, the Buddhist gatehouse was adapted for use in Shinto shrines but the roof above the first floor
was abandoned in favour of a simple balcony that was more in keeping with
Shinto needs, a style termed *rōmon*. Unlike the *rōmon* associated with other
shrines, which were Wayō in style, the Yōmeimon at Nikkō is Zenshūyō. This
is hardly surprising in view of its builder and the sponsorship of Zenshūyō by
the *bakufu*. Even the *rōmon* of the Tōshōgū built at Mt Kunō as the temporary

Fig 7.15
Tōshōgū,
Nikkō.
Yōmeimon.
Side elevation
(Source:
Bunka-chō,
*Kokuhō jūyō
bunkazai
[kenzōbutsu]
jissoku zushū*)

189

Fig 7.16
Tōshōgū,
Nikkō.
Yōmeimon.
Detail of
bracket sets
and sculpture
above entrance

Fig 7.17
Tōshōgū,
Nikkō.
Yōmeimon.
Detail of
sculpture
above entrance

mausoleum for Ieyasu in 1616 was Wayō in form. To this unique gateho
Nikkō no fewer than four *karahafu* have been added, the ultimate step in invest-
ing the gatehouse with declaratory power; it wedded the single most potent
architectural symbol of the day to the most expressive building style of the age.

Beyond the style and siting of the Tōshōgū buildings, one of the clearest
indications of deliberate drawing upon Shinto authority at Nikkō is the fact
of the 1634–1636 rebuilding itself. The decision to rebuild the shrine, to
mark the twentieth anniversary of its initial construction, reflected the pervasive Shinto tradition of periodic renewal. We have seen this custom sanctioned
by the highest level of authority at the Ise shrines. The timing of the decision to rebuild the Tōshōgū may itself have been directly prompted by Ise,
for it seems to have been made immediately after the periodic rebuilding of
that shrine which had been completed in 1633. Thus imperial custom became
Tokugawa custom.

With the Tōshōgū the Tokugawa also carried forward their strategy of
defining authority in relation to the daimyo by requiring them to pay periodic obeisances to Ieyasu at Nikkō. Daimyo were even obliged to establish
Tōshōgū in their own domains. The Nikkō Tōshōgū was the logical culmination of the process of defining Tokugawa authority in relation to the imperial
institution which we witnessed in its earlier stage at Nijō Castle, when the
emperor came to the Tokugawa court. Nikkō became the focus for a Tokugawa
theocracy. The revelation of that deified authority became the Tōshōgū. By
this means the Tokugawa countered the most powerful tool of imperial
authority – its direct association with Amaterasu through worship at the Inner
Shrine of Ise – by creating a monument with pretensions to equivalent status
and political significance. At Nikkō, Ieyasu was doctrinally equated with
Amaterasu, the Sun Goddess, by use of the image of the sun shining in the

191

east, the *Tōshō daigongen*, and by a range of tectonic strategies such as the use of *torii* and shrine buildings which reinforced the Shinto association with Tokugawa divinity.

The consummation of this process was to come in 1645, just nine years after the major building activity at Nikkō had been completed. By the simple expedient of having existing Tōshōgū ceremonies 'regulated' by an imperial proclamation, the Tōshōgū acquired status equal to that of Ise Shrine.[32] The shrine was officially proclaimed as a *gū* rather than a *sha*, a title hitherto reserved for Ise Jingū and redolent with imperial nuance. The following year the imperial court began a practice of sending an envoy to make annual offerings at Nikkō.[33] This in effect promoted the Tōshōgū to the same level as Ise Shrine, with Ieyasu assuming religious significance of the order of the ancestor of the Imperial House, Amaterasu. In practical terms this meant that imperial emissaries henceforth had to be dispatched to both Ise and Nikkō annually as well as on special occasions, such as the birth of an imperial heir or the death of an emperor, to report to the respective tutelary deities of the two shrines. In 1633 the Tokugawa had enjoyed the sight of an imperial envoy bringing Buddhist sutras, lighting incense and praying before the steps of Hidetada's recently completed mausoleum, in the presence of an audience of the most powerful daimyo.[34] At Nikkō each visit by an imperial envoy to the steps of the Yōmeimon became a ritual demonstration of imperial confirmation of Tokugawa authority.

Shogunal and Daimyo Gateways 8

The Intersecting Spheres of Arbitrary Will and Technical Necessity

The relationship between architects and authority has not always been a case of sympathetic accommodation of building design and process to governmental needs. Today we are not unaccustomed to vituperative disagreement between government and architects. For instance, Yoshimura Junzō, a leading postwar architect, had one such difference of opinion in 1965 while participating in the building of the new Imperial Palace in Tokyo, within the precincts of the former Edo Castle:

> With the basic design done for the palace, I began tackling interior details that were crucial to me. Then bureaucracy in the palace began meddling with my work. I protested – in vain. In the end, I realised that I could not be honest to myself if I continued to work under such conditions. So I walked out of it. What else could you do with those stone-headed government functionaries?[1]

A most modern dilemma but there were similar conflicts between master builders and government officials earlier in Japanese history.

The master builder as designer or architect emerges from the historical records with increasing definition as we move into the late sixteenth and seventeenth centuries.[2] Not surprisingly, so too does the evidence of disagreement. Research by Kate Nakai has identified one instance of conflict over architectural design which arose between Arai Hakuseki (1657–1725) and the official master carpenters of the Tokugawa shogunate.[3] Hakuseki was a dedicated Neo-Confucian scholar who, under Ienobu and Ietsugu, the sixth and seventh Tokugawa shogun respectively, set out to bring stricter order to Tokugawa government. For him the ambiguity of authority between the shogunate at Edo and the imperial court at Kyoto demanded resolution. His Confucian philosophy convinced him that political authority should rest on a well-defined hierarchy, clearly codified in a unified system of social and ceremonial observances. This inflexible conviction guaranteed that tension would arise between his views on the way in which architectural style should reflect hierarchical order and the equally inflexible precedent based on experience of the master builders responsible for carrying out government architectural projects.

Hakuseki's reforms involved the adoption of certain ceremonies and rituals associated with the imperial court, including the substitution of *gagaku* court music for the Nō favoured by the warrior class as their official entertainment, and certain architectural changes to elevate shogunal building protocol to conform with imperial court practice. During Yoshimune's reign as eighth shogun, the tension between architecture and authority came to a head over the issue of the style of a gateway in front of the Ōhiroma as part of Hakuseki's plans to elevate the status of the shogun. Nakai, who has followed the dispute in close detail, notes that Hakuseki had special furnishings made in Kyoto for the shogun's reception hall at Edo Castle and a *yotsuashimon* built within the walls of the castle.[4] This particular gateway type, with its gabled roof and two principal and four flanking pillars, was the most elaborate ceremonial gateway of the day, reserved for the shogun during his *onari* visits to the daimyo palaces (Figure 8.1), and for reception of the emperor at shogunal establishments such as the palace of Nijō Castle. By custom it was positioned in the outer walls of a palace compound, not directly in front of the Ōhiroma, where convention dictated the erection of a more simple gateway without roof, a *heijūmon* or 'single level gateway'[5]. For Hakuseki, construction of a roofed gateway arbitrarily promoted the architectural status of the shogun to the same level as that of the emperor by elevating the style of gateway in front of the Ōhiroma to the same style as the gateway built at Nijō Castle for Emperor Go Mizunoo's visit of 1626.

Hakuseki's Edo Castle gateway sparked a heated debate with the official master carpenters charged with its construction, and eventually with the shogun Yoshimune himself, over the propriety of such an action. According to Hakuseki's records,[6] the only surviving evidence of the dispute, he disproved the claim by the official master builders that the precedent of building *heijūmon* in this inner location went back to the Kamakura shogunate. In this Hakuseki was probably correct, because the convention appears to have been established in the later sixteenth century under the Toyotomi.[7] The shogunal carpenters may have been aware of this but tactfully wished to avoid citing a Toyotomi precedent for a Tokugawa convention. Hakuseki, while relying on the Go Mizunoo gateway of 1626 as his precedent, overlooked, or chose to ignore the fact that a roofless gateway led to the Ōhiroma garden of the shogun's palace on the other side of the ornamental lake at Nijō Castle: this would have confirmed the claims made by the shogunal master carpenters.

The carpenters ultimately bowed to the will of Hakuseki and constructed the grand gateway. Ironically, the steps Yoshimune later took to eradicate Hakuseki's changes to protocol led him to have the gateway dismantled and removed from Edo Castle simultaneously with his efforts to restore the traditional shogunal protocol.[8] Here again the rationale may have been observance of precedent, but the motivation was political, namely to achieve reconciliation with the *fudai daimyō* against whose power shogunal ascendancy had been asserted by Hakuseki. We have seen a similar architectural accommodation with the interests of the *daimyō* in the decision to postpone the rebuilding of the *tenshu* of Edo Castle after the Meireki fire of 1657.

The key issue for architecture and authority raised by the Hakuseki gateway controversy is 'What is the relationship between the way a building is made and what the government authority believes it should look like?' Addressing this question adds an important dimension to the study of the relationship between architecture and authority in that it compels an examination of the relationship of the authority of the customary traditions of the master carpen-

Fig 8.1
Edozu byōbu,
detail. Daimyo
palaces in the
vicinity of Edo
Castle
(Courtesy of
National
Museum of
Japanese
History,
Sakura)

ters to the political will of the state. Each sphere may be absolute in its own
way. Government has its own political agenda and imperatives while architecture is ruled by the iron law of structural viability and stylistic acceptability
observed with the strictness of a religious faith handed down from generation
to generation. Suggesting a change to accepted architectural protocol, such
as a decision to build a grand gateway with a roof where no such gateway
would normally be constructed, constituted more than a simple clash between
political innovation and architectural conservatism. It amounted to an infringe-
ment upon, even a heresy against, the inherited and inviolate architectural
order.

By the middle of the Edo period the circumstances were ripe for confrontation between architecture and authority because of the changes in the nature
of the profession of master builder. We have observed the increasing prominence and power of such families such as the Kōra in the consolidation of
the Tokugawa order. The early Edo period was not only an age of castles
and palaces; it was also the age of the master carpenter as designer, builder

195

and bureaucrat. In other words the master builder had become the equivalent of the chief architect in Western tradition. The profession of carpenter broadened and diversified in response to insistent demand from the state for increasingly costly and idiosyncratic architectural works. Family workshops of elite master carpenters, particularly the Kōra, enjoyed privileged status as official government builders. Their household heads became the proud peacocks of the artisan profession, strutting across the stage of history with their tail feathers preened for all to see. At the same time they were charged with considerable administrative responsibility in the *bakufu* building bureaucracy which had been created to manage state projects, and were rewarded with hereditary stipends often equivalent to mid-ranking members of the warrior class serving the shogunate. Kōra Munehiro was honoured with the court title of 'Lord of Bungo Province' for his services to the state. The heirs to these traditions were naturally dedicated to preserving the integrity of their family building practice. It is understandable that they would not willingly surrender their power over the shape of the built environment to the whims a new ruler.

What happens, therefore, when the arbitrary ruler decides he wants something that is beyond the realm of architectural possibility as defined by the necessities of the traditions of the master builders? Logic dictates three possible answers: the patron supervenes, the builder wins, or the result is a compromise between the two. It is this last resolution to the dilemma which is most common, that is, an intersection between the sphere of arbitrary will and the sphere of technical necessity. The building completed under such circumstances is the product of compromise. This dynamic of compromise between political and architectural process opens up new stylistic possibilities in architecture and refines the spatial and symbolic parameters of authority itself.

It was no coincidence that Hakuseki's architectural controversy concerned the style of a gateway. The Tokugawa paid considerable attention to gateway style as the most visible representation of status in their political order. As a consequence, and as the Edo period progressed, there was a complex and protracted dynamic of interaction between the political and architectural spheres over gateways and status within the Tokugawa socio-political order.

In Japan the gateway or *mon* has long been seen as far more than a transitory point of arrival and departure. It is a critical point of intersection between public and private domain, between *soto* and *uchi*. In its architectural style, structure, size, decoration, location, and material used, it is a dynamic representation to the outside world of that which lies within. As a natural consequence of this outward exhibition, gateways have penetrated deeply into the Japanese perception of authority. The association between the architecture of the gateway and the expression of authority has lead to the word *mon*, or gateway, entering the basic vocabulary for government and status. We have seen that one title for the emperor was *mikado*, or 'honourable gateway', an example of metonymic usage. The characters for *kenmon*, meaning a person of influence, read literally a 'gateway of power'. Fame is equated with the gate in the term *meimon*, literally a 'famed gateway', and disgrace in the form of expulsion or excommunication is *hamon*, or a 'broken or violated gate'. The *mon* as the entry to a residence is the logical symbol for family in the term *ichimon*, 'one gate'. Similarly *shūmon* 'religion gate' is a metaphor for religion or a sect, and *bumon*, 'warrior's gate', was used to signify the military class as a whole. *Mon* also has the common meaning of school so that a pupil or disciple is a *monka*, 'beneath the gateway', or *monjin*, 'person of the gate'. The gateway is therefore a vital indication of group and individual identity in Japanese society and acts as a physical manifestation of latent power relations. This association is central to the understanding of the reciprocal relationship between architecture and authority.

Imposing gateways have functioned throughout Japanese history as compelling symbols of both religious and secular authority. As we saw in the Nara period, *mon* stood at the entrance of Buddhist temple and imperial palace alike to proclaim their patron's prestige to the outside world with that flair for the dramatic and decorative which distinguishes effective declamatory architecture. Gateways were also an important feature of aristocratic mansions, and ecclesiastical and government buildings. In the Heian capital they lined the great avenues and were subject to government regulation to ensure accord between status and gateway style, as we have already seen.[9]

Perhaps of all periods of Japanese history, the gateway came most into its own as a symbol of status in the Edo period. *Mon* built for the daimyo mansions in Edo were some of the most effective and compelling examples of declamatory architecture ever created. Gateway construction reached a climax under the third Tokugawa shogun, Iemitsu. Any daimyo upon whom he chose to bestow the honour of official visitation or *onari* was required to spend lavishly in anticipation of the visit by building special audience and entertainment facilities for the shogun and his entourage, a situation reminiscent of Elizabeth I of England's enthusiasm for impoverishing her greater lords by protracted formal visits to their carefully prepared country estates. In Edo the most important building symbolically was the most visible, namely the elaborate gateway which was reserved for receiving the shogun, the *onarimon*. The *Kōra oboegaki* describes such gateways as follows:

> An *onarimon* – a large *yotsuashi*[*mon*] with *karahafu* set into the front and rear eaves – was built facing the carriage entrance of the hiroma. On the occasion of onari visits the *hiroma* was entered and exited directly via this gateway.[10]

None of the Edo *onarimon* survives, but a gateway built for a planned shogunal visit by Iemitsu to Nishi Honganji in Kyoto still stands as the best evidence for this type of structure (Figure 8.2). The cost of the *onarimon* must have been precariously close to ruinous for many daimyo. A description of an *onarimon* erected at the city of Fushimi, in the same style and at about the same time as the Edo gateways were built, is included in Saikaku's *Eitaigura*. This notes that 'the work is said to have consumed three years' revenue from the lord's five hundred and fifty thousand *koku* fief'.[11] Although information such as this must be treated with reserve it does give some idea of the cost relative to income of the gateways prepared for Iemitsu's official visits.[12]

There were three distinct phases in the relationship between gateway architecture and Tokugawa authority. In the first phase, the era of the establishment of Tokugawa authority, we have seen the way in which the daimyo were skilfully coerced into extravagant gateway construction in order to absorb their

Fig 8.2
Karamon,
Nishi
Honganji,
Kyoto. Rebuilt
for planned
visit by
Tokugawa
Iemitsu in
1632

resources and signify their subordination to the shogun. In this process gateway architecture proved a faithful servant of the state.

In the second phase, coinciding with the middle of the Edo period and the era of Hakuseki's reforms, we have seen hints of a more complex interaction between the political and architectural establishments and a more troubled accommodation between political purpose and architectural convention. Although the will of the state was to prevail, there are hints of loss of political control over the built order.

As we turn to the last century of Tokugawa government, after about 1760, we enter a third phase in the relationship between gateway architecture and the ruling order, one characterised by the eventual and perhaps inevitable assertion of the primacy of technical needs and architectural custom over political needs and governmental custom. In the same way as it had been agent of change in the Heian period, fire was the catalyst. From the middle of the seventeenth century a series of devastating fires in Edo, of which the Meireki fire of 1657 was the most destructive, had effectively dampened the enthusiasm of shogun and daimyo alike for costly, rhetorical building projects. Pragmatism replaced polemics in architecture, as state and daimyo resources were stretched to the limit to rebuild the city with its palaces and religious buildings. Instead of free-standing ceremonial gateways, more modest

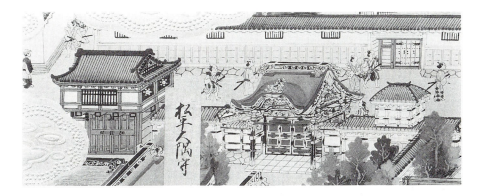

entrances set into the walls of the row houses, or *nagaya*, that surrounded the mansion complexes became the principal point of entry for the daimyo and important visitors. These had been used as service entrances to daimyo palaces in the early Edo period (Figure 8.3), but gateways built in this style were now elevated to a role of highest symbolic importance. According to Thomas McClatchie, a visitor to Tokyo in 1878, a typical daimyo mansion had a *nagaya* 'forming the whole of the street frontage, except where at intervals a fire-proof storehouse, with thick mud sides, or a short strip of fencing or ordinary wall is to be seen'.[13] These gatehouses, or *nagayamon*,[14] lacked the expressive power of the *karamon* but acquired certain structural and stylistic details which spelled out in a quieter symbolic language the identity and rank of the daimyo for whom they were built. The massive timbers of their entrances and the flanking guard houses, or *bansho*, became a substitute for the polychrome grandeur of the earlier gateways.

Heavy framing had come into general use for the buildings of the warrior class in the later sixteenth century when nationwide castle construction accompanied the wars of unification.[15] Multistorey castle gatehouses required sturdy framing at the entrance level to support the upper levels of the structure and to provide protection against attack (Figure 8.4). With the establishment of unified national government under the Tokugawa the age of castles passed but the influence of castle architecture is still evident in the heavy timber framing of the entrance vestibules of *nagayamon*. The *nagayamon* became a key symbol of status in the Tokugawa political order, but only three gateway structures from Edo survive today in historically and architecturally viable condition. Two of these, the Ikedamon, and the Akamon (Figure 8.5), are conspicuous landmarks in modern Tokyo. The Ikedamon, popularly known as the Kuromon or 'Black Gateway' because of its sombre aspect, stands in the outer wall of the Tokyo National Museum complex at Ueno. It was first built as the principal entrance to the mansion of the daimyo of Tottori to the immediate southwest of Edo Castle. It was moved to the Tōgū Gosho at Shiba Takanawa in 1891, and finally to its present site in 1952. The second gateway, the Akamon, is the famed 'Red Gateway' of the main campus of the present University of Tokyo. It was originally built in 1823 to commemorate the marriage of Maeda Nariyasu, daimyo of Kaga, to the twenty-fourth

199

Fig 8.4
Himeji Castle,
Hyōgo prefec-
ture.
Two-storey
gatehouse.
Rear view

daughter of the shogun Ienari. The Akamon, because of the special shogunal privilege bestowed upon the Maeda, was built as a free-standing structure, but the Ikedamon, as the entrance to a daimyo mansion, is a *nagayamon*.

The third surviving gateway is known as the Rōjūmon or 'Gatehouse of the Senior Councillor' (Figure 8.6). Like its black and red contemporaries, it is registered under the Cultural Properties Law as an 'important cultural property' (*jūyō bunkazai*), but it enjoys neither the popular prestige nor the central location of the Ikedamon and Akamon. It is now situated some 75 kilometres east of its original site in Edo near the coast of the scenic Bōsō peninsula at Kujūkuri, rusticating in bucolic isolation at the Yamawaki Gakuen summer camping ground. It was moved to this site and fully restored in 1973–1974. Documents and other sources establish that this gatehouse has been moved three times since 1867, once during the Meiji period when it was drastically reduced in size. After the Meiji Restoration the daimyo mansion of which it was part became the site of the building of the Ministry of Justice of the Meiji government. The gatehouse served as its main entrance until the ministry was transferred to new, Western-style premises at nearby Kasumigaseki in 1889. A map of 1883 shows that the gatehouse occupied the full length of the main street frontage of the Justice Ministry compound, making it some 120 metres in length, over 100 metres longer than the present structure (Figure 8.7).[16]

In 1897 the vacated Justice Ministry site was donated to a private prepara-tory school, the Kaigun Yobikō (later renamed Kaijō Gakuen), but two years later the school, like the Justice Ministry before it, was moved to Kasumigaseki. It was proposed to move the gatehouse to the new school site also but it proved either too large, or too costly, to relocate in its entirety and only the central section eventually ended up at the new site. After the Meiji period,

Fig 8.5
Ikedamon
(above) and
Akamon
(below),
Tokyo.
Oblique front
view

in 1930, it was moved again to the home of Fujiyama Raitarō at Shirogane
before passing finally into the hands of Yamawaki Gakuen in 1973.[17]

Both the Rōjū and Ikeda gatehouses are therefore remarkable not only for
their survival but for the number of moves they weathered. Together they
constitute the last examples of the *nagayamon* type to remain in good condition, and afford a rare opportunity to compare extant buildings with written
documents to assess the relationship between the spheres of arbitrary will and
technical necessity during the last century of Tokugawa government.

Style and Symbolic Significance of the Nagayamon

The Ikedamon and the Rōjūmon are built in the same basic *nagayamon* form.
Both gatehouses are 21.82 metres long or exactly 12 *ken* in the standardised
Meiji system (see Figure 8.8). This indicates that the Ikedamon, like the
Rōjūmon, was cut down to its present length after 1886, presumably when it
was resited in 1891. The identical length of the two gatehouses suggests
that 12 *ken* was considered the optimum size for moving buildings of this

201

Fig 8.6
Rōjūmon,
Chiba prefec-
ture. Oblique
front view

type in the late nineteenth century. The Ikedamon, like the Rōjūmon, is
equipped with two *bansho*, but these are crowned by elaborate *karahafu*, the
style of cusped gables which originally dominated the entrance of the early
Edo-period gateways of shogunal visitation. Both gatehouses differ from the
Akamon of Tokyo University which is a free-standing structure.

Edo-period documents assist in establishing the specific iconography of these
gatehouses and the political circumstances of their evolution. Thomas
McClatchie noted in 1878 that the gateways and their *bansho* 'have for years
been the subject of so many notifications and such minute regulations, that
it is not too much to say that more attention has been bestowed on them
than on any other portion of the feudal mansions'.[18] The considerable body
of Tokugawa government edicts directed at the gateways of the daimyo is an
important indication of their symbolic importance in the Tokugawa socio-
political order. Regulations reveal that consistency and conformity of
architectural style became paramount concerns in a society in which doing
things 'according to one's status' (*bungen ni ōjite*) was an exhortation frequently found in government edicts.[19] The *mon* as the most publicly visible
part of a daimyo residence had thus become the primary object of official
concern by the later eighteenth and early nineteenth centuries.

Fig 8.7
Rōjūmon. Plan
from 1883
map showing
original
dimensions
(Source:
Bunkazai
kenzōbutsu
hozon gijutsu
kyōkai (ed.)
*Jūyō bunkazai
buke yashiki
mon shūriki*)

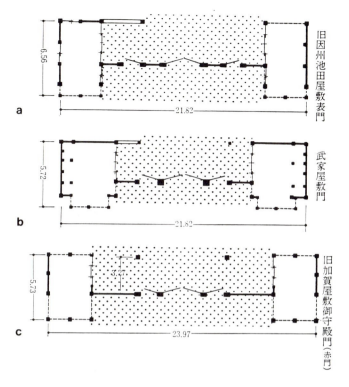

旧因州池田屋敷表門

武家屋敷門

旧加賀屋敷御守殿門(赤門)

Fig 8.8 Plans
of Ikedamon
(a), Rōjūmon
(b) and
Akamon (c)
(Source:
Bunka-chō,
*Jūyō bunkazai
15*)

The *Aobyōshi* ('Blue Cover Book'), a woodblock printed compendium of
regulations and etiquette published in 1840–1841 as a handbook for the
convenience of members of the samurai class, is the most relevant and valuable source for understanding the style of the Rōjūmon.[20] The fact that one
section is entirely devoted to daimyo gateways could in itself underline their
significance. Charts of gateway styles with accompanying explanation were
published in the *Aobyōshi* in much the same way that military forces publish
charts showing badges of rank. The *Aobyōshi* includes eight diagrams illustrating various gate styles, and lists details of their characteristics (Figure
8.9).[21] The main text of the section on gateways is actually a government
edict issued in 1809, over 30 years earlier, prior to the publication of the
compendium. According to the text, daimyo of 50,000 to 100,000 *koku* status
were permitted to build a *nagayamon* with two *bansho* and two single-door
side entrances for their main entrances. The *bansho* were to have single sloping
roofs and projecting grill windows. Stepped-out stone foundations were also
permissible. The Rōjūmon conforms with this prescription except that the
bansho lost their elevated masonry foundations during one of the relocations.
The pertinent diagram in *Aobyōshi* shows a gatehouse identical in form to the
extant building except for the *bansho* foundations and the position of the side
doors which are set in the outside bays of the vestibule (Figure 8.9, second
left, lower row). The caption to the diagram states unequivocally that this
style of gatehouse was 'used as the mansion of a *rōjū* and others in official
position', providing written confirmation of the function which the gatehouse
served.

203

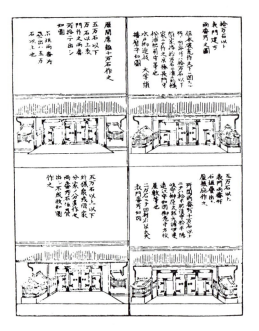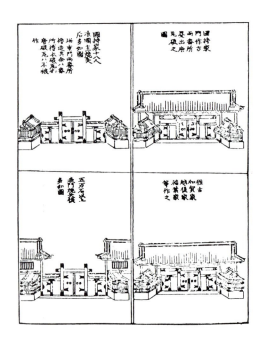

Fig 8.9
Aobyōshi,
1840–41.
Pages illustrating daimyo gateway styles according to status
(Source: *Edo sōsho*, II)

Aobyōshi also establishes the fact that the Rōjūmon conforms with Tokugawa law with regard to building width. A three-bay width limit for the *kunimochi*, or highest-ranking daimyo, first established in 1657, is retained in the 1809 edict; all other daimyo, however, were required to reduce their nagaya to two and a half bays.[22] The extant Rōjūmon is two and a half bays wide, the appropriate width for the gatehouse of a daimyo below *kunimochi* status, which was the rank of the *rōjū* incumbents of this mansion.

The *Aobyōshi* thus provides both written and pictorial explanation for the symbolism of the gatehouse now standing at the Yamawaki Gakuen site. Furthermore it confirms that in general style and specific detailing the gatehouse complies with the 1809 law. This handbook also offers another valuable clue about the relationship between the status of the owner and style of the gatehouse. The preface to the edict of 1809 quoted in its entirety in the *Aobyōshi* states that 'in the sixth month of 1809 a memorandum was given to the *ōmetsuke*[23] by Doi Ōi no Kami concerning the method of building mon *bansho*'. 'Doi Ōi no Kami' was the honorific title for the senior councillor Doi Toshiyoshi.[24] In 1809 Doi himself was the occupant of the *Daimyō kōji* mansion of which this gatehouse was part, a fact which may well account for the close correlation between the style of the extant gatehouse and the prescriptions of the 1809 Tokugawa law. It would have been unlikely that the *rōjū* responsible for the law would disregard its injunctions as regards the style of his own official gatehouse.

The memorandum quoted in the *Aobyōshi* indicates that a gatehouse conforming to its stylistic prescription stood on the *rōjū* mansion site at the time the 1809 regulation was issued. It is not clear whether this gatehouse, or a successor, provided the main section of the present building. The original gatehouse may have been rebuilt after the devastating fire of 1862. However, the Edo-period timbers of the extant gatehouse may well date to the time of Doi as the incumbent (1802–1822). There are many instances in which *mon* survived the destruction by fire of the edifices which they guarded because of their physical distance from the main buildings, and the Rōjūmon could be another such example.[25]

The 1809 memorandum was aimed specifically at *nagaya* and their *bansho*, whereas earlier edicts had sought to restrict building widths in general. In fact it had been official policy since a major fire in 1772 for even the highest ranking daimyo to build *nagaya* rather than the more elaborate free-standing type of gateway. An edict issued shortly after that fire stated:

> Concerning rebuilding in the areas recently destroyed by fire: this should be done in accordance with social status and should not be gaudy throughout. . . . Concerning the front gateways of daimyo mansions: a *nagaya* should be built, even in the case of *kunimochi* daimyo. Building widths and all the rest of the rebuilding should not be turned into a major undertaking.[26]

This written evidence is all we need to conclude that *bansho* came into general use in gatehouse architecture between 1772, when the *nagayamon* law was promulgated, and 1809, when the edict (later reprinted in *Aobyōshi*) was issued. The latter document contains the first specific written references to *bansho* in any Tokugawa document, and as the preface indicates, is intended to correlate *bansho* style with daimyo status. Interestingly no *bansho* are depicted in any early Edo-period paintings showing *nagayamon*, such as the *Edozu byōbu*. From the Tokugawa laws, therefore, it may be inferred that construction of *bansho* became common following the ban on free-standing gateways in 1772, and that by 1809 it was necessary for the shogunal bureaucracy to issue a detailed law establishing precise correlations between daimyo rank and *bansho* style. In the later Edo period the *nagayamon* was thus adapted for its new role as principal entry and symbol of authority in the Tokugawa order by the addition of *bansho* watch-houses. The *bansho* is a case of a creative response to the economic and legal strictures of an era.

The status gradations revealed in these edicts are evident not only in the general architectural form of the Rōjūmon but also in that of the two other late-Edo gateways that survive in Tokyo. The Rōjū and Ikeda gatehouses are both *nagayamon*, in conformity with the 1772 law (Figure 8.10). However, because of differences in status between the Ikeda and the Doi, they differ in their architectural detail. The two *bansho* of the Ikedamon are covered with *karahafu*, the cusped gable that had been used for the free-standing ceremonial gateways of the early Edo period (Figure 8.11). The 1809 edict actually banned such extravagance but the *Aobyōshi* diagrams indicate that the upper-ranking daimyo were ignoring this provision and still using *karahafu*, at least on their *bansho*. By contrast the simple roofs of the Rōjūmon appear humble in concept and execution, an effect now exaggerated by the loss of

205

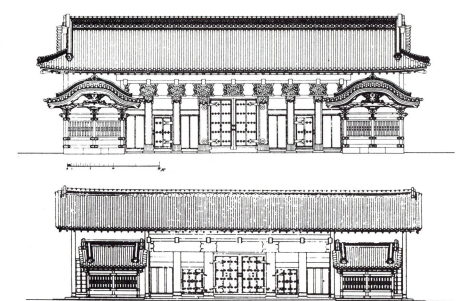

Fig 8.10
Ikedamon
(top) and
Rōjūmon
(bottom).
Front
elevations
(Source:
Bunka-chō,
*Kokuhō jūyō
bunkazai
[kenzōbutsu]
jissoku zushū*)

the original stone foundations which would have elevated the structures by some further 50 centimetres (Figure 8.11). This difference in style reflects the differences in rank between the daimyo of the two gatehouses in the manner described in the *Aobyōshi*. The Ikeda, as daimyo of Tottori, had a status of 325,000 *koku* whereas the *rōjū* were listed as below 100,000 *koku*.[27]

In their turn both these gatehouses are markedly different from the Akamon, which by virtue of its special function as the entrance to the quarters of the shogun's daughter at the Maeda mansion, is more ornate than other daimyo gateways of its time (Figure 8.12). It is, in fact, the type of independent gateway structure which the 1772 edict sought to discourage. Its style is not even listed in the *Aobyōshi* among the gateways used by daimyo.

Fig 8.11
Bansho of
Ikedamon
(left) and
bansho of
Rōjūmon
(right)

Today these three *mon* demonstrate the role of gateway architecture as a visible and articulate representation of Tokugawa authority. Together they show the detailed and controlled language of status in the Tokugawa hier-

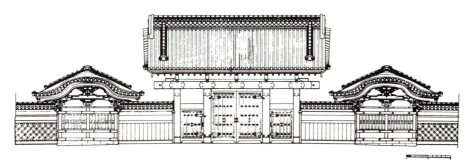

Fig 8.12
Akamon,
Tokyo. Front
elevation
(Source:
Bunka-chō,
Kokuhō jūyō
bunkazai
[kenzōbutsu]
jissoku zushū)

archy. They also reveal the dynamics of late Tokugawa architectural policy with their distinctive architectural features formed by the interaction of stylistic traditions and political forces within an overall context of declining economic power. Ultimately a reciprocal causality governing the relationship between architecture and authority from the middle of the Edo period may be identified. These gateways and the written record together offer a fascinating insight into the intersection of the two spheres, each dependent on the other but proudly reluctant to acknowledge that mutual dependence or symbiosis. It is a revealing study of the relationship between how a building is made and what a patron wants.

9 Building the Meiji State

The Western Architectural Hierarchy

The Meiji period (1868–1912) was unmistakably and decisively an era of construction. Its 45 years witnessed the construction of a new state, a new society and a new built environment to express its identity and ambitions. It saw the semi-closed military and bureaucratic state of the Tokugawa shogunate replaced with a Westernising nation under a restored imperial authority. This entailed the establishment of new political institutions, a reordering of the political and social hierarchy beginning with the dismantling of the status and privileges of the warrior class, and the putting in place of the political, industrial and economic infrastructure for a modern nation-state defined in Western terms. The Imperial Charter Oath of April 1868, which set out the objectives of the new government, stated, '[all our actions] shall follow the accepted practices of the world. . . . Knowledge shall be sought throughout the world so as to broaden and strengthen the foundations of imperial rule'.[1] Not since the Nara period had Japan embarked upon so ambitious a redefinition of itself in terms of foreign models.

The adoption of Western industrial technology went hand-in-hand with the forging of new social and political institutions. A major slogan of the earlier part of the Meiji period was 'civilization and enlightenment' (*bunmei kaika*), developed by Fukuzawa Yukichi (1834–1901), that great exponent of Westernisation. The slogan was firmly grounded at a practical level in the passage from craft industries to factory-based mass production, and the government was to provide strong guidance in setting detailed objectives for this process and in concentrating capital for major projects.

At the beginning of the new era one of the most urgent tasks facing the Meiji leaders, who were drawn largely from the former samurai class, was the construction of a new built environment for the conduct of the affairs of state and the development of modern industry, commerce and education. The 'accepted practices of the world' meant the creation of Western-style urban plans and buildings, particularly for the newly designated capital city of Tokyo. The old shogunal headquarters of Edo had lost its political rationale with the curtailment of the *sankin kōtai* system in the 1860s and the collapse of the Tokugawa shogunate in 1867. It was reborn as Tokyo, the 'Eastern Capital', with the shogun's castle transformed into the emperor's palace.

Initially the affairs of the new state were conducted from the old daimyo palaces and mansions, with carpet spread over *tatami* floors and chairs and tables standing on them. The Meiji leaders, most of whom were former samurai of the great outer domains of Satsuma, Tosa, Hizen and Chōshū, or members of the imperial court, and some of whom had already been to the West on fact-finding missions, quickly brushed aside the architectural framework of the old order. The daimyo gatehouses, which had been such important symbols of authority and status under the Tokugawa, made way for fences of wrought iron, stone and brick, although some, like the Rōjūmon, were more reluctant to go than others. The Western-style buildings of powerful new government ministries and the burgeoning commercial empire of Mitsubishi lined the broad gas-lit avenues in the heart of Tokyo. Together with public facilities like post offices and railway stations, they became the new architecture of authority. Gracious buildings of stone or brick presented to the world the new imperial and commercial order. Their uncompromising vertical façades and strictly symmetrical wings proclaimed their importance with an architectural vocabulary of Greek columns and Renaissance-inspired porticos and pediments. Soon the sounds of the locomotive were to punctuate the deliberations of the busy bureaucrats and entrepreneurs, signalling that the transportation revolution was gathering momentum.

Not since the eighth century had there been so concerted a national effort to redefine the image Japan displayed to the world. This period also shares with the Nara period an extraordinary level of government commitment to architecture as a means of defining identity and achieving official goals. The driving force in the transfer of Western architectural styles and engineering technology to the new state was the authority of the government and the growing power of the commercial and industrial sector.

The primary motivation for the Meiji programmes of Westernisation was survival against encroachment of foreign powers, followed by international recognition and acceptance as a modern nation. The urgency and energy with which building ventures of the new state were undertaken showed a thorough appreciation of the implications for Japan of the fate of China at the hands of Britain, France, Germany, Russia and the United States. The struggle between the shogunal and imperial restoration factions had intensified when the shogunate displayed apparent weakness in 1853 by granting unlimited foreign access to the ports of Nagasaki, Kobe, Shimoda, Yokohama and Hakodate in the manner of the Chinese foreign concessions. The decimation of Satsuma defences at Kagoshima by a British naval squadron in 1863 delivered a stern warning of Japan's military vulnerability to the West. It was clear that Japan had to become an economic and military power with the institutions and trappings of Western civilization if it were to survive in the international order of the later nineteenth century.

Japan may have entered the industrial age belatedly, but wasted no time in pursuing the new goals of Western-style progress. The Industrial Revolution and the Economic Revolution, which had taken more than a century of evolution in Europe and America, were telescoped into half that time in Japan. This created an explosive demand for buildings to house the new forms of government, commerce, industry and education. Architecture became an essential tool of state for convincing the flood of foreign visitors entering Japan of its reincarnation as an urban and urbane civilization. Architecture was charged with a mission of the highest national significance: proclaiming

209

loudly on every city block and street corner Japan's assurance and authority as a modern state.

The New Hierarchy of Architectural Authority

It is tempting to dismiss summarily Western-style Meiji architecture because its form seems so familiar to us. If we are to apprehend fully its significance in the definition of Meiji authority we should not think of these buildings as simply imitative or derivative. The Japanese architectural achievement of Meiji deserves due recognition because, in the context of place and time, it was nothing short of remarkable. After the first halting steps Meiji architecture was neither quaint in style nor inept in execution. It was authoritative as architecture and architectonic as authority.

Japanese government ministries and banks, railway stations and factories, schools and churches, libraries and hospitals, were as convincing in their formal attributes as any buildings of similar purpose in Europe or America. The Japanese had already mastered the architectural vocabulary of classical revival by the time they had spelled out their new governmental order in the constitution of 1889; before the ink had dried on the Imperial Rescript on Education of 1890 Japanese primary school students throughout the nation were engaged in the joys of inscribing their names into Western-style lift-top desks in 28,000 timber-floored schools with sash-windows and hinged doors. So effective are these buildings as models of Western-style architecture that, after spending only a few minutes inside, it is easy to forget that one is actually in Japan.

The new architecture undoubtedly had a dramatic impact upon the way people thought and felt about their relationship to the state and its new organs of government, the conduct of their daily lives and perhaps ultimately about themselves. Western-style homes may have still been confined to the residences of the elite by the early twentieth century, but for most Japanese, Western architectural forms had become an inescapable daily reality. *Tatami* mat floors may not have surrendered to carpet in the majority of Japanese homes until a generation after World War II, but from the 1870s, the social and behavioural consequences of architectural Westernisation were experienced from the moment a citizen had dealings with a local municipal hall or post office, primary school or bank, or travelled on the new steam locomotives.

Meiji architecture poses a special challenge when it comes to the selection of representative examples for analysis of authority. More buildings survive than from earlier periods in history by virtue of their temporal proximity to our own age and the use of more fire-resistant building materials. There has also been active preservation of Meiji buildings, including the creation of the vast outdoor museum of Meiji Village near Inuyama, because the Japanese have formed a special, almost sentimental, attachment to early Western architecture in Japan, identifying the exotic forms with the foundation of their modern state and persona. With Meiji we also enter the age of the photograph and the Western architectural blueprint which make it much easier to reconstruct the appearance of destroyed buildings.

The selection process is further complicated by the varied character of Meiji architecture. This may be due in part to the confusion arising in any great era of rapid change, but equally it reflects the complex technological and stylistic developments in construction and architecture taking place in nineteenth-century Europe and America. This was a period of remarkable technological invention arising from the advances of the industrial revolution, particularly in iron- and steel-frame engineering, which culminated in the construction of the epoch-making tower by Gustave Eiffel for the Paris Exhibition of 1889. This was also an era which was prey to an uneasy ebb and flow of enthusiasm for reviving the great architectural styles of classical antiquity and the middle ages in the light of contemporary fashion, technology and political needs. Classical columns and pediments, as used by Alberti and Sangallo, Michelangelo and Palladio during the Renaissance, enjoyed virtually unchallenged dominance as the international style of architecture until the middle decades of the nineteenth century when the grandeur of the Gothic style of the middle ages was rediscovered. In Britain, church-like buildings with pointed arches and lancet windows became the secular architectural vocabulary for law courts and municipal chambers, museums and railway stations.[2] The Gothic style, as revived in Britain by Scott and Burges and extolled by Ruskin, was challenged on the European continent and in America by another wave of classical revivalism. The renewed confidence of 'Second Empire' France under Napoleon III and of a Germany unified under Bismarck found architectural expression in a new international style of the Baroque idiom. It had heavily ornamented Greek temple façades set against the new fashion of ambitiously angled mansard roofs capped with cupolas and an occasional ribbed dome. The interiors of these buildings had a Rococo frivolity with gilded arabesques and other surface flamboyance given greater effect by dramatic placement of windows and mirrors.[3] In the United States a more pristine Neo-Classicism, which came into vogue as a result of the World Columbian Exposition held in Chicago in 1893, exploited the forms of classical antiquity to claim that America was replacing Europe as the new frontier of Western civilization.

The confusion and complexity of architectural styles in the West paralleled confusion and complexity in the nature of authority. In the same way as the Japanese who became architects were exposed to the ferment of style and counter-style, the Japanese who became Meiji political leaders were exposed during their energetic foreign travel and studies to the nineteenth-century ferment of ideas about the nature and workings of the modern nation-state. These ideas ranged from constitutional monarchy in Britain to monarchical absolutism in Prussia, and from the liberalism which inspired the 1830 and 1848 revolutions in Europe to the ideology of entrepreneurial capitalism in the post-Civil War United States.

It is not surprising then, that Meiji architecture reflects the complexity of the contemporary architectural scene in Europe and America, but in the context of our discussion of authority in Japan the sometimes confusing assemblage of styles and materials takes on a logical hierarchy corresponding to the hierarchy of the state. For this chapter a building representing each level in this hierarchy has been selected for detailed examination to identify the architectural and political character of the new Western order. Stone was reserved for buildings of paramount importance to the state, most notably the Akasaka Detached Palace, where it was used in conjunction with a Neo-Baroque façade. In the next category, slightly lower in status, were the red-brick buildings with steel or timber frames and Gothic or Classical details, the supreme example being the Tokyo Station building. Below this category of red-brick construction were the timber-frame weatherboard buildings. They were the most numerous of all Meiji Western-style buildings, cheaper and easier to construct than brick structures. It was this type of architecture, with numerous variations on the Classical and Baroque themes, which served as the official architecture of the Ministry of Education. It is exemplified by the Sōgakudō, the first school of Western music. Finally, the restoration rebuilding of our old friend the Great Buddha Hall of Tōdaiji affords special insights into the authority of tradition in the overtly Westernising age. Each of these building types addressed a particular political need and each will be discussed in turn, starting at the pinnacle of hierarchy.

The Akasaka Detached Palace: Architecture Exceeding its Authority

The Akasaka Detached Palace was built in the last decades of the Meiji period, allowing us to assess Japanese success in achieving their goal of Westernising the official state environment (Figure 9.1). The palace has become well known internationally since its refurbishment in 1968–1974 as the Geihinkan, or State Guesthouse. Its marble entrance portico has provided a dignified back-drop for welcoming speeches by visiting heads of state, while its sumptuous interior, bedecked in crystal chandeliers and gilded arabesques, has served as the setting for summit meetings of the great powers.

Fig 9.1 Akasaka Detached Palace, Tokyo. Oblique view of front façade. (Courtesy: Geihinkan and Masuda Akihisa)

The palace was never intended for this role. It was abandoned by its government almost at its birth. It had been built to serve as the official residence of the Crown Prince. The idea for an 'East Imperial Palace' (Tōgū Gosho) as the official palace of the Crown Prince first took root in 1893, as the reign of the Meiji emperor moved towards its thirtieth year. A planning committee was formed in 1896 consisting of government officials, mostly from the Imperial Household Ministry (Kunaishō), together with architectural specialists. Design work started two years afterwards, and construction was completed eleven years later in June 1909.[4] Prior to completion its name was officially changed to the 'Akasaka Detached Palace' (Akasaka Rikyū) by the Imperial Household Ministry.

From the political point of view the motivation for the creation of the Akasaka Detached Palace was eminently practical. As the accession of the Crown Prince Yoshihito to the throne became more imminent, it became imperative to promote the importance of the next emperor. What better way to achieve this than by the construction of an impressive new palace? The Akasaka Palace was, therefore, conceived as an architectural tool for strengthening the authority of the imperial institution beyond the death of the incumbent emperor. It was to be one of two buildings designed to bolster the Crown Prince's authority with an emphatic architectural presence in Tokyo. The second of these buildings, completed in 1909 just prior to the Akasaka Palace, was the Hyōkeikan, a Neo-Baroque hall crowned by a great copper dome which is now the Archaeological Wing of the Tokyo National Museum at Ueno. It was officially a 'gift' from the people of Tokyo to commemorate the wedding of the Crown Prince, paid for in part by public subscription, thereby heightening public involvement with and loyalty to the next emperor and his new consort.[5]

Today, as we look at the magnificent masonry edifice at Moto-Akasaka from the old parapets of the outer moat of Edo castle at Yotsuya, there can be no doubt that the design and construction were eminently suitable for its political purpose. The new palace was surrounded by an aura of national euphoria at the attainment of the objectives of the Meiji Restoration. It exudes the vaunting pride of a modern nation-state enjoying the success of the far-reaching process of Westernisation which had born fruit with its recognition as a great power by Britain in the Anglo–Japanese Alliance of 1902 and in its success in vanquishing the forces of Czarist Russia in 1905. The building has a powerful, immovable presence as it sits seemingly oblivious to the crowded city surrounding it amidst four square kilometres of carefully landscaped gardens in the best French aristocratic tradition, complete with manicured lawns and formal flower-beds bordered by neat border hedges. The site had previously been that of one of the mansions of the daimyo of Kii, a collateral family of the Tokugawa but, like so much of the Tokugawa and other daimyo land in Edo, was appropriated by the Meiji state following the Restoration.

The palace building itself is unashamedly Neo-Baroque, emulating the decorative exuberance of Versailles while fastidiously observing the axial symmetry of nineteenth-century German palaces such as the Neue Hofburg (1894) in Vienna (Figure 9.2). It rises two stories in height to a discrete copper-tiled

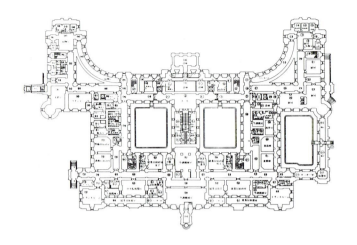

Fig 9.2
Akasaka
Detached
Palace, Tokyo.
Plans of
basement
(above),
first (centre)
and second
floors (below)
(after
restoration)
(Source:
Geihinkan
(ed.)
*Geihinkan
Moto-Akasaka
Rikyū kaishū
riryoku*)

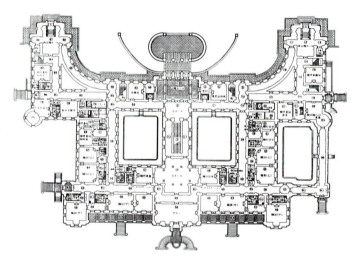

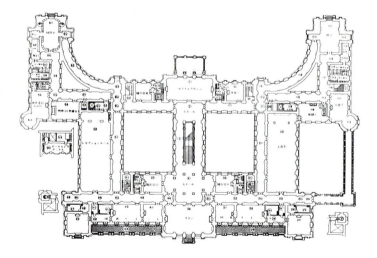

Fig 9.3
Akasaka
Detached
Palace, Tokyo.
Detail of inte-
rior showing
the grand
stairway
leading to the
second floor
(Courtesy:
Geihinkan and
Masuda
Akihisa)

roof. The central structure pays homage to Classical Greece, with the pillars
and triangular pediment of the archetypal Greek temple. Its two wings spread
out on each side, reaching forward at the ends in a graceful arc. The granite
walls and lines of pedimented windows are a model of order and symmetrical balance. It is this same sense of order and balance which permeates the
official architecture of the Meiji period, from its palaces to post offices. It is
reminiscent of the way that the Nara state turned to symmetrical planning to
express its notions of order and authority.

Within the palace, the staterooms, the grand ballroom on the second floor,
and the private suites intended for the Crown Prince and Princess in the
opposing wings, are all fluent, self-indulgent Rococo in style, with gold highlighting the Corinthian capitals on marble columns, the arabesque carvings
on the walls and the plaster mouldings on the vaulted ceilings. The floors,
altogether 15,000 square metres in surface area, vary from marbled mosaic
and burgundy carpet along the corridors and in the entrance area to precisely
crafted, highly polished parquet in the main chambers.

The palace was a remarkable technical achievement as well as a decorative
tour de force. Electricity replaced gas-light, with clusters of electric lights
illuminating the pillars of the entrance portico and the great marble staircase
leading to the second floor (Figure 9.3). In addition to electricity, the palace
also had hot and cold running water, central heating and air conditioning,

215

although initially possessing only one bathroom. Presumably this was a design oversight rather than an indication that the Japanese had adopted the contemporary bathing habits of the European aristocracy along with their architectural styles.

Building the Akasaka Detached Palace: Architects and the Meiji State

It was a singular achievement that a building of such essential 'foreignness' was constructed little over one generation after the first tentative attempts at Western-style building in Japan. The achievement is all the more striking when it is compared with the first attempt by the Meiji government to build an official guesthouse for foreign visitors 40 years earlier. The Tsukiji Hotel, constructed in the centre of Tokyo near the Sumida River in 1868, was a curious yet predictably eclectic building (Figure 9.4). It employed traditional Japanese timber-frame construction to imitate the Western-style buildings which by then graced the Treaty Ports of Yokohama and Kobe. The conventional Japanese tiled roof was surmounted by a Western-style belvedere, complete with wrought-iron weather-vane. The walls were covered with terracotta tiles, a feature used to protect buildings against fire in the Edo period but which did not save the Tsukiji Hotel from a fire in 1872 which reduced its modest Westernising pretensions to ashes.

By the turn of the century the Japanese were able to achieve such dramatic improvements in the quality of their Western-style buildings, as demonstrated by the Akasaka Palace, largely because of the success of the policy of employing foreign experts (*oyatoi*). During the Meiji period some 3,000 specialists in many fields from Europe and the United States came to Japan at the invitation of the government to provide the Meiji state with knowledge and guidance in government and law, finance, investment, the army and navy, science and technology, industry and commerce, learning and culture. By far the greatest number of *oyatoi* were associated with the Ministry of Construction and were specialists in the fields of engineering and architecture, itself an indication of

Fig 9.4
Tsukiji Hotel,
Tokyo
(Source: *The
Far East*,
1872)

the importance of building to the state.[6] They planned and supervised the major projects in the first two decades of the modern transformation of Japan, and bequeathed their skills to the first generation of Japanese experts in architecture, engineering and urban planning.

The Akasaka Palace was the fruit of this process. It was designed using technical drawings in the Western manner. Its construction was directed by Katayama Tōkuma, the official architect for the Imperial Building Bureau (Naishōryō) of the Imperial Household Ministry and one of the first Japanese to be trained in Western architectural practice at the Kōbu Daigakkō, the Imperial College of Engineering, predecessor of the Faculty of Engineering of the modern University of Tokyo.

The programme at the Imperial College of Engineering was established by Josiah Conder, a young British architect who had arrived in Japan at government invitation in 1877. With Conder's arrival we encounter one of the least visible but most far-reaching of changes to Japanese architecture in the Meiji period, namely the adoption of Western design practice. Government policy was to establish in Japan the profession of 'architect', as defined in contemporary Europe and America, in order to take charge of the building of Western-style buildings. The logic seemed impeccable: Western-style architects were needed to make Western-style buildings. However, the architects of nineteenth-century Europe and America were the product of the Renaissance tradition of the artist who designed, rather than the builder who built, a separation still affecting architectural practice today. This offered scope for individual artistic expression in architecture as an art, but also seriously weakened the traditional building professions, particularly the top level of master builders because they lost their design prerogatives, and along with this, their prestige and on-site power. This was to become a particularly serious problem in Japan, with its strong tradition of architectural attainment by the master carpenter.

Josiah Conder was the seminal influence on the practice of Western-style architecture in Meiji Japan, establishing a course at university level on European architectural styles along with providing practical training in Western drafting techniques.[7] He changed the initial Japanese emphasis on utilitarian engineering to doctrinaire architectural style. With Conder, Japan entered the international forum of architectural ideology as well as design practice.

At that time, matters architectural were being argued in Europe and America with a vehemence rivalling the theological controversies of medieval Christendom. This ensured the informed attention of politicians and the public alike to the details of new buildings. National as well as individual prestige was at stake, with John Ruskin and William Burges ascribing the highest nobility and civic virtue to the Gothic style at the same time as it drew the scorn of Henry Van Brunt, apologist for the Columbian Exposition. From his committed classical and New World position he scornfully dismissed Burges' life and work as nothing but 'a beautiful early Gothic masquerade'.[8]

To understand Conder's own design predilections is to understand much of the stylistic nuance of Western architecture in Meiji Japan. After training at the University of London, in 1875 Conder had entered the architectural firm of none other than William Burges, champion of the Gothic Revival in England. The next year Conder won the prestigious Soane Prize, awarded by the Royal Institute of British Architects for the most distinguished entry in an annual design competition.[9] The Meiji government probably selected Conder to establish Western architectural training in Japan because of the award of the Soane Prize. For a young architect like Conder, the Japanese offered considerably more scope for carrying out his own more classically orientated work than did the prospect of remaining in England as part of Burges' Gothic Revival firm.

Conder was only 25 years of age when he arrived in Japan and was to remain there for the rest of his professional life. His principal works were to include the completion of the epoch-making Rokumeikan in 1883, a Western-style club for interaction in a Western manner between the Japanese elite and their foreign associates in government, business and high society. Although the Rokumeikan does not survive, contemporary photographs reveal that it had the symmetrical façade with arcades of rounded arches set on Classical columns inspired by Palladio's revival of the Ancient, as well as the more pronounced hipped gambrel roofs over the central structure typical of the French Second Empire style.[10]

Katayama Tōkuma was a student in Conder's first class at the nascent Imperial College of Engineering. After gaining experience as an assistant for some of Conder's architectural commissions for the Meiji government, he embarked upon his own architectural career which was to be based on a close association with the most influential circles of Meiji government. Japanese Western-trained architects came to occupy a place of privilege in the Meiji establishment because of the political significance of the service they provided. At the same time, patronage by powerful members of the ruling elite was essential for the success of architects in gaining major public commissions. This symbiosis between architect and state is a universal phenomenon. It would be impossible, for instance, to imagine the great architectural and artistic outpourings of the Italian Renaissance without the patronage of individual architects by the Roman Papacy or by the mercantile houses of Florence.[11] If patronage forms the crucial link between architects and authority, for Katayama it was the patronage of Yamagata Aritomo which guaranteed the commission for the Akasaka Palace. Yamagata was a dominating force in the Meiji-period government, serving as Home Minister, two terms as Prime Minister, and at the end of his career, as president of the Privy Council (1909–1922).[12] Yamagata's support therefore ensured Katayama's placement at the heart of the imperial bureaucracy, a support which he enjoyed in part because both came from Chōshū. Loyalty between former samurai from the outer domains of Chōshū, Satsuma, Tosa and Hizen of the Tokugawa system is an abiding characteristic of Meiji government.

After initial training with Conder, Katayama visited Europe in 1882 for a period of seven months to make a special study of palace architecture.[13] In 1886 he was appointed to the team working on the Imperial Palace building project, an eclectic Japanese-Western style building, eventually destroyed by bombing in World War II. Katayama had particular responsibility for the interior design, spending eleven months in Germany studying the interior decoration and furnishings of palaces. After the completion of the Imperial Palace project in 1887, Katayama remained in the service of the Imperial Household Ministry and was promoted to supervisor of the newly formed Imperial Building Bureau. From this position he was to direct a team of talented technical experts in constructing such important architectural milestones of the Meiji state as the Japanese Red Cross Central Hospital (1890), the Nara Imperial Museum (1894), and the Kyoto Imperial Museum (1895). Not surprisingly, he was also responsible for the official residence of his political mentor Yamagata in 1891.

The Akasaka Palace was to be Katayama's largest and most important project. From the inception of the project in 1896 he was made a member of the planning committee. He spent the following year once again in Europe, studying palace architecture while completing the basic drawings for the Akasaka project. In 1898 a new Bureau for the Construction of the Eastern Palace (*Tōgū gosho gozōei kyoku*) was created to manage the project, and Katayama was placed in charge of the design and construction as *gikan*, a title best translated here as 'Chief Architect'.[14] This promotion coincided with the apogee of Yamagata's own power, as he assumed office as Prime Minister for the second time on 5 November 1898.

Beyond Foreign Models

Katayama coordinated the technical work of a veritable army of architectural draughtsmen, engineers and specially organised groups of craftsmen skilled in making the intricate details of carvings and mouldings essential for each room. He made two further trips to Europe and the United States to investigate the technical aspects of central heating and air conditioning, and to finalise details of interior decoration. He also purchased antique French and German furniture for each chamber.

The use of steel framing for the building was a technological breakthrough. In the United States Katayama consulted specialists in newly developed steel framing techniques, including Edward Shankland, who had developed the steel framing of the Manufacturing Building, the largest building of the 1893 Columbian World Exposition.[15] He also arranged the export to Japan of the 3,000 tonnes of steel framing needed for the project from the Carnegie Works at Pittsburgh, and for the despatch of two American engineers to assist in its erection on site.

The long-accepted interpretation in both Japanese and Western architectural circles of the structural system used for the Akasaka Palace is that the walls were made of brick, which was then faced with stone and clipped onto a steel framework to give them resilience against earthquake. In other words the conventional wisdom has it that the building is something of a carefully engineered architectural pretense of a masonry structure.[16] This interpretation assumes that the palace was built using the same structural system that had been employed for the main building of the Bank of Japan, constructed between 1890 and 1896. Some brick may have been used for subsidiary parts of the Akasaka Palace and there is no denying the reliance on a great deal of imported steel. However, Katayama's own technical explanation of the building, given in a long interview with the *Nihon shinbun* on 17 May 1907 after the main construction work on the palace had been completed, reveals a very different structural logic to the building:

> Strictly speaking, steel-frame structures are a pure American system but here at the Akasaka Palace it is to a large extent very different in the composition of the components. What I mean by this is that in the United States the steel framing performs the principal [structural] role [in a building] and the stone is little more than a [non-structural] wall attached to it on the outside. But here at the Akasaka Palace the stone itself has been made the main structure of the building and the steel framing is used only to strengthen the weak parts of the stone [at the interfaces]. As a result it is not unusual for parts of the wall to be as much as 9 *shaku* (2.73 metres) thick. . . . We were aware from studying recent cases of earthquakes [in Japan] . . . that, although steel frame structures had been used, these were not really safe and caused a lot of problems. At the Bureau for the Construction of the Eastern Palace we therefore thoroughly considered this defect in the American system [of steel framing] and have been careful to give thorough consideration [to solving the problem].[17]

The use of structural steel in Japan in the 1890s was the first occasion on which this new engineering technology had been employed in an earthquake-prone region. Although Sir Henry Bessemer had invented a method for producing steel for large-scale buildings as early as 1855, Hitchcock notes that 'the full architectural possibilities of the use of structural steel were hard to grasp before the nineties'.[18] The transfer of this technology to Japan stimulated developments to improve its aseismic potential. The existing method for its use was neither rigid enough to withstand earthquake shocks, nor flexible enough to vibrate and absorb the seismic energy. Steel-frame structures built in Japan using the American technology before 1907 had been caught in this danger zone between rigidity and flexibility, and as Katayama himself noted in the interview, for the Akasaka Palace it was necessary to devise a new system of steel-reinforced masonry capable of sustaining high wall loading from earthquakes. It is a matter of historical record that the Akasaka Palace was to survive without damage the devastating force of the Great Kantō Earthquake of 1923, which registered 7.9 on the open-ended Richter scale.

In addition to its technical innovations in seismic engineering, it is the consummate mastery of interior detail which distinguishes the Akasaka Palace from other Meiji Western-style buildings. It is the best example of official Meiji architecture because the interior detail is so fully developed. Other buildings had impressive exteriors but their interiors were much less complete and impressive. For example, the interior of the Hōheikan, built in 1880 under the supervision of an American, Louis Boenmer, as a hotel and official guesthouse for the Hokkaidō Colonisation Commission (*Kaitakushi*) in Sapporo, was a competent timber-frame weatherboard building, which from the outside could easily be mistaken for the residence of a wealthy Massachusetts family of the same era. Inside, however, the walls and ceilings are quite stark in appearance, with decoration confined to half columns and plaster mouldings at the anchor points for the chandeliers.

The Akasaka Palace displays complete mastery of the idioms of the European palace interior but goes an important stage further in adapting these to Japanese stately requirements. Aided by traditional Japanese craftsmen who had carefully studied European decorative techniques, Katayama did not merely reproduce the grand style of European Baroque and Rococo. He added to it his own Japanese motifs and subject matter. African lions of British empire pedigree may prowl the ceiling apses of the ballroom, but one lion sits contentedly beneath a suit of samurai armour. The oil paintings which are set into the polished cypress-wood panels of the state dining room are variations of the birds and flowers themes used so effectively by the Kano painters for Nijō Castle (Figure 9.5). There are even profusely blossoming peonies which offer a Japanese complement to antique French furniture. The more one understands of the Akasaka project, the more one is reminded not of European palaces but of the great palace projects of Japanese history. The Akasaka Palace is heir to the same tradition as the Daigokuden of Nara and the Palace of the Second Compound of Nijō Castle. Its creation exhibits the same competence at organising architectural projects for state purposes, and its completed form the same attention to the theatre of government in the hierarchy of spatial transition and decorative programmes.

Fig 9.5
Akasaka
Detached
Palace. Detail
of the State
Dining Room
(Courtesy:
Geihinkan and
Masuda
Akihisa)

221

Authority Exceeded

The Akasaka Palace was, therefore, an exuberant expression of late Meiji-period imperial authority and self-confidence, earning Katayama the acclaim of his architectural peers.[19] Ironically, the very success of the building as palace architecture called into question its suitability as a residence for the Crown Prince. As early as 1902, when the original budget estimate of 2.5 million *yen* was revised to double this figure, it was deemed too costly and ostentatious for its avowed purpose by the emperor himself. After an audience with the emperor, the Minister for the Imperial Household Tanaka Mitsuaki, issued the following instructions to the Imperial Building Bureau:

> The construction and ornamentation of the Palace should be appropriate to the status [of the Crown Prince]. However, it is essential to concentrate exclusively on simplicity and sturdiness and to avoid ostentation in order to conform to the emperor's wishes. His Majesty has refused to authorise any increase in the construction budget and has given strict orders that henceforth no further requests will be entertained.[20]

This is an extraordinarily blunt statement in the generally restrained official records of the Meiji emperor. The phrasing of these objections has a familiar ring to it, recalling the efforts of the Tokugawa shogunate to curb architectural extravagance by the daimyo in order to maintain the correspondence between architectural form and status in their political order. Whatever the reality of contemporary European palaces which the Akasaka Detached Palace so competently reflects, the inference in the official imperial records is that it was too grand for its purpose. When finished, at just slightly more than the 5 million *yen* authorised by the emperor in 1902, the new building became an acute embarrassment at the highest levels of state. It was not politic to permit the Crown Prince to reside in his new palace as long as the Meiji Emperor lived, and once Yoshihito ascended his father's throne he was obliged to reside in the Imperial Palace. Katayama's palace stood unoccupied from the time of its completion in 1909. It was not until the summer of 1917 that it was used for official purposes when it provided the grand setting for a state banquet in honour of the Korean Crown Prince. The Akasaka Detached Palace is a fascinating illustration of architecture exceeding its authority.

Tokyo Station: Temple to Progress and Empire

The construction of the Central Station in Tokyo (*Chūō teishajō*), or Tokyo Station (*Tōkyō eki*) as it is now universally known, coincided with the building of the Akasaka Palace. However it was to prove a more pervasive and powerful demonstration of the authority of the late Meiji state than was the Palace because of the particular national and international circumstances prevailing at the time of its construction.[21]

There was to be no crisis of authority with this late Meiji building, conceived in 1898 but not completed until 1914, two years after the Meiji period had

ended. Tokyo Station was to become no less than a temple to progress and a monument to empire (Figure 9.6). It paid homage to the power of rail in the development of the state through its mastery of Western transportation technology and civil engineering. The main building, with its grand scale and warm red-brick walls held together securely by steel framing, became the visible and functioning focus of a growing empire of communication, capitalism and colonialism, reminiscent of the role of Tōdaiji at the centre of the Nara *kokubunji* system over eleven centuries earlier. The steel tracks which radiated from Tokyo were soon to connect the length and breadth of the main Japanese islands in a vast and efficient transportation network and, via steamship at Moji at Shimonoseki, to Pusan in Korea, with the growing sphere of influence on the Asian mainland. By the 1920s passengers could purchase return tickets at Tokyo Station to twenty-five destinations in China, including Beijing.[22]

When completed in 1914, Tokyo Station occupied an area of approximately 19,800 square metres, including the station building on the Marunouchi or west side, four large platforms and multiple tracks, and the freight yards on the Yaesu or east side (Figure 9.7). The station opened onto a wide plaza almost as large as the area occupied by the actual station building and its railway tracks. This was to be the focus for the development of a Western-style commercial district in the later 1920s. The station building itself had a north-south frontage of some 350 metres in length, and the tracks, platforms and freight facilities extended eastwards over 100 metres. The domes at the north and south entrances each had an ambitious span of 36 metres. Tokyo

Fig 9.6
Tokyo Station and Marunouchi Plaza *ca* 1926 (Courtesy: Transportation Museum, Tokyo)

223

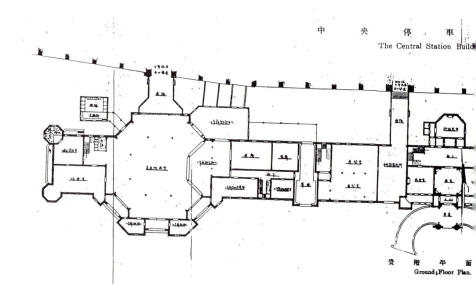

中　央　停　車　車
The Central Station Build

Fig 9.7
Tokyo Station.
Plan by
Tatsuno Kingo
(Source:
*Kenchiku
zasshi*, no.
286, 1900)

Station was thus executed on the same grand scale as London's St Pancras Station and Washington's Union Station. Its construction coincided with that of Washington's Union Station, completed in 1908, Melbourne's Flinders Street Station, finished in 1910, and New York's Grand Central Station, completed in 1913. Tokyo Station therefore was built in an international context of railways and their capital-city stations as an expression of national confidence, as a part of a strategy of centralising state power and as a demonstration of national mastery of advanced building technologies.

The importance of Tokyo Station has been underestimated as a work of architecture and as witness to the political, technological and artistic imperatives of the late Meiji and early Taishō periods. Until recently it was overshadowed by other buildings in histories of late nineteenth- or early twentieth-century architecture. Subsequent changes to imperial authority and the plans of Marunouchi have diminished its once powerful political and planning role at the centre of Tokyo. As a railway station it was relegated to secondary transportation significance by Shinjuku and Ueno Stations. As a work of architectural design its carefully calculated proportions were grossly disfigured by war-time bombing and subsequent clumsy postwar repairs (Figure 9.8), leading to the mistaken impression that its design was based on that of the central railway station in Amsterdam.[23] By the mid-1980s there were plans to demolish the original Meiji building and replace it with a more 'cost-effective' structure. A vigorous preservation campaign ensured its survival and new Shinkansen lines have since re-established its importance as a transportation hub.

Tokyo Station and Imperial Authority

Tokyo Station was built against a background of growing Japanese competence in transportation technologies, the increasing importance of transportation to

224

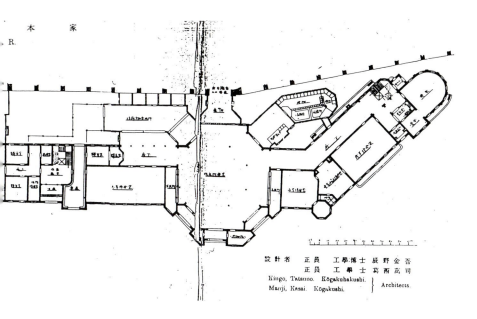

設計者　正員　工學博士 辰野金吾
　　　　正員　工學士 葛西萬司
Kingo, Tatsuno. Kōgakuhakushi. ⎫
Manji, Kasai. Kōgakushi.　　　⎬ Architects.
　　　　　　　　　　　　　　 ⎭

the centralisation of state power, and the international context of railways and
capital-city stations as the expression of national confidence and authority.
These were years in which the authority of the Japanese state matured and was
projected into the international sphere with the expansion of its economic,
political and military interests on the Asian continent. The central role of Tokyo
Station in nation and state was accentuated by its role as the emperor's own
station, from which he embarked on state visits. The main entrance faced the
Imperial Palace across the moat, and at the heart of the station complex were
the grand portico and reception rooms for the emperor and members of the
imperial family (Figure 9.9). The architectural design paid unequivocal homage
to the authority of the imperial institution, with the design focused on the
central Imperial Entrance with its emphatic portico and flowing Neo-Baroque
pediment. The reservation of the most impressive and central entrance for the
exclusive use of the imperial family is a familiar strategy in the use of architecture to enhance authority. The gateways of the Imperial Palace in Kyoto and
the *onari* gateways of Edo derived much of their effectiveness as symbols of
authority by the exclusiveness of their entry. Exclusion and exclusiveness is also
the basis for the special sense of place created at the inner precincts of the
shrines at Ise.

Tokyo Station was to serve as the visual centrepiece of the business
and administrative district of the city of Tokyo, the area now known as
Marunouchi. In so doing it emphasised the relationship between the Imperial
Palace and the emerging status of Japan. The district in front of the Imperial
Palace, where many of the daimyo palaces had been located in the Edo period,
was destroyed by a disastrous fire in 1872. It remained a burnt-out waste-
land until purchased in its entirety by Iwasaki Yanosuke, son of the founder
of the powerful Mitsubishi commercial firm. In 1893 Iwasaki consolidated
Mitsubishi into an even more powerful financial empire, and undertook the

225

Fig 9.8
Tokyo Station.
Building after
bombing in
1945 (above)
and after post-
war repairs
(below)
(Courtesy:
Mishima Fujio
and Nagata
Hiroshi,
*Tetsudō to
machi Tōkyō.*)

redevelopment of this area as the centre of its corporate power. Josiah Conder was placed in charge of constructing the new Mitsubishi buildings. In collaboration with one of his former students, Sone Tatsuzō, Conder designed a series of three-storey red-brick buildings along the spacious avenues in conscious emulation of the financial district in contemporary London. Starting with Mitsubishi Number One Building in 1894, 13 more buildings of the same style were to be built there in the course of the next 17 years.[24]

Tokyo Station was situated at the end of the grand avenue, 70 metres wide, which cut through the new Marunouchi district to the palace moat plaza.[25] At the completion of Tokyo Station an axis of authority had been created through the heart of central Tokyo, running from Sakashita Gatehouse of the palace to the emperor's entrance at the station, a distance of 900 metres. The pomp and circumstance of the emperor processing in horse-drawn carriage down the central boulevard of the city to be received by officials at the station invested the buildings in the public mind with a close association with the authority of the emperor. The greatest of these spectacles were the grand processions accompanying the imperial departure and return on the occasion of the enthronement of the Taishō and Shōwa emperors at the Imperial Palace

Fig 9.9
Tokyo Station.
Central Hall
and Imperial
Entrance

in Kyoto (Figures 9.10–9.12). The processional boulevard leading to Tokyo
Station itself reflected the dramatic vista-planning in contemporary European
cities – notably Baron Haussmann's Paris of the Second Empire – but it
also recalled Suzaku Avenue in imperial Nara which bisected the city
from the Rajōmon in the south to the Suzakumon at the entrance to the
Imperial Palace in the north. The Marunouchi and Nara avenues were approximately the same width. Similar processional routes, highlighted by triumphal
gateways and arches, were also a feature of the projection of authority in
ancient Mesopotamia, Egypt and imperial Rome. For the opening of Tokyo
Station on 18 December 1914, a three-bay triumphal arch, 34 metres high
and 25 metres wide, adorned with gold imperial chrysanthemums and
festooned with flags, was erected in the station plaza in front of the imperial
entrance.[26]

Tokyo Station and Steam Power

To understand fully the importance of Tokyo Station to imperial authority it
is vital to appreciate the power of the locomotive and the authority of railway-
station architecture to the contemporary nation-state. Internationally, by the
turn of the twentieth century, the railway had created a new standard for
judging progress and power by virtue of its revolutionary speed, carrying
capacity and reliability as compared with horse-drawn transportation. The
railway was the ubiquitous symbol of the Machine Age and this elevated the
station building to the company of the highest authority. The most important railway stations in Europe and America became the cathedrals of the
industrial age, with grand façades of stone and brick expressing their political, economic and social importance and their cavernous, smoky interiors,
spanned by the modern miracle of cast-iron framing and glass, replacing the

227

Fig 9.10
The procession
of Emperor
Shōwa and
entourage
leaves Sakashita
Gatehouse of
the Imperial
Palace for
Tokyo Station
on the occasion
of travel to
Kyoto for the
Enthronement
Ceremonies,
November
1928
(Source:Official
publication,
*Shōwa tairei
shashinchō*.
Tokyo, Ōtsuka
kōgeisha,
1930)

Fig 9.11
Official party
farewelling the
Emperor and
Empress at
Tokyo Station,
1928
(Source:
Official publi-
cation, *Shōwa
tairei
shashinchō*)

Fig 9.12
Emperor
Shōwa and
entourage
returning to
the Imperial
Palace, Tokyo,
from Tokyo
Station,
following the
Enthronement
Ceremonies in
Kyoto,
November
1928
(Source:
Official publi-
cation, *Shōwa
tairei
shashinchō*)

sacred spaces of incense-filled cathedrals in homage to the new gods of progress. Every city needed an impressive central railway station as its gateway on the world and as the focus of the comings and going of both the high and the low in society. These stations became an opportunity for propaganda in fierce international competition.[27]

The station created a new urban phenomenon, the railway square, with hotels, offices and shops springing up around the entrance to the transport artery, redefining the centre of cities in the way that cathedrals and government houses had once defined the urban hierarchy. From Victoria and St Pancras Stations in London to Flinders Street Station in Melbourne, from Union Station in Washington DC to Victoria Terminus in Bombay, the railway station vaunted the material triumph of new technology in spanning continents and carrying people, goods and information in ways unprecedented in human history. By the 1880s and 1890s the railway was conquering the land in the way that the caravel had conquered the oceans four centuries earlier. The Orient Express and the Trans-Siberian Railway inaugurated a new era in international transportation, rapidly traversing formerly sacrosanct borders. The railway quickly became a tool for economic and political expansion, a mainstay of colonialism as well as capitalism, and an artery for rapid troop deployment in arenas of competing colonial interests, including East Asia, giving rise to the concept 'railway diplomacy' as part of the language of international confrontation.

In the climate of heightening international tension after the turn of the twentieth century, railways played their part alongside dreadnoughts as stepping-stones for the extension of national influence. The Trans-Siberian Railway, which reached Lake Baikal in 1902, was serving as an artery for

Czarist Russia's expansion into continental East Asia. Japan had learned the Western lesson of the importance of colonial power as an arm of national policy, and now sought to counterbalance this growing Russian influence. This culminated in the outbreak of the Russo-Japanese War in 1904. Japan's victory in 1905, along with British recognition of Japan as a great power in the Anglo-Japanese Alliance signed three years earlier, had secured Japan the international recognition which had been at the core of national concerns throughout the Meiji period. The Treaty of Portsmouth of 1905, which concluded the Russo-Japanese War, gave Japan the right to maintain guards on its railway interests on the Asian mainland and led to the establishment of the South Manchurian Railway Company. Strategic concern with railways continued with the conclusion of a secret treaty with Russia in 1907, which effectively divided Manchuria into a northern Russian zone of influence and a southern Japanese sector in response to fears of American railway expansion in the region.[28]

It was entirely in keeping with the growing tide of colonialism, supported by railway expansion in China, that the occasion of the official opening of Tokyo Station on 18 December 1914, was used to welcome back Lieutenant-General Kamio Mitsuomi (1855–1927) and his staff from the successful military expedition in China against the German-occupied railhead at Qingdao. By securing this coastal city, situated between Beijing and Shanghai, in support of the Allied war effort against Germany following the outbreak of World War I, Japan gained access to the Chinese hinterland along the German-built railway to Jinan.[29] The account of the opening of Tokyo Station given in the *Tokyo Asahi* newspaper shows the clear connection in the public mind between Tokyo Station and the growing Japanese empire:

> The grand spectacle of the opening, the brilliance of a triumphant return! On this day, the eighteenth [of December, 1914], Commanding Officer Kamio and his general staff, were joyously welcomed back to the Imperial Capital after their grand and triumphant military expedition, and marked the first step in the opening for business of the grand Tokyo Station, the largest station in Asia.[30]

Building Tokyo Station

The construction of the central station was part of a comprehensive plan to complete the missing link in the Tokyo urban rail system from Shinagawa to Ueno. The creation of a modern national steam-railway system had been a high priority for the new Meiji state, with far-reaching implications for Western technology transfer and the formation of industrial infrastructure. In the early stages, all equipment including engines, rolling stock and rails, were imported from Britain, along with drivers and engineers. Finance was also heavily underwritten by loans floated in Britain. The first railway line was opened between Shinagawa and Yokohama in 1872, a distance of 29 kilometres. This became the main transportation artery between the old Tōkaidō post town on the boundary of the former city of Edo and the treaty port of Yokohama.

Politically, the opening of this line was an event of the first magnitude, with the emperor and his retinue boarding the train with all the pomp and pageantry of a grand state occasion. The fact that the distinguished passengers stepped neatly out of their shoes on to the Shinagawa platform as they boarded their gilded rail coach, and had to be provided with substitutes upon their arrival in Yokohama, hinted at the social adjustments new technology was to force upon time-honoured custom.

The Japanese were understandably anxious to break free of foreign dependence. In the early 1870s a machinery hall for the Japanese National Railways was built at Shinbashi to begin local manufacture of engine and carriage parts. The building itself, however, had to be constructed using iron pillars and beams imported from Hamilton's Windsor Ironworks in Liverpool. But by the time that the railway network linked Kobe with Yokohama in 1889, the Shinbashi Factory of the Japan Railway Bureau had been built using locally manufactured cast-iron pillars and roof trusses.

The government objective was to complete a unified national railway reaching from Kyushu through Tokyo to link up with the expanding railway systems in the north of Honshu.[31] As early as 1886 plans had been drawn up for this link, with a 'Central Station' proposed for a site in what became the Ginza. This proposal was put forward by the German, Wilhelm Böckmann who, together with Hermann Ende, had been invited by the Japanese Government to devise a master-plan for the government and administrative district of central Tokyo with a parliament building as its focus.[32]

It was to be another 28 years of stop–start work and negotiations before Tokyo Station was finally opened in December 1914, two years after the death of the emperor Meiji. From 1893 the leading Prussian railway engineer Herman Rumshöttel, first invited to Japan in 1887 to work on the expansion of the railway system in Kyushu, was commissioned to survey the rail line between Shinagawa and Ueno.[33] After various delays caused by the Sino-Japanese War, it was decided to proceed with Rumshöttel's plan for an overhead railway using steel-frame and brick bridges to cross the major roads in the city.

In 1898 the government invited another German, Franz Baltzer, to prepare the detailed designs for the main station and tracks and to supervise their construction. Baltzer had recently completed the overhead urban line in Berlin, as well as the Köln Station, and was considered to be ideally suited to this task.[34]

Railroading Authority: Tatsuno and Proper Station

It was Balzer who drew up the first detailed plans for Tokyo Station, with the main building situated on the west side of the site, facing towards the imperial palace, and a rational arrangement of through-tracks, platforms and freight-yards located on the Yaesu or east side. Balzer's design unwittingly precipitated a crisis in the architecture of Meiji authority. Perceiving a need to reconcile contemporary political needs with traditional Japanese architecture, he produced a design for the station building comprising a series of structures similar to the architecture of the palaces of the daimyo, many of which were still extant in Tokyo. The chambers to receive the emperor were marked by a grand *karahafu* set over the entrance (Figure 9.13).

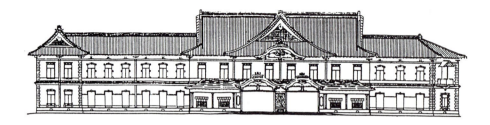

Fig 9.13 Franz Baltzer's designs for the Tokyo Station Building (1898–99). (Main building and entrance to railway platforms (above), and Imperial Entrance (below). (Source: Kajima (ed.) *Tōkyō eki tanjō*)

The magnificently expressive flowing form of *karahafu* had been central to the architectural iconography of Momoyama and Edo period authority. We have seen from the *Aobyōshi* that as late as 1841 the *karahafu* was still reserved as a status symbol for daimyo of highest status. Balzer's design for Tokyo Station was therefore entirely in keeping with Japanese traditions of architecture and authority, but it was entirely out of step with the intention of the Meiji imperial state to represent its new authority as a modern, Westernised nation. The plans were rejected by the committee responsible for the station development. It was decided to retain only Balzer's general layout for the station complex, rails, platforms and freight-yard, and to employ a Japanese architect to design a red-brick, Western-style building instead.

This was similar to the situation which had occurred when Ende and Böckmann had presented to the government their detailed designs for a new Diet Building in Tokyo in 1887. After careful consideration of the Japanese tradition of architecture and authority, they had proposed an European-style building with traditional Japanese hip-gable tiled roof and a central hall capped with a fanciful pagoda-like tower. A *karahafu* graced the classical columns of the central entrance.[35] This proposal had also been rejected out of hand.

After the failure of Balzer's Tokyo Station plans to win the committee's approval, the task of designing the new Tokyo Station building was put in the hands of a Japanese, Tatsuno Kingo. Along with Katayama, it is Tatsuno who best symbolises the Meiji architectural establishment. He had been a member of the governmental committee responsible for drafting the architectural requirements for the new Diet Building, and was no doubt involved in the decision to turn down the Ende–Böckman proposal.[36] It was now considered that he could be relied upon to give the Tokyo railway building its proper station in the Meiji state.

Tatsuno was an architect of authority in both the literal and metaphorical sense, so strong was his contribution in giving tangible expression to the authority of the Meiji period. His background and career closely conform to the pattern typical of most Meiji leaders whatever their field. Like Katayama, he had been born of a samurai family, in 1854, in Karatsu of the province of Hizen. He was part of the first student intake for the newly established Imperial College of Engineering. In 1879 he graduated at the head of his class and received a travel scholarship from the government which enabled him, along with nine other members of his graduating class, to travel in England and Europe and gain first-hand experience of Western architectural practice. In May 1880 he entered the architectural firm of Burges in London, while undertaking courses in architecture and art at the University of London. In 1883 he returned to Japan after a period of study of architecture in France and Italy. His sketch-books include precise drawings of corbelling, pediments and towers.[37] Upon his return to Japan he quickly became the central Japanese figure in the adoption of Western architectural styles, succeeding Conder as Professor in the Faculty of Engineering of the University of Tokyo. He was co-founder of the Japan Architects Association, later serving as President, and helped to establish *Kenchiku zasshi*, the journal through which technical information on Western building practice was disseminated throughout the architectural profession.

In 1888–1889 Tatsuno visited Europe and America in order to make a special study of bank buildings, paralleling the way Katayama had made a special study of European palaces. The establishment of a new Western style banking system, with the Bank of Japan at its centre, was crucial to the economic programmes of the Meiji state, so new bank buildings loomed large on the political agenda. It is clear that Tatsuno's study of Western bank buildings was part of a well-concerted policy directing the acquisition of Western architectural skills in mid-Meiji, in preparation for a Japanese take-over of responsibility for building projects from foreign teachers and mentors. Approximately two-thirds of the 140 buildings with which Tatsuno was associated over his long career were to be bank buildings. The rest were a mixture of commercial and institutional buildings together with four major railway station buildings. Tatsuno designed not only the Main Building of the Bank of Japan (1890–1896), the central institution for Japan's modernising economy, but also its branches in Osaka, Kyoto, Nagoya, Kanazawa, Hakodate and Hiroshima. The main building was built in a Classical Revival style. It was the first major application of structural steel to architecture in Japan had brick walls faced with stone.[38] Thereafter the basis of Tatsuno's architectural practice was to become red-brick buildings with steel frames. The exteriors were complete with the horizontal bands and stone Classical Revival details characteristic of 1880s London, but more flamboyant and overtly decorative than the one employed by Conder. Tatsuno's combination of experience in Western institutional architecture and the expressive power of his design work made him preeminently suited to the challenge of designing the Tokyo Station building.

Surviving drawings reveal three distinct stages in the evolution of Tatsuno's design (Figure 9.14).[39] In the initial stage, little more than a conceptual sketch, a three-storey Neo-Baroque hall, capped by a short clock-tower, was placed at the centre. The structure had a Classical Revival porticoed entrance for receiving the emperor and imperial family when they travelled around the nation on

official tours. The central hall was flanked by a pair of large identical buildings, each with its own central hall and matching wings. One was to be reserved for departures and the other for arrivals by the general public, a rational approach to crowd control retained in the final design. The three main buildings were connected by two-storey buildings and a corridor one storey in height. Overall, there was little stylistic unity in the façade; it was more a collection of buildings loosely conjoined, than a single unified structure.

The second stage of the design process did little to unify this overall design. It concentrated instead on giving visual emphasis to the emperor's hall by means of an arched pediment set over the entrance, with a squat, Gothic Revival tower situated above it. The third stage of the evolution of the design, however, reveals the design of the building as it was to be constructed. The Gothic tower on the emperor's hall has been replaced with a high mansard, Second Empire-style roof more in keeping with the Neo-Baroque style of the rest of the station. The entrance portico is given heavier pillars closer in style to those used at the Akasaka Palace. The scattered collection of buildings shown in the earlier stages has now been integrated into a uniform façade. The third design redrafting coincided with Japanese victory in the war against Russia and the re-establishment of public control over the national railway system in 1906, a factor which increased the need for administrative space within the building. As a result the building is approximately one-third higher than in the earlier designs, comprising three storeys in all, and additional rooms with dormer windows have been worked into the roof.

Despite Tatsuno's unquestionable authority over the project it would be a mistake to think of the Tokyo Station building as simply the work of one person. The scale alone suggests that this would have been impossible. Moreover in 1903, when planning began, Tatsuno was still completing the large Osaka Branch building of the Bank of Japan. During the final design and construction phase at Tokyo Station from 1906, Tatsuno was also responsible for building two other stations in Tokyo and one in Pusan in Korea, as well as the National Sumo Stadium in Tokyo.

Fig 9.15
Tokyo Station
showing
construction of
the steel
framing
(Source:
Transportation
Museum,
Tokyo)

In order to carry out this heavy work-load Tatsuno established two architectural offices, one in Tokyo and the other in Osaka. Each office had a junior partner and several assistants. Tatsuno was aided in the drafting of the Tokyo Station drawings by Kasai Manji, his junior partner at the Tokyo Office. Kasai, a graduate from Tatsuno's own architectural course at the University of Tokyo in 1903, had immediately upon graduation become the junior partner to his former professor.

Tatsuno's Tokyo office developed a standardised design for its railway station buildings as a result of the experience of designing and redesigning Tokyo Station. The characteristic hall with the flanking wings used at each end of Tokyo Station are to be found again at Tatsuno's Manseibashi Station, completed in 1911, and the new Shinbashi station building at Karasumori, finished in 1914. All three buildings even had similar Neo-Baroque pediments, windows and arches. The design of Tokyo Station also shows influences from Tatsuno's other work: the grand arched pediment over the emperor's entrance at Tokyo Station, which is such an important feature of the building in symbolic terms, is a larger version of the entry to the Kyoto branch of the Bank of Japan, a banded red-brick building completed in 1906 under the direction of his Osaka Office.

The most distinctive feature of Tokyo Station, apart from the red-brick, are the ribbed domes which crown the north and south wings and which rest upon the sturdy steel-frame structure of the walls (Figure 9.15). The domes were added to the station design to bestow greater visual impact and appropriate symbolic importance to the station than that presented by the other red-brick buildings of Marunouchi which it faced across the railway square.

The dome became paramount in the architectural vocabulary of authority in the first decade of the twentieth century in Japan. Tatsuno had first experimented with a dome on the Bank of Japan headquarters building (1890–1896), but this was a rather modest and tentative example of the genre. His colleague Katayama put the dome to greater visual effect for the Hyōkeikan, completed in 1909. Here a large ribbed dome, complete with Baroque oriels, was set over the central hall, and a smaller dome rose at the end of each wing.

235

The dome had been rediscovered during the Renaissance, and enjoyed enduring prominence on such great edifices as St Peter's in Rome and St Paul's in London. During the Baroque revival it was used with considerable enthusiasm because of the exciting curved emphasis it gave to roof-lines and the opportunity afforded by its interior for painting and gilded embellishment. Young Japanese architects were introduced to the dome during their visits to European cities after 1877, but it took nearly a generation of building practice to master the engineering technology needed to create a structurally stable dome in Japan. The first dome designed and built by a Japanese was the octagonal ribbed dome which crowned the central tower of the Hokkaidō Development Commission headquarters, later to serve as the headquarters of the Hokkaidō prefectural government (Hokkaidō-chō). Completed in 1888, it was the tallest structure in the city of Sapporo, a spectacular symbol of authority with its copper roof gleaming in the sun surrounded by a forest of tall brick chimneys billowing coal smoke on a winter's day.

This first dome may have been a public-relations triumph but structurally it proved an unmitigated disaster. It was built with a timber frame, each piece carefully crafted by traditional master carpenters. The pillars of the dome tower were set into the base of a Western-style rigid triangular truss roof, in much the same manner of the belvederes which had been added to conventional framed structures to create the early castle keeps in the sixteenth century. Unfortunately the Japanese did not realise that the Western trussing required strong lateral bracing to counteract the lateral pressure exerted by the dome and its tower. In 1895, seven years after its completion, the dome and tower collapsed, falling dramatically to the earth below, the inherent structural instability exacerbated by rain damage.[40]

Although Conder completed the large ribbed dome of the Russian Orthodox Cathedral in Tokyo, the St Nicholas Cathedral, in 1891, and Tatsuno the more modest Bank of Japan building soon afterwards, the real breakthrough in dome construction was Tatsuno and Kasai's National Sumo Stadium, completed in 1909 just as the framing operation for the Tokyo Station domes was commencing. The sumo stadium was covered by a giant semi-circular steel frame clad in glass, with a span of 66 metres. The stadium, when finished, had a seating capacity of 13,000 people, making it easily the largest such structure to have been built in Japan to that date. With the experience gained at this project, the Japanese were able to proceed without foreign supervision in the erection of the intricate earthquake-proof, steel-framing of Tokyo Station (see Figure 9.15). The logistics of the project alone indicate the enormity of the engineering undertaking. The construction work was in the hands of Ōbayashi-gumi, with an average of 3,000 workmen employed at the site each day, a tribute once again to the Japanese ability, demonstrated from time immemorial, to organise monumental construction projects.[41]

The feature for which Tokyo Station is best known is its red-brick walls. The walls were actually supported by steel framing, much of it imported from England. However, as a result of further experience gained in erecting rigid steel framing during the construction of the Sumo Stadium, the Japanese were now confident of their ability to construct a steel-frame structure in a seismic region. In addition, building with bricks posed few of the immense loading problems presented by the granite walls of the Akasaka Palace. The bricks themselves were of two types, wall bricks, and veneer bricks used to decorate their outer surface. In all 8,332,000 wall bricks and 934,500 veneer bricks were used in the construction of the station. These bricks were specially prepared by five different companies. The Japan Brick Manufacturing Company was responsible for the wall bricks and four other firms received contracts for the various types of ornamental brick used to enliven the walls.[42]

From the early years of Meiji, brick played an increasingly important part in the creation of the new Westernised cities. Brick imported from Shanghai had first been used for godowns in the foreign treaty ports in the 1860s[43] but as a construction material it assumed political importance for the Meiji government when it was used in the rebuilding of what is now known as the Ginza district of central Tokyo following a devastating fire in 1872. The rebuilding was the first concerted urban modernisation project of the Meiji government, transforming part of the old artisan district of Edo into a show-piece of large-scale, Western commercial enterprise. The project was under the supervision of a British engineer, Thomas Waters, who laid out a broad avenue southwest from the old Kyōbashi and lined it with the simple, Classical Revival-style buildings preferred by engineers. The walls were made of brick, selected because of its fire-proof quality. The bricks were covered with a veneer of Portland cement, a common practice in Europe used to disguise this distracting vernacular material, but the Japanese, no doubt captivated by its quintessential foreignness, quickly elevated brick in the hierarchy of building materials and flaunted it as an exotic exterior cladding.

Thereafter brick assumed iconic significance as a physical embodiment of things Western and modern, of the civilization and enlightenment extolled by the Japanese political and intellectual leaders. Red-brick became for the Meiji state what red pillars had been for the Nara state. Brick construction was used in a wide range of public and commercial buildings as well as more humbly utilitarian structures. The most extensive use of brick was found in the new Mitsubishi commercial district in Tokyo, across from which Tokyo Station was to rise, but brick was employed in an extraordinary range of other structures. These included those for government ministries such as the Ministry of Justice, and for local government, of which the Hokkaidō Prefectural headquarters of dome fame is best known, along with banks, university libraries and chapels, post offices and museums, railway bridges and aqueducts, and the large water-front warehouses in the treaty ports of Hakodate and Yokohama, a number of which still stand today.

The Japanese may have perceived brick as foreign, and therefore exotic and desirable, but it is equally possible that its rustic textured surface struck an aesthetic resonance because of its similarity to the familiar earth walls of farm-houses and the consciously rustic walls of tea-houses and aristocratic retreats in the Japanese tradition. Brick walls had, moreover, a great practical advantage; they were quick to erect, the same quality which had made brick the preferred material for European rulers in a hurry like the Roman emperors and France's Henri IV. And the Meiji Japanese were certainly in a hurry to build their new environment. Brick also raised none of the procurement problems posed by stone which had beset the castle-builders of Edo nearly 300 years earlier and it was easy to manufacture, especially for a nation with a long-established tradition of terracotta tiling. Western-style bricks were being manufactured as early as the 1850s in daimyo domains such as Saga, Satsuma, and at Nirayama in Izu, for the making of reverberatory blast furnaces. The first known use of brick for an actual building in Japan was at the Nagasaki Ironworks in 1857.[44] Ende and Böckmann persuaded the Japanese Government to send a brick-maker, Ōtaka Shōemon, to study brick-making and laying in Germany. He was one of a group of 20 Japanese which included 17 craftsmen sent abroad to study stone paving, stained glass, etching, painting (of buildings) and masonry techniques. Upon his return to Japan in 1887 Ōtaka established the *Nihon renga seizō kaisha* (Japan Brick Manufacturing Company) with a large, Hoffman-style circular kiln at its factory in Saitama prefecture near Tokyo. The main share-holder was that indefatigable industrialist and company director, Shibusawa Eiichi (1840–1931). The company was to supply the wall bricks for most of the important red-brick buildings of Meiji-period Tokyo, including Conder's Mitsubishi Number One Building, Tatsuno's Bank of Japan, of which Shibusawa was a director, and the wall bricks for Tokyo Station itself.[45]

For the Japanese of the time it mattered little that brick walls, when made in the Western load-bearing manner, collapsed during earthquakes. Comfort also seemed to be a secondary consideration to image, for solid brick wall buildings, with their poor air circulation and problems of inherent dampness, were unsuited to Japan's humid summers and extended wet and typhoon seasons. Traditional Japanese construction methods, with their flexible timber framing to carry the load of the roof and light-weight non-bearing walls of moveable screens and plaster infill, were infinitely stronger seismically and more suitable climatically to Japan's conditions than were load-bearing brick walls. The Japanese soon found, however, that brick walls could be strengthened by supporting them with traditional timber frames in one of those processes of adaptation of foreign ideas for which Japanese civilization is renowned.[46] By the turn of the twentieth century steel framing had replaced the timber.

The completion of the Shinagawa-Ueno line, with Tokyo Station at its centre, was another major milestone. It marked the swing away from private enterprise to renewed state control of major trunk lines. From the beginning of the Meiji era the state had adopted a financial policy of concentrating capital to facilitate the growth of nascent Western-style industries. Once on their feet, privatisation was to follow, in keeping with prevailing Western practice. This had been the strategy employed for heavy industry and was applied with equal success to railways. By the 1880s there was a steady growth in private railway lines, with 1,864 kilometres of lines in private hands by the end of the decade compared with 887 kilometres in state hands.[47] In 1905–1906 the policy was reversed and Tokyo Station was completed as the focus of the renationalised railway system.

The construction of Tokyo Station took place against the background of financial shortages created by the high cost to the economy of the Russo–Japanese War, exacerbated by the absence of war indemnities as a result of the American-engineered Treaty of Portsmouth. The final cost of Tokyo

Station was 2.7 million *yen* – slightly more than half the cost of the Akasaka Palace, and modest if the scale of the engineering as well as architectural work is taken into account.[48] Although the war itself had stimulated military-related industries, it was followed by inflation and problems of industrial transition. The cost of nationalising the railways also placed a heavy burden on the state. In 1905 the economy too was at a critical point of transition from traditional to modern industry.[49] Tokyo Station may have been grand in scale, but cost-cutting because of the general economic situation is also apparent in the use of plaster for some of the detailing normally reserved for stone. Tatsuno himself complained of lack of finance to make alterations to the design of the Imperial Entrance after the third phase drawings were completed. He obviously felt the inadequacy of an entrance which was little different from that of the Kyoto Bank upon which it was modelled.[50]

It may be appreciated, therefore, that the creation of the new railway station at the heart of Tokyo was a momentous achievement for nation and state as Japan moved into the twentieth century. Tokyo Station transcended its immediate function as the focus of a national transportation system to assume iconic significance as a statement of technological power and national authority sanctioned by the imperial presence and emphasised by its dramatic urban setting.

Marching to a Different Tune: The Ministry of Education and the Sōgakudō

The impression which may be gained from the study of Akasaka Palace and Tokyo Station is of a monolithic projection of authority by the Meiji establishment – using certain officially approved Western architectural styles mastered by architects trained at the official university, and modified by structural necessity, stylistic preferences and a certain amount of domestic politics. A third Meiji-period building reveals another and lower level of Western-style architecture in the hierarchy of the Meiji establishment, the significance of which has only recently been realised. This building is the Sōgakudō, constructed in 1889–1890 as the main building of what was to become the Tokyo University of Fine Arts (Tōkyō Geijutsu Daigaku). The Sōgakudō, or 'Hall for Instrumental Music', served as the college where most Western-style musicians were trained in Japan. Moreover, it contained Japan's first Western-style concert hall, and served as the virtual 'National Theatre' of Western music until after World War II. This finely crafted building, dedicated to the musical arts, typifies the broad genre of education buildings built for the Meiji government in pursuit of the goals of a Westernised system of learning for the modern state.

Today the Sōgakudō stands on a site in Ueno Park in Tokyo, close to its original location, but considerably reduced in size (Figure 9.16). It was originally some 80 metres in length but the left wing was amputated to allow the erection of a new university building in the inter-war period. During the 1983–1987 restoration it was decided to reduce the length of the remaining wing and use the timbers salvaged to build a shorter version of the lost wing.[51] This at least re-established the symmetrical integrity of the original

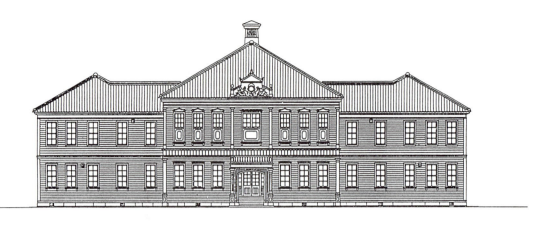

Meiji-period design. Despite this major surgery it is clear even from a study of the truncated structure that the Sōgakudō was a remarkably mellifluous accomplishment in Western-style architecture. The overall style is Classical Revival, with a Palladian portico, carefully crafted timber mouldings, cornices and applied pilasters, and an impressive Baroque pediment set into the eaves over the central entrance (Figure 9.17).

The Sōgakudō exemplifies the official architectural style adopted by the Ministry of Education (Monbushō) from the middle of the Meiji period for most of its prestige buildings. The style was based on the French Classical Revival of the first Napoleonic empire, rather than that of the Second Empire of Napoleon III which was at the time becoming popular in Japan through the Imperial College of Engineering architectural programme.

The reform of education was a fundamental and far-reaching policy of the Meiji state in its pursuit of Westernisation. The 1872 Education Ordinance outlining this policy of a fully Westernised system of primary-school education was immediately implemented. Detailed studies of the European and American education systems were conducted. By 1877 a large education museum had been established in Ueno Park near the present site of the

Sōgakudō. Edward Morse, brought to Japan under the government foreign empolyees scheme to teach botany at the University of Tokyo, commented that the museum building included:

Fig 9.17
Sōgakudō.
Front oblique
view after
1983–87
restoration

> a long and spacious hall [which] was filled with an extensive and interesting collection of educational apparatus from Europe and America – modern schoolhouses in miniature, desks, pictures, maps, models, globes, slates, blackboards, inkstands, and the minutest details of school appliances abroad. . . . What a wise conception of the Japanese, entering as they were on our methods of education, that they should establish a museum to display the apparatus used in the work. Here was a nation spending nearly a third of its annual budget on education, and in contrast Russia spending a half of one percent on the same department. [52]

Construction of the Sōgakudō began just two years after Morse made these observations. The completed building provides a clear illustration of the government's educational priorities of the 1880s as revealed in Morse's comments, that is, the creation of Western-style buildings appropriate to Western-style education. The architects of the Sōgakudō were Yamaguchi Hanroku and Kuru Masamichi. Of the two, Kuru was the junior, joining the Ministry of Education after graduating from the University of Tokyo in 1883. He later became influential as an architect and was responsible for the Hōōdō-den of the Japanese Pavilion of the 1893 Columbian World Exposition. However in the late 1880s and 1890s it was Yamaguchi who was the more significant. He was employed as 'Chief Architect' (*gikan*) of the Ministry of Education, the same title later received by Katayama to mark his status as chief architect of the Imperial Household Agency. Yamaguchi was plagued by poor health, which restricted his architectural output to a mere ten years, yet

241

his contribution between entering the Ministry of Education in 1885 and leaving it for private practice in 1892, was to prove decisive in forging the official architectural style of the Ministry of Education. Yamaguchi's professional training had been very different from that of the mainstream Conder group, resulting in a notably different nuance to the architectural language of Ministry of Education authority. At the age of 18, in 1876, Yamaguchi was selected as a member of the second group of Monbushō-sponsored students to study abroad. He entered the famed École Polytechnique (École Centrale) in Paris, and completed the three-year course in civil engineering, followed by two years' practical experience in Paris. The timing is significant, since 1876 was the year before Conder's arrival in Japan and the early programme in architecture at the forerunner to the Imperial College of Engineering was still dominated by pragmatic engineering.

Yamaguchi returned to Japan and from 1885 to 1892 was Chief Architect in charge of the construction of educational buildings throughout Japan. In this capacity he was responsible for the Main Building of Rika Daigaku, or Science Faculty of the University of Tokyo in 1888; the Fifth National Middle and High School built in collaboration with Kuru in 1889; the First National Middle and High School of 1890; the Second National Middle and High School of 1891, and the Fourth National Middle and High School, in collaboration with Kuru once more, in 1891.[53] The Physics and Chemistry Theatres of this Fourth National High School survive in restored form at Meiji Village. The Sōgakudō therefore belongs to a stream of architectural projects flowing from the Ministry of Education under the direction of Yamaguchi.

Yamaguchi's work directly reflected his French background as an engineer trained in the Classical Revival forms of the first half of the nineteenth century. This classicism was less emphatic, simpler in form and decoration than the Classical Revival of the Second Empire, with its ornate Neo-Baroque forms. In fact Yamaguchi's work springs directly from the École Polytechnique tradition. This famed engineering school had been founded by Napoleon and was dominated by J.-N.-L. Durand. His treatises became 'a sort of bible of Romantic Classicism that retained international authority for a generation or more'.[54] Although in the way of most timber-frame Western-style buildings of the 1880s it was built using traditional Japanese joinery and carpenters' tools, the roof trussing and spanning of interior space – particularly in the concert hall – is based on Western engineering techniques (Figure 9.18). The use of the tensioning rods in the concert hall and in the trussing system is particularly indicative of Durand's influence.

Durand's Classical Revival forms have a strong sense of utility, but the fenestration, pilasters and colonnades lack real stylistic conviction. The pragmatic classical features of the Sōgakudō clearly reflect this; the façade is competent but uninspired. Its style becomes explicable as a distant descendant in wood of the masonry palaces of the Roman Renaissance, interpreted by the École Polytechnique. Together with the Victorian brick and the French Second Empire style, this earlier Classical Revival, already out of fashion in Europe, exerted an enduring influence on the Meiji-period educational establishment. It resulted in a distinctive genre of weatherboard school buildings which assumed a lower level in the architectural hierarchy of the Meiji state

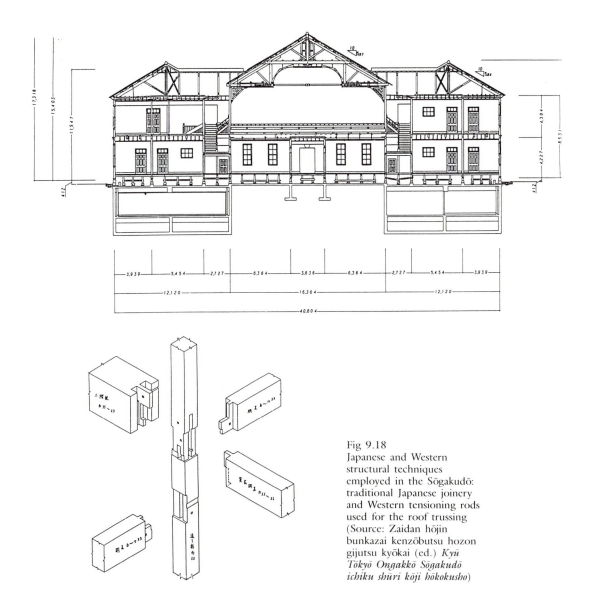

Fig 9.18
Japanese and Western
structural techniques
employed in the Sōgakudō:
traditional Japanese joinery
and Western tensioning rods
used for the roof trussing
(Source: Zaidan hōjin
bunkazai kenzōbutsu hozon
gijutsu kyōkai (ed.) *Kyū
Tōkyō Ongakkō Sōgakudō
ichiku shūri kōji hōkokusho*)

than the grand stone and red-brick buildings, in much the same way as daimyo gatehouses in the late Edo period were differentiated in status by the presence or absence of *karahafu*. Many of these school-buildings were to survive well into the post-World War II period in towns and villages dispersed throughout the nation, evidence of the widespread impact on perceptions of the establishment wrought by the Meiji educational reforms.

The Disestablished Daibutsuden

In the meantime, it is pertinent to ask what had been the fate of Japanese traditional architecture in this period of such prodigious construction of Western-style buildings? The Japanese adoption of Western architectural styles

243

was pragmatic in terms of national needs, but became autocratic, developing its own momentum and direction and threatening much that was valuable in tradition. New architecture was inexorably challenging the bases of Japanese society, contributing its own particular dynamic to the process of Westernisation but at the same time exacerbating the problem of accommodation with tradition. A decade after the completion of the Sōgakudō, at broadly the same time as the Akasaka Detached Palace and Tokyo Station were being built, another project of equal importance to the understanding of architecture and authority in the Meiji state was being undertaken at Nara. This project was the repair and reconstruction of the Daibutsuden of Tōdaiji, a process which continued for seven years from 1906 to 1913. Unlike the Akasaka Palace and Tokyo Station, which stood in the limelight of Meiji authority, the Daibutsuden of Nara was lost deep in the shadows, its importance only begrudgingly and belatedly acknowledged by the state. Radically different in architectural style and religious and political meaning from the officially sponsored building projects, the Daibutsuden survived a dual crisis of identity and technology to reassert its moral authority over government by the end of the Meiji period.

Tōdaiji was the antithesis of everything that the Meiji state espoused as important. Its religious and architectural character was at cross-purposes both with State Shinto as official belief and Western building types as the establishment environment. It is therefore most instructive to revisit the Tōdaiji as it stood in the Meiji period, in order to ascertain how time and circumstance were treating it in an age preoccupied by Western-style palaces, railway stations and concert halls.

Tōdaiji had proved remarkably resilient, surviving the abandoning of Nara as the national capital and the consequent loss of state patronage in the ninth century. During the civil wars of the late twelfth- and later sixteenth-centuries most of its principal buildings, including the Daibutsuden, were destroyed by fire. The Daibutsuden had on each occasion risen from the ashes, its Great Buddha repaired and recast. Each time it had been a combination of a charismatic monk raising sizeable private donations and the patronage of the reigning shogunate which had enabled rebuilding to proceed.[55]

The Daibutsuden as it survived into the early Meiji period had itself been rebuilt under Tokugawa patronage between 1688 and 1707. Although it retained something of the flavour of the earlier twelfth-century building, with such features as multiple-tier bracket sets, it also reflected Tokugawa architectural symbolism, particularly and predictably, the addition of a *karahafu* over the central bay (Figure 9.19).[56] It is unarguably the Tokugawa-sponsored Daibutsuden which stands at Tōdaiji today, but it survives only because of the Meiji-period rebuilding. By the late nineteenth century the Edo-period building was in danger of structural failure. The huge upper roof was collapsing under a load of tiles which weighed 2,000 tonnes. The bracket sets at the corners, which took the brunt of this load, were bent as much as 20 degrees from the horizontal. The main roof truss was no longer stable. As a temporary measure extra struts had been pushed in to prop up the ends of the roof, but rain-water was seeping into the truss, causing many timbers to rot and exacerbating the structural problems.

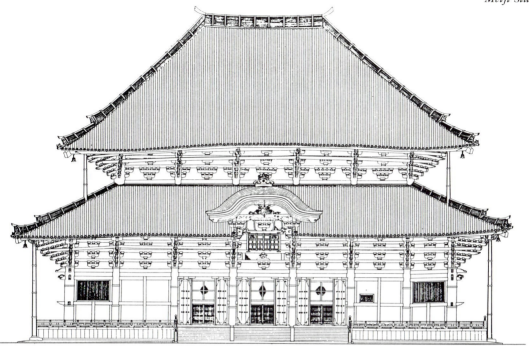

Fig 9.19
Daibutsuden,
Tōdaiji. Front
elevation prior
to Meiji period
restoration
work
(1906–1913)
(Source:
Tōdaiji
Daibutsuden
Shōwa daishūri
iinkai (ed.)
*Kokuhō Tōdaiji
Kondō
[Daibutsuden]
shūri
hōkokusho)*

The building had to be completely dismantled and reconstructed. The project was carried out under the direction of the national government's Ministry of the Interior (Naimushō) with site work supervised by a special bureau based in Nara. Technical direction was in the hands of the new generation of Japanese specialists, trained in Western architecture and armed with doctorates in engineering from the University of Tokyo. Tsumaki Yorinaka was technical director, Itō Chūta and Sekino Tadashi were assistant directors while Amanuma Shun'ichi was a technical consultant.[57] Itō, Sekino and Amanuma were to be responsible for the first major studies in the modern field of Japanese architectural history.

In view of their training in Western architecture and engineering, it is not surprising that the solution found for the structural dilemma of the Daibutsuden by this able team was drawn from outside the Japanese architectural heritage (Figure 9.20). Detailed Western-style scale drawings were made, including calculations of mechanical stress using the principles of Western engineering. Structurally weakened members were replaced with new timbers and steel bracing was inserted to strengthen the roof truss and the eaves bracket sets. A box truss of imported Shelton steel was inserted in the roof framing to support the traditional timber truss. This ingeniously contrived foreign intrusion was hidden from view by a suspended ceiling of traditional Japanese design. In addition to reinforcing the main truss, diagonal bracing was added to the side bays and the upper levels of the roof structure. Bolts

Fig 9.20
Daibutsuden,
Tōdaiji.
Transverse
section prior
to Meiji period
restoration
work (top) and
after reinforce-
ment using
Shelton steel
box truss
(bottom)
(Source:
Tōdaiji
Daibutsuden
Shōwa daishūri
iinkai (ed.)
*Kokuhō Tōdaiji
Kondō
[Daibutsuden]
shūri
hōkokusho*)

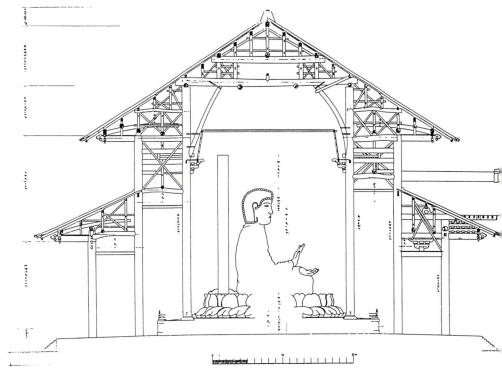

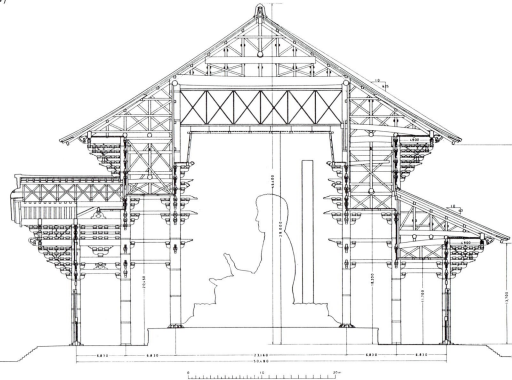

246

and metal plates strengthened the traditional wood joinery at the intersection of critical load-bearing members. Iron tensioning rods were set at an angle of 45 degrees above the outer pivot points of the bracket arms in order to provide additional support to the overworked cantilevers. Concrete was used to secure the ornamental ridge-tiling. The load of the roof was reduced 12 per cent by cutting down the number of roof tiles from 128,000 to 112,000 through the use of composite tiles in place of the separate pan and cover tiles traditionally used for projects of this type.[58]

One can only sympathise with the restorers of the Daibutsuden in their recourse to this Western solution. The scale of the problems they faced was daunting in the extreme. There had been attempts to repair the building in 1882 using conventional means but these had been unsuccessful.[59] There were simply no timbers available anywhere in Japan suitable for the restoration of a structure the size of the Daibutsuden. Further, by the early twentieth century, the master carpenters capable of building on that scale had all passed away leaving no heirs to their tradition of monumental construction. There had been no large-scale traditional architectural project in the earlier part of the Meiji period to keep the special skills of large-scale structure construction alive. The Tokugawa master carpenters had been able to rebuild the Daibutsuden in the late seventeenth century because they were less than two generations removed from the builders of the great castles, palaces and religious buildings of the early Edo period. Their fathers and grandfathers would have transmitted to them knowledge gained from building the vast halls of Nishi Honganji and Fushimi Castle. The master carpenters of the end of the Meiji period were reaching back beyond their collective experience and as a consequence were found sadly lacking.

The Tōdaiji project may have represented a failure of traditional building technology but it was a remarkable demonstration of the newly acquired Japanese mastery of advanced Western engineering techniques. The use of steel framing to solve the problem of preservation of the Daibutsuden was an ingenious but inevitable result of Meiji concern with Western technology. It reveals that the fundamental objective of architectural restoration was the maintenance of the appearance of the original Japanese building while resorting to artificial means, that is, methods outside the original techno-aesthetic complex, to preserve it. This philosophy may not be acceptable to restorationist architects today but it reflected the approach common in Europe at the time.

Behind this remarkable technical process was an even more remarkable process of confrontation between the Westernising state and Japanese tradition. The problem of the repair and preservation of Japan's traditional architectural treasures forced the Meiji government to come to terms with its Japanese heritage. The structural crisis of the Daibutsuden occurred when the government and all who were seen as 'progressive' were concerned with Westernisation, so that Japanese traditions, many of them still relevant, were abandoned in the frantic pursuit of things foreign. Even the master carpenters who had created Japanese architecture were now deemed by the Meiji state to be ancillary to the new breed of Japanese 'architect'. A wedge was being driven into the hitherto organic process of design and construction, with master carpenters downgraded to the humble status of manual workers while the government sponsored the development of a Western-style architectural profession to replace them in service to their new political ends.

In an age of systematic construction of Western-style buildings, the sagging, rotting, leaking Daibutsuden cried out for attention like an abandoned old man. Only after a long and difficult re-evaluation of the place of tradition in the modern technological world of a Westernising Japan was it eventually rehabilitated by the new state.

At the outset it had not been the intention of the Meiji leaders to abandon long-established traditions so completely. Their aim had been modernisation rather than whole-scale Westernisation, summed up in the words of Sakuma Shōzan's slogan 'Eastern ethics and Western science' (*Tōyō no dōtoku, seiyō no gakugei*). Consistent with this broad objective, traditional culture was to be protected by the new government. As early as 1871 the Dajōkan issued an edict ordering temples and shrines to help in the compilation of a national register of important buildings and art treasures. The process ground to a halt in the face of the more radical Westernising priorities of 'civilization and enlightenment'. Japan plunged headlong into what we would now call a development boom in which Westernisation was to be achieved irrespective of the cost to traditional culture and civilization. It was partly the insistence of foreigners like Ernest Fenollosa, the wealthy Boston art connoisseur who had arrived in Japan in 1877, and the perplexing problems thrust on them by German architects who insisted on using traditional Japanese architectural features for their state commissions, which forced reappraisal of official attitudes. After 1885 the Ministry of the Interior began making appropriations for the preservation of temples and shrines. A number of significant ancient buildings in the Kyoto-Nara area were repaired, including the Kondō of Tōshōdaiji, the Five Storey Pagoda of Daigoji, and the Hondō of Kiyomizudera.[60] Initially the funds for repairs were allocated through the Kunai-shō, but in 1888 a *Rinji zenkoku hōmotsu torishirabe-kyoku* ('Provisional Bureau for Investigation of National Treasures') was established within the Imperial Household Ministry, marking the consolidation of government preservation and restoration activities.

With the enactment of the first systematic laws for preservation of historically significant art and architecture in 1897, these activities were rationalised. The laws were formulated under the guidance of Itō Chūta, who was to play an important role in the restoration of the Daibutsuden. The *Koshaji hozonhō*, or 'Law for the Preservation of Old Shrines and Temples' was promulgated on 5 June 1897 (Law Number 49) in order to protect religious buildings and the works of art they contained. The 20 articles of this law established a system of providing national government financial support for preservation and restoration of buildings and other works of art. Application for financial support was to be made to the Minister of Internal Affairs (Article One) for works of architecture and related art of historical uniqueness and exceptional quality (Article Two). Responsibility for the process of preservation and restoration was to be in the hands of local officials (Article Three). Restoration work was to be financed directly from the national coffers (Article Eight). Responsibility for implementation of the law was vested in the Ministry of the Interior but in 1914 was transferred to the Ministry of Education. This law was followed on 15 December of the same year, 1897, by a second law giving supplementary provisions for designating architecture and art as *kokuhō* or 'national treasures' (Law Number 420).[61] Together these two laws of June and December 1897 established a comprehensive system for designating and protecting cultural properties which was to be the foundation of the modern preservation of Japan's artistic and architectural heritage.

The restoration of the Daibutsuden, beginning in June 1906 and ending in May 1913, shortly after the death of the Emperor Meiji, was carried out under the provisions of these laws. However it would be incorrect to interpret this as a case of careful formulation of a cultural properties preservation policy followed by its orderly enactment at Tōdaiji. The technical requirements of the building process dictated policy as much as policy was to govern building. The sequence of events leading to the construction work, which is recorded in detail in the official record of the restoration published by Tōdaiji in 1915,[62] shows that the national government laws for preservation of temples and shrines evolved only in response to the financial and architectural crisis posed by the actual condition of the Daibutsuden. The key preservation laws were formulated during the course of nearly a decade-long debate between the chief abbot of Tōdaiji and the national government concerning the importance of the building, and ways and means of funding its restoration. A desperate letter from the temple authorities, sent directly to the Minister of Internal Affairs in 1892, pleaded for financial assistance. It cited the unique historical significance of the building and reminded the government of the major role played by eminent figures in Japanese history, from Emperor Shōmu to Tokugawa Tsunayoshi, as patrons in past rebuilding projects.[63]

The first detailed estimate of the cost for restoring the Daibutsuden, made in 1891, was for a total of 32,800 *yen*. The temple had been able to raise a mere 4,600 *yen* during its concerted fund-raising activities over the preceding six years. Spiralling inflation caused by the Sino-Japanese and Russo-Japanese Wars, together with the high cost of the new technology required, meant that construction costs reached a final figure of 728,429 *yen*, 36 *sen* and 7 *rin*.[64] This was a considerable sum in contemporary terms but modest when compared to construction expenditure on the Akasaka Palace and Tokyo Station. The total preservation and restoration budget of the national government under the 1897 laws was initially 150,000 *yen* but this rapidly increased to 200,000 *yen* per year, of which three-quarters was devoted to building projects.[65] From this budget Tōdaiji received a regular annual payment of 30,000 *yen* for five years from the inception of the law, as well as additional special grants in response to specific requests.[66]

The rebuilding of the Daibutsuden, therefore, contributes an alternative picture of the relationship between authority and architecture to our understanding of the Meiji period. The agonising process of financing its restoration, which spanned much of the era, acted as a catalyst for reappraisal of official priorities, leading to the establishment of a national system for protection and preservation of cultural properties. This was a case of the authority of traditional architecture wearing down the power of the modern state.

249

Continuity and Change at the End of Meiji

By the end of the Meiji period and the completion of the Akasaka Palace and Tokyo Station, Japan had become a fully competent practitioner of international architecture. Moreover it contributed its own particular skills in banded red-brick and sophisticated earthquake-proof framing to the family of Second Empire Neo-Baroque buildings which were to be found, in cities as far apart as Paris and Melbourne, Washington and London, as the universal architectural language for expressing national authority.

The driving force behind the adoption of Western architectural styles was the authority of the Japanese state working in tandem with the power of the industrial and commercial sectors. The architectural achievement of the Meiji period is a direct measure of the determination of the leaders of government and industry to modernise their nation along Western lines, as well as a yardstick of their ability to mobilise and manage human and material resources in the construction of new buildings and cities. The key to this success was a coherent programme in Western architectural training and the selective use of competent foreign experts in the key professions of architecture and engineering. The experts, only some of whom it has been possible to discuss here, were to train the first Japanese architects who then continued to learn 'on the job' as they built the masterpieces of Western-style architecture in the later years of the nineteenth and the first decades of the twentieth century.

We have seen that the official desire for a new architecture of authority came into conflict with that most articulate of traditional architectural symbols, the *karahafu*, when the design for new civic buildings was concerned. The cusped gables of castles and gateways commanded the attention of the German architects and engineers but was spurned by the Japanese themselves. However, it is likely that the emphasis upon roof size and shape in traditional architecture informed the Japanese preference for high pitched roofs and curved cupolas in their new Western-style architecture. Similarly the fondness for heavily accented Neo-Baroque entablatures, replete with curved mouldings, fulfilled the need for gable grandeur created by an almost subliminal awareness of the grace and expressive power of traditional gables. The Classical orders as interpreted in the Baroque idiom were entirely consistent with the traditional pillar and beam system in Japanese architecture. Both the Japanese and the Classical traditions were orders in the same sense; they were systems of design based on modules translated by ratios into a comprehensive set of measurements determined by proportions, and ultimately, by the propriety of status. This greatly facilitated their adoption into the Japanese architectural vocabulary of authority and eased the transition into the iconoclastic modernism of the twentieth century.

Tange Kenzō's Tokyo Monuments   10

New Authority and Old Architectural Ambitions

Time has not yet imposed its own interpretation on the staggering succession of events and changes which have occurred since the end of the Allied Occupation in 1952. Study of the recent past presents its own peculiar problems and opportunities. An historical perspective, using the focus of the relationship between architecture and authority, uncovers much in contemporary Japan which is consistent with the past, particularly with the experience of buildings as a projection of identity and authority and as the built environment in which the power of the state and of big business operates.

From an historical viewpoint, the second half of the Shōwa era, from the mid-1950s to 1989, could be called a new Nara period of modernisation using foreign prototypes. It may equally be described as a new Momoyama period, an epoch in which the resources of the state and the nation were mobilised to rebuild after war and to attain national stability and international stature. This era may also be likened to the Meiji period, as an era of consciously planned, government-engineered modernisation and Westernisation.

There have been profound changes to Japanese government and society in the 50 years since the end of the Pacific War in 1945. The trends over this period are well known and need to be only briefly touched on here. The immediate postwar era was characterised by a grim struggle to rebuild cities devastated by bombing raids. The Allied occupying powers redefined Japanese state authority. The emperor, in their terms, became a mere symbol of the sovereignty of the people and, in the same way that the Charter Oath at the beginning of the Meiji period had exhorted the people to abandon evil customs of the past, the Occupation authorities reworked political, educational and social institutions to abandon custom and tradition in favour of political democracy and economic capitalism in an all-embracing social engineering programme.

The Occupation was followed in the 1950s by recovery stimulated by the Korean War. This culminated in the 'economic miracle' of the 1960s during which the GNP doubled, but at a cost of environmental pollution and uncontrolled urban growth. The typical family dreamed of home ownership, a dream fuelled by American influence and the desire of the 'salaryman' middle class to share in the new prosperity of great industry and corporations.

The 1970s were characterised by the economic shocks caused by the oil crises of 1973 and 1978 which shattered the illusion of limitless progress of

251

the 1960s. By the 1980s however, there was a return of seemingly uncon-strained economic ebullience. This was particularly true after 1985 as a result of the dramatic increase in the value of the *yen* and government stimulation of the domestic economy to offset the trade imbalance with the United States. These measures also precipitated excessive economic liquidity which caused rampant real estate speculation and a chronic cost and tax spiral for land. By the 1990s a new realism took over, as the 'bubble economy' burst and the country entered a period of recession followed by slowed growth, lower eco-nomic expectations and the savage reminder of the fragility of human society inflicted by the Kobe earthquake of 1995.

From the viewpoint of architecture and authority there are two overriding characteristics of this half century, namely, the importance of construction and the dominance of cities, the two being closely interrelated.

Building and the Postwar Nation

Probably more buildings have been constructed in Japan in the second half of the twentieth century than at any other time in its history. The construction and architectural sectors of the economy are major pillars of the GNP. Their achievements range from huge engineering projects to link the four main islands of the Japanese archipelago by means of some of the world's longest suspen-sion bridges and undersea tunnels, to the application of new technologies in industrial automation and robotics to manufactured home construction. The output of a single general contractor such as Shimizu or Takenaka today would equal the entire production programme of the official builders for the Tokugawa shogunate during its phase of frenetic building activity in the first half of the seventeenth century. This is obviously a function of industrialisation and mechanisation, but it also reflects a modern preoccupation with building projects akin to that of the Nara, Momoyama, early Edo and Meiji periods. Economic and industrial growth has generated large-scale construction while government policy at national, prefectural and local level has placed heavy emphasis on the building of new urban facilities and infrastructure. The cen-trality of construction to economic vitality has stimulated research and devel-opment of new building technologies and materials. There has been careful coordination of the construction activities across the board in the government and private sectors, a type of collaboration which has generated much of the dynamic growth during the last decades. The Japanese construction industry is now a powerful force internationally, building palaces and public facilities in the oil-rich Middle East countries, and large-scale projects in developing nations, funded through official development aid. 'Japanese architecture' under these circumstances encompasses work by architects of Japanese nationality both in Japan and abroad, as well as collaborative ventures between foreign architects and construction companies in Japan itself. The palaces by Tange Kenzō in Kuwait and the Kansai Airport Terminal by Renzo Piano are part of the wide spectrum of architectural activity in Japan today.

The great national wealth of modern Japan, together with its search for iden-tity both internationally and in terms of its own traditions, has meant that the field of construction has also been a major arena for corporate and national self-definition. The leading trading and industrial houses of Mitsubishi, Sumitomo and Mitsui are multinational corporations, each with economic power and corporate authority equal to that of many small and medium-sized nations. For them, as for any institution of authority, buildings have been both the essential workplace and a means of promoting corporate image.

Economic pluralism, an aggressive consumer society and a degree of cultural schizophrenia have contributed to a bewildering diversity of architectural expression. Coherence created by traditional design or by international architectural influences has been shattered by consumerism and commercialisation. Buildings are now seen as consumer products, with form following the capricious aesthetic, seasonal and financial dictates of current fashion. It is often difficult to distinguish the genuinely experimental from the crassly commercial by appearance alone.

The trend toward the indulgent and the idiosyncratic in architecture was facilitated by changes in the nature of the architectural profession itself. Economic prosperity and technological progress in both design and construction techniques allowed the architect a much fuller range of individual expression. Iconoclastic design motifs became a way for younger architects to secure professional acceptance internationally, and thereby, recognition and commercial success at home. The cult of the architect is very much bound up with the Western concept of individualism and of projection of the image of a client through construction of distinctive buildings. In the 1980s this was exacerbated by *nouveau-riche* corporations and local governments which translated new-found wealth into particularly self-indulgent buildings.

Copious quantities of information for the understanding of new buildings, and of course, the architects themselves, now includes photographic and film archives, the popular press and television, as well as advertising and promotional material on a lavish scale. In their apologia of new and often experimental buildings, architects frequently bemuse us with their explanations. Moreover, some architects, among whom are Kurokawa Kishō and Isozaki Arata, speak in a language heavily larded with Western metaphor and allusion, impenetrable to reasoned historical analysis because it subsumes traditional Japanese architecture in a Western matrix of spatial analysis devised only in this century.

Cities and the Concentration of Authority

The second general characteristic of the past half-century has been the overwhelming dominance of cities. The population has shifted from a predominantly agricultural to an urban basis. The focus of government and society is in the cities, many of which now boast considerable concentrations of capital, power and people.

These cities are pulsating centres of population and commerce, political and cultural power, yet their surface appearance is jagged and disturbing, a riot of free enterprise and often unconstrained growth (Figure 10.1). The visual disunity of Japanese cities, with their disordered superstratum of construction activity and wild juxtapositions of geometric and curvilinear forms, creates the

253

Fig 10.1
Tokyo-
Yokohama
postwar urban
growth

type of fragmented environment which is ideal for fostering the cult of individual expression in architecture, particularly where considerable capital is
available for development. Ironically, the architectural theory of contextualism
has provided a convenient rationalisation for idiosyncratic design; some architects have deliberately taken the theme of chaos from their surroundings and
expressed it in their own work, thereby providing a convenient justification
for quite arbitrary designs. *Nouveau-riche* cities also fell victim to a landmark
mentality, engaging architects to construct idiosyncratic buildings in the belief
that this would stimulate civic consciousness. These buildings invariably
became the 'talk of the town' but to the detriment of traditional townscapes
and frequently of good taste as well.

An example of this is the 75-storey Landmark Tower at the centre of the
high-technology port city at Yokohama, Minato Mirai 21 ('The future city of
the 21st century') (Figure 10.2). The name conveys exactly what the purpose
is, a shining tower rising to the heavens like a large exclamation mark, to draw
attention to Yokohama and to proclaim to its nearby giant neighbour Tokyo
that it is also to be taken seriously as a city. The creative design of this building was the work of the American architect Hugh Stubbins. The choice of a
foreign architect by the city of Yokohama was like the preference of younger
Japanese for clothes with foreign 'designer labels'. The Landmark Tower is
architecture as fashion, and in Japan it is the foreign labels which attract the
greatest kudos. In fashion terms, Stubbins' Landmark Tower promotes the

image of Yokohama as somewhere trendy and a little exotic, even foreign. This is not an inappropriate symbol for a city with a history as a nineteenth-century treaty port and foreign enclave, but it is also a manifestation of older concerns. It is a building driven by the political imperative of propaganda to mouth vertical discourse at the surprised horizontal city beneath. There is nothing new in this, for such must also have been the effect of the soaring *tenshu* of Edo Castle in the seventeenth century.

Fig 10.2
Landmark
Tower, Minato
Mirai 21,
Yokohama

255

All these developments, both in individual buildings and entire urban centres, are in part manifestations of deliberate and sustained attempts to make tangible the identity and authority of local government and private corporations. It is a primal human urge to draw attention to one's self through buildings, their size and style and materials. It seems that the more people have in common, and the more readily they can travel between points of the compass, the more they seek to accentuate minor differences of place and perception with architectural statements of identity and power. In these circumstances a few metres in height, a different shade of marble or an idiosyncratic massing of shapes, can become a consuming passion. This leads to the experimentation and indulgence which is at the heart of the architecture of authority. The reactions of the citizens of Yokohama to their Landmark Tower would not have been fundamentally different from the reaction of the citizens of Edo to the glittering, polychromed and exotically eclectic ceremonial gateways, shogunal mausolea and castle keeps.

Although Osaka has had considerable importance as the focus of the Kansai region, it is Tokyo which has been the focal point for contemporary Japan, the centre of government, business, fashion and culture, education and publishing. This has been a result of the circumstances of authority. Tokyo has been capital of both the nation, with a concentration of the organs of national government and administration situated in the Kasumigaseki and Hibiya districts, and the capital of a large local spread comprising the urban region, the hinterland of the Kantō Plain, and the peppering of small islands of the Ogasawara chain south of Kantō in the Pacific. The Tokyo Metropolitan Government is responsible for a population of some 15 million people, comparable to that of many smaller nations.

The importance of Tokyo has been both reflected in and enhanced by a large number of buildings of architectural and civic significance, but the association between architecture and the Japanese state at the dual level of authority in Tokyo, the national and the metropolitan, is most clearly illustrated by two particular building complexes. The first is the Gymnasium complex at Yoyogi constructed for the 1964 Tokyo Olympics, and the second, the Tokyo Metropolitan Government and City Hall complex at Shinjuku, completed in 1991. Both are internationally well known but neither has, as yet, been interpreted in the matrix of the authority which spawned their physical form. They are two of the most important building projects to be completed in the city of Tokyo during the postwar era. They can also claim special architectural significance in postwar Japan because of their close relationship to the time and circumstance of authority which created them.

Tange Kenzō and the Tokyo Olympics Buildings

The 1964 Tokyo Olympics provided Japan with a golden opportunity to demonstrate its national resurrection from the devastation of the Pacific War, and its full re-entry into the international community. As Yasukawa Daigoro, president of the Olympics Organising Committee, announced, the Tokyo Olympics 'will not only be a display of sportsmanship by the world's athletes,

Fig 10.3
Gymnasium
Buildings,
1964 Tokyo
Olympics,
Tange Kenzō
and URTEC

but will also highlight the continuing efforts of the Japanese people as a worthy member of the world family of nations'.[1] The Olympic Gymnasium Buildings, designed by Tange Kenzō, became an eloquent reaffirmation of Japan's dignity and authority as a nation (Figure 10.3). They represent a particular moment in postwar history, standing at the watershed between recovery and renewed national self-confidence and international acceptance.

Through much of modern history the hosting of the Olympic Games has provided nations with a special opportunity to project national character onto the international stage. The post-World War I Games held in Paris, the subject of the film *Chariots of Fire*, allowed the victorious nations to preen their national pride through athletic competition. The infamous 1936 Berlin Games were intended by Hitler as an opportunity to demonstrate the physical superiority of the Aryan race and of its Nazi creed, although the realisation of this intention was to be thwarted. For the Japanese people, at both the national and the personal level, the decision to allow Tokyo to host the XVIIIth Olympiad provided a great opportunity and challenge. Less than 20 years earlier most of Central Tokyo and much of the surrounding area west, as far as Yokohama and east towards Chiba, had been reduced to ashes by fire bombing. The Olympics provided the opportunity to use new architecture together with the transportation technology of the new, high-speed Bullet Express Train system and monorails linking Haneda Airport to the Yamanote City loopline, to project a renewed national self-confidence to the host of foreign visitors, and through the international television and print media to the rest of the world.

The planning for the Olympic Games began in 1960, at the beginning of a momentous decade of unprecedented national industrial and economic development. The triumphant sculptured forms of Tange's Gymnasium Buildings were to help muster and focus national energy and confidence in the task of doubling the GNP.

Tange had emerged as a leading architect in Japan in the 1950s. He helped pioneer the adoption of the functional forms of the International Style or 'Modern Movement' to Japanese postwar needs. The International Style originated in the Bauhaus in Weimar Germany, espousing an ideology of functionalism. Tange had been a student of Maekawa Kunio, who had studied under Le Corbusier, one of the giants of the International Style. Tange's Hiroshima Peace Centre, begun in 1949 and completed in 1956, had shown a rare ability to articulate the severe modernist materials of steel-frame, concrete and glass to replicate the dignified spacing of traditional timber-frame buildings. Tange's interpretation of the International Style opened up long vistas on Japan's architectural past rather than closing off tradition, which had been a common feature of the movement since the 1930s. The inspired solemnity of the Memorial Museum building at Hiroshima, its rectilinear forms rising above the sombre setting of the atom bomb site, marked Tange as an architect with the genius to capture the special moment of a time and place.

In 1959 Tange completed the designs for the first Tokyo Metropolitan Government Headquarters, located at Yurakuchō. This was to be a set of steel-framed buildings elevated on pilotis, revealing the influence of both Le Corbusier and Mies van der Rohe, but demonstrating an ability to create a civic building able to satisfy the functional needs of government administration, while projecting the desired message to the public. In 1960 Tange's success at Hiroshima and Tokyo made him the obvious choice of the committee responsible for the design of the Gymnasium complex for the Tokyo Olympics.

This complex was to be an official government project under the aegis of the national Ministry of Education in collaboration with the Ministries of Construction and Finance. National reputation and individual reputations were equally at stake. In the administration there was tension over finance between the Ministry of Education, which had overall responsibility for the project, and the Ministries of Construction and of Finance. The Ministry of Construction estimated that the buildings required a budget of three billion *yen*. The Ministry of Finance would only approve finance of two billion *yen*. It required a direct appeal by Tange to the Minister of Finance to resolve the stalemate and assure budgeting at the necessary level. Tange argued that, 'Since the Olympics would be the first major international event Japan had sponsored, half way measures would not do'.[2]

The Finance Minister was Tanaka Kakuei, who later became one of Japan's most controversial prime ministers. Tanaka was one of those politicians who seemed well able to grasp the importance of construction to nation building, no doubt a direct result of his own construction industry background. Tanaka's vision for the construction of a new Japan led to sweeping plans for remodelling the Japanese archipelago in the 1970s. However Tanaka's disgrace, brought about by involvement in the Lockheed scandal, and nation-wide land speculation caused by his plans together conspired to ensure that only part of his vision was ever realised.

The design brief prepared for Tange placed stress on the importance of the symbolic meaning of the buildings. Tange responded to this responsibility by exploiting the power that a building can exercise over its audience:

> My thought on the design went farther than the conception of a large space as a mere expanse. I wanted the space to have an exhilarating influence on the people participating in sports events within it, while promoting a sense of excitement and union with the spectators . . . for some time I had devoted thought to communications between architectural space and the human spirit. And these thoughts inevitably led to consideration to the topic of symbol. . . . Symbols are crystallisations of images of historical periods in the evolution of civilisations.[3]

Yoyogi Park in Tokyo, the location chosen for the Olympic buildings, was itself symbolically significant. In the immediate postwar years it had been known as the Washington Heights Occupation Forces housing estate and, along with Grant Heights, had been one of the major sites for the housing and administrative offices of the US army personnel stationed in the Tokyo area. The scars of defeat and occupation were therefore to be removed from the Tokyo landscape and instead would rise a set of buildings which even today, a generation later, capture the magic and excitement of that Olympic moment. Tange's design consisted of two separate buildings which are closely interrelated in materials and form. They are set on a large, multi-level, pedestrian concourse providing access on two levels for athletes and spectators and conveniently close to rapid mass transit.

The Main Gymnasium is the larger of the two buildings, designed to seat 15,000 people and containing the Olympic Swimming Pool. It is approximately 150 metres in length and encloses an area of 20,620 square metres (Figures 10.4–10.5). The roof, with its great sweeping slopes, dominates the design, providing a powerful and expressive form which lingers in the imagination. The Small Gymnasium, with a seating capacity for 4,000 spectators, included the Olympic basketball court and tennis courts and conference rooms (Figure 10.6). It used another distinctive form, that of the snail-shell spiral, which was designed to complement in plan the dynamic swirling form of the main gymnasium building. It had a single central column and a suspension roof system similar to that of the main building.

The speed with which the project was completed was a triumph of organisation and management, with construction beginning in January 1963, little more than 18 months before the Olympics were to commence.[4] Its construction was as much a triumph of engineering as of architectural design, the product of a close collaborative work between Tange and his architectural design firm, and the seismic engineer Tsuboi Yoshikatsu.

The structural system used for the roof of the main building was a cunning adaptation of the principle used in suspension bridges. It is a suspension membrane roof carried by two multi-strand, steel cables stretched between two columns set almost 125 metres apart (Figure 10.7). These cables rise 42 metres above the ground and are anchored by massive concrete blocks at each end. By keeping the cables under tension, their strength is greatly increased and they are able to carry an extraordinarily heavy load. From the two high-tensile cables smaller cables project at right angles to carry the roof

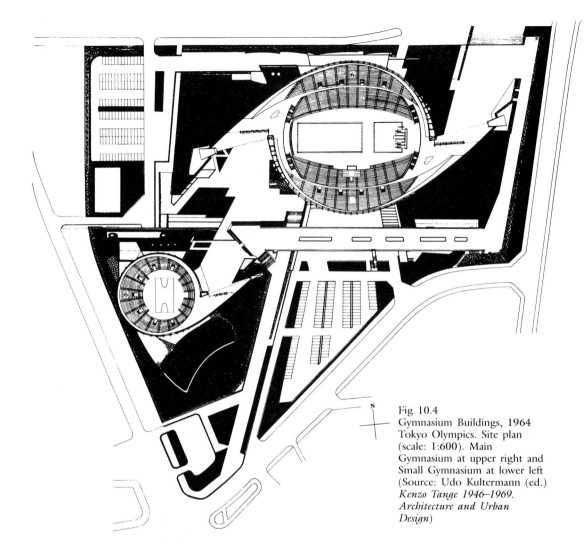

Fig 10.4
Gymnasium Buildings, 1964
Tokyo Olympics. Site plan
(scale: 1:600). Main
Gymnasium at upper right and
Small Gymnasium at lower left
(Source: Udo Kultermann (ed.)
*Kenzo Tange 1946–1969.
Architecture and Urban
Design*)

skin of compressed steel and aluminium panels, each panel one by three metres
in size. The seating areas have strong concrete foundations laid in a circular
plan acting as compression rings to anchor the edges of the roof. A skylight
is formed at the centre of the top where the two main cables run parallel to
each other. This allows natural light to flood the interior, creating something
of a mystical spatial effect not dissimilar from that created in medieval cathedrals as the interior spaces soar upwards to the light. For the swimmers
competing for national honour below in the Olympic Pool, and even for the
general public to whom the pool is open in summer, swimming back-stroke
down the pool is like being transported into an ethereal domain where gravity
and mass are effortlessly defied.

The technology of suspension-roof structuring had been experimented with
internationally in the 1950s, most particularly by Le Corbusier for the 1958
Brussels World's Fair and by Eero Saarinen for the 1958 Hockey Stadium at

Yale University.[5] It was to be used again for the 1972 Munich Olympic Stadium by the German engineer Frei Otto. However, it was Tange and his collaborator Tsuboi who were first able to put the technology into practice on a monumental scale, an important demonstration of Japanese assimilation of foreign technology to its own needs. When completed in 1964 it was the largest tensile structure in the world, an achievement made all the more remarkable because it is the only such structure to remain standing in an earthquake-prone region.

Tange was convinced that tensile structures offered the greatest potential for large-scale spanning of interior spaces, but it was the close collaboration with Professor Tsuboi and his assistant Kawaguchi Mamoru which allowed the experimentation necessary to create the final shape. As Tange himself notes:

> The nature of the structure plus the weight of the materials resulted in complicated deformations at the construction stage. Therefore, all connections between main cable and subordinate cables had to be effected by means of three-dimensionally flexible steel balls.[6]

The buildings were an amazing achievement in terms of the interplay between structure and aesthetics, technology and tradition. The forms grew from the need to enclose an Olympic audience and its activities, the wish to express structural logic in aesthetic form, and the desire to come to terms with national tradition. In this Tange was extraordinarily effective in invoking the traditional sense of authority conveyed by the great tiled roofs of temples (Figure 10.8). The roof-ridge of the Olympic building drew inspiration from the tile-capped

Fig 10.5 Main Gymnasium Building, 1964 Tokyo Olympics. Transverse section (above) and longitudinal section (below) (Source: *The Japan Architect*, November, 1964)

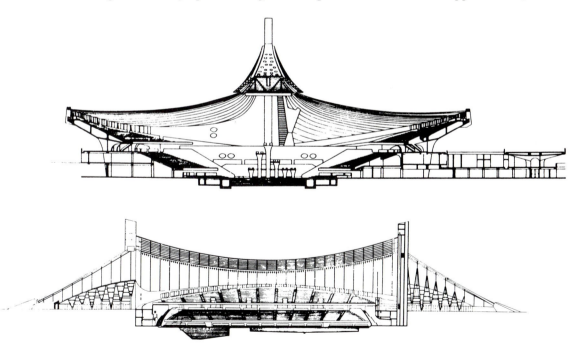

261

Fig 10.6
Small
Gymnasium,
1964 Tokyo
Olympics.
Exterior view
and roof plan
(Source: Udo
Kultermann
(ed.) *Kenzo
Tange
1946–1969.
Architecture
and Urban
Design*)

Fig 10.7
Main
Gymnasium,
1964 Tokyo
Olympics.
Tensile steel
cables

ridges of Buddhist temples, while its classical curvature echoed the graceful lines of the temple roofs. The cables seem to hang languidly between the two columns, their catenary curve creating the impression of a sweeping temple roof. This curvature, which continues in the downward sweep of the roof membrane, also streamlined the roof against the force of strong winds, to which suspension-membrane roofs had always hitherto been particularly vulnerable.

Tange's Olympic Gymnasium and the Daibutsuden of Tōdaiji constitute a similar phenomenon: the use of imported technology with an emphasis upon the visual impact of the forms to proclaim the importance of the buildings and their purpose to the rapidly modernising nation. It is a brilliant culmination of ideas in common currency in the international architectural community in the late 1950s and 1960s. This was a period when architects in the International Style were searching for more organic forms, so that buildings, while acknowledging the dictates of function, would also accept the requirements of place with a reawakened awareness of the past. Le Corbusier had explored this approach in his planned State Capital for the Punjab in India, particularly his Chandigarh Assembly Building. It was to inspire the Danish architect Jørn Utzon in his design for the Sydney Opera House with its distinctive shell-like roof forms, which he began drafting at about the same time as the Tokyo Olympic buildings were being planned.

Not content with invoking the authority of Buddhist tradition only, Tange also searched for other motifs in both Japanese and European architectural traditions, an approach which a generation later would have been labelled 'post-modern'. The avenues leading to the gymnasium are fortified by stone-faced walls with the distinctive curvature of those of the Japanese castle, thereby invoking the symbolism of the castle as well as the Buddhist temple (Figure

263

Fig 10.8 Main
Gymnasium,
1964 Tokyo
Olympics
(above) and
ridge tiles,
Kakushōan,
Enryakuji
(below)

10.9). Tange also sought associations with the gymnasia of classical antiquity.
Of his distinctive curved plan for the main gymnasium building, he said:

> The hint for this comma form came from the Circus Maximus in Rome. Viewed
> from a certain angle, because of partial destruction, the shape of the building
> seems to be out of alignment. I found this attractive and decided that a similar
> composition would make possible the desired openness and smooth pedestrian
> movement'.[7]

This easy eclecticism – drawing together the International Style, classic antiquity, and temple roofs and castle walls from Japanese tradition – is one of the
universal characteristics of architecture and authority. In concept it is similar

Fig 10.9 Stone walls of Osaka Castle (above left), Olympic Gymnasium Buildings (above right) and Tokyo Metropolitan Government Headquarters (below)

to the way in which the *tenshu* of Azuchi Castle was created, drawing together elements of religious and secular building practice for the walls, timber-frame and roofing to serve the ends of Nobunaga's authority.

The New Tokyo Metropolitan Government Headquarters and the Victory of Local over National Authority

The New Tokyo Metropolitan Government Headquarters (Shintochō) opened its high-tech doors for business in April 1991. Not a single building, but a city in its own right, it is a fortress of government authority and administrative power comprising a series of skyscrapers and interlinked buildings and surrounding a civic plaza. It is the largest single set of buildings to be constructed in Japan in the twentieth century. The scale and sophistication is a direct index of their importance as a centre of government and as a metaphor for authority. There could be no more appropriate work of architecture with which to conclude this study.

The late 1980s, which witnessed the planning for a new headquarters for the Tokyo Metropolitan Government, was, like the 1960s, another period of optimism in society and ebullience in the economy and culture. Information technology became a vehicle for government-initiated structural reform and social engineering. New urban planning ventures used fibre-optic cable information networks to link government, business and education. If knowledge is power, then information had become the new authority of postindustrial Japan. From early in the decade, the creation of new cities with information technology system infrastructures was an important platform of national and local government policy. In fact throughout Japan, construction commenced on 19 'technopolis' cities which were designed to integrate all aspects of life, from work to leisure, within the matrix of information technologies. The most ambitious of the new generation of urban plans was that for a 448 hectare artificial island-city to be completed in the centre of Tokyo Bay by the middle of the next century. Other projects around the great waterfront sweep of the Bay from Yokohama in the southwest to Kisarazu on the western side of the Boso peninsula are now closer to completion. These projects addressed the problem of the chronic land-shortage by creating more inner-city residential land, and combined redevelopment of old harbour facilities and waterfront zones with large-scale land reclamation. The Tokyo metropolitan government allocated some 7.37 trillion *yen* for waterfront planning and construction in 1989–91 alone. Objections to the environmental impact of massive land-fill required for the larger projects led to some reconsideration of technical details, while the recession of the early 1990s slowed the rate of progress.

It is at Shinjuku, now the main commercial, transportation and entertainment centre of Tokyo, that the urge to govern by information network has been made most manifest in the monumental architectural form of the Tokyo Metropolitan Government Headquarters. This complex covers an area of 14,349 square metres, or three full city blocks of some of the most expensive land in the world (Figures 10.10–10.11). City Hall Tower I soars skyward

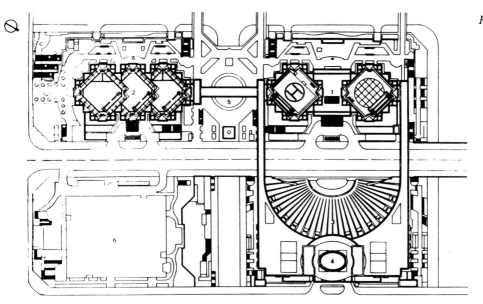

Fig 10.10   New Tokyo Metropolitan Government Headquarters, Shinjuku. Tange Kenzō. Plan
(scale: 1 : 2,500)
(Source: *The Japan Architect*, No. 3, 1991)

1. City Hall Tower I   2. City Hall Tower II   3. Citizens' Plaza
4. Assembly Building   5. Central Mall   (6. NS Building)

Fig 10.11   New Tokyo Metropolitan Government Headquarters. View of Tower I (left) and
Tower II (right) from west

Fig 10.12
New Tokyo Metropolitan
Government Headquarters.
Front façade of Tower I (above
left)

Fig 10.13
New Tokyo Metropolitan
Government Headquarters.
Tower I. Detail (above right)

Fig 10.14
New Tokyo Metropolitan
Government Headquarters.
Tower II. (below)

to a height of 243 metres, making it at the time of completion the tallest building in Japan. One hundred and fifty metres from the ground the main tower separates into two towers of equal size, reminiscent of the twin-towered Gothic cathedrals of medieval Europe (Figures 10.11–10.12). These towers have been off-set at an angle of 90 degrees to the main façade to provide a dramatic accent to the top of the building. A cluster of satellite dishes grow like wild mushrooms in seemingly random arrangement around the upper levels (Figure 10.13).

Beside the main skyscraper is a stepped building, City Hall Tower II, which is 163 metres in height (Figure 10.14). Like its neighbouring City Hall Tower I, it contains the offices of the Tokyo Metropolitan Government. The two buildings have a combined total floor area of some 380,000 square metres, making them the largest set of buildings in Japan in terms of floor space. A semi-oval plaza extends in front of Tower I across to the Assembly Building which, although smaller in scale, invokes the Baroque ambience of the plaza of St Peter's Cathedral, Rome (Figure 10.15). The buildings are all unified in the choice of materials, with granite and marble for most of the solid surfaces and mirrored glass for the windows.

The Tokyo Metropolitan Government Headquarters is a bold assertion by the Tokyo government of its own identity and authority separate from that of the national government located in the Kasumigaseki, Toranomon, Hibiya and Marunouchi districts, so methodically planned in the Meiji period. With the establishment of the new metropolitan headquarters at Shinjuku the two centres of authority in Tokyo, the national and the metropolitan, are clearly differentiated.

Shinjuku was founded in 1698 as a new post-town, as the name denotes, on the Kōshū kaidō heading northwest out of Edo in the direction of the

Fig 10.15
New Tokyo
Metropolitan
Government
Headquarters.
Assembly
Building

269

central alpine provinces. It was brought inside the official boundary of the city of Tokyo only as late as 1932. Since then the rapid westward expansion of the city along the new private rapid electric-rail transit lines radiating from Shinjuku, particularly the Seibu and Odakyū Lines, has redefined the actual population centre of the city to a point west of Shinjuku. Locating the new city government buildings at Shinjuku has made it more accessible to all citizens. Commuters pass through Shinjuku station at the rate of over three million each day, whereas less than one-third of this number pass through Tokyo and Yūrakuchō stations where the old offices were located.

By the early 1980s it was apparent that new buildings were needed to cope with the major overcrowding at the existing buildings at Yūrakuchō. As city government had grown in size and complexity, additional buildings had been added behind Tange's original structure. There were no fewer than 32 buildings coopted into government use, many of them old and inefficient in design and equipment. Corridors were being used for storing documents. The decision to build a new headquarters was precipitated by two problems facing the authorities. Firstly, the increased need for space created by the new information technologies with their fibre-optic cable networks and computer work stations, and secondly, the realisation that the existing buildings were totally unsuitable as an earthquake disaster centre. The reasoning may have been eminently rational in terms of space and function, but the Governor of Tokyo, Suzuki Shun'ichi, was able to exploit the practical reasons for relocation for his political advantage and create a crowning monument to himself and the glory of his vision of greater Tokyo.

A decision to relocate the government functions eventually at Shinjuku had already been made in 1950 when a new city plan was adopted to deal with the anticipated recovery and growth of Tokyo. A three-block site was set aside at Shinjuku, when the area to the west of the main station was designated as a special 'urban sub-centre' (*fukutoshin*) in 1960, as part of a policy to establish satellite cities within the metropolitan region in order to alleviate the problem of over-concentration of business and finance in the Marunouchi and Hibiya areas. At that time, the large 330,000 square metre sewerage treatment works, situated close to what is now the Yodobashi northwest exit to the station, were relocated, and the land so freed was laid out in the grid plan favoured since time immemorial for such city projects. The urban development plan for west Shinjuku coincided with changes to building regulations which permitted the construction of the first high-rise buildings in Japan. In 1971 the Keio Plaza Hotel became the first of a series of skyscrapers over 100 metres in height built in the area. There are now 11 such buildings, which include the headquarters of a number of Japan's largest corporations such as Mitsui, and of one of the biggest general contractors in Japan, Taisei Corporation.

Design and Construction

When a special committee of the Metropolitan Government met to consider a field of nine candidates, Tange was the obvious choice for the appointment of chief architect for the new Tokyo Metropolitan Government Headquarters complex in 1986. He had, after all, been responsible for the first government building completed in 1959, as well as for the epochal Olympic buildings. He was also a friend of governor Suzuki, an association which went back to the time of the Tokyo Olympics when Suzuki had been vice-governor of Tokyo and played an important role in their organisation.

The buildings were constructed under a special ordinance issued by the Tokyo Metropolitan Government to permit rapid completion of the project. The planning phase took 18 months and the construction phase some 35 months. The pace of this construction was staggeringly fast when the size of the buildings is taken into account. Tange had the key design role, but working drawings and construction were undertaken by a large number of contractors and sub-contractors, normal practice in the case of any large-scale commission. The project required the mobilisation of virtually all general building contractors in Japan as well as other specialist companies, a formidable array of expertise and resources. The main contractors engaged for Tower I were Taisei, Shimizu and Takenaka, while Kajima and Ōbayashi-gumi were responsible for Tower II. The Assembly Building was constructed by Kumagai-gumi and Tōkyū Construction.[8] Major construction firms in Japan have a consistent record of working together effectively for fixed-period projects, despite a carefully cultivated public image of intense competitiveness. This is no accident, for the ability to coordinate the building expertise of many seemingly disparate and competitive groups is one of the persistent features of the realisation of the architecture of authority in Japan, encountered at Nara, in Momoyama castles, and again with Tokugawa mausolea. So is the urgency with which such projects of political importance can be completed. Many of the personnel who worked on the new government buildings were smoothly transferred to Shinjuku immediately upon the completion in 1989 of the Makuhari Messe project in Chiba Prefecture, the large trade-fair venue and international convention complex built as part of urban development around Tokyo Bay. This is a striking parallel with the rapid transition of personnel from the Taitokuin mausoleum to the Nikkō Tōshōgū more than 350 years before.

The completed buildings, despite their obvious beauty, size and symbolism, also convey a sense of practical purpose. This is particularly true of the stepped second building, which houses many of the functioning administrative departments of the metropolitan government. The space and structure of the plaza have a calculated, methodical sense to them with the air bridges spanning the avenues running between the buildings, allowing for easy movement of people. The buildings used sophisticated flexible-frame structural technologies to allow them to withstand severe earthquakes. They also incorporated sophisticated intelligent building-service functions, ranging from highly automated climate systems to fibre-optic cable information networks which allow for better emergency and disaster management and planning of facilities and services. The Earthquake Disaster Headquarters was equipped with a map information system with a geographic database for every part of the metropolitan region. In an emergency, detailed information may be projected instantly onto large video screens for planning response. Control of detail is essential for any local government but, prior to the building of the Metropolitan Headquarters, it had been an overwhelming problem for the vast metropolis of Tokyo. On a

Fig 10.16
New Tokyo
Metropolitan
Government
Headquarters.
Tower I.
Detail of
Governor's
Suite

more routine level, a computerised database currently contains graphics for each and every road, street and lane in the entire metropolis, with automated annotation of the state of repair and service records.

Tange himself said that the lattice-like pattern of windows, and of marble and granite on the exterior of the buildings, was intended to invoke the memory of geometric timber-frame buildings of Edo as well as the circuit board of a computer, an apt metaphor for the age of information and technology in Tokyo over which these government headquarters now presides.[9] In addition to symbolising the information age, the small geometric patterning of these rectangular shapes in contrasting light grey and dark blue-grey granite, enhance the overall sense of size of the towers.

The governor's office itself extends across the entire width of Tower I, occupying an area of 195,000 square metres and projecting boldly from the exterior walls on both sides. The crest of the City of Tokyo decorates both front and rear (Figure 10.16). The office is palatial in character, with ceilings 6.4 metres in height, and is lined with marble. It looks out over the plaza and captures the attention as anyone enters the building, an unmistakable visual suggestion that the focus of metropolitan government is its governor. One is reminded of the habit of medieval lords in Europe of placing their personal suites over the main entrances to their castles for better control and supervisory purposes.

A special feature of the buildings is the lavish use of granite and marble for the exterior surfaces and the entrance and reception area, as well as for the governor's offices. The plaza is also faced with marble, imported from Korea. The outside walls are faced with imported granite, including the blue granite which creates the exterior pattern. Stone and marble became the prestige materials in the later 1980s for government and business alike as they strained to find ways to express their authority through their buildings. The use of expensive and rare materials is not surprising in view of the consistent use of a hierarchy of materials in the language of architectural authority. Between 1986 and 1989 the amount of granite and marble imported for architectural use increased approximately 1.7 times; 1.35 million tonnes of granite were imported in the fiscal year 1989 at a cost of 36 billion *yen*.[10] In fact 90 per cent of the granite and 99 per cent of the marble used for the buildings was imported, primarily from Korea and Italy, adding its own symbolic meaning in an age of deliberate internationalisation.

As a result of this prodigious use of marble and granite, a new hierarchy in materials was created in Tokyo, with buildings clad in granite and marble ranking above those surfaced in ceramic tiles and sheet metal. The Tokyo Metropolitan Government Headquarters Buildings, particularly Tower I and the Assembly Building, stand supreme because of the amount of stone and marble used in their construction and also employed extensively on the interior. There is an obvious parallel with architecture and authority of the Meiji period. The supreme standing of the Akasaka Detached Palace in the hierarchy of authority was achieved in part because of Katayama's unprecedented reliance on granite for the walls. Red-brick buildings such as Tokyo Station were ranked one clear level lower in the status hierarchy, but well above a weatherboard establishment. A century later history repeated itself, with unequivocal authority proclaimed by buildings of granite and marble over those of ceramic tile and metal cladding. It is interesting to note in passing that the most common colour for ceramic tiles used for facing the exterior of Tokyo buildings in the 1970s and 1980s was that of red brick.

The new Tokyo Metropolitan Government Headquarters invokes authority in certain other notable ways. For, whatever the dictates of political correctness as a building complex to serve the needs of the people of Tokyo, in silhouette it bears a strong resemblance to the multiple keeps of Himeji Castle. Both the castle and the skyscraper represent to their own age the application of cutting-edge building technology to meet the government imperative to proclaim its own importance, and protect and administer its people. The emphasis placed on the Earthquake Disaster Centre by Governor Suzuki may be seen as a logical requirement of any Tokyo government, but it also invokes that most ancient of all responsibilities of authority to protect its people from danger. Both the castle and the skyscraper complex were built with the same urgency, responding to the needs of a particular moment. In the case of Himeji emphasis was placed upon military preparedness but there is a certain sense of security and impregnability about the new Metropolitan Headquarters building as well. In an age of increased international terrorism all governments need to plan for the security of their administrative and governmental buildings and this headquarters is no exception. At the same time its extensive disaster-management facilities offers the promise of protection and leadership against earthquake, the insidious enemy.

There is also more than a passing formal similarity in appearance between Himeji Castle and the metropolitan government complex, whatever the parallels drawn by critics at the time of its completion with the Notre Dame in Paris. Each combines an eye-catching high-rise complex, consisting of several distinct towers, with extensive horizontal buildings set at its base. The similarity arises from a shared need to address the requirements of political symbolism and government administration. Himeji with its palaces and administrative buildings laid out at the foot of the great multi-towered keep, and the Tokyo Metropolitan Government Headquarters with its high-rise towers and multiple levels of horizontally organised offices, disaster centres, and international congress facilities, have far more in common both in function and in design than would at first appear. Perhaps this is what Tange is signifying in placing castle walls around the boundary of his architectural domain. For the base of the main tower of the Tokyo Government Complex was made with walls of finely cut granite shaped with the slight hint of the curvature and inward slope which is characteristic of Japanese castle architecture (see Figure 10.9). There is a strong connection between this feature and the walls of the Olympic Gymnasium Buildings, and ultimately with castles like Himeji.

Both the Olympic Buildings and the Tokyo Metropolitan Government buildings are the product of the design vision of Tange Kenzō who, on the basis of these two monumental works and the numerous other local, national and international commissions of his prolific career, has assumed the stature of the architect of the Japanese postwar establishment. His standing in the creative interstices between architecture and authority, his ability to capture and monumentalise in built form a particular moment of political importance, places him historically on a level with Katayama and Tatsuno, architects of the late Meiji period, the Kōra in the early Edo period, and with the more shadowy master builders of eighth-century Nara.

The Edifice Complex: Governor Suzuki and the Architectural Projection of Power

The Metropolitan Government complex marked the culmination of a 12-year career of Suzuki Shun'ichi as governor of Tokyo. A member of the Liberal-Democratic Party which had been in power at the national level almost continuously throughout the postwar era, Suzuki proved to be both a tough metropolitan administrator and a powerful political force within his own party. A glance at the method of financing the headquarters building project illustrates his inspired pragmatism. The initial budget estimate was 136.5 billion *yen*, excluding the price of the land which had been allocated to the Metropolitan Government as its right. The buildings would therefore occupy some of the highest priced real estate in the world: in 1991 estimated to be worth 38.5 million *yen* per square metre by the National Land Agency at the time the buildings were completed.[11] The cost of purchasing such a site would have been beyond the resources of even the largest corporations – eloquent testimony to the special prerogatives of those who rule, in this case the power of Tokyo Government to command the most precious of all resources in Tokyo. When completed, the final official cost of the buildings was stated to be 157 billion *yen* (approximately 1.2 billion US dollars in 1991 terms), a sum apparently 15 percent higher than the original estimates. The increased cost was caused by spiralling labour costs occasioned by the shortage of skilled construction workers during the four years of the project, part of an endemic, nationwide labour shortage.[12]

Significantly, the project was not deficit-funded, as this would have made it a political liability for Governor Suzuki. Suzuki had inherited a huge met-ropolitan government debt but had made himself famous by halving the governor's salary and undertaking other cost-cutting measures, eliminating the debt in three years. The new government buildings were paid for by the sale of small, unused pockets of government-owned land, scattered through-out the metropolitan area – left-overs from infrastructure redevelopment projects, and savings made by scrupulous fiscal management during his three terms as governor. Suzuki quite justifiably made much political capital of this. Here was a governor who could provide the citizens of Tokyo with new admin-istrative, cultural and recreational facilities and supplied guaranteed leadership in the event of natural disaster. All this could be supplied at no financial burden to ordinary, hard-working Tokyoites. This was not a building complex constructed at the expense of the people of the metropolis, but created for their security, safety and better government.

The project was a logical extension of Suzuki's dedication to a 'My Town' concept for Tokyo. Under his guidance, the Tokyo government promoted pro-vision of amenities and the diffusion of services to each of the many constituent parts of Tokyo, combined with fostering a rebirth of a sense of identification with the city in which people live. The new Tokyo Metropolitan Government Headquarters was the largest of a series of building projects begun in the 1980s by the metropolitan government to foster this civic consciousness by creating new urban facilities. The timing expediently coincided with the 400th anni-versary of Tokugawa Ieyasu's march into the Kantō Plain to establish his new military headquarters at Edo in 1590, an historic fact also used to political advantage. Other new facilities built throughout the Tokyo metropolitan region included the monolithic Edo-Tokyo Museum designed by Kikutake Kiyonori, the Tokyo Metropolitan Gymnasium by Maki Fumihiko, Taniguchi Yoshio's Tokyo Metropolitan Seaside Aquarium, and Ashihara Yoshinobu's Art and Culture Centre. There is a direct parallel with the use of architecture to rein-force authority in the late sixteenth century; both Ieyasu and Suzuki consoli-dated their authority on the Kantō Plain by resorting to architectural projects on a massive urban scale. The Metropolitan Government Headquarters was the new castle *tenshu*, while the Edo-Tokyo Museum coopted the past to strengthen Tokyo's sense of identity in the present. The sports, leisure and cultural facil-ities provided by the other large-scale buildings fulfilled the responsibility of the beneficent ruler concerned for the well-being of his subjects.

Suzuki's building campaign parallels the series of government projects carried out in Paris to coincide with the bicentenary of the French Revolution, an indication of the universal nature of this phenomenon. I. M. Pei's contro-versial glass pyramid additions to the Louvre, the monumental arch at La Défense and the Opéra at the site of the Bastille were all part of President François Mitterrand's concerted campaign to leave a lasting architectural legacy of his reign as national president to the city of Paris. To speed up the approval process Mitterrand resorted to issuing building permits for these projects under a special ordinance, a strategy with which Suzuki seems also to have been fully conversant because the new government buildings were, in the same way, constructed under a special ordinance.

275

The circumstances surrounding the completion of the building in early 1991 and the opening of government business there in April are in themselves a dramatic illustration of the way in which buildings can serve as an active player in the game of politics. After 12 years in power and having reached the age of 80, Suzuki ran into strong opposition from the Liberal Democratic Party national headquarters on the question of his renomination for a further term as governor of Tokyo. With the election fixed for April 1991, the national body of the LDP overturned Suzuki's renomination and installed its own candidate, Isomura Hisanori, a respected news correspondent of NHK, the Japan Broadcasting Corporation. Suzuki was urged, at first in private, and then more publicly, to consider if it was not time for him to retire gracefully.

With an election looming and the outcome highly uncertain, the new government buildings became a major political issue, so strongly were they identified with Suzuki and his policies. Suzuki was sharply attacked for creating an architectural extravagance. Professional reaction to the buildings was muted, in deference to Tange's senior position in the Japanese architectural world, but the press and opposition groups were highly vocal in their criticism, particularly of the magnificent suite of offices for the governor. It was even proposed initially to make the bath in Suzuki's private suite of marble, prompting one critic to quip that he did not know why he did not use gold instead. The *Japan Times* of 9 February 1991 declared that 'construction of the palatial new Metropolitan Government buildings in Shinjuku and his [Suzuki's] failure to check the steadily deteriorating living environment in the metropolis in particular have been drawing critical responses from among Tokyo citizens'. It appeared that the Tokyo Metropolitan Government Headquarters would become the gravestone marking the end of Suzuki's political career. Suzuki himself increased the political stakes by declaring publicly that he would not set foot in his new office suite until he was re-elected. His opponent Isomura responded by stating that he would use another, more modest office if he were elected. The term 'office politics' took on a more literal meaning.

Suzuki refused to stand down and ran his campaign as an independent member of the LDP, with the support of his local party organisation, in opposition to the nationally sponsored candidate Isomura. The media and opinion polls favoured Isomura but Suzuki won a comfortable victory. There were many factors contributing to this victory, including the strength of local party organisation, increasing dislike of the national LDP at the local level, and Suzuki's record of competent fiscal management coupled with the success of the 'My Town Tokyo' policy.

However, one cannot overlook the role of the new government buildings as a factor contributing to Suzuki's re-election. The headquarters building was a direct campaign issue, the focus of much media attention and debate. His opponents attacked its creation as monument-building by an ageing patriarch, but Suzuki used its construction as a tool for re-election by employing the construction process as a metaphor for good government. The completion of the buildings and the move of government to its new headquarters just prior to the April election was impeccably timed from a political point of view for its greatest impact. Now the political rationale for the relentless pressure for on-time completion was clear; it had been imperative for the government to meet the construction deadline by March 1991 because of the April election. The timing of the completion, just three weeks before the election, the opportunity this afforded for an open-day for the citizens of Tokyo to visit and admire their new government buildings, and not least the trouble-free transfer of the physical accoutrements of government and administration to the new building over the course of two weeks, using 2,000 Nippon Express removal trucks, were a triumph of organisation and public relations. The move was referred to in the popular press as the 'mini-shift of the capital of the Heisei era' (*Heisei mini sento*) invoking language associated with the movement of capitals in the Nara period. What citizen would not have been impressed? This was an election campaign in which the management competence and civic concern of the incumbent governor were convincingly demonstrated by architecture. The spectacle of the new sparkling silver towers against the bright blue spring skies of Shinjuku, seen either directly or as the ubiquitous visual background to television news and weather forecasts, kept Suzuki's achievement before the public eye. The buildings had become the new symbol of Tokyo itself, expressing stability and assuredness and Suzuki's own authority over both metropolis and political party.

Such grand architectural statements as the Tokyo Metropolitan Government Headquarters inevitably act as a spur to the architectural ambitions of others. It was replaced in 1993 as Japan's tallest building by the Landmark Tower at the heart of Minato Mirai 21 in Yokohama. Some 296 metres in height, or 53 metres higher than the government building, the Landmark Tower was built as part of the strategy of Yokohama to compete with Tokyo for a greater share of the economic boom.

Now, just a few years later, all this has passed into history. The age of extraordinary economic and cultural vitality of the 1980s, of which the Tokyo government buildings are both product and symbol, ended abruptly with the onset of the economic recession in 1991. This was followed by a period of increasing political uncertainty marked by the fall from power of the Liberal Democratic Party after a record term in office, and a series of unlikely coalition governments. The disastrous Kobe earthquake of early 1995, although confirming the safety of many newer buildings, nevertheless shook public confidence in the ability of buildings to withstand earthquake shocks. Yet from this economic and political uncertainty new projects are emerging, some on an even greater scale than the Tokyo government buildings. Such has always been the fate of great architectural ambition. In the long term the buildings created in response to the urgent needs of one era take on a life and meaning of their own, fated to attract envy and competition, and destined to acquire new significance with the passing of time.

11 Beyond Vanity and Evanescence

Exploration of the ideas and institutions of authority as embodied in and moulded by architecture has offered considerable scope for identifying the fundamental motive forces at work in Japanese history. In so doing the centrality of the architectonic impulse in Japan, springing from those fundamental human attributes of ambition and creativity, of awe for the intangible and respect for the palpable, has been revealed. Both architecture and authority exhibit a dynamic and cumulative character, grounded in tradition and continuity, sometimes arbitrary and forceful, sometimes mannered and lacking power. In drawing together the relationship between architecture and authority as revealed by a range of architectural achievement, from the oldest buildings of Nara to the newest in Tokyo, it is salutary to return to the sombre warning made explicit at the opening of the *Tale of Heike* that 'all is vanity and evanescence'. What is the meaning of the architecture of authority when so many of the most vaunting architectural statements of religious and political authority have proved so short lived? It would almost seem that buildings created by the greatest ambition proved the most transitory. The fate of the palaces of eighth-century Nara, and the castles of sixteenth-century Azuchi and seventeenth-century Edo, prompts us to ask whether the architecture of authority contains within itself the seeds of its own destruction. This was the question which concerned Kamo no Chōmei, retired court poet and Buddhist monk, in the year 1212:

> Whence does he come, where does he go, man that is born and dies? For whose benefit does he torment himself in building houses that last but a moment, for what reason is his eye delighted by them? This too we do not know. Which will be first to go, the master or his dwelling? . . . Of all the follies of human endeavour, none is more pointless than expending treasures and spirit to build houses in so dangerous a place as the capital.[1]

We have seen bountiful evidence of the prodigious expenditure of inspiration and resources on the building of houses of state and of religion, in the centres of authority of Japan over the course of almost 1,500 years. Equally we have seen that, in historical terms, many of these great buildings endured only briefly although they created great excitement and delight during their lifetime. For whose benefit should we go to all this trouble, to paraphrase Kamo no Chōmei?

In addressing this question it should be emphasised that vanity and evanescence are not in themselves peculiarly Japanese phenomena, however important they may seem. 'Lo, all our pomp of yesterday / Is one with Nineveh and Tyre' proclaims Kipling's *Recessional* hymn. Permanence is not the basis for judging the effectiveness of the architecture of authority, although concerns of survival and longevity may loom large in the minds and plans of its builders and patrons. In fact the more effective the architecture as authority the more likely it was to be destroyed by countervailing authority. So directly did some buildings personify their patrons, their prestige and power, that to overthrow their authority meant that the towering castle keeps, the gilded roofs, the glittering gateways, also had to be destroyed. The failure of many of the great works of architectural authority to survive as more than a screen painting, or a faded memory is, perversely, a testimony to their very success in embodying the authority which created them. When that authority crumbled the physical frame that personified and housed it also collapsed. Such was the fate of the Nara Palace. It was also the fate of many of the Tokugawa mausolea after the Meiji Restoration, as A.B. Mitford (Lord Redesdale) wrote in his account of a visit on 1 July 1870 to the Shiba Tokugawa mausolea. His comments reveal how decisively a change in authority can eviscerate the architectural form of its power:

> Three years ago, admittance to see these temples and shrines was only to be obtained with difficulty, even by the highest foreign officials. . . . Even two years ago, when we first visited them, we did so only after much trouble; and these priests were numerous, two occupying each step of the gateway and the entrance to the temple. They knelt, or sat after Japanese fashion on their heels, and facing each other one on each side of each step; and we were permitted to go to a certain spot; beyond that was the 'holy of holies'. Now it is far otherwise. Anyone may go who is willing to tip the attendant priests, and although they exact, what all are willing to pay, every respect to the names of the proud ones in whose honour these edifices have arisen, nothing is hidden or kept from the curious gaze of the liberal paying barbarian.[2]

Such is the fate of architecture associated intimately with the prevailing political order. Mitford's account shows that, in just three years from 1867 to 1870, the Shiba mausolea had slipped from the status of sacred structures dedicated to founders of the ruling order to objects of mere curiosity in a new age.

The corollary of vanity is jealousy, and this has often been a cause of the destruction of buildings. Even as it impresses, the ability to build a splendid palace or mansion attracts envy: 'Men who love buildings are their own undoers, and need no other enemies', as Marcus Crassus observes in Plutarch's *Lives*.[3] There was certainly an element of envy in the vehemence with which the Tokugawa destroyed the Toyotomi castle of Osaka in 1615, and of an almost inordinate love of buildings by members of the House of Toyotomi.

Jealousy alone does not account for the evanescence of most buildings of this type however. Historically it is clear that much of the architecture of authority was summoned forth by special needs which themselves had brief duration. This was the case with the palaces of Imperial Nara and the *tenshu* of Iemitsu's Edo Castle. So well attuned were these buildings to the specific political circumstances which spawned them, so much were they creatures of their time, that once the circumstances of authority changed, they too faded away – in the words of the *Tale of Heike*, 'as insubstantial as a dream on a Spring night' to become 'one with Nineveh and Tyre' (to permit a cross-cultural metaphor).

At this point we would do well to seek an answer to the question whether there was any ethical or moral correlation drawn in Japan between the evanescence of architecture and a failing of authority. As has been discussed, there was a clear correlation between architecture and authority in the Sino-Confucian world-view, to which Japan was, in various periods, both heir and debtor. In Chinese civilization correct government required the correct built environment. If the ruler was not virtuous there would be disorder in the physical world. Although not as comprehensively articulated there are elements of this philosophy within the Judeo-Christian tradition. A hint of this is seen in the way Matthew Arnold accounted for the decline of empires in the nineteenth century:

> And Empire after Empire, at their height
> Of sway, having felt His boding sense come on.
> Have felt their huge frames not constructed right,
> And droop'd and slowly died upon their thrones.[4]

We may well ask whether the Japanese make a similar connection between government failing and architectural foible? Chōmei certainly recognised the apparent folly of architectural aggrandisement in the capital, but his criticism is directed at the wastefulness and futility of the exercise rather than at any perceived moral or ethical failure by its sponsors. It seems that the Japanese adopted the Chinese correlation between virtuous governments and correct architectural principles but happily ignored its corollary. Extravagance in building materials and styles was easily justified as homage to the gods or as a responsibility of high office but much of the architecture of authority in Japan was spawned by exultation in new power and resources. Such is the nature of the *nouveau-riche*. However, there was convenient justification to be found in giving glory to the gods or one's ancestors, who, in the case of the Tokugawa, most satisfactorily happened to be identical. There was clear political advantage in constructing the Tōshōgū, or the Tōdaiji of Nara for that matter, but it may be unfair to dismiss this as completely self-serving. Did there not exist a similar balance between glorifying God and glorifying Mammon in the case of the builders of the cathedrals of Christendom? Praise of God may have raised those soaring spires but the authority of the local bishop was greatly enhanced with each additional course of masonry in the walls. The frightening chorus of creatures sculptured on the gateways of Nikkō may have warned of the awesome authority of the tutelary god enshrined within, but simultaneously sang the praise of his successors in shogunal office to each daimyo and imperial emissary pausing beneath to pay obeisance.

Beyond the correlation between the fortunes of authority and the fate of architecture, the evidence of the great architectural monuments we have considered establishes that architecture is an integral and exalted function of institutions of human governance and spiritual belief. Raw ambition and subtle political manipulation, fierce spiritual yearnings and distended doctrinal disputes, all have architectural emanations as well as political consequences. In the Japanese experience architecture is an attribute, not merely a sign or symbol of authority. Architecture is inseparable from the form, purpose and activities of authority, as the contained is from the container. Since we have experienced in this study some of the greatest works of architecture in Japanese history, it is possible to restate in an unequivocal fashion that, as an attribute of authority, some buildings became an incarnation of authority in their own right in Japan. In making authority tangible, architecture took on a life and authority of its own. Architecture became the reification of authority, whereby something most immaterial, in this case authority, is apprehended. Thus the authority of the imperial institution is inseparable from the architecture of Ise Shrine. It is impossible to imagine Emperor Shōmu without Tōdaiji. We cannot envisage Fujiwara Michinaga without the Tsuchimikado-dono nor Oda Nobunaga without Azuchi Castle. The Tokugawa shogunate loses its most powerful projection of divine authority without the brilliance of the Nikkō Tōshōgū. The Meiji state and the Akasaka Palace seem inseparable. Time may well prove a similar, if slightly more modest, association between Governor Suzuki and Tange's glittering Tokyo Metropolitan Government Headquarters.

As an attribute of authority, architecture has played a central role in giving tangible expression to ideas of rule and to defining these ideas in practice. This is a dynamic process, particularly crucial at the alpha and omega of authority. At the beginning of a government, architecture helps effect a transition from *de facto* power to *de jure* authority, establishing a pervasive image of the new order which becomes a tool of power, particularly when, in addition, spatial relationships are manipulated by built form to create hierarchy in the social and political order. At this point architecture injects its own special vocabulary into political nomenclature and discourse, and forms its own hierarchy of styles, features and materials which are homologous with the structure of authority itself. This is as true for Tokugawa palaces and mausolea as it was later for Meiji palaces and railway stations. For it was unfailingly to architecture that the rulers of Nara and Kyoto, Edo and Tokyo turned for a working definition of authority. At times the reliance on architecture bordered on obsession, spawning complex expressions of built genius.

As we have seen in the case of Nijō Castle, architecture can continue to convince and coerce through its configuration of space and structure, and the effects of colours and materials, long after the initial and urgent need for its creation has passed. It continues inexorably to mould the behaviour of subject and ruler alike. In this way a building can assert an intellectual independence, an autonomous authority to proclaim its own message without necessarily referring back to its original purpose. And, in the era of decline of authority, a building may serve to buttress a weakened establishment with its solid physical forms, to foster an illusion of strength and order which is no longer the political, economic or military reality. Such was the role of Tokugawa gateway architecture as it became the eviscerated projection of an authority from which real power had ebbed.

281

The dynamic in the process of the architectural relationship to authority in Japan is pinpointed by Lewis Mumford's statement that:

> In an age of social disintegration . . . architecture loses much of its essential character; in an age of synthesis and construction it steps forward once more as the essential commanding art . . . architecture becomes a guide to order in every other department of activity.[5]

Mumford's observations, although based on Western experience, nevertheless characterise the circumstances of authority in Japan in both the eighth and seventeenth century. Architecture became a guide to the process of state formation at Nara, with the ordering of architecture into different departments being a central role of state, and the preoccupations of state under Shōmu with extending central authority over the provinces by the vehicle of the official temple system. In the sixteenth century, consistent with Mumford's characterisation, decline in architecture followed the fragmentation of central power in the age of civil wars. Architecture 'steps forward once more' with the re-establishment of centralised authority under Nobunaga. The castles of Azuchi, Himeji and Edo in this new period of 'integration' commanded attention as a palpable demonstration of the new order.

The process of consolidation, with architecture as the 'essential commanding art', reached its rhetorical culmination during the primary phase of the consolidation of the new government under the first three Tokugawa shogun. From 1600 until the death of Iemitsu in 1651, the Tokugawa were extraordinarily effective in translating their political ambitions into physical forms, with a glittering array of castles, palaces and mausolea created in rapid and staggering succession. Rarely has authority created such spectacular edifices as the *tenshu* of Edo Castle, and the mausolea of Taitokuin and Tōshōgū in less than a single decade. In stark contrast a loss of direction, the decline of certitude, is reflected in the architecture of the late Edo period, and it is not until the Meiji period that we find architecture once more stepping out to take the lead in the building of a new state.

We have also seen that the relationship between religious and secular authority is reflected in shared architectural forms. The technology and aesthetics of great temples and shrines is held in common with that of great palaces and castles. Buildings, like rulers, have refused to observe an artificially imposed distinction between the sacred and the secular, exposing the artificiality of such modern distinctions to the nature of premodern authority itself.

There have been many traditions in Japan and elsewhere which have denied the monumental as an attribute of authority, seeking in apparent simplicity a more elemental communion with nature or a spiritual order. Some of the world's great religions, including Christianity and Buddhism, had their origins among the meek and humble. Ephemeral simplicity was also at the animistic heart of ancient Shinto. As these beliefs became codified and institutionalised, however, they acquired impressive building traditions as the physical matrix for their spiritual and temporal authority. For a kingdom not of this world, Christianity showed considerable ingenuity in redefining Heaven on Earth through the medium of churches and cathedrals. Such was also true of Shinto, as it succumbed to the blandishment of architectural and iconic expression as part of the institutionalisation of centralised imperial and bureaucratic authority in the Nara period.

In Shinto we encounter one of those paradoxes of Japanese civilization which gives it special meaning. Some of the most enduring expressions of authority have stood the test of time not through any permanence of their materials but because of a dynamic tradition of regeneration and renewal. Authority and architecture have sustained each other down the centuries; when one faltered the other has managed to struggle on. With the ritual of 20-year rebuilding, the Ise Shrine provides the most extended example of this thesis. However the same process is evident, if not so well ordered, in the Nara temples and in all historic buildings which developed parallel systems of human organisation to support their physical forms.

The building process itself furnishes a further dimension to understanding the relationship between architecture and authority in Japan and is an effective way of demonstrating that authority. At times the actual process of building was so important politically that the very activity may be said to be an attribute of authority. In the case of Ise and of the first building and rebuilding of the Daibutsuden, this activity became an act of worship, a ritual homage to authority. Once a building is completed, it is easy to overlook the significance of the processes of construction in the workings of state, of the laying down of foundations, the assembly of pillars and beams, the raising of ridge-poles and the spreading of tiles and shingles. But the making of a monument constituted as dramatic and palpable a demonstration of authority as the finished building. The ability to organise people and materials on a monumental scale is a hallmark of most great civilizations from Mesopotamia and Egypt to China and Japan. The palaces and temples of Nara and the castles of Momoyama, the city of Edo and its reincarnation in Meiji and modern Tokyo, required the wholesale mobilisation of the resources of state. The national polity in each instance was as much the product of the collective sweat of tens of thousands of artists, artisans and labourers as it was the product of statecraft.

We may recall particular historical instances in which the process of building has required governments to rethink their administrative organisation as in the Nara and Edo periods. Social and economic historians can learn much from a study of the building process about the cost of labour, the ranking of professions and society, and the system of education in the training and transmission of technical skills and social values from one generation of master builders to the next. There are also fascinating instances in which the effectiveness of government itself may be assessed by comparison of statements of intent contained in written policy documents, laws and edicts, with the ability to translate these policies into the reality of the built environment. How we regard government today to a large extent depends upon assessing the effectiveness of policy implementation. In Japan, we are afforded the rare opportunity to accomplish this historically by recourse to architecture as a primary source. It is notable that an examination of Tokugawa policy in relation to Edo architecture also uncovered a fundamental tension between the official order and the architectural order, with the latter as much the product

283

of building traditions and technical requirements as it was a response to government dictates. Comparison of stated intention with architectural form revealed a special dynamic in the relationship between government and architecture. The internal organisation and technology of the building professions has always responded to its own dictates, and the relationship between technical necessity and the arbitrary will of government provides new and fruitful ways of examining architecture and authority. Architecture has been seen to impose its own rules upon what can be accomplished, acting as a constraint on ideology and institutions at the same time as it creates its own institutional organisation and logic.

As we pay our last obeisance to this deep and many-faceted tradition of architectural authority, we should resolve that such buildings must no longer linger in the shadow of Japanese history, isolated from the mainstream of modern historical investigation. They demand to stand in the full light of analysis and recognition which is their proper due. Having relived and recreated some of the special moments in Japanese civilization through its buildings, and discerned the ambition which animated them and the processes which built them, we can no longer claim surprise at the vigour and creativity of contemporary Japan. The builders of Japanese civilization, the makers of the monuments great and small, high and low which have been the subject of this study, have shown many times over that they were capable of achieving a sublimity of architectural expression which, transcending the needs of a particular occasion and patron, equalled any of the most exalted architectural creations in human experience. It is interesting, and salutary, to ponder on the question of how time will impose its own ordering on the architecture of the present age. A millennium from now, which works of architecture will remain intact, or in memory, to speak the language of authority of our times?

Notes

1 Authority in Architecture: Container and Contained

1 The term *mikado* is used to refer to gateways and, by extension, to the emperor as early as the *Man'yōshū*, the collection of imperial court poetry compiled in the Nara period. The earliest known reference to *kenmon* meaning a powerful person rather than an impressive gateway occurs in an order issued from the Dajōkan in 902 AD. See further, Kokushi daijiten henshū iinkai, *Kokushi daijiten* (14 vols), Yoshikawa kōbunkan, 1984–1993, s.v., 'kenmon seike', 'heika'; *Nihon kokugo daijiten* (20 vols), Tokyo: Shōgakukan, 1972–1976, s.v. 'ken'i', 'kenryoku', 'kenmon', 'mikado', 'heika'.

2 John Ruskin, *Lectures on Art*, London: George Allen, 1889, p. 67.

3 Yoshida Kenkō (1283–1350), *Essays in Idleness (Tsurezure-gusa)*, in Donald Keene (compiler and ed.) *Anthology of Japanese Literature*, Rutland, Vermont and Tokyo: Charles E. Tuttle, 1956, p. 233.

4 Leon Battista Alberti, *On the Art of Building in Ten Books* (trans. Joseph Rykwert, Neil Leach and Robert Tavernor), Cambridge, Mass. and London: MIT Press, 1988, p. 5.

5 John James, *Chartres. The Masons who Built a Legend*, London, Boston, Melbourne and Henley: Routledge and Kegan Paul, 1982, p. 85.

6 See further Françoise Tallon, 'Art and the Ruler: Gudea of Lagash', *Asian Art*, vol. 5. no. 1, Winter, 1992, pp. 35–41.

7 See Paul Frankl, *Principles of Architectural History: the Four Phases of Architectural Style, 1420–1900* (trans. J. Fane. O'Goorman) Cambridge, Mass., The MIT Press, 1973. Originally published in 1914 as *Die Entwicklungsphasen der Neueren Baukunst*.

8 See further Thomas A. Markus, *Building and Power. Freedom and Control in the Origin of Modern Building Types*, London: Routledge, 1993, pp. 57–66.

9 B.W.P. Wells, 'The Psycho-Social Influence of Building Environment: Socio-Metric Findings in Large and Small Office Spaces', *Building Science* 1, 1965, pp. 153–165. Reprinted in Robert Gutman (ed.) *People and Buildings*, New York and London: Basic Books, 1972, pp. 97–119. Another pioneer in the analysis of the psychological implications of architectural form was Edward T. Hall, who developed the study of 'proxemics' or 'the study of ways in which man gains

285

knowledge of the content of other mens' minds through judgements of behaviour patterns associated with varying degrees of proximity to him'. See Edward T. Hall (ed.), 'Silent Assumptions in Social Communication', in *Disorders of Communication*, Research Publications, Association for Research in Nervous and Mental Disease 42, 1964, pp. 41–55. Reprinted in Gutman, (op. cit.) pp. 135–151. See also *The Hidden Dimension*, Garden City, New York: Doubleday, 1966. Although Hall's theories are worth pursuing into an Asian context, his own such pursuit into the Japanese field is a useful warning of the danger of superficial generality endemic to work carried out without appropriate linguistic and historical background.

10 Christopher Alexander *et al.*, *A Pattern Language. Towns, Buildings, Construction*, Oxford: Oxford University Press, 1977; Rudolf Arnheim, *The Dynamics of Architectural Form*, Berkeley, Los Angeles and London: University of California Press, 1977; Joseph Rykwert, *On Adam's House in Paradise*, Cambridge, Mass.: MIT Press, 1981 (first published in 1972).

11 O. Newman, *Defensible Space*, New York: Macmillan, 1972. See also Alice Coleman, *Utopia on Trial. Vision and Reality in Planned Housing*, London: Hilary Shipman, 1985.

12 Kim Dovey, 'Seduction, Surveillance and Segregation: Researching Power and Built Form', paper presented at IAPS 12 International Conference, Marmaras, Greece, 11–14 July, 1992.

13 *Shorter Oxford English Dictionary*, s.v. 'authority'.

14 Baldwin Smith, *Architectural Symbolism of Imperial Rome and the Middle Ages*, New York: Hacker Art Books, 1978. (Originally published by Princeton University Press in 1956.)

15 Ronald Harry Graveson, 'The House of Law', in Roscoe Pound *et al.*, (eds) *Perspectives of Law: Essays for Austin Wakeman Scott*, Boston: Little Brown, 1964, p. 131.

16 Peter Stein, 'Elegance in Law', *The Law Quarterly Review*, vol. 77, April, 1961, p. 254.

17 From *Yoshida Shoin zenshū*. Quoted in Maruyama Masao, *Studies in the Intellectual History of Tokugawa Japan*, Tokyo: University of Tokyo Press, 1974, p. 362.

18 John Ruskin, *The Seven Lamps of Architecture*, London: J. M. Dent and Sons. (Originally published in 1849 with a second edition in 1855.)

19 For example, the essays in Henry A. Millon and Linda Nochlin (eds) *Art and Architecture in the Service of Politics*, Cambridge, Mass. and London: The MIT Press, 1978.

20 Recent examples of this approach include Janet Southorn, *Power and Display in the Seventeenth Century: the Arts and their Patrons in Modena and Ferrara*, Cambridge and New York: Cambridge University Press, 1988; Clare Robertson, *'Il Gran Cardinale': Alessandro Farnese, Patron of the Arts*, New Haven and London: Yale University Press, 1991.

21 See further Thomas A. Markus (op. cit. note 8); Robin Evans, *The Fabrication of Virtue: English Prison Architecture, 1750–1840*, Cambridge: Cambridge University Press, 1982.

22 James S. Ackerman, *The Villa: Form and Ideology of Country Houses*, The A.W. Mellon Lectures in the Fine Arts, 1985, the National Gallery of Art, Washington DC, Princeton: Princeton University Press, 1990. This study traces the evolution of the villa typology and its meaning from Palladio to Frank Lloyd Wright and Le Corbusier. See also Reinhard Bentmann and Michael Müller, *The Villa as Hegemonic Architecture*, Atlantic Highlands: Humanities Press, 1992, a translation of a 1970 New Left view of Palladio and his architecture. Another building type now recognised to have been of political consequence was the town hall in England. See Robert Tittler's *Architecture and Power: The Town Hall and the English Urban Community c. 1500–1640*, Oxford: Clarendon Press, 1991.

23 Lois Craig and the staff of the Federal Architecture Project, *The Federal Presence. Architecture, Politics, and Symbols in United States Government Building*, Cambridge, Mass. and London: The MIT Press, 1978; William Searle, *The White House: The History of an American Idea*, Washington: AIA, 1992; Vincent Scully, *Modern Architecture: The Architecture of Democracy*, New York: Braziller, 1973.

24 See Thomas R. Metcalf, *An Imperial Vision. Indian Architecture and Britain's Raj*, London, New York and Berkeley: University of California Press, 1989.

25 John Ruskin, *The Seven Lamps of Architecture*, (op. cit. note 18), p. 182.

26 Michael Cooper (ed.) *They Came to Japan: An Anthology of European Reports on Japan 1543–1640*, Berkeley and Los Angeles: University of California Press, 1965, p. 134.

27 Walter H. Pater, *Studies in the History of the Renaissance*, London: Macmillan, 1873, p. viii.

28 Bruno Taut, *Houses and People of Japan* (2nd edn), Tokyo: Sanseido Company, 1958 (first published in 1937), p. 278.

29 Ibid., p. 158.

30 John Ruskin, *The Stones of Venice*, edited and introduced by Jan Morris, Boston and Toronto: Little Brown and Company, 1981 (first published 1853), pp. 89–90.

31 Edward S. Morse, *Japan Day by Day, 1877, 1878–79, 1882–83*, Boston and New York: Houghton Mifflin Company and the Riverside Press: Cambridge, 1917, p. 72.

32 George Steiner, *Real Presences*, London and Boston: Faber and Faber, 1989, p. 229.

33 Richard Aldington (comp.), *The Religion of Beauty. Selections from the Aesthetes*, Melbourne, London and Toronto: William Heinemann, 1950, p. 9.

34 For example, Amanuma Shun'ichi, *Nikon kenchiku shiyō* (2 vols), Kyoto: Asuka-en, 1927; Robert Treat Paine and Alexander Soper, *The Art and Architecture of Japan*, Harmondsworth: Penguin Books, 1955.

2 The Grand Shrines of Ise and Izumo: The Appropriation of Vernacular Architecture by Early Ruling Authority

1 *Izumo fudoki*, (trans. Michiko Yomaguchi), Tokyo: Monumenta Nipponica Monograph, 1971, p. 80.

2 The most detailed analysis available in English of the technical features of the Ise and Izumo shrines is Watanabe Yasutada, *Shinto Art: Ise and Izumo Shrines*, (trans. Robert Ricketts), Tokyo: Weatherhill, 1974. *The Heibonsha Survey of Japanese Art.* (Katsuichirō Kamei *et al.*, eds) Originally published by Heibonsha under the title *Ise to Izumo* in 1964. The first major study of Ise to appear in English was Kenzō Tange and Noboru Kawazoe, *Ise: Prototype of Japanese Architecture*, Cambridge, Mass.: MIT Press, 1965, a translation of a book published in 1961 by Asahi Shinbun. Tange was one of Japan's leading modernist architects of the postwar period, and this study reflects his concern with relating Japanese modernism to traditional architecture.

3 J. J. Coulton, *Ancient Greek Architects at Work. Problems of Structure and Design*, Ithaca, New York: Cornell University Press, 1977, p. 30.

4 Cf. 'Christianity was only following a precedent in adapting the symbolic forms and glory of palace concepts to the service of God, for these had always been in the [near] East a close correlation in men's minds between palaces and temples, kings and gods'. Baldwin Smith, *Architectural Symbolism of Imperial Rome and the Middle Ages*, New York: Hacker Art Books, 1978, p.12. (Originally published by Princeton University Press in 1956.)

5 Nihon daijiten kankōkai, *Nihon kokugo daijiten*, Tokyo: Shōgakukan, 1975, s.v. 'matsurigoto'. G. B. Sansom first drew this to the attention of Western scholarship in 1931. See G. B. Sansom, *Japan. A Short Cultural History*, (rev. edn), Rutland, Vermont and Tokyo: Charles E. Tuttle, 1973, p. 50. (First published in 1931.)

6 Fukuyama Toshio, 'Jingū no kenchiku to sono kenchiku', in Gomazuru Junshi (ed.) *Jingū. Dai rokujūkai jingū shikinen nengū*, Tokyo: Shōgakukan, 1975, p. 118. Fukuyama reaches this conclusion from analysis of the *Kō daijingū gishiki-chō* of 804.

7 See Edwina Palmer, 'Land of the Rising Sun: The Predominant East–West Axis among the Early Japanese', *Monumenta Nipponica*, vol. 46, no. 1, Spring 1991, pp. 69–90.

8 See Sey Nishimura, 'The Way of the Gods: Motoori Norinaga's Naobi no Mitama', *Monumenta Nipponica*, vol. 46, no. 1, Spring 1991, pp. 21–41.

9 This association is clearly articulated in *Imperial Precepts to Soldiers and Sailors* formally accepted by Yamagata Aritomo from the emperor in 1882 and reflecting Yamagata's views in the ethos for a modern military force: '. . . with single heart fulfil your essential duty of loyalty, and bear in mind that duty is weightier than a mountain, while death is lighter than a feather'. Quoted in Ryusaku Tsunoda, W. T. de Bary and Donald Keene (comp.) *Sources of Japanese Tradition* (2 vols),

New York and London: Columbia University Press, 1964, vol. 2., p. 199.

10 The two shrines were treated as separate entities in the earliest known written record of the ceremonies carried out at Ise, the *Kō daijingū gishiki-chō* and *Toyouke-no-miya gishiki-chō* of 804 AD. In the *Engi-shiki* of 927 AD these records are integrated into a single section (Book IV), and the 'Shrine of the Great Deity' (*Ōmikami-no-miya*) and the Toyouke Shrine are treated as part of the same institutional entity, together with 40 other minor shrines. See Felicia Gressit Bock (trans. and ed.) *Engi-shiki. Procedures of the Engi Era*, Book I-V, Tokyo: Sophia University, 1970, pp. 44–56, 123–150.

11 Adapted from W.G. Aston, *Nihongi. Chronicles of Japan from the Earliest Time to A.D. 697*, London: George Allen and Unwin, 1956, p. 176. (First published as a *Supplement to the Transactions of the Proceedings of the Japan Society*, London, by Kegan Paul, Trench, Trubner, 1896.)

12 Tange and Kawazoe draw attention to the early practice of suspending bronze mirrors from sacred *sakaki* trees to welcome the emperor as an example of the direct association of these mirrors with imperial authority. See Tange and Kawazoe, (op. cit. note 2), p. 175.

13 Information supplied by Ise Jingū Shichō.

14 See further E. Satow, 'The Shintō Temples of Isé', *Transactions of the Asiatic Society of Japan*, First Series, 1874, pp. 113–119. For analysis of the documentary sources for architectural change at Ise see Fukuyama Toshio, 'Jingū no kenchiku to sono rekishi' (op. cit. note 6), pp. 118–132.

15 The thesis that the form of the Ise sanctuary buildings was based on the vernacular storehouse was first advanced by Fukuyama Toshio who, with his mentor Sekino Masaru, conducted the excavation of the Toro site in the immediate postwar era. Fukuyama drew attention to the close similarity between the Mikeiden of the Outer Shrine of Ise and the reconstruction of a typical rice storehouse at Toro by Sekino. There is no question of the similarity between the two building styles but some caution is necessary regarding the architectural detail because Ise itself was under periodic reconstruction at the same time as the Toro excavations. As a result there may have been some over-enthusiasm for the parallels.

16 Tatsumi Hirokazu, *Taka-dono no kodaigaku. Gōzoku no kyokan to ōken no saigi*, Tokyo: Hakusuisha, 1990, pp.10–32.

17 See further Ishino Hironobu, 'Rites and Rituals of the Kofun Period,' *Japanese Journal of Religious Studies*, 1992, vol. 19, nos. 2–3, pp. 193–194.

18 Jingū shichō (ed.) *Koji ruien*, Tokyo: Jingū shichō, (reprint) 1936, vol. 52, p. 1005.

19 Nishina Shinmeigū is registered as a National Treasure by the Japanese government. See further Ōta Hirotarō (ed.) *Nagano-ken no kokuhō jūyō bunkazai: kenchikubutsu hen*, Matsumoto: Kyōdo shuppansha, 1987, pp. 77–79, 244–245.

20 Tange and Kawazoe, (op. cit. note 2), pp. 168–169.

21 See Felicia G. Bock, (op. cit. note 10), especially Book IV and note 95.

22 Aston, *Nihongi*, (op. cit. note 11), pp. 301–381. Note especially p. 307. This struggle is also recounted in Tange and Kawazoe, (op. cit. note 2), pp. 198–200.

23 Book IV, 'The Shrine of the Great Deity in Ise'.

24 *Shunki*, 10th day, 8th month, 1040. Quoted in Ōta Hirotarō, 'Shikinen zōteisei shikō,' *Kenchikushigaku*, no. 19, September, 1992, pp. 94, 107.

25 Ōta Hirotarō, 'Shikinen zōteisei no chōsa hōkoku', *Kenchikushigaku*, no. 18, March 1992, pp. 33–45.

26 Ibid., p. 3. The other disruptions to the regularity of the rebuilding interval occurred after fire (792 – after seven years); the change of capitals from Nara to Kyoto (810 – after 18 years); in the middle of the Heian period for reasons which are unclear (1057 – after 17 years), in the fourteenth century during the period of disputed imperial succession (1364 – after 21 years, and 1391 – after 27 years); at the turn of the seventeenth century with the establishment of the Tokugawa shogunate (1609 – after 24 years), and as a result of World War II (1953 – after 24 years). See ibid., pp. 33–45.

27 Recounted in Sansom (op, cit. note 5), p. 49.

28 Joan R. Piggott, 'Sacral Kingship and Confederacy in Early Izumo', *Monumenta Nipponica*, vol. 44, no. 1, Spring 1989, pp. 45–74.

29 Adapted from Aston, *Nihongi*, in De Bary *et al.* (op. cit. note 11).

30 De Bary, ibid., p. 29.

31 Ibid., p. 30.

32 Ibid.

33 According to the *gishiki-chō* and other early records. See Fukuyama Toshio (op. cit. note 6), pp. 123–124.

34 The rebuildings of Izumo as documented by Fukuyama Toshio are: 659, 822, 987, 1036, 1067, 1096, 1115, 1145, 1175, 1190, 1227, 1248, 1278, 1282, 1325, 1386, 1412, 1442, 1467, 1486, 1519, 1550, 1580, 1609, 1667 and the present buildings in 1744. All dates are completion dates. See Fukuyama Toshio and Ōbayashi-gumi (eds) *Kodai Izumo Taisha no fukugen*, Tokyo: Gakuseisha, 1989, pp. 144–145.

35 Wealth measured in terms of estimated rice yield for taxation purposes of 1 *koku* = 180 litres or 5.96 bushels.

36 Ōta Hirotarō and Itō Yōtarō (eds) *Shōmei* (2 vols), Tokyo: Kajima shuppankai, 1971, vol. 2, p. 308.

37 An annotated plan is included in *Shōmei*, the secret family records of the Heinouchi, the master builders in charge of many of the most important projects of the late sixteenth and seventeenth centuries. These records were compiled in 1610. See *Shōmei*, ibid., vol. 1, p.123; vol. 2, p. 309.

38 Ōta Hirotarō, *Kenchikushigaku* (op. cit. note 25), pp. 33–45.

39 Fukuyama Toshio and Ōbayashi-gumi, (op. cit. note 34'), pp. 89–191. Evidence used by Fukuyama includes the *Izumo kuni nikki*, and a painting dated to *ca* 1250 depicting the Izumo shrine (*Izumo Taisha kingō ezu*).

40 See for example Tange and Kawazoe, (op. cit. note 2), p. 195.

41 Ishino Hironobu, (op. cit. note 17), p. 194.

42 *Izumo fudoki* (op.cit. note 1), p. 123.

43 Fukuyama and Ōbayashi-gumi (op. cit. note 34), pp. 72–73.

44 Ibid., p. 234.

45 Ibid., p. 140.

46 Ibid., pp. 176–206.

3 Great Halls of Religion and State: Architecture and the Creation of the Nara Imperial Order

1 Historic Nara is now generally referred to as *Heijō-kyō* and the palace precinct as *Heijō-kyū*. It is considered likely that the characters for these names were read *Nara no miyako* and *Nara no miya* in the eighth century. See Tsuboi Kiyotari and Tanaka Migaku, *The Historic City of Nara. An Archaeological Approach*, (trans. David W. Hughes and Gina L. Barnes), Tokyo: The Centre for East Asian Cultural Studies, 1991, pp. 5–6.

2 The first-known archaeological survey of the palace site was carried out in 1852 by Kitaura Sadamasa, the official of the Tokugawa *bakufu* in charge of the Yamato district. After the Meiji Restoration, in 1897 Sekino Tadashi surveyed the site and established the location of the perimeter of the palace compound. In 1922 the palace site was designated as an 'historic site' by the Ministry of Education and protected from further urban encroachment. Initial excavations took place in 1924 and the archaeological potential of the site was confirmed. Since 1955 systematic archaeological work has been carried out by the government agency now known as the *Nara kokuritsu bunkazai kenkyujo* (Nara National Cultural Properties Research Institute). Approximately 300,000 square metres, amounting to some 30 percent of the palace site, has now been excavated and details of many of the buildings reconstructed. The results of the surveys are published regularly as *Heijō-kyū hakkutsu chōsa hōkoku*. A summary of the findings is available in Tsuboi and Tanaka, ibid.

3 *Shoku Nihongi*, in Kuroita Katsumi (ed.) *Shoku Nihongi, Kokushi taikei*, Tokyo: Yoshikawa kōbunkan, (rev. edn), 1935, vol. 2 (henceforth cited as *Shoku Nihongi*). I have been assisted by the earlier translations and commentaries of G. B. Sansom ('The Imperial Edicts in the Shoku-Nihongi [700–790 AD]. Translated with Introduction and Notes', *Transactions of the Asiatic Society of Japan*, 1924, Second Series, vol. 1, pp. 5–39); B. Snellen ('Shoku Nihongi. Chronicles of Japan, continued, from 697–791 AD', *Transactions of the Asiatic Society of Japan*, 1934, Second Series, vol. XI, pp. 151–239; 1937, vol. XIV, pp. 209–278. Snellen's work covers the first six *kan* of forty) and Richard A. Ponsonby-Fane, (*Imperial Cities: the Capitals of Japan from the Oldest Time Until 1229*, originally written *ca* 1930; reprint edn Washington DC: University Publications of America, 1979). See also Sakamoto Tarō, *The Six National Histories* (trans. John S. Brownlee), Vancouver and Tokyo: University of British Columbia Press and the

University of Tokyo Press, 1991. (Originally published as *Rikkokushi*, Tokyo: Yoshikawa kōbunkan, 1970.) In addition to the official history, further information is now becoming available to historians from *mokkan*, the tens of thousands of wooden tablets with written inscriptions recovered from the palace site.

4 *Shoku Nihongi* (op. cit. note 3), 2nd month, 707, p. 27.

5 Ōta Hirotarō, 'Kodai kenchiku no seisan', suppl. to vol. VI, *Nara rokudaiji taikan,* Tokyo: Iwanami shoten, 1968, pp. 9–12.

6 By the eighth century supplies of *hinoki* were dwindling in the Nara region and fresh forests, close to the rivers which were essential for transportation to Nara, had to be found in the provinces around Lake Biwa to the north.

7 Recent research conducted by Ōbayashi-gumi, using computer-aided graphics and sophisticated labour and cost projections, has determined that the construction of the earlier palace compound at Naniwa would have required 590,000 workers if modern construction techniques had then been available. In 645, when it was actually built, it would probably have required three times that number.

8 Many of the details of the arrangement of buildings with Nara Palace are still unclear. Several buildings were sometimes erected on the same site and the organisation of the principal compounds underwent substantial change over the course of the eighth century.

9 *Dai-ichiji Daigokuden.* The date of construction of this 'first Daigokuden' is not clear. There is some evidence of an earlier structure beneath its foundations, possibly the Daigokuden of the Fujiwara palace which was dismantled and brought to Nara when the capital was moved. The archaeological evidence for determining the location and reconstructing the architectural characteristics of the Daigokuden is published as *Nara kokuritsu bunkazai kenkyūjo sanjūshūnen kinen gappō (gappō yonjū-satsu), Heijō-kyū hakkutsu chōsa hōkoku XI: Dai-ichiji Daigokuden chiiki no chōsa,* Nara: Nara kokuritsu bunkazai kenkyūjo, 1981 (henceforth cited as *Daigokuden Archaeological Report*). See also Okada Shigehiro, *Tojō kokufu, Fukugen Nihon taikan,* Tokyo: Sekai bunkasha, 1988, vol. 3, pp. 40–41.

10 'The Emperor held Court in the Daigokuden; the officials and Koma [Korean] ambassadors did homage . . . . His Majesty went to the Kō-mon and gave a banquet in the Chōdō to those above the fifth rank, the foreign ambassadors and the officials [1st day, 1st month, 763]'; 'The Emperor went to the Jūkaku-mon [?Kō-mon] and was graciously pleased to witness shooting on horseback [5th month, 777]. *Shoku Nihongi,* cited in Ponsonby-Fane, (op. cit. note 3), pp. 66–67, 70.

11 G. B. Sansom, (op. cit. note 3).

12 Miyamoto Nagajirō, *Heijō-kyō. Kodai no toshi keikaku to kenchiku,* Tokyo: Sōshisha, 1986, pp. 56–57.

13 'The Emperor went to the Kō-mon of the Daigokuden and witnessed the dancing and singing of the Hayato [6th month, 729]'. *Shoku Nihongi,* cited in Ponsonby-Fane, (op. cit. note 3), p. 66.

14 Tsuboi and Tanaka, (op. cit. note 1), p. 53.

15 See further Cunrui Xiong, *Sui-Tang Chang'an (582–904)*, unpublished doctoral dissertation, the Australian National University, 1988, p. iv.

16 K. C. Chang, *The Archaeology of Ancient China*, New Haven and London: Yale University Press, 1977, pp. 321–350.

17 James Legge, *The Chinese Classics*, vol. 32, *The Sho King* [Shu Jing] (Book of Documents) (2nd edn), Hong Kong: Hong Kong University Press, 1960; *The Book of Chow*, Book IV, 'The Great Plan', pp. 320–344.

18 The 'Four Deities' (*shi-shin* [*si shen* in Chinese]) were: the Red Bird (*suzaku*, also *shujaku* [*zhu qiao*]), governing the south and propitiated by a body of water; the Black Warrior (*gembu* [*xuan wu*]), associated with the north and geomantically placated by an area of high ground; the White Tiger (*byakko* [*bai hu*]), governing the west and topologically satisfied by a road; and the Green Dragon (*seiryū* [*qing long*]), governing the east and associated with a river.

19 Xiong, (op. cit. note 15), pp. 84–85.

20 *Daigokuden Archaeological Report*, (op. cit. note 9), p. 228.

21 Ibid., Fig. 109.

22 Koizumi Kesakatsu, *Monosashi: Mono to ningen no bunka-shi*, Tokyo: Hōsei daigaku shuppankyoku, 1977, pp. 164–165, 168.

23 *Shoku Nihongi* (op. cit. note 3), [3rd month, 702], p. 14. See also, Nihon gakushiin Nihon kagakushi kankōkai (ed.) *Meiji-zen Nihon kenchiku gijutsushi*, Tokyo: Inoue shoten, 1982, p. 204. (First published in 1961.)

24 *Daigokuden Archaeological Report*, (op. cit. note 9), p. 220. The foundation dimensions of the building (51.48 x 21.20 metres) may be subdivided into 153 x 70 *shaku*, each unit of 29.45 centimetres. Mochizuki Nagayo, *Nihonjin no shakudo*, Tokyo: Rokugei shobō, 1971, p. 166.

25 *Shoku Nihongi*, (op. cit. note 3), [2nd month, 713], p. 51. See also Mochizuki, (op. cit. note 24), p. 166.

26 *Shoku Nihongi*, (op. cit. note 3), [8th day, 11th month, 724], p. 102.

27 There were few direct imperial proclamations given in the Nara period. These were reserved for the notification of imperial accession or events of extraordinary national significance such as the first discovery of gold in Japan in 749. Protocol demanded that more routine matters would receive imperial attention in seclusion and only the written request would be recorded for posterity. See further, G. B. Sansom, (op. cit. note 3), pp. 5–39; J. B. Snellen (op. cit. note 3), pp. 164–167.

28 The temple's record of its formation, *Tōshōdaiji kenritsu-engi*. See Nara-ken kyōiku iinkai jimukyoku, Nara-ken bunkazai hozon jimusho, *Kokuhō Tōshōdaiji kōdō shūri hōkokusho*, Nara: Kyōdō seihan, 1972, p. 2.

29 Nara rokudaiji taikan kankōkai (ed.) *Tōshōdaiji*, vol. 1, *Nara rokudaiji taikan*, Tokyo: Iwanami shoten, 1969, vol. 12, p. 28.

30 For technical analysis of the condition and restoration of the Tōshōdaiji Kōdō see Nara-ken kyōiku iinkai jimukyoku, Nara-ken bunkazai hozon jimusho, (op. cit. 28) The *Tōshōdaiji senzaiden dendō-hen* records that extensive repairs were carried out in 1275 and in the Empō era (1673–1680). See also Ōta Hirotarō (ed.) *Nihon kenchiku kiso shiryō shūsei*, Tokyo: Chūō kōron bijutsu shuppan, 1981, vol. 4, pp. 126–145.

31 Cited in Ponsonby-Fane, (op. cit. note 3), p. 76.

32 Koizumi (op. cit. note 22), pp. 60–78, Mochizuki (op. cit. note 24), pp. 161–254.

33 Nishikawa Kōji, *Nihon toshishi kenkyū*, Tokyo: Nippon hōsō kyōkai, 1972, pp. 33–46.

34 *Shoku Nihongi*, (op. cit. note 3), [26th day, 12th month, 743], p.176.

35 Ibid., [26th day, 12th month, 743], p. 176.

36 Ibid., [2nd day, 5th month, 745], pp. 182–183. The confusion surrounding the location of the capital is described delightfully by Ponsonby-Fane, (op. cit. note 3), pp. 94–105.

37 The politics of the court factions has been analysed by Takashima Masato, *Nara jidai shoshizoku no kenkyū*, Tokyo: Yoshikawa kōbunkan, 1983. See also the useful summary in Ross Bender, 'The Hachiman Cult and the Dōkyō Incident', *Monumenta Nipponica*, 1979, vol. XXXIV, no. 2, p. 133.

38 As with city walls, the Japanese never adopted the practice of erecting masonry bases for their gatehouses, although the stone-faced chambers and outer surfaces of the great burial mounds of the fifth and sixth centuries furnish indisputable evidence of adequate technical skills to do this. The absence of masonry at Nara may simply have been caused by a shortage of suitable stone in the region, although impressive monoliths are used on some of the fifth- and sixth-century burial sites.

39 Tsuboi Kiyotari, *Heijō-kyū no ato*, *Nihon no bijutsu*, 1975, no. 115, pp. 33–35 and Figure 12; Okada Shigehiro, *Tojō to kokufu*, (op. cit. note 9), pp. 42–45.

40 Ōta Hirotarō (op. cit. note 30), vol. 4, p. 43. The *Ryūki shizai-chō* identifies a 'Lady Tachibana' (*Tachibana-fujin*) as donor of the building to Hōryūji. Her identity is not clear but she may have been a consort of Emperor Shōmu.

41 Ōta Hirotarō, ibid., pp. 43–51. Asano Kiyoshi, *Nara jidai no kenchiku*, Tokyo: Chūō kōron bijutsu shuppan, 1969.

42 Takashima Masato, (op. cit. note 37), pp. 51–59.

43 Ōta Hirotarō, *Nihon kenchikushi josetsu*, Tokyo: Shōkōkusha, (2nd rev. edn), 1989, pp. 94–95.

44 On the religious and artistic significance of Tōdaiji see further John M. Rosenfield *et al.*, *The Great Eastern Temple. Treasures of Japanese Buddhist Art from Tōdai-ji*, Bloomington, Ind.: The Art Institute of Chicago in association with Indiana University Press, 1986.

45 The reconstruction was by Professor Amanuma Shun'ichi in the Meiji period.

46 The Buddha, the Buddhist Law and the Buddhist Priesthood.

47 From *Shoku Nihongi*, (op. cit. note 3), trans. in Ryusaku Tsunoda, W. T. de Bary and Donald Keene (comp.), (2 vols), *Sources of Japanese Tradition*, New York and London: Columbia University Press, 1958, vol. 1, pp. 104–105.

48 The Sanskrit may also be translated as 'flower ornament'. See *The Flower Ornament Scripture. A Translation of the Avatamsaka Sutra*,

(trans. from the Chinese by Thomas Cleary), (3 vols), Boulder and London: Shambhala, 1984.

49 Stanley Weinstein, *Buddhism under the T'ang*, London, New York, New Rochelle, Melbourne, Sydney: Cambridge University Press, 1987, p. 45.

50 Ibid., pp. 44–45.

51 Ibid., pp. 38–39.

52 De Bary (op. cit. note 47), p. 105.

53 Bender (op. cit. note 37), p. 132.

54 *Shoku Nihongi*, (op. cit. note 3) [12th month, 757], p. 244.

55 Daigan Matsunaga and Alicia Matsunaga, *Foundations of Japanese Buddhism*, vol. 1, The Aristocratic Age, Los Angeles and Tokyo: Buddhist Books International, 1974, pp. 22–23. The authors note that the legend that Shōmu despatched the monk Gyōgi to Ise to receive the blessing of Amaterasu for the Great Buddha project is without foundation in historical sources.

56 Archaeological evidence of the casting of the Great Buddha has only come to light at Tōdaiji since 1988. See further Chiyonobu Yoshimasa, 'Recent Archaeological Excavations at Tōdai-ji', *The Japanese Journal of Religious Studies*, Summer 1992, vol. 19, 2–3, pp. 245–254.

57 Recorded in *Shoku Nihongi* (op. cit. note 3) and recounted in Sansom, (op. cit. note 3), pp. 128–29.

4. Heian Palaces and Kamakura Temples: The Changing Countenances of Aristocratic and Warrior Power

1 See further Jeffrey P. Mass, 'The Kamakura Bakufu', in John W. Hall *et al.*, (eds) The Cambridge History of Japan, Cambridge and New York: Cambridge University Press, 1988, vol. 3, *Medieval Japan*, edited by Kōzō Yamamura, pp. 46–88.

2 See William H. Coaldrake, *The Way of the Carpenter: Tools and Japanese Architecture*, Tokyo and New York: Weatherhill, 1990, pp. 115–18.

3 See further Toshio Fukuyama, *Heian Temples: Byōdō-in and Chōson-ji* (trans. Ronald K. Jones), New York and Tokyo: Weatherhill/ Heibonsha, 1976. The Heibonsha Survey of Japanese Art. (Originally published by Heibonsha under the title *Byōdō-in to Chūson-ji* in 1964.) Mimi Yiengpruksawan, 'The House of Gold: Fujiwara Kiyohira's Konjikidō', *Monumenta Nipponica*, vol. 48, no. 1, Spring, 1993, pp. 33–52.

4 Although the two characters comprising the term *shinden* may now be translated as 'sleeping hall', in the eighth century, when the term was adopted from China, its meaning would have been closer to original Tang usage of 'house or building of the aristocracy or government'. The addition of *zukuri* to the term occurred in the Edo-period popular compendia, *Kaoku zakkō* and *Teijō zakki*. In these copious but unreliable works the term *zukuri* means simply 'the way of building', a contraction of *tsukuri-kata*. It is only since the Meiji period that

architectural historians have translated the term as 'style' as a result of the influence of Western architectural theory. See further Sekino Masaru, 'Jūtaku kenchiku kara mita Man'yōshū', *Tōyō kenchiku*, vols 1–3, 1937, pp. 100–106. *Kaoku zakkō* was compiled by Sawada Natari and published in 1841. See Imaizumi Sadayoshi (ed.) *Zōtei kojitsu sōsho*, Tokyo: Yoshikawa kōbunkan, 1928, vol. 15, pp. Ê221–322. *Teijō zakki* was compiled by Ise Teijō and published in 1842. See *Zōtei kojitsu sōsho*, ibid., vol. 2. See also Inoue Mitsuo, 'Zukuri ni tsuite', *Kenchikushi kenkyū*, no. 23, 1956, pp. 20–23; Maeda Matsuoto, 'Shinden zukuri no kōkyū', *Kenchiku zasshi*, no. 491, 1927, pp. 2–3.

5 'Sanjō-den youchi no emaki', from the *Heiji monogatari emaki*. Hand scroll 41.3 x 699.7 cm. Fenollosa-Weld Collection, Museum of Fine Arts, Boston.

6 The scrolls are also known as the *Heiji monogatari ekotoba*. See Komatsu Shegemi (ed.) *Heiji monogatari ekotoba*, *Nihon no emaki*, vol. 12, Tokyo: Chūō Kōronsha, 1988.

7 See Mary Neighbour Parent, *The Roof in Japanese Buddhist Architecture*, New York and Tokyo: Weatherhill and Kajima, 1983.

8 *Nihon kiryaku* [23rd day, 4th month, 1030] (Chōgen 3), Jingū shichō, *Koji ruien*, reprint, Tokyo, Jingū shichō, 1935–36, vol. 52, p. 1023. See also Nihon gakushiin Nihon gakujitsu shinkōkai (ed.) *Meiji-zen Nihon kenchiku gijutsushi*, Tokyo: Nihon gakujutsu shinkōkai, 1961, pp. 76–77.

9 *Koji ruien*, ibid., vol. 52, p. 822.

10 Maeda Matsuoto (op. cit. note 4).

11 To date the most comprehensive study which collates archaeological and literary evidence is: Ōta Seiroku, *Shinden-zukuri no kenkyū*, Tokyo: Yoshikawa kōbunkan, 1987. The epoch-making archaeological discovery was the uncovering of a ninth-century *shinden-zukuri* mansion at a site in the grounds of Yamashiro High School in Kyoto in 1979. This mansion was found to have the characteristic central building (the 'shinden') which was 21 metres long. Six other buildings were arranged around it symmetrically and all were interconnected by raised-floor galleries.

12 *Sesshō* or regent to a child emperor and *kampaku* or regent to an adult emperor.

13 Helen Craig McCullough (trans.) *Ōkagami. The Great Mirror. Fujiwara Michinaga and His Times*, Princeton, New Jersey: Princeton University Press, 1980, p. 185. The importance of the Fujiwara has led historians customarily to call this age the 'Fujiwara period' or 'Fujiwara era'. The appropriateness of the family name to designate the middle Heian period has recently been challenged, although the centrality of the family itself has not. See Mimi Hau Yiengpruksawan, 'What's in a name? Fujiwara fixation in Japanese cultural history', *Monumenta Nipponica*, vol. 49, no. 4, Winter, 1994, pp. 423–453.

14 The palace was sometimes referred to using both avenue names. Hence 'Tsuchimikado Higashi no Tōin-dono'. See Heibonsha chihō shiryō sentaa (ed.) *Kyōto-shi no chimei, Nihon rekishi chimei taikan*, vol. 27, Tokyo: Heibonsha, 1979, pp. 556–557.

15 These details have been established by study of contemporary documents including Michinaga's own diary and collation with site evidence and buildings of similar type which have been recently discovered. See further, Ōta, (op. cit. note 11), pp. 159–163.

16 Ōta, (op. cit. note 11), pp. 305–307. Note especially Table 7, p. 306; *Kyōto-shi no chimei* (op. cit. note 14), p. 556.

17 Ōta (op. cit. note 11), pp. 159–160.

18 Ibid., p. 306.

19 For details of the gradual destruction of the Imperial Palace and the shift to the present-day site see Kokushi daijiten henshū iinkai, *Kokushi daijiten*, vol. 4, Tokyo: Yoshikawa kōbunkan, 1984, pp. 235–35.

20 See G. Cameron Hurst III, *Insei. Abdicated Sovereigns in the Politics of Late Heian Japan 1086–1185*, New York and London: Columbia University Press, 1976.

21 On the use of private palaces by Emperor Toba see further: Hirayama Ikuo, 'Toba tennō gosho ni tsuite', *Kenchikushigaku*, no. 18, March, 1992, pp. 17–32.

22 Ōta Seiroku (op. cit. note 11), pp. 312–314, 519–525.

23 Detailed records of these ceremonies survive, including plans of the different chambers in which they were conducted. This affords considerable scope for further study of the relationship between the design of the interior of *shinden-zukuri* mansions and palaces and the activities carried out within them. See Ōta Seiroku, ibid., pp. 314–352.

24 It was near this site that Yorimichi had been responsible for the building of the Byōdō-in, completed in 1053.

25 Hiroshi Kitagawa and Bruce T. Tsuchida (trans.) *The Tale of the Heike*, Tokyo: University of Tokyo Press, 1975, vol. 1, p. 5.

26 See further Mass (op. cit. note 1).

27 Jeffrey P. Mass, *Antiquity and Anachronism in Japanese History*, Stanford: Stanford University Press, 1992, p. 74.

28 Ibid., pp. 75–76.

29 See Nagazumi Yasuaki and Shimada Isao (eds) *Hōgen monogatari, Heiji monogatari, Nihon koten bungaku taikei*, vol. 31, Tokyo: Iwanami Shoten, 1960, pp. 468. Ishii Ryōsuke, *A History of Political Institutions in Japan*, Tokyo: University of Tokyo Press, 1980, pp. 38–39. English translation by the Japan Foundation. First published by the University of Tokyo Press in 1972 under the title *Nihon kokkashi*.

30 Kokushi daijiten henshū iinkai, *Kokushi daijiten*, Yoshikawa kōbunkan, 1984, s.v. 'buke no tōryō'.

31 See further Fumiko Miyazaki, 'Religious Life of the Kamakura Bushi: Kumagai Naozane and His Descendants', *Monumenta Nipponica*, vol. 47, no. 4, Winter, 1992, pp. 453–455.

32 Articles one and two. *Goseibai shikimoku* (also known as the *Jōri shikimoku*). K. Asakawa, 'Some Aspects of Japanese Feudal Institutions', in *Transactions of the Asiatic Society of Japan*, 1st Ser., vol. 46 (1918), pp. 92–93. Cited in David John Lu (ed. and comp.) *Sources of Japanese History*, vol. 1, New York: McGraw-Hill Book Company, 1974, pp. 102–103.

33 Nihon rekishi henshū iinkai (ed.) *Nihon rekishi daijiten*, Tokyo: Kawade shobo shinsha, vol. 3, 1974, s.v. 'Kamakura Daibutsu'.

34 The perception of threat by the Mongols was to continue for several more years. It ultimately contributed to the destabilization of Kamakura rule by exhausting its resources and by its failure to produce booty with which to reward the armies of warriors who had responded to the Kamakura cause to save Japan from invasion.

35 Martin Collcutt, *Five Mountains. The Rinzai Zen Monastic Institution in Medieval Japan*, Cambridge, Mass. and London: Harvard University Press, 1981, p. 26 ff.

36 See detailed discussion of records of destruction and rebuilding of Engakuji in Kanagawa-ken kyōiku iinkai (ed.) *Engakuji Shariden shūri chōsa tokubetsu hōkokusho*, Yokohama: Boku insatsu kōgyō, 1970, pp. 9–27.

37 Ibid., pp. 2–37. Also Ōta Hirotarō, *Nihon kenchiku josetsu*, (rev. edn), Tokyo: Shōkokusha, 1989, pp. 110, 270.

38 The date 1407 (Ōei 14) written on one of the hidden surfaces of a cantilever arm, was discovered during restoration work in 1914. This indicates that considerable repairs to the roof and roof supports were carried out at the beginning of the fifteenth century.

39 *Sentai Jizō bosatsu ryaku engi*.

40 Collcutt (op. cit. note 35), pp. 57–58.

41 The cypress shingles were changed to reed thatch in 1859 as a result of restoration work under Tokugawa patronage. The roofing was changed back to the original wooden shingle type in 1932.

42 Ōta Hirotarō (ed.) *Nagano-ken no kokuhō jūyōbunkazai: kenchikubutsu hen*, Matsumoto: Kyōdo Shuppansha, 1987, pp. 168–69.

5 Castles: The Symbol and Substance of Momoyama and Early Edo Authority

1 Article six of the *Buke shohatto*, Ryusaku Tsunoda, W. T. de Bary and D. Keene (comps) *Sources of Japanese Tradition*, New York and London: Columbia University Press, vol. 1, p. 327.

2 Michael Cooper, (ed.) *They Came to Japan: An Anthology of European Reports on Japan 1543–1640*, Berkeley and Los Angeles: University of California Press, 1965, pp. 131–132.

3 See Fujiki Hisashi with George Elison, 'The Political Posture of Oda Nobunaga', in John Whitney Hall *et al.* (eds), *Japan Before Tokugawa: Political Consolidation and Economic Growth, 1500 to 1650*, Princeton, New Jersey: Princeton University Press, 1981, pp. 149–193.

4 Michael Cooper, 'Cultural Survey, 1994', *Monumenta Nipponica*, vol. 50, no. 1, Spring, 1995, p. 108.

5 Naitō Akira, 'Azuchijō no kenkyū', *Kokka*, no. 987 (March, 1976), Section ll-3.

6 Kodama Kōta, *Shiryō ni yoru Nihon no ayumi*, Tokyo: Yoshikawa kōbunkan, 1955, pp. 68–69.

7 Naitō Akira, 'Azuchijō no kenkyū', *Kokka*, nos 987–988 (February and March, 1976).

8 The stupa hypothesis was supported by the eminent historian Asao Naohiro but skepticism was expressed by Willem Jan Boot. See Willem Jan Boot, 'The Deification of Tokugawa Ieyasu', Research Report, *The Japan Foundation Newsletter*, vol. xiv, no. 5, 1987, p. 10.

9 Miyakami Shigetaka, 'Azuchijō no tenshu no fukugen to sono shiryō ni tsuite. Naitō-shi Azuchijō no kenkyū ni taisuru gimon'. *Kokka*, nos 998–999, March–April, 1977.

10 Miyakami's reconstruction drawings were not available for publication in this study.

11 Rudolph Arnheim, *The Dynamics of Architectural Form*, Berkeley, Los Angeles and London: University of California Press, 1977, p. 208.

12 Basil Hall Chamberlain, *Things Japanese, Being Notes on Various Subjects Connected with Japan for the use of Travellers and Others* (5th edn, rev.), London: John Murray, 1905, p. 319.

13 See Motoo Hinago, *Japanese Castles* (trans. and adapted William H. Coaldrake), Tokyo, New York and San Francisco: Kodansha International, 1986. Appendix by translator, pp. 187–88.

14 Kodama, *Shiryō*, (op. cit. note 6), pp. 68–69. A slightly different translation is rendered in: George Elison and Bardwell L. Smith, (eds) *Warlords, Artists and Commoners: Japan in the Sixteenth Century*, Honolulu: The University Press of Hawaii, 1981, pp. 64–65.

15 See further, Carolyn Wheelwright, 'A Visualisation of Eitoku's Lost Paintings at Azuchi Castle', in George Elison and Bardwell L. Smith, (eds) *Warlords, Artists and Commoners: Japan in the Sixteenth Century*, ibid., pp. 87–111.

16 Kodama, *Shiryō* (op. cit. note 6), p. 68.

17 Naitō, *Kokka*, no. 987 (op. cit. note 5), p. 21.

18 Ibid., p. 17.

19 Kimura Yukihiro, 'Anōshū-zumi ishi-gaki to Kurita Monkisabu', in Kawasaki Tōrū (ed.) *Hieizan monzenmachi Sakamoto*, Ōtsu: Ōmi bunkasha, 1980, pp. 92–95. This includes a transcript of an interview held with the last surviving hereditary stone-mason of Anō.

20 The surviving history and genealogy of the Okabe family were compiled in 1827 (*Okabe Mataemon keifuryaku* cited in Mizuno Yasutsugu, 'Okabe Mataemon', in *Rekishi to tabi*, no. 1, 1977, pp. 166–168). Although this work was written some 300 years after the life of Okabe, it may be reasonably presumed to have a degree of veracity as it would have been based upon carefully transmitted oral history, perhaps supported by written records and drawings which themselves no longer survive. According to this source, the Okabe served as the head master builders to the Ashikaga *bakufu* from the time of the eighth shogun Yoshimasa (1436–1490). Okabe Mataemon had the title of *banshō-gashira*, or Head Master Carpenter, to the Ashikaga court and was engaged in building work at the Imperial Palace in Kyoto, on the residences of the Ashikaga shogun, as well as on castle fortifications and temple and shrine construction in several

regions. Other records (Mizuno, ibid., p.166.) establish that, after the outbreak of civil war in Kyoto in 1467, the Okabe family shifted its building activities to temple and shrine projects in the Mikawa and Owari regions of central Japan (present-day Aichi prefecture), presumably as a result of the disorder in the capital which caused a temporary cessation of all building activities.

21 Kodama, *Shiryō* (op. cit. note 6).

22 Ibid., p. 69.

23 See further, Satō Jirō, *Kawara to yane kōzō*, Tokyo: Gakugei, 1978, pp. 150–153.

24 These dates are based on family records of the Ikeda, such as the *Ikeda-ke nenpu*, together with dated inscriptions which were discovered on timbers during the exhaustive restoration of the castle. This latter work began before World War II and was eventually completed in 1965. See Bunkazai hogo iinkai (ed.) *Kokuhō jūyō bunkazai Himejijō hozon shūri kōji hōkokusho III: tenshu oyobi sono shūhen no shoyagura mon nado shūri kōji hōkoku*, (henceforth *Himejijō Restoration Report*), Kyoto: Shin'yōsha, 1965, pp. 2–5.

25 See *Himeji-kō*, cited in *Himejijō Restoration Report*, pp. 4–5.

26 See further Hinago Motoo (op. cit. note 13), pp. 107–110.

27 Ibid., p.107.

28 See further, Naitō Akira, *Edo no tōshi no kenchiku*. Complementary volume to Naitō Akira and Suwa Haruo (eds) *Edozu byōbu*, Tokyo: Mainichi Shinbunsha, 1972, pp. 17–19.

29 Murai Masuo, *Edojō: Shōgun-ke no seikatsu*, Tokyo: Chūō kōronsha, 1964, p. 46–58.

30 Naitō Akira, *Edo no toshi no kenchiku* (op.cit. note 28), pp. 139–150.

31 Now held in the Tokyo Metropolitan Library, Hibiya, Tokyo.

32 The plan is preserved in the collection of the Tokyo Metropolitan Library. See also Naitō (op.cit. note 28), p. 28.

33 Kuroita Katsumi (ed.) *Kokushi taikei*, Tokyo: Yoshikawa kōbunkan (rev. edn), 1929–1935, vol. 39. *Tokugawa jikki I*, p. 241.

34 Fujino Tamotsu, *Bakuhan taiseishi no kenkyū*, Tokyo: Yoshikawa kōbunkan (rev. edn), 1975, p. 227.

35 Naitō, *Edo no toshi no kenchiku* (op.cit. note 28), pp. 28–31.

36 Ibid., pp. 33–34.

37 *Chitose no matsu*, the biography of Hoshina Masayuki, cited by Naitō, ibid., p. 34. Various editions survive, the oldest dating to 1691.

38 See further Fujino (op. cit. note 28), p.409; Kitajima Masamoto, *Edo bakufu no kenryoku kōzō*, Tokyo: Iwanami shoten, 1964, pp. 468–471 and 649–650; Harold Bolitho, *Treasures Among Men: The Fudai Daimyo in Tokugawa Japan*, New Haven and London: Yale University Press, 1972, pp. 164–169.

39 John James, *Chartres. The Masons who Built a Legend*, London: Boston, Melbourne and Henley: Routledge and Kegan Paul, 1982, p. 1.

6. Nijō Castle and the Psychology of Architectural Intimidation

1 A palace was not built in the Inner Compound of Nijō Castle until 1633–1634. It was a private retreat in the *sukiya* or tea-house influenced style but was destroyed by fire *ca* 1780. The present buildings on this site were moved to Nijō Castle from the Kyoto Gosho in the 1860s.

2 B.W.P. Wells, 'The Psycho-Social Influence of Building Environment: Socio-Metric Findings in Large and Small Office Spaces', in *Building Science*, vol. 1, 1965, pp. 153–165. Reprinted in Robert Gutman (ed.) *People and Buildings*, New York and London: Basic Books, 1972, pp. 97–119.

3 Without discarding the *Five Classics* hitherto given central importance in Confucian thinking, Zhu gave new prominence to the *Analects* (*Lun yu*), the *Mencius* (*Meng Zu*), the *Greater Learning* (*Da Xue*) and the *Doctrine of the Mean* (*Zhong Yong*), which had been part of the *Book of Rites* (*Li Ji*). These he republished with his own exegesis as *The Four Masters* (*Si Zi*), and became the foundations for government orthodoxy as the classical curriculum for the civil service examinations. See Daniel K. Gardner, *Chu Hsi: Neo-Confucianism Reflection on the Confucian Canon*, Council on East Asian Studies, Harvard University, Cambridge, Mass. and London: Harvard University Press, 1986, pp. 3–16.

4 W. T. de Bary (ed.) *Sources of Chinese Tradition*, New York and London: Columbia University Press (2 vols), 1964, vol. 1, pp. 481–483.

5 See Beatrice Bodart-Bailey, 'The Persecution of Confucianism in Early Tokugawa Japan', *Monumenta Nipponica*, vol. 48, no. 3, Autumn, 1993, pp. 293–314.

6 The framework for interpretation of Tokugawa government was created by Kanai Madoka, Kitajima Masamoto and Fujino Tamotsu. They defined the system as a balance of power between *bakufu* and daimyo, characterised by the term *bakuhan* system. See Kitajima Masamoto, *Edo bakufu no kenryoku no kōzō*, Tokyo: Iwanami shoten, 1964; Fujino Tamotsu, *Bakuhan taiseishi no kenkyū*, Tokyo: Yoshikawa kōbunkan (rev. edn), 1975. The relationship between shogun and emperor has been characterised more recently by Kate Nakai in terms of bifurcation, while Asao Naohiro and Marius Jansen prefer the term 'dualism'. See Kate Wildman Nakai, *Shogunal Politics: Arai Hakuseki and the Premises of Tokugawa Rule*, Harvard East Asian Monographs 134, Cambridge, Mass. and London: Harvard University Press, 1988; Asao Naohiro with Marius B. Jansen, 'Shogun and Tennō', in John Whitney Hall *et al.*, (eds) *Japan Before Tokugawa: Political Consolidation and Economic Growth*, 1500–1650, Princeton: Princeton University Press, 1981, pp. 248–270. On fudai daimyo see Harold Bolitho, *Treasures among Men: The Fudai Daimyo in Tokugawa Japan*, New Haven and London: Yale University Press, 1974. Herman Ooms has shown how the Tokugawa

appropriated Shinto mythology and the universal notions of divine kingship. See Herman Ooms, *Tokugawa Ideology. Early Constructs, 1570–1680*, Princeton: Princeton University Press, 1985.

7 Kuroita Katsumi (ed.) *Kokushi taikei*, Tokyo: Yoshikawa kōbunkan (rev. edn), 1929–1935, vol. 39. *Tokugawa jikki*, vol. 1, p. 237 (1602, 5th month, 1st day).

8 Ibid., p. 73.

9 Ibid.

10 The most impressive of these was the Daibutsuden of Hōkōji built in emulation of the Nara Great Buddha Hall.

11 The Tokugawa-sponsored rebuilding of the Gosho, spanning most of the first half of the seventeenth century, is fully documented in the records of the Nakai, the shogunal master builders in charge of Kansai-area projects. See Hirai Kiyoshi (ed.) *Daiku-gashira Nakaike monjo no kenkyū* (10 vols), Tokyo: Chūō kōron bijutsu shuppan, 1976. See also Fujioka Michio, *Gosho*, Tokyo: Shōkokusha, 1956.

12 The most spectacular use of *gokyō* by Hideyoshi was at his newly completed palace-castle of Jurakudai in Kyoto in 1587 on which occasion the famous portable gilded teahouse was built.

13 Ōta Hirotarō *et al.*, *Nihon kenchikushi kiso shiryō shūsei*, Tokyo: Chūō kōron bijutsu shuppan, 1974, vol. 17, pp. 17–18.

14 The *Kan'ei gokyōki* records the details of the visit. See also Hirai Kiyoshi, *Nihon jūtaku no rekishi*, Tokyo: NHK Books, 1974, pp. 105–106; In English see Kiyoshi Hirai, *Feudal Architecture of Japan* (trans. Hiroaki Sato and Jeannine Ciliotta), New York and Tokyo: Weatherhill/Heibonsha, 1973, pp. 124–134. For further details of the Gokyō Goten see Soga Tetsuo (ed.) *Nijōjō*, Tokyo: Shōgakukan, 1974, pp. 252–256, 406–408, 413–415.

15 According to carpenters' inscriptions on the roof truss the original gateway, dating to 1625, was extensively rebuilt in 1687. However, the delicate carvings seem from their consummate execution to belong more to the first half of the seventeenth century. See Kyōto-shi moto-rikyū Nijōjō jimusho (ed.) *Jūyō bunkazai Nijōjō shūri kōji hōkokusho*, vol. 5, Kyoto: Nakanishi insatsu, 1976, pp. 14–19.

16 Ōta Hirotarō and Itō Yotarō (eds) *Shōmei* (2 vols), Tokyo: Kajima shuppankai, 1971, vol. 1, p. 304.

17 See Kōra Munetoshi, *Ōhiroma hinagata narabi oboegaki* [henceforth the *Kōra Memorandum*]. His descriptions of Edo daimyo architecture were compiled between 1703 and 1707 and are published in *Nihon kenchikushi kiso shiryō shūsei*, (op. cit. note 13), vol. 17, pp. 7–8, n. 4.

18 Kaempfer, Book 5, Chapter XII, (BL SL 3060, Folio 354 v-355) (trans. Beatrice Bodart-Bailey).

19 Christopher Alexander *et al.*, *A Pattern Language. Towns, Buildings, Construction*, New York: Oxford University Press, 1977, pp. 645–646.

20 Latest research on the Ōhiroma and Kuroshoin of Nijōjō Ninomaru Goten is contained in: *Nihon kenchikushi kiso shiryō shūsei* (op. cit.

note 13), vol. 17, pp. 17:3–9, 17–32. See also Soga Tetsuo, (op.cit. note 14), which publishes photographs of early plans and diagrams.

21 *Yaezakura* (*Prunus donarium*).

22 *Tokugawa jikki*, (op. cit. note 7) vol. 5, pp. 282–283.

23 Michael Cooper (ed.) *They Came to Japan. An Anthology of European Reports on Japan, 1543–1640*, Berkeley and Los Angeles: University of California, 1965, pp. 116–117.

24 Ōta, Hirotarō (ed.) *Traditional Japanese Architecture and Gardens*, Yokohama: Kokusai Bunka Shinkōkai, 1972 (trans. Kirishiki Shinjirō), p. 224.

25 For example, *onari* visits on the Owari (2nd month, 1623), Date (12th month, 1623 and 2nd month, 1624), Kii (1st month, 1624) and Mito (2nd month, 1624). *Tokugawa jikki* (op. cit. note 7), vol. 1, pp. 247–248; Satō Osamu, *Kinsei bushi jūtaku*, Tokyo: Sōbunsha, 1979, pp. 47–50.

26 Takayanagi Mitsukoshi *et al.*, *Nambokuchō, Muromachi, Momoyama, Edo jidai*. Kokuhō, vol. 6, Tokyo: Mainichi shinbunsha, 1968, p. 111.

27 See Konpira Kunio, *The Noh Theater: Perspectives and Principles*, Tokyo and New York: Weatherhill, 1983, pp. 115–116.

28 *Shōmei* (op. cit. note 16), vol. 1, pp. 298–299.

29 For example, the official description of the final audience of daimyo with the last Tokugawa shogun (21st day, 10th month, 1867), *Tokugawa jikki* (op. cit. note 7), vol. 5, p. 282.

30 *Kōra Memorandum* cited in *Nihon kenchikushi kiso shiryō shūsei* (op. cit. note 17) vol. 17, pp. 7–8, n. 4.

31 Ibid.

32 Ibid.

33 Ibid.

34 See further, Tōkyō kokuritsu hakubutsukan (ed.), *Tokubetsu tenkan. Edojō shōhekiga no shitae*, Tokyo: Tōkyō kokuritsu hakubutsukan, 1988, pp. 23–25.

7 Tokugawa Mausolea: Intimations of Immortality and the Architecture of Posthumous Authority

1 As recorded in Sūden's diary *Honkō kokushi nikki*. Quoted in Ōkawa Naomi, *Tōshōgū*, Tokyo: Kajima kenkyū shuppankai, 1970, p. 96, n. 1.

2 *Gongen-zukuri* was a term taken from Ieyasu's posthumous title of Tōshō-daigongen, but the first recorded use of *gongen* to indicate the style of mausoleum architecture, rather than the spirit of Ieyasu, occurs in the *Sharui tatechi-wari*, a 1739 compendium on the siting of Shinto shrines. In this document the term *gongen gosha*, or 'the shōgun's gongen shrine' is used. See Adachi Kō, 'Gongen-zukuri to ishima-zukuri,' *Kenchikushi*, no. 3, 1941, pp. 393–397.

3 Kondō Yutaka, *Kokenchiku saibu goi*, Tokyo: Taiga shuppan (rev. edn), 1972, pp. 156–157; Ōta Hirotarō, *Nihon kenchikushi josetsu*, Tokyo: Shōkokusha (rev. edn), 1969, pp. 75–76.

4 Tōkyō-fu (ed.) *Tōkyō-fu shiseki hozonbutsu chōsa hōkokusho*, vol. 11, 'Shiba-Ueno reibyō', Tokyo: Chūgai insatsu, 1934. (Henceforth the *Tanabe Report*.)

5 Tanabe later incorporated the material in this report with additional photographs of the extant buildings together with discussion of other Tokugawa mausolea at Shiba and Ueno under the title *Tokugawake reibyō* (Tokyo: Shōkokusha, 1942). Information in Tanabe's original report was collated with other Government records by Itō Nobuo in a Bunka-chō publication on registered cultural properties destroyed during the war. See Bunka hogo iinkai (ed.), *Sensai ni yoru shōshitsu bunkazai kenzōbutsu (reibyō: Tōshōgū)*, Kyoto: Benridō, 1965.

6 The model was dismantled and placed into storage in 1936. It was placed in the care of English Heritage in 1984 and is now in the process of being reassembled and its condition stabilised by conservation architects. It is planned to place it on permanent display in the Horniman Museum, London.

7 Cited in full in *Tanabe Report*, pp. 22–25.

8 Hayashi Jusai (comp.) *Kansei chōshū shokafu*, Tokyo: Eishinsha, 1917–1918, vol. 5, p. 249.

9 Naitō Akira, *Edo no toshi no kenchiku*, complementary vol. to Naitō Akira and Suwa Haruo (eds) *Edozu byōbu*, Tokyo: Mainichi shinbunsha, 1972, p. 98.

10 Details recorded in the *Kōra oboegaki*, edited in the early eighteenth century on the basis of earlier written records. Cited in full in Ōta Hirotarō *et al.*, (eds) *Nihon kenchikushi kiso shiryō shūsei*, Tokyo: Chūō kōron bijutsu shuppan, vol. 17, 1974, pp. 7–8, n. 4.

11 It is difficult to distinguish between the Heinouchi and Tsuru contributions without broader understanding of the Tsuru tradition. One avenue of exploration would be a detailed analysis of the Sendai projects of Date Masamune with which they were associated before coming to Edo. However, their position on the list of *Shimo tōryō*, lower than the Kōra and Heinouchi, suggests a subsidiary rather than principal role in the Taitokuin project.

12 Ōta Hirotarō and Itō Yōtarō (eds) *Shōmei* (2 vols), Tokyo, Kajima shuppankai, 1971, vol. I, pp. 54–56; vol. II, pp. 98–99. Both the Shiba and *Shōmei* gateways are *yatsuashimon* executed in the Wayō mode with *mitsumune-zukuri* ceilings. There is also a suggestive correlation between specific details of the two *mon*, such as the three level bracket sets and the distribution of rafters over the central bay. Rafter arrangement is a key indication of proportions used in building design. It amounts to the artistic signature of a workshop when it acts as a module for determining the dimensions of the rest of the building. The *Shōmei* specifies, and the Shiba Sōmon uses, 18 rafters set above the entrance bay. Such precise correlation is more than coincidence. It should be noted, however, that the *suehafu*, the pointed gables with cusped flair set into the roof planes of the Sōmon, are not part of the Heinouchi design in *Shōmei* and must be attributed to another source, possibly the Kihara family, who were supervisors of

the overall project and designed similar gables for the Haiden of the
Sanshū Iga Hachimansha (1636) and the Haiden of the Sanshū Iga
Gosho Jinja (1641).

13 *Kōrake shiryō*, quoted in 1965 Bunka-chō Report, (op. cit. note 5), p.14.

14 *Kase* may also be read *segare*, meaning son.

15 *Hōtō no koto*, *Shōmei* (op. cit. note 12), vol. I, p. 162–164; *Tōki-shū*,
vol. II, Figs. 15–23. The description of the reliquary pagoda concludes
by noting that the example given was built by Heinouchi Yoshimasa
for the interior of the Daibutsuden of the Hōkōji constructed for the
Toyotomi in Kyoto at the beginning of the Keichō era.

16 *Shōmei* also includes detailed descriptions of the system of proportions
used in designing this type of nine-ring arrangement on top of the
roof. *Shōmei*, ibid., vol. I, pp. 165–172.

17 Kodama, Kōta (ed.), *Shiryō ni yoru Nihon no ayumi. Kinsei-hen*, Tokyo:
Yoshikawa kōbunkan, 1955, pp. 81–83 and 127–130; Zaisei keizai
gakkai, (eds) *Nihon zaisei keizai shiryō* (10 vols), Tokyo: Zaisei keizai
gakkai, 1922–1933, vol. 3, pp. 821–822; Shihōshō (ed.) *Tokugawa
kinreikō* (11 vols), Tokyo: Sōbunsha, 1959–61, especially edict no.
157, and Fujino Tamotsu, *Bakuhan taiseishi no kenkyū*, Tokyo:
Yoshikawa kōbunkan, 1961, pp. 241–64.

18 Hideyoshi's mausoleum served as a rallying point for the Toyotomi
cause in the period before their defeat at the sieges of Osaka Castle in
1614 and 1615, and, like the castle, was demolished immediately after
the Tokugawa victory.

19 *Kansei chōshū shokafu* (op. cit. note 8), vol. 9, p. 106; vol. 16,
pp. 218–219; vol. 2, p. 60.

20 Quoted in full in Tanabe Yasushi, 'Edo bakufu sakuji-kata shokusei ni
tsuite', *Kenchiku zasshi*, no. 598, 1935, p. 28; summarised in Kuroita
Katsumi (ed.), *Kokushi taikei*, Tokyo: Yoshikawa kōbunkan, (rev. edn),
1929–1935, vol. 40, *Tokugawa jikki*, vol. 2, p. 568.

21 On the specialist nature of building trades and professions of the early
Edo period see William H. Coaldrake, *The Way of the Carpenter: Tools
and Japanese Architecture*, Tokyo and New York: Weatherhill, 1990,
pp. 13–18, 137–48.

22 Sakuma was rewarded with 20 pieces of gold in 1640 for the speed
with which Honmaru palaces and *tenshu* were rebuilt. See *Kansei
chōshū shokafu* (op. cit. note 8), 9, p. 106.

23 *Nikkōsan kyūki*, quoted in Tōshōgū shamusho (ed.) *Tōshōgūshi*,
Hamamatsu, kaimyōdō, 1927, pp. 59–62.

24 Nikkō shaji bunkazai hozonkai (ed.) *Kokuhō Tōshōgū Yōmeimon*, *dōsayū
sode-kabe shūri kōji hōkokusho*, Kyoto: Benridō, 1974. (Henceforth
Yōmeimon Restoration Report), pp. 9–10.

25 *Yōmeimon Restoration Report*, ibid., p. 9. The original document, held
in the archives of the Akimoto family, was destroyed in World War II,
but a photographic copy is preserved in the archives of the Tōshōgū.

26 *Gozōeichō*, quoted in *Tōshōgūshi* (op.cit. note 23), pp. 112–135.

27 Fujino Tamotsu, *Edo bakufu*, Iwanami kōza Nihon rekishi, vol. 10,
Tokyo: Iwanami, 1963, p. 33 ff.; Kitajima Masamoto, 'Tokugawa

bakufu chokuryō no seijiteki seiritsu', *Rekishigaku kenkyū*, vol. 4, no. 5, 1935, pp. 27–49.

28 Quoted in *Tōshōgūshi*, (op. cit. note 23), p. 136

29 See details in *Tōshōgūshi*, (op. cit. note 23), p. 44, 136.

30 *Yōmeimon Restoration Report*, (op. cit. note 24), pp. 8, 207. The *Gozōeichō* lists costs of silver 118 *kan* 990 *momme* 'for cross land transportation from Edo to Nikkō of timbers, lacquered objects and sculpture, and for landscaping (the Yōmeimon site)'.

31 The Haiden bays are either 7.02 *shaku* or 7.06 *shaku* and the kōhai bays are 13.00 *shaku*. The centre bays of the Honden are 19.00 *shaku*, reflecting the width of the Ishinoma, and the flanking bays are either 7.59 *shaku* or 8.71 *shaku*.

32 Asao Naohiro, *Sakoku*, Nihon no rekishi, vol. 17, Tokyo: Shōgakukan, 1975, pp. 271–278. For a broader discussion of Tokugawa policies towards the imperial institution see Asao Naohiro and Marius Jansen, 'Shogun and Tennō', in John Whitney Hall *et al.*, (eds) *Japan Before Tokugawa: Political Consolidation and Economic Growth, 1500 to 1650*, Princeton: Princeton University Press, pp. 248–270. See also Hermann Ooms, *Tokugawa Ideology, Early Constructs 1570–1680*, Princeton: Princeton University Press, 1985.

33 *Tokugawa jikki* (op. cit. note 20).

34 24th day, first month, 1633. *Tokugawa jikki*, ibid., vol. 2, p. 583.

8 Shogunal and Daimyo Gateways: The Intersecting Spheres of Arbitrary Will and Technical Necessity

1 Junzō Yoshimura, 'Twilight over Architecture', *Koreana*, vol. 3, no. 3, 1989, p. 33.

2 See further, William H. Coaldrake, *The Way of the Carpenter: Tools and Japanese Architecture*, New York and Tokyo: Weatherhill, 1990. See also Spiro Kostof (ed.) *The Architect: Chapters in the History of a Profession*, Oxford: Oxford University Press, 1977.

3 Kate Wildman Nakai, *Shogunal Politics: Arai Hakuseki and the Premises of Tokugawa Rule*, Council on East Asian Studies, Harvard University, Cambridge Mass. and London: Harvard University Press, 1988, pp. 191–192, 226–267.

4 Ibid., p. 192.

5 *Shōmei*, the secret written records of the Heinouchi, compiled in the first decade of the seventeenth century, states that a *heijūmon* was to stand 'in front of the *shuden* (main audience hall)'. Ōta Hirotarō and Itō Yotarō (eds) *Shōmei* (2 vols), Tokyo: Kajima shuppankai, 1971, vol. 1, p. 35.

6 Recorded in the *Tōryō-domo kōjōgaki fushin jō*. I am grateful to Professor Nakai for furnishing me with a copy of the original document. See further details in Nakai (op. cit. note 3), pp. 226–227.

7 *Shōmei* (op. cit. note 5).

8 Nakai (op. cit. note 3), p. 220.

9 See further William H. Coaldrake, 'Edo Architecture and Tokugawa Law', *Monumenta Nipponica*, vol. 36, no. 3, Autumn, 1981, p. 262.

10 Ōta Hirotarō, *et al.*, *Nihon kenchikushi kiso shiryō shūsei*, Tokyo: Chūō kōron bijutsu shuppan, 1974, vol. 17, pp. 7–8, n. 4.

11 Ihara Saikaku, *The Japanese Family Storehouse* (trans. G.W. Sargent), Cambridge: Cambridge University Press, 1959, p. 67.

12 None of the Edo gateways of this type survives but in Kyoto the extant Karamon of the Nishi Honganji was prepared for an official visit by Iemitsu in 1632 and provides tangible illustration of the magnificence of these *onarimon*, its sweeping *karahafu* enlivened by richly polychromed sculpture of heroic mythological beasts and Chinese sages.

13 Thomas McClatchie, 'The Feudal Mansions of Yedo', *Transactions of the Asiatic Society of Japan*, 7, 1879 (1964 reprint), p. 164.

14 The term *nagayamon* is best translated as 'gatehouse' rather than simply as 'gateway' because it provided both entry to the mansion complex and residential barracks for lower ranking retainers of the daimyo.

15 See further Hinago Motoo, *Japanese Castles* (trans. and adapted William H. Coaldrake), Tokyo, New York and San Francisco: Kodansha International, 1986.

16 Bunkazai kenzōbutsu hozon gijutsu kyōkai (ed.) *Jūyō bunkazai buke yashiki mon shūriki*, Chiba: Yamawaki Gakuen, 1976, Figure 4.

17 Ibid., pp. 6–8.

18 McClatchie (op. cit. note 13), p. 167.

19 See further Donald H. Shively, 'Sumptuary Regulations and Status in Early Tokugawa Japan', *Harvard Journal of Asiatic Studies*, vol. 25, 1964–1965, pp. 123–165.

20 The *Yōgō benshi* is the other major source for gateway styles in the late Edo period. Several versions written by different hands dating to and beyond the end of the Bunsei era in 1818 exist in the archives of the Department of Architecture, the University of Tokyo. *Yōgō benshi* includes detailed descriptions of the mon built by many daimyo in the late Edo period but furnishes no specific information about the Rōjūmon.

21 This study is based on the first edition held in the Archives of the Department of Architecture, the University of Tokyo. I am grateful to Inagaki Eizō, Professor Emeritus of the University of Tokyo, for locating this document for me. Another version of the document is published in Zōtei kojitsu sōsho henshū iinkai (ed.) *Edo sōsho*, Zotei kojitsu sōsho, Tokyo: Yoshikawa kōbunkan, 1928, vol. II, pp. 22–24. The gateway section of the published version is translated in full in Coaldrake, 'Edo Architecture' (op. cit. note 9), pp. 275–276.

22 25th day, 1st month, 1657. Zaisei keizai gakkai (ed.) *Nihon zaisei keizai shiryō* (10 vols), Tokyo: Zaisei gakkai, 1922–1923, vol. 3, pp. 829–830.

23 Officials charged with supervision of daimyo affairs.

24 Ishii Ryōsuke (ed.) *Bunka bukan* (12 vols), Tokyo, 1982, vol. 3, p. 183. This register of daimyo families issued during the Bunka era

(1804–1818) gives names, titles, coats of arms, status, and other details for purposes of official protocol.

25 Examples include the Nandaimon and Tegaimon of Tōdaiji in Nara, the Tayasumon and Sakuradamon of Edo Castle, the Karamon of Nishi Honganji, and gateways to the residences of lower ranking samurai in the castle towns of Hagi in Yamaguchi prefecture and Matsushiro in Nagano prefecture.

26 27th day, 3rd month, 1772. *Nihon zaisei keizai shiryō* (op. cit. note 22), vol. 4, p. 748.

27 *Bunka bukan* (op. cit. note 24), vol. 3, p. 137.

9 Building the Meiji State: The Western Architectural Hierarchy

1 David John Lu (ed.) *Sources of Japanese History*, New York: McGraw-Hill, 1974, vol. 2, p. 36.

2 The most influential projects were George Gilbert Scott's St Pancras Station and Hotel (London, 1865–1875) and William Burges's competition design for the Royal Courts of Justice (London, 1866).

3 The 'Second Empire Style' is typified by L-T-J Visconti and Hector-Martin Lefuel's massive additions to the Louvre, the Pavillons Turgot, Richelieu and Colvert (1850–1857) and Charles Garnier's Opéra (1861–1874).

4 Yoshikawa Seiichi and Mizuno Shintarō (eds) *Tōkyō eki to Tatsuno Kingo: ekisha no naritachi to Tōkyō eki no dekiru made*, Tokyo: Higashi Nihon ryōkaku tetsudō, 1990, p. 131.

5 'Public subscription' in reality meant a coalition of business and political interests dedicated to forging closer associations with the imperial institution. There was a similar trend in Osaka, as well as Tokyo, with the mayor and the head of the house of Sumitomo forming a committee in 1900 to build a park on Nakanoshima to commemorate the Crown Prince's wedding. See Hara Kei, *Hara Kei nikki*, Tokyo: Fukumura shuppan, 1965, vol. 1, p. 293.

6 Kokushi daijiten henshū iinkai (ed.) *Kokushi daijiten*, Tokyo: Yoshikawa kōbunkan, 1985, s.v. 'oyatoi'.

7 Muramatsu Teijirō (ed.) *Nihon no kenchiku-Meiji, Taishō, Shōwa*, 10 vols, Tokyo, Toppan insatsu, 1983, vol. 2, pp. 101–102.

8 William A. Coles (ed.) *Architecture and Society: Selected Essays of Henry Van Brunt*, Cambridge, Mass.: Belknap Press of Harvard University Press, 1969, p. 177.

9 Yoshikawa and Mizuno (op. cit. note 4), p. 129.

10 Onogi Shigekatsu, *Meiji yōfū kyūtei kenchiku*, Tokyo: Sagami shobō, 1983, pp. 162–170.

11 See Francis Haskell, *Patrons and Painters. A Study in the Relations Between Italian Art and Society in the Age of the Baroque*, London: Chatto and Windus, 1962.

12 See Roger F. Hackett, *Yamagata Aritomo in the Rise of Modern Japan (1838–1922)*, Harvard East Asian Series 60, Cambridge, Mass.: Harvard University Press, 1971.

13 Yoshikawa and Mizuno (op. cit. note 4), pp. 130–131.

14 His appointment was reported in the *Kokumin shinbun* of 19 August 1898. Nakayama Yasuaki (ed.) *Shinbun shūsei Meiji hennenshi*, Tokyo: Zaisei keizai gakkai, 1936, vol. 11, p. 42. *Shinbun shūsei Meiji hennenshi*, vol. 10, p. 275.

15 Muramatsu (op.cit. note 7), p. 164. See also David B. Stewart, *The Making of a Modern Japanese Architecture, 1860 to the Present*, Tokyo and New York: Kodansha International, 1987, pp. 59–62.

16 Muramatsu (op. cit. note 7), pp. 161–62.

17 Interview with Katayama Tōkuma, *Nihon shinbun*, 17 May, 1907. *Shinbun shūsei Meiji hennenshi* (op. cit. note 14), vol. 13, p. 257.

18 Henry Russell Hitchcock, *Architecture: the Nineteenth and Twentieth Centuries*, (4th edn), Harmondsworth, Mdd: Penguin Books, 1977, p. 169.

19 Tatsuno told Katayama that 'in England you would be knighted for this meritorious deed. This one building is sufficient to earn you immortality'. Cited in Onogi Shigekatsu (op. cit. note 10), p. 166.

20 Kunai-chō (ed.) *Meiji Tennōki*, Tokyo: Yoshikawa kōbunkan, 1974, vol. 10, p. 346.

21 Tokyo Station was seriously neglected as an historical building until the 1980s when it was threatened by redevelopment plans for the centre of Tokyo. David Stewart, for example, dismisses it by saying that 'nothing need be said except that its facade *must* be preserved as both a record of Tatsuno's period style and an element of townscape'. Stewart (op. cit. note 15), p. 54. Dallas Finn's *Meiji Revisited. The Sites of Victorian Japan*, Tokyo and New York: Weatherhill, 1995, published as this study went to press, includes a useful section on the station building as well as featuring it on the front cover.

22 Japanese Government Railway, Japan Travel Bureau, *Pocket Guide to Japan*, 1925, Tokyo: Japan Hotel Association, 1925, pp. 118–119.

23 There is no mention of a relationship with Amsterdam Station in any newspaper accounts or guide books before 1945. For a detailed comparison of the Amsterdam and Tokyo Stations, and definitive rebuttal of anything other than the general similarity of most railway station buildings of this turn of the twentieth century genre, see Aart Oxenaar, 'Amsterdam Central and Tokyo Central–different members of the same family', in Yoshikawa Seiichi and Mizuno Shintarō (eds) *Tōkyō eki to Tatsuno Kingo. Ekisha no naritachi to Tōkyō eki no dekiru made*, Tokyo: East Japan Railway Company, 1990, pp. 22–29.

24 Fujimori Terunobu, *Meiji no Tōkyō keikaku*, Tokyo: Iwanami shoten, 1982, pp. 209–214.

25 The district was named 'Marunouchi' in 1929.

26 *Jiji shinpo*, 18 December 1914. Taishō nyūsu jiten hensan iinkai (ed.) *Taishō nyūsu jiten*, Tokyo: Mainichi komyunikeshonzu, 1986, vol. 1, pp. 562–563. Yoshikawa and Mizuno (op. cit. note 4), p. 70.

27 Typical are the two murals added to the monumental entrance hall of Strasbourg central railway station in 1883 depicting 'an idealised German view of relations with Alsace . . . a dozen years after the forced incorporation of Alsace into Bismarck's New German Reich'. See James Wilkinson, 'The Uses of Popular Culture by Rival Elites: The Case of Alsace, 1890–1914', *History of European Ideas*, Oxford: Pergamon Press, 1990, vol. II, p. 606.

28 E. H. Harriman, the railway magnate, wanted a Korean concession. See Mikiso Hane, *Japan. A Historical Survey*, New York: Charles Scribner's Sons, 1972, pp. 377–378. Hackett (op. cit. note 12), p. 168.

29 See further, Peter Duus *et al.*, (eds) *The Japanese Informal Empire in China, 1895–1937*, Princeton: Princeton University Press, 1989, pp. 220, 344.

30 *Tokyo Asahi shinbun*. 19 December 1914. *Taishō nyūsu jiten* (op. cit. note 26), p. 563

31 The governing clique at the time comprising the former imperial courtier Iwakura, and former samurai from the outer domains, Itō, Ōkubo, Ōkuma and Matsukata, were all enthusiastic supporters of an extended steam railway system. Nevertheless, railway construction had proven difficult, with only some 130 kilometres of tracks completed in the first decade. The Kobe–Osaka link followed the Yokohama one in 1874 and three years later it reached Kyoto. The next link with Ōtsu, built entirely by Japanese engineers, was opened in 1880, and though limited in distance the system as completed to that date was already of great importance to the developing economy. In the same year two million passengers were carried on the Shinagawa-Yokohama run and three million on the Kobe–Osaka link. See further, Thomas C. Smith, *Political Change and Industrial Development in Japan: Government Enterprise 1868–1880*, Stanford: Stanford University Press (rev. edn), 1965, p. 43 ff.

32 Nakajima Hisao, 'Kanchō shūchū keikaku to chūō teishajo', in Yoshikawa and Mizuno (op. cit. note 4) p. 43.

33 Ibid., p. 44.

34 Horiuchi Masaaki, 'Maboroshi Tōkyō eki keikaku', in Yoshikawa and Mizuno (op. cit. note 4), pp. 46–59.

35 Fujimori (op. cit. note 24), pp. 228–247.

36 Tatsuno was to continue to grapple with the problem of the Diet Building until his death in 1919. He also served as a member of numerous committees which failed to reach agreement on the desirable form of the central building of Japanese elected government.

37 The drawings were exhibited at the Tokyo Station Gallery (11/90–1/91).

38 Muramatsu Teijirō, *Nihon kindai kenchiku gijutsushi*, Shinkenchiku gijutsu sōsho, no. 8, Tokyo: Shōkokusha, 1976, pp. 68–69.

39 Yoshikawa and Mizuno (op. cit. note 4), pp. 55–58.

40 Fujimori Terunobu, 'Akarenga monogatari: dōmu ni kaketa gishitachi', *Hokkaidō supesharu*, NHK Sapporo, 4 July, 1988.

41 Tōkyō suteshon gyararii (ed.) *Tōkyō eki to renga. JR Higashi Nihon de meguru Nihon no renga kenchiku*, Tokyo: Higashi Nihon ryōkaku tetsudō, 1988, p. 48.

42 Ibid. p. 49.

43 Harold S. Williams, *Tales of the Foreign Settlements in Japan*, Rutland Vermont and Tokyo: Charles E. Tuttle, 1958, p. 77. Williams also notes that thousands of Glasgow bricks found their way to Japan as ballast in ships.

44 Muramatsu (op. cit. note 38), pp. 55–57.

45 Ibid., pp. 48–59. It was only from 1897, ten years after its foundation, that the company started making a profit. This would have been due to the series of late Meiji official projects for which it supplied brick.

46 Examples include the chapel and classrooms built at Dōshisha University between 1884 and 1894.

47 Paul Akamatsu, *Meiji 1868, Revolution and Counter-revolution in Japan*, London: George Allen and Unwin, 1972, p. 286.

48 Cost as reported in *Jiji shinpo*, 2 October, 1914. Taishō nyūsu jiten hensan iinkai (ed.) *Taishō nyūsu jiten*, Tokyo: Mainichi komyu-nikeshonzu, 1986, vol. 1, p. 562.

49 Kazushi Ohkawa and Henry Rosovsky, 'A Century of Economic Growth', in William Lockwood (ed.) *The State and Economic Enterprise in Japan*, Princeton: Princeton University Press, 1965, pp. 77–78.

50 Letter to Hirai Seiichirō, 1907, Archives: Department of Architecture, University of Tokyo.

51 See Zaidan hōjin bunkazai kenzōbutsu hozon gijutsu kyōkai, *Kyū Tōkyō Ongakkō Sōgakudō ichiku shūri kōji hōkokusho*, Tokyo: Shin'yōsha, 1987.

52 Edward S. Morse, *Japan Day by Day (1877, 1878–79, 1882–83)*, Boston and New York: Houghton Mifflin Company, and Cambridge: Riverside Press, 1917, vol. 1, pp. 282–283.

53 Muramatsu Teijirō, *Nihon kindai kenchiku no rekishi*, Tokyo: NHK bukkusu, 1977, pp. 116–117.

54 *Précis des leçons d'architecture données à l'École Polytechnique* (2 vols), 1802–1805. See further Henry Russell Hitchcock, (op. cit. note 18), p. 47.

55 See further William H. Coaldrake, 'The Architecture of Tōdai-ji', in John M. Rosenfield *et al.* (eds), *The Great Eastern Temple. Treasures of Japanese Buddhist Art from Tōdai-ji*, Indiana and Chicago: The Art Institute of Chicago in association with Indiana University Press, 1986, pp. 42–47.

56 This addition may have been prompted by use of a *karahafu* on the Daibutsuden built in Kyoto by the Toyotomi.

57 See further *Nara rokudaiji taikan*, Tokyo: Iwanami shoten, 1968–1972, vol. 9, Tōdaiji 1.

58 Tōdaiji Daibutsuden Shōwa daishūri shūri iinkai (eds) *Kokuhō Tōdaiji Kondō (Daibutsuden) shūri hōkokusho*, Nara: Meishinsha, 1980, vol. 1, p. 37.

59 Ibid. p. 36.

60 See Bunkazai hogo iinkai jimukyoku kenzōbutsuka (Itō Nobuo), 'Bunkazai (kenzōbutsu) hogo jigyō no gaiyō', *Kenchiku zasshi*, December, 1959, pp. 1–2.

61 On the two laws see Bunkazai hogo iinkai (ed.) *Bunkazai no ayumi*, Tokyo: Bunkazai hogo iinkai, 1960, pp. 473–74, 476–77.

62 Washio Ryū and Hiraoka Myōkai (eds) *Daibutsu oyobi Daibutsudenshi*, Nara: Nara Daibutsu kyōkai kinen hakkō, 1915, pp. 85–120.

63 Quoted in full in ibid., pp. 91–94.

64 Ibid., Appendix, p. 5.

65 See Bunkazai hogo iinkai jimukyoku kenzōbutsuka (Itō Nobuo) (op. cit. note 60), p.1.

66 Washio and Hiraoka (op. cit. note 62), p. 99.

10 Tange Kenzō's Tokyo Monuments: New Authority and Old Architectural Ambitions

1 Daigoru Yasukawa, 'Message from Tokyo Olympic Committee', *Contemporary Japan*, vol. XXVII, no. 4, October, 1963, p. 641.

2 Kenzō Tange, 'Recollections: Architect Kenzō Tange', *The Japan Architect*, No. 341, September, 1985, p. 6.

3 Ibid.

4 Udo Kulterman (ed.) *Kenzō Tange 1946–1969: Architecture and Urban Design*, New York, Washington and London: Praeger, 1979, p. 200.

5 Ibid., pp. 200–204.

6 *The Japan Architect* (op. cit. note 2)

7 Ibid.

8 See data in *The Japan Architect*, New Series No. 5, 1992, pp. 88–93, 244.

9 *The Japan Architect*, New Series No. 3, 1991, p. 31.

10 Figures from the Ministry of Finance, as reported in the *Asahi shinbun*, 26 January 1991.

11 Official government land values are always lower than actual market value.

12 In addition to the cost of 1.57 billion *yen* for the buildings there was considerable cost incurred in the purchase and installation of office automation, landscaping of the surrounding area and the removal of records and equipment from the old government buildings at Yūrakuchō. The final cost was to be in the vicinity of 2.39 billion *yen*. It is not clear how this additional expense was underwritten but it was kept separate from the cost of constructing the buildings. See Sasaki Nobuo, *Tochō mo hitotsu no seifu*, Tokyo: Iwanami shinsho, 1991, p. 2.

1 Kamo no Chōmei, *An Account of My Hut in 'Hōjōki'*, Donald Keene (comp. and ed.), *Anthology of Japanese Literature*, Tokyo and Rutland, Vermont: Charles E. Tuttle, 1956, pp. 196–199. On Kamo no Chōmei see further, Hilda Katō, 'The Mumyōshō of Kamo no Chōmei and its significance in Japanese literature', *Monumenta Nipponica*, vol. XXIII, nos 3–4, 1968, pp. 321–430.

2 *The Far East*, vol. 11, no. 1, June 1871, p. 10.

3 Chapter 2, section 5.

4 Matthew Arnold, *The Poems of Matthew Arnold 1840–1867, with an Introduction by Sir A. T. Quiller-Couch*, London: Humphrey Milford, Oxford University Press, 1913, p. 185.

5 Lewis Mumford, *The Culture of Cities* (rev. edn), New York and London: HBJ Books, 1970, p. 403.

CHRONOLOGICAL TABLE

11 Beyond Vanity and Evanescence

1 Kamo no Chōmei, *An Account of My Hut in 'Hōjōki'*, Donald Keene (comp. and ed.), *Anthology of Japanese Literature*, Tokyo and Rutland, Vermont: Charles E. Tuttle, 1956, pp. 196–199. On Kamo no Chōmei see further, Hilda Katō, 'The Mumyōshō of Kamo no Chōmei and its

Historical Periods AD	Political and Religious Authority	Major Architectural Projects
ca 200–552 Later Yayoi and Kofun Period	Yamato and Izumo emerge as regional centres	Monumental tomb construction
	Assertion of Yamato hegemony	Fortified regional power bases
	Continuous contact with mainland Asia via Korean peninsula	
552–710 Asuka Period	Introduction of Buddhism and growing political and cultural relations with Korean kingdoms	Foundation of Hōryūji Earliest recorded periodic rebuilding of Izumo Shrine (659)
	Centralization of government authority under Emperor Temmu (reigned 673—686)	First state-sponsored periodic rebuilding of Ise Shrine (completed 690)

Historical Periods AD	Political and Religious Authority	Major Architectural Projects
710–794 Nara Period	Foundation of city of Nara as imperial capital	Construction of Nara city and imperial palace with Daigokuden (Imperial Audience Hall)
	Consolidation of institutions of a centralized, bureaucratic and imperial state on the Tang dynasty Chinese model under Emperor Shōmu (reigned 724–749)	
	Intensified factional struggle at imperial court. Capital moved to Kuni, Naniwa and Shigaraki consecutively (740–745)	
	Return of capital to Nara (745)	Rebuilding of Nara Palace. Construction of Tōdaiji with Daibutsuden (Great Buddha Hall)
	Nara abandoned as capital	
794–1185 Heian Period	Kyoto as imperial capital	Development of *shinden-zukuri* palaces in Kyoto
	Relations with China severed	
	Flourishing of aristocratic culture	

Historical Periods AD	Political and Religious Authority	Major Architectural Projects
Heian Period (continued)	Domination of court by Fujiwara. Michinaga as Regent	Tsuchimikado-dono. Frequent reconstruction after fire. Designated Imperial Palace early thirteenth century
		Byōdōin at Uji
	Insei (rule by retired emperors) established (1086)	
	Decline of central government and rise of regional power. Heiji Incident (1159–1160)	Honden of Izumo Shrine rebuilt on increasingly monumental scale, reaching 48 metres in height in 1115. Collapses 6 times between 1031 and 1235 due to structural failure
	War between Taira and Minamoto (1180–1185)	Partial destruction of Tōdaiji including Daibutsuden
1185–1333 Kamakura Period	Kamakura shogunate Renewed contacts with China	Building of city of Kamakura. Rebuilding of Tōdaiji under patronage of Kamakura shogunate
	Increasing influence of Zen Buddhism	
	Defeat of Mongols (1266 and 1281) and assertion of Hōjō power	Monumental building programme in Kamakura
		Shōfukuji founded
		Destruction of Kamakura by Ashikaga forces

Historical Periods AD	Political and Religious Authority	Major Architectural Projects
1333–1467 Muromachi Period	Ashikaga shogunate established in Kyoto Flourishing of Higashiyama and Kitayama court culture	Rebuilding of Jizōdō of Shōfukuji
1467–1573 Period of Civil War	Ōnin Rebellion (1467–1477) and civil war Arrival of Portuguese at Tanegashima (1543)	Hiatus in periodic renewal of Ise Shrine (1462–1585) Periodic renewal of Izumo Shrine performed 6 times (1467–1609)
1576–1600 Momoyama Period	Process of national unification under Oda Nobunaga, Toyotomi Hideyoshi and Tokugawa Ieyasu	Age of castle construction. Azuchi and Himeji castles. Destruction of Daibutsuden of Tōdaiji
1600–1868 Edo Period	Tokugawa shogunate (1603) Consolidation of political authority	Explosive development of Edo city Tokugawa-sponsored periodic renewal of both Ise and Izumo Shrines Construction of Edo Castle. *Tenshu* rebuilt twice (1622–1623, 1637–1638). *Shoin-zukuri* palaces built for daimyo in Edo as part of *sankin kōtai* system

Historical Periods AD	Political and Religious Authority	Major Architectural Projects
Edo Period (continued)		Nijō Castle and Palace of the Second Compound built in Kyoto Taitokuin Mausoleum Nikkō Tōshōgū
	Meireki Fire (1657) destroys central Edo including most of castle	
	Increasing use of sumptuary regulation	
		Tokugawa sponsored rebuilding of Daibutsuden of Tōdaiji (1707) and Honden of Izumo Shrine (1744)
	Kyōhō Reforms (1716–1745)	Development of simpler daimyo gate-house style; Ikedamon and Rōjūmon
	Tempō Reforms (1841–1843)	
	Increasing foreign pressures contribute to destabilization of Tokugawa shogunate. Collapse of Tokugawa shogunate (1867)	
1868–1912 Meiji Period	Restoration of imperial government	Edo becomes new national capital and renamed Tokyo
	Establishment of State Shinto	Akasaka Palace
	Far-reaching process of modernization, educational reform and industrialization	Tokyo Station Sōgakudō

Historical Periods AD	Political and Religious Authority	Major Architectural Projects
Meiji Period (continued)	Meiji Constitution and establishment of parliamentary government Colonial expansion	Daibutsuden of Tōdaiji rebuilt
1912–1926 Taishō Period		Rebuilding of Tokyo after Great Kantō Earthquake
1926–1989 Shōwa Period	War with China (1937–1945)	
	Pacific War (1941–1945)	Taitokuin Mausoleum destroyed in U.S. fire-bombing of Tokyo (1945)
	Allied Occupation (1945–1952)	Post-war rebuilding
	Tokyo Olympiad (1964)	Olympic Gymnasium Buildings by Tange Kenzō
		Shōwa restoration of Daibutsuden of Tōdaiji
	Bubble economy (until 1991)	Building boom. Post-industrial waterfront development projects on Tokyo Bay
1989–present Heisei Period	Re-election of Suzuki Shun'ichi as Governor of Tokyo	New Tokyo Metropolitan Government Headquarters (Shintochō) (1991)
	Era of unstable coalition governments at national level	Completion of 61st periodic renewal of Ise Shrine (1993)

Index

Note: Page references xvi–xviii are to the Glossary

320